THE BORDER GUIDE

A GUIDE TO LIVING, WORKING AND INVESTING ACROSS THE BORDER

THE BORDER GUIDE

A GUIDE TO LIVING, WORKING AND INVESTING ACROSS THE BORDER

Robert Keats, CFP® (US), CFP™ (CDA), RFP (CDA), MSFP

Self-Counsel Press Ltd.
(a division of)
International Self-Counsel Press
USA   Canada

Printed in Canada.

Self-Counsel Press acknowledges the financial support of the Government of Canada through the Book Publishing Industry Development Program (BPIDP) for our publishing activities.

Seventh edition: 2004; Reprinted 2004

Eighth edition: 2007

Library and Archives Canada Cataloguing in Publication

Keats, Robert
     The border guide : a guide to living, working and investing across the border / Robert Keats. — 8th ed.

(Self-counsel reference series)
ISBN-13: 978-1-55180-765-2
ISBN-10: 1-55180-765-3

     1. Canadians—United States—Finance, Personal. 2. Finance, Personal—United States. 3. Canadians—Legal status, laws, etc.—United States. I. Title. II. Series.

HG179.K42 2006   332.02400973   C2006-905364-2

Self-Counsel Press
(a division of)
International Self-Counsel Press Ltd.

1704 North State Street	1481 Charlotte Road
Bellingham, WA 98225	North Vancouver, BC V7J 1H1
USA	Canada

This book is dedicated to my late father and mother,
Gordon Keats (1922–1992) and Anne Keats (1924–2006).
May they rest in peace with our heavenly Father.

Dad and Mom, I miss you.

Contents

Acknowledgements

No man is an island. This book in its eight editions would not have been possible without the assistance of many people. I have been blessed with a lovely family — my wife, Barbara, and my children, Sarah, Daniel, Carl and Rebekah — who have been my inspiration. My only regret in writing this book was the time I had to spend away from them all.

The research required to prepare any book of this scope is enormous, even under ideal circumstances. Taking highly technical topics such as immigration, tax planning and estate planning between Canada and the United States, and presenting them in a format that is both logical and readable, have been formidable tasks. I would like to acknowledge Dale Walters, my partner of 11 years, for assistance in editing and providing a great deal of research.

Brad Flecke, an immigration attorney for our firm, reviewed all of the immigration issues presented in Chapter 7. I thank him for both his time and his prudent counsel.

The vast majority of this book was conceived and written in a wonderful little cabin nestled among the tall pines of northern Arizona. I would like to thank Teresa Bertocchi, a long-time family friend, for the use of her cabin. I will never forget the fresh mountain air, the spectacular thunderstorms and the warmth of the fireplace.

I would also like to thank all of you who read previous editions of this book for your positive comments and enthusiastic support. My final and biggest thank-you goes to all of our cross-border Canadian and American clients. Without their interest and encouragement, I would never have been in a position to write this book.

Introduction

Because our social and cultural institutions are so similar, many Americans and Canadians feel completely at home on either side of our two nations' border. Many incorrectly assume that the laws governing investment, taxation and immigration are the same as well. Unfortunately, this can lead to some unpleasant surprises, particularly when conducting basic financial transactions such as buying or selling real estate. The North American Free Trade Agreement (NAFTA) has only served to fuel the fires of cross-border commerce. Many Canadians migrate to the Sunbelt, seeking respite from harsh winters, and many Americans migrate to Canada for the pleasant summers.

The Border Guide was written for both Canadians and Americans, regardless of which direction they may be moving or investing across the 49th parallel. It is a particularly great resource for Canadians who are considering some form of permanent or seasonal residency in the United States or have resided there for employment or other reasons and are contemplating returning to Canada. It will also prove extremely useful for U.S. citizens living in, investing in or moving to Canada, or those who are married to Canadians. It will be of particular value to Canadians who intend to invest or do business in the United States, even if your financial curiosity is limited to an occasional shopping trip or vacation. Whatever your interest, the information contained in these pages will help you to transact your cross-border business affairs with competence and confidence. It is the only step-by-step guide for people who want to understand and take advantage of American and Canadian tax, financial and medical institutions. It will also show you how to avoid many of the common pitfalls of having assets and spending extended periods of time in both countries.

Chapters 1 through 6 deal primarily with Canadians visiting and investing in the U.S., and Chapters 7 to 9 address Canadians moving and immigrating to the U.S. Although many of the issues discussed in these chapters are not relevant to Americans immigrating to or investing in Canada, Americans face many similar cross-border issues when they move north. I therefore recommend that American readers review these chapters, paying particular attention to the concerns of U.S. citizens and green card holders living in Canada and the differences in both income and estate taxation between Canada and the United States. Chapters 10 and 11 discuss the residency status of new or returning immigrants to Canada and certain Canadian tax regulations that apply to Americans who invest in Canada. To get the full picture, both these chapters should be read by Americans moving to Canada for the first time. Chapters 12 to 14 address investment, social benefits, medical coverage, estate tax and issues relating to small business ownership for cross-border residents. The book concludes with Chapter 15, which highlights the key role of a cross-border financial planner in helping you get the most benefits from living or investing across the Canada/U.S. border.

To prevent this book from becoming a dry technical manual that is factually accurate but functionally useless, I have presented my ideas in a non-technical fashion. Certain concepts have occasionally been simplified in the service of readability. Sound professional advice is recommended for applying any of the ideas or techniques detailed in this guide. Please be aware that tax and other rules in both Canada and the U.S. are constantly changing, which can make some of this information outdated the minute the book reaches the shelves. Please rely on your advisors to keep you current on all these issues.

At the end of many of the chapters I have included some typical questions from readers, along with my responses, to illustrate and broaden the concepts presented. The majority of these questions were posed by readers of my numerous newspaper and magazine columns and articles or by readers of a previous edition of *The Border Guide*. Most were looking for advice relating to their own specific problems or situations, but I hope that my responses to their questions will help to answer yours, as well.

Crossing the Border

AN INTRODUCTION TO PERSONAL
CROSS-BORDER FINANCIAL PLANNING

After many years of cross-border financial planning between Canada and the United States, I have come to the conclusion that the U.S. is the best tax haven for Canadians. The same tax advantages that are available to Canadians by going to a remote island in the middle of nowhere can be had by driving across the U.S. border. Ninety percent of Canada's population is located within 100 miles of the U.S. border, so the United States is a very accessible tax haven. In addition, Canadians are familiar with U.S. cities, modes of transportation, the primary language and other cultural similarities.

The economic and tax environment of the United States and Canada has grown in breadth and complexity over the past few decades and, with it, the need for comprehensive personal cross-border financial planning. The intent of such planning is to capitalize on the most satisfactory mix of savings plans, insurance coverage, investment vehicles, tax strategies, retirement plans and estate-planning techniques available in each country. Applied to your own specific needs and goals, these cross-border planning opportunities can reap great financial rewards for you and your heirs.

Cross-border financial planning encompasses all the basic individual financial planning requirements of both Canada and the United States in the areas of net worth, cash flow, risk management, retirement goals, taxation, estate planning and investments. It analyzes each area according to your particular situation, and then weighs option against option, completes timely currency conversions, factors in your immigration status, examines applicable tax treaty rules, and develops a road map for you to follow to achieve your financial goals with maximum income, safety and tax savings.

One of the major difficulties inherent in cross-border financial planning is that the rules change depending on immigration status and in which direction the cross-border movement is going. For example, a winter visitor to the United States who marries a U.S. resident dramatically alters his or her financial planning options, and a new cross-border financial plan becomes necessary in order to take advantage of new opportunities and to avoid any costly mistakes. In addition, performing a seemingly simple task such as purchasing a home in the U.S. can greatly affect a person's tax status with respect to both income tax and estate tax in the United States. Figure 1.1 depicts all the major immigration status possibilities. A person who is your typical winter visitor from Canada has different sets of tax rules and immigration rules applying to him or her than would apply to the same visitor if he or she had a U.S. visa or green card. All the important planning issues for each respective status category are discussed in detail in subsequent chapters of this book.

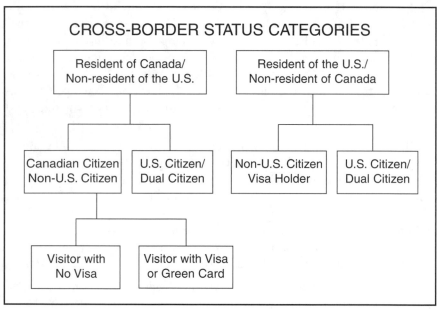

Figure 1.1

HOW LONG CAN YOU REMAIN IN THE UNITED STATES AS A VISITOR?

Few things cause more confusion and controversy among visitors to the United States than how long they can legally remain in that country without breaking any rules. (For Americans visiting or moving to Canada, see Chapter 11.) The source of this confusion is primarily the fact that there are at least four sets of rules governed by various government agencies that deal with residency. These residency rules sometimes conflict, and adherence to one set of rules does not automatically mean compliance with the others. The four sets of rules that tell you how much time you can legally spend in the United States as a visitor are the following:

1. **The Immigration Rules.** Canadian visitors to the United States may enter the country without any actual visa being issued. However, in the post-9/11 war-on-terrorism era this privilege for Canadians is being changed with current and pending rules from the new U.S. Department of Homeland Security. (More about these changes will be discussed later in this chapter.)

   Technically, Canadian visitors currently fall into the B-2 visitor category (or B-1 for those entering for business purposes), allowing them to remain in the United States legally for up to six consecutive months without a visa. The B-1 business visitors can conduct business on behalf of their Canadian employers only and all compensation must come from the Canadian side of the border. Business visitors are likely to fall into one of the income-tax filing requirements discussed in Chapter 3, particularly if the U.S. entity for which they are working reimburses the Canadian company for services rendered and the business visitor's expenses.

   Extensions to the six-month limit, primarily for medical reasons, may be granted by applying to the U.S. Citizenship and Immigration Service (USCIS, formerly the Immigration and Naturalization Service or INS). However, USCIS is taking so long to process these extensions currently that even if you applied for the extension the day you arrived in the United States, it already would have expired by the time it was granted. If you leave the United States and re-enter at any border crossing, including those between Mexico and the United States, the six-month clock starts over again with each re-entry.

   This does not mean you can legally keep leaving the United States and re-entering every six months perpetually because you want to change from a casual visitor to a resident. You will be stopped from re-entering the country if it appears that you may have taken up permanent residency, and you may be asked to show proof that you have not done so. With the new rules being implemented at the border, all visitors entering and leaving the U.S. will be required to show a passport or similar identification so they will be checked in and out of the country. This means that whether you are entering or leaving the U.S., each immigration official will know the exact time, place, purpose and mode of transportation for each and every time you have crossed the border in either direction. This information is on immigration officials' computers and available at their fingertips. Proof that you have not become a U.S. resident can be whatever the immigration official at the border decides, but it will likely include providing one or more of the following: your last three months' utility bills, a provincial driver's licence, a recent Canadian tax return or a property tax notice or lease agreement. It is also extremely important not to have anything in your possession that indicates any U.S. residential connections such as a U.S. driver's licence, business cards with a U.S. address, U.S. credit cards and so on. As you will read in Chapter 7, it is recommended that you carry a Border Kit every time you enter the United States to mitigate any hassles you may have with U.S. customs and immigration personnel.

New rules that came into effect in April 1997 and that were heightened by the 9/11 attacks give low-level immigration officials at U.S. borders greater powers. They have the right to act as prosecutor and judge in order to refuse entry to the United States for up to five years or more to those persons they feel are not telling them the truth about why they want to enter the United States. Hundreds of Canadians have been refused entry to the United States under these new rules, without the right to appeal, as U.S. border agents, spurred by their new powers and new technology, become more vigilant. Many people ask if U.S. and Canadian customs and immigration personnel share information. The answer is a definite yes; in fact, they share exactly the same computer database. Chapter 7 provides further direction for those Canadian visitors who wish to become green card holders, technically known as legal permanent residents of the United States. It also discusses other, less permanent visas.

2. **The Income Tax Rules.** Generally speaking, a person will be classified as a U.S. resident for tax purposes if he or she is regularly present in the country for more than four months each year under the "substantial presence test" detailed in Chapter 3. Note that the number of days present in the United States need not be consecutive. An individual can be deemed a resident of the United States for tax purposes, although he may not have any right to remain in the country under the immigration rules. Thus a person may become subject to income tax in the United States on his world income without having the right to remain legally within its borders for more than six months as a visitor. Consequently, it is much easier to become a resident of the United States for tax purposes, as noted in Chapter 3, than to become a permanent resident under immigration rules as explained in Chapter 7. It is also possible to be a resident for tax purposes of both Canada and the United States at the same time, with the Canada/U.S.

Tax Treaty providing the tiebreaker rules to settle this issue. Article IV of the treaty has four separate rules or tests to determine residency. You need pass only one of these tests, as taken in the order listed, to pass the residency test. If, after applying the four treaty tests, it is still unclear whether you are a resident of Canada or the U.S., a competent authority consisting of a panel of Canadian and U.S. tax officials makes the final determination. These treaty tiebreaker rules are outlined in detail in Chapter 3. Canada Revenue Agency (CRA) has a critical rule that states that once you are a treaty resident of the U.S., you are automatically considered a non-resident of Canada for tax purposes, and you could be forced to go through a Canadian tax exit — with all its consequences. (See Chapter 9 for more details.)

3. **The Estate Tax Rules.** What estate tax is and how it applies to non-residents is covered in detail in Chapter 4 and in Chapter 9 for U.S. residents. Unlike income tax and immigration, there is no clear set of rules of residency for estate taxes. Residency is based on a series of facts and circumstances. Some of the factors that determine residency or "domicile" for estate tax purposes are the relative size and nature of your permanent homes in Canada and the United States; the amount of time spent in each country; your immigration status in the United States; written declarations on such documents as wills or tax returns; the locations of your significant assets and important papers, and your personal, family and business connections. Generally, Canadians who are clearly visitors to the United States, have no U.S. green cards and whose intent is to routinely return to Canada each year could not be considered to have given up domicile in Canada, and would not be subject to American estate tax on their worldwide assets. Court cases in which the IRS has challenged a Canadian winter visitor's estate by attempting to tax worldwide assets of the deceased have failed. The IRS was unsuccessful in those cases, because the deceased must have shown a clear intent to give up one domicile for another. A 2003 U.S. Internal Revenue Service (IRS) ruling stated that a Canadian living in the U.S. on an L-1 visa (see Chapter 7 for details on how an L-1 visa works) could be considered domiciled in the U.S. for estate-tax purposes, even though the L-1 visa would expire after a maximum of seven years and the Canadian would have had to move back to Canada. This ruling appears to be a liberal extension of these domicile rules in a similar manner to the income tax rules that may determine you to be a resident of the U.S. for income tax purposes, without any legal immigration status to allow you to stay in the U.S.

Visitors to the United States may still be subject to the non-resident estate tax on their assets located in the U.S. This will be explained in greater detail in Chapter 4.

4. **The Provincial Medicare Rules.** These sets of rules are unique because they act in direct opposition to the tax and immigration residency rules by stipulating that you cannot be away from your home province for longer than a specified period of time. To remain eligible for provincial medicare, most Canadian provinces require that you must be present in the province for a minimum of six months a year and have a permanent residence available to you there. In 1999 Ontario added a thirty-day grace period, allowing someone to be out of the province for 212 days a year without affecting his or her Ontario Health Insurance Plan (OHIP) coverage. Newfoundland allows its residents to stay out of province for up to eight months in twelve before they lose coverage. Your medicare coverage depends on the amount of time you spend out of province, which includes the time you spend in other provinces as well as out of the country. (However, due to pressure from travelling Canadians, some provinces currently do not count travel in other Canadian provinces as time out of the province for their provincial medicare coverage.) In most provinces, once you've lost provincial medicare, you have to wait three months as a returning resident to reinstate your coverage. (Alberta has no waiting period for coverage to start for returning residents.)

For those moving to the United States, your provincial medicare coverage generally ceases within thirty days of your leaving Canada, and in some provinces it ceases at the end of the month in which you leave. Check with your local medicare office and plan accordingly so you don't have any gaps in your coverage.

We are often asked, "How does a particular government department responsible for enforcing any of the above rules know how much time you are spending out of your province and where you are spending your time?"

The fact of the matter is they do not always necessarily know, or need to know. Instead, they pass the burden of proof on to you by asking you to declare, under penalty of perjury, that the facts you present regarding your travel itinerary are true. As discussed below, you should also remember that we live in a computer age in which information is easily stored and retrieved. This information is continually being shared by various government agencies and government-owned corporations.

CROSSING THE 49TH PARALLEL WILL NEVER BE THE SAME AS IT WAS

The time when Canadians and Americans could be confident of crossing the Canada-U.S. border with a wave and a smile or by simply showing a valid driver's licence are numbered. The U.S. Homeland Security Administration has introduced new rules that require all persons entering the United States to have a valid machine-readable passport or other authorized ID card with biometric identifier information on it. These rules come into effect January 8, 2007, for all border-crossings at airports and seaports. For all other border-crossings this requirement will take effect June 1, 2009. These deadlines may be moved back one or two years to give Homeland Security more time to develop technology for the new ID card.

The biometric identifiers for the ID cards (and eventually the passports) may be fingerprint scans, retina or iris scans, or even face-recognition scans. A system called US VISIT (United States Visitor and Immigration Status Indicator Technology) has been in effect since early 2005, photographing and fingerprinting every visitor entering the U.S. through airports and other points of entry. Fortunately, Canadian citizens have not been required to submit to this US VISIT program. (Canadian permanent residents who are not citizens of Canada or the U.S. are subject to these requirements.) However, unless changes are made for technical or political reasons, the new passport requirement will be totally enforced by June 1, 2009, for Canada and 26 other countries whose citizens do not currently require visas when entering the United States.

Since less than 20% of Americans and less than 40% of Canadians currently have passports, this requirement to allow only visitors with passports to enter the United States is a major hurdle and may slow border traffic significantly. Because of this, the Homeland Security Administration has embarked on developing a new ID card for U.S. citizens that will be much cheaper and quicker to produce. Canada is considering similar plans to develop an ID card for Canadians that will be acceptable for cross-border Canada-U.S. travel. Experimentation is ongoing as to which biometric identifiers on the ID cards and passports will provide the most security at the least cost without severely impeding the flow of cross-border traffic.

Considering that there are over 53 million crossings from Canada to the U.S. every year, this program is massive, technologically complicated and extremely expensive. However, once all travellers have the new passports or ID cards, it is expected that immigration clearance between countries will actually be much quicker and safer. These passports and ID cards will be very difficult for anybody to forge or steal. A U.N. agency that sets travel standards on a worldwide basis is also working on new passport formats so that the biometric identifiers can be incorporated into them. The United States has developed a new passport with a computer chip that will carry all pertinent personal information. This new passport will replace all current passports as they come up for renewal. These new e-passports, as they are called, will be read electronically even before you take your passport out of your pocket. Together with a simultaneous face scan, this will enable U.S. customs and immigration officials to identify you and assess whether you are a risk or not before you even talk to them. Canada and the U.S. are working out programs for frequent border-crossers under similar rules to the current Nexus programs, where frequent travellers complete special forms, go through background checks and pay an annual fee to go through "fast lanes" at the border by swiping ID cards and doing a fingerprint or retina scan at an kiosk without needing to even talk to a border agent. The billions of dollars of imports and exports that go through the Canada-U.S. border daily are also targeted by a program called FAST (Free and Secure Trade) as a way of expediting the passage of precleared commercial trucks to ensure the border remains secure but open for business.

Behind the scenes of the U.S. Patriot Act will be many immigration agents with very advanced computer systems that will attempt to identify every individual against known data from airline and ship manifests to weed out potential terrorists before they arrive at a U.S. entry point. Visitors in general will be pre-profiled as to their potential security threat so border personnel can focus on those travellers who score high in the risk profile score. Where you might fit into this profile system will be kept secret, but you can greatly lower your risk profile and help expedite your border crossings if you do such things as join a Nexus program, travel on a recently issued passport, pay for airline tickets well in advance with a well-established credit card, travel with other people with an equally low profile, and if travelling across the border by car, ensure your auto registration matches yourself and your place of residence. Another issue to watch for, particularly in light of Canada's much more liberal marijuana laws, is having a clean criminal record, as criminal databases are now integrated into the profiling system. Minor marijuana convictions that are misdemeanors in Canada may be considered a felony by U.S. authorities and bar you from entering the U.S. and/or obtaining a green card. Similarly, non-Canadian citizens entering Canada from the U.S. or other countries may be refused entry if they have a "driving under the influence" offence (DUI) appearing on their record (in Canada, DUI is more commonly known as "impaired driving"). Consequently, Americans with a DUI or other offense should contact the Citizenship and Immigration Canada (CIC) office at their entry point into Canada well in advance to get a waiver that will enable them to enter Canada without delay. As you may recall, President George W. Bush had a DUI in his youth; he had to get a waiver to visit Canada. Likewise, Martha Stewart, with her short stint in jail for insider trading, was also required to get a waiver when she was subsequently scheduled to speak in Halifax. She chose not go through the waiver process and dropped her Canadian speaking engagement.

WHERE TO LIVE OR WINTER IN THE UNITED STATES

The nature of cross-border financial planning will often be determined by which U.S. state you choose to reside or vacation in. This guide is not meant to provide you with a visitor's bureau brochure about which Sunbelt state is the best, but it examines some of the major tax implications of the most popular Sunbelt states: Arizona, California and Florida. In Appendix B, we will provide tax rates and other technical data on these and another popular state, Hawaii. The reasons that Arizona, California and Florida are popular with Canadians can be summarized in a collection of comments from long-time residents or visitors to one or more of these three states:

ARIZONA

- Offers the most sunshine of almost any populated area in North America. Expect clear skies nearly 85% of the time, and an annual rainfall of 6 inches (15 cm) in the desert southwest. Winter daytime temperatures range from 65° to 85°F (18° to 30°C) in the Phoenix and Tucson areas.

- Great for people with arthritis because of the dry climate. Not so good for allergy sufferers, since something is always in bloom.

- Golfers' paradise. There are more than 250 golf courses in the Phoenix area alone that are open 365 days a year.

- Geographically diverse state from the Grand Canyon to mountain high country to Sonoran desert. There is decent snow skiing in northern parts of the state during winter at elevations in excess of 10,000 feet, and plenty of year-round water sports on the numerous man-made reservoirs and lakes. Arizona has the most boats per capita of any state in the U.S.

- Arizona has a relatively kind tax regime. In a 2005 in-depth national survey of all 50 states, completed by *Bloomberg Wealth Manager* magazine (now called *Wealth Manager Magazine*), Arizona scored an A-, considering all forms of taxes combined, including state income, sales and property taxes. Arizona is a very tax-friendly state to Canadians, and if you take into consideration this fact and the special tax credits for Canadian taxes paid, Arizona would likely have been rated A+ on the Bloomberg survey had the survey included Canadian issues.

- The most frequently mentioned drawback about Arizona is that if you choose to stay in the Phoenix area during the summer, you can face average daily high temperatures of over 100°F (38°C). However, popular retirement communities such as Prescott in the central part of the state offer four distinct seasons (although snow is rare) and an ambience not unlike that of a small town in New England.

- Arizona has one of the lowest unemployment rates in the country with plenty of opportunity for permanent or part-time employment in all areas of the economy.

- Several airlines now have non-stop flights from most major Canadian cities.

CALIFORNIA

- Plenty of sun and ocean. Temperatures vary considerably from the coast to the inland desert, with the coastal areas having less extreme temperature changes because of the moderating effect of the Pacific Ocean. The Palm Springs area has a climate almost identical to that of southern Arizona.

- Major man-made and natural tourist attractions abound, such as Disneyland, Hollywood and Big Sur.

- The ocean provides plenty of opportunity for sailing, fishing and whale watching.

- Geographically diverse state from the miles of spectacular coastlines to the mountains, farmland, vineyards and desert.

- The major drawback of this state is its population, which is greater than all of Canada's. In the past decade, it has seen more than its fair share of earthquakes, floods, mudslides and wildfires. California is also noted for its high cost of living and relatively high taxes.

- California scored only a D+ on the 2005 Bloomberg survey. It is also not very friendly taxwise to Canadians who have assets and income from Canada.

- For those seeking employment in the computer industry, Silicon Valley, near San Francisco, although greatly diminished after the dot-com bust of the early 2000s, remains a great innovative computer technology centre.

- California is easy to fly to from any city in Canada and is accessible by car from Vancouver and Calgary.

FLORIDA

- Very mild climate with a minimal difference between winter and summer temperatures, 70° to 90°F (20° to 32°C) on average. Expect plenty of rain year-round, and high humidity during summer.

- Provides two surprisingly different coasts, the Atlantic and the Gulf. Each has miles of beautiful beaches, islands and keys and all the year-round water sports that go with them.

- Like California, major man-made tourist attractions such as Disney World, Universal Studios and Cape Kennedy are located there.

- Florida has no personal income tax but has a small intangible personal property tax. It rates an A- on the Bloomberg survey, the same as Arizona, and is just as Canadian tax friendly.

- It's easy to drive to Florida from Ontario, Quebec and the Maritimes.

- This state offers the most services for Canadians. It has several radio and TV stations broadcasting Canadian news in both French and English. In addition, it has a good distribution of Canadian daily newspapers.

- The major complaint about Florida seems to be that it is getting too crowded — particularly on the Atlantic coast, and its hurricane season. With respect to the hurricanes, it is important to note that the U.S. Federal Emergency Management Agency (FEMA) does not provide any aid to seasonal residents who are not U.S. citizens.

Nevada, Washington, New York and Hawaii, other popular states with Canadians, received scores of A+, A, D- and B+ respectively on the *Bloomberg Wealth Manager* magazine survey.

POPULAR CROSS-BORDER MISCONCEPTIONS

One of the primary purposes of this book is to dispel many of the popular misconceptions Canadians have about living, visiting and investing in the United States. Some of the more common misconceptions are:

- **You lose money changing Canadian dollars to U.S. dollars!** No, there is no loss in exchanging one currency for another, other than the commissions you pay as a transaction cost. You don't make a profit changing U.S. dollars to Canadian dollars either. See Chapter 2 for a more complete explanation of this popular misconception.

- **Canada has no estate or inheritance taxes!** Wrong — Canada's deemed disposition tax on death on RRSPs or RRIFs and appreciated property can be as high as 50%. Many provinces also levy significant probate or estate administration fees. For a combined husband and wife estate of less than $5 million Canadian estate taxes are frequently much higher than those in the United States. Only about 1% to 2% of the population in either Canada or the U.S. would have estates greater than this amount. See Chapters 4 and 9 for further details on this tax.

- **The 1995 amendment to the Canada/U.S. Tax Treaty eliminates the U.S. non-resident estate taxes.** No, some Canadians are actually worse off under this new treaty, but many are unaffected by the new rules. These rules are much more complex than the old rules, so a new level of understanding is required to determine if you are any better off. See Chapter 4 for the real scoop.

- **RRSPs can be left alone if you move to the United States!** Leaving your RRSPs in Canada when you move to the United States can create many potentially costly tax problems, and you may miss opportunities to withdraw them at no or very low tax rates. Chapter 8 will discuss how to remove your RRSPs at very low or even no net income tax, once you have taken up residence in the United States.

- **Canadian exit tax is too high for you to leave Canada.** This misconception is frequently perpetuated by Canadian accountants who emphasize this exit tax as an obstacle rather than as a great planning vehicle that could actually reduce taxes. The CRA does impose a deemed disposition tax when exiting Canada to go live in another country. However, this tax is not an additional tax; it is tax one would normally pay if the appreciated asset were sold. The

CRA allows you to defer any tax that might be due upon exit to the date the asset is actually sold. The CRA may require collateral for this tax deferment but also requires that you pay no interest on any tax due, so you get the equivalent of a interest-free loan. In addition, as noted in Chapter 9 and Chapter 10, proper planning before you leave Canada can help you avoid this tax altogether.

- **You will earn lower rates of interest investing in the United States!** Canadian banks sometimes pay slightly higher rates on term deposits and GICs. However, overall diversified investment portfolios earn about the same rate of return for a similar level of risk in both Canada and the United States. Chapters 6 and 12 provide further insight into this misconception.

- **Wills are all you need for a complete estate plan!** Wills are very necessary, but there are more effective estate-planning vehicles, such as living trusts and living wills, that may provide for lower estate settlement costs and better estate management. See Chapters 4 and 9 for further explanation.

- **Investing in the United States means you must file U.S. tax returns!** No — there are a large number of investments you can put money into in the United States that are exempt from taxes and any filing or reporting requirements. Chapter 6 lists the investments that are exempt from U.S. taxes for non-residents.

- **You can't be a citizen of Canada and the United States at the same time!** Wrong — dual citizenship is possible and has been for several years. Chapter 7 explains dual citizenship status.

- **You lose your CPP/QPP and OAS by moving to the United States!** No, you keep all these benefits, and in reality you will likely keep much more of your Canada Pension Plan/Quebec Pension Plan and Old Age Security after taxes once you have become a resident taxpayer of the United States. Chapter 8 provides the calculations to show you some of the tax savings available on CPP/QPP and OAS when a Canadian moves to the United States. You will not be subject to the OAS clawback if you are a U.S. resident, regardless of your income. You can also double dip and qualify to receive CPP/QPP, OAS and U.S. Social Security payments with good cross-border planning. See Chapter 13 for more details.

- **Medical insurance is too expensive in the United States!** Some U.S. health insurance is expensive; however, those under 65 can obtain very good coverage with high deductibles for less than $250 per month for up to a $2-million limit of coverage, depending on an absence of pre-existing conditions, age and other factors. Those over 65 are usually eligible for U.S. Medicare, at no or reasonable costs. Chapters 5 and 13 provide further details for those needing health insurance in the United States.

- **Investments in the United States are riskier than in Canada!** No, the same rules of prudent investing apply in both countries. Because there are more investment choices in the United States, there can be greater opportunity to choose an inappropriate investment. However, this greater selection also allows prudent investors to find a greater number of safe investments in the United States at lower costs, which can actually help lower risk.

WHAT IS THE CANADA/UNITED STATES TAX TREATY?

One of the most important documents for the protection of a Canadian's financial assets in the United States is the Canada/U.S. Tax Treaty. Most Canadians, however, are completely unaware of its existence and the benefits that it gives them. Even though tax planning is an important part of cross-border planning, it is my experience that few financial advisors on either side of the Canada-U.S. border have ever cracked the cover of this treaty on behalf of their clients. They tend to focus instead on the tax rules of their own individual countries.

Canada and the United States signed their first full tax treaty in 1942, with amendments in 1950, 1956, 1966, 1980 and 1994. The most recent amendment was written in 1994 and 1995 and took effect in 1996. New treaty negotiations commenced in October 1998 to discuss unresolved issues in the 1996 amendment. Some minor amendments to the treaty were finalized in late 2000, but have yet to be ratified by both governments. The tax treaty is the most important business treaty for both Canada and the United States. Millions of Canadians and Americans are affected by this agreement, and as long as Canada and the United States continue as each other's major trading partner, its impact will only increase.

The Canada/U.S. Tax Treaty attempts to accomplish the same goals as any tax treaty — the prevention of tax measures that may discourage trade and investment, reaching a common ground on the taxation of non-residents to avoid double taxation on the same income, and to protect the domestic treasury. To a large extent the Canada/U.S. Tax Treaty has accomplished these goals, as long as one embarks on extensive cross-border planning.

The two countries negotiated an estate tax article that was added to the existing treaty in 1995. For some people this will resolve the potentially high non-resident estate tax and/or capital gains tax that Canadians face if they hold U.S. real estate and stocks. The U.S. non-resident estate tax and the effects of the latest treaty are covered in greater detail in Chapter 4.

Up until 1996, Canadian winter visitors were able to use the Canada/U.S. Tax Treaty protection by default, without having to make any active filings or declarations. Current regulations now require that formal statements be filed with the Internal Revenue Service (IRS), forcing Canadians who spend four to six months in the United States to become more aware of the treaty and how it can help them if they do not wish to be taxed on their world income in both the United States and Canada. Chapter 3, in addition to explaining more benefits of the Canada/U.S. Tax Treaty, has been designed to show you who must file returns or statements in the United States, and under what circumstances these returns must be filed.

The Canada/U.S. Tax Treaty is one of the most important tools used in cross-border financial planning for two key reasons:

- The terms of the treaty take precedence over almost all the Canadian Income Tax Act (ITA) rules in Canada and the Internal Revenue Code (IRC) tax rules in the United States. It is an important trump card to play at appropriate times when doing cross-border planning. The value of this cannot be over emphasized for any cross-border planner.

- The terms of the treaty seldom change. The Canada/U.S. Tax Treaty has been amended only six times in its more than 65-year history and can be relied on to a much greater degree for long-term planning than either the ITA or the American IRC. The ITA and IRC are subject to constant revision without notice and are affected by annual budgets, bipartisan politics and election campaigns. In fact, since the last major treaty negotiations of 1989 the IRS has changed the U.S. domestic tax rules an estimated 15,000 times and the CRA has probably made an equal number of changes to Canadian rules.

Take a look at Figure 1.2 for an illustration of how the treaty is structured.

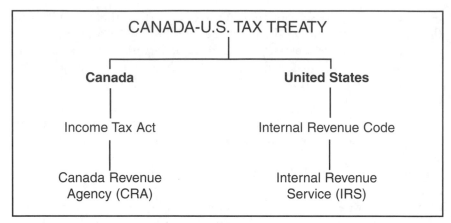

Figure 1.2

CROSS-BORDER Q&A

RULES GOVERNING U.S. RESIDENCE

I am a Canadian, female, 48 years old. I have been in Florida since September 2005 and intend to stay here permanently if all problems can be solved. Unfortunately, I do not qualify for a green card. I do have a Social Security Number. I intend to cross the border every six months to fulfill Canadian legal requirements. My health insurance terminates as of March 26, 2006, and most American health insurance companies require you to be a permanent resident.

Problem 1: Is health insurance possible to attain? If so, could you please recommend an insurer?

Problem 2: Am I considered a full-time resident?

Problem 3: My car has Ontario plates and registration. Am I better returning my car to Canada and buying one here or can I change the plates and registration here? What does it entail?

Problem 4: Do I need specific documents from Canada to obtain car insurance in Florida?

Problem 5: I would like to buy a house in Florida with a friend. What must I do to ensure my heirs have no problems?

— Susan G., Kissimmee, Florida

Problem 1: This can be solved through the use of either a U.S. health insurance carrier who requires that you have only a U.S. address or using a non-U.S. insurance company such as Lloyd's of London or a Danish company called Danmark International Health Insurance.

Problem 2: This problem has a yes, a maybe and a precautionary answer depending on which perspective you are looking from. You would be a resident of the United States for tax purposes since you will be spending more than 183 days there. For insurance purposes, the answer is a maybe, because each company has its own definition of what constitutes a resident, but most require legal U.S. residence. For immigration purposes, you would likely be classed as an illegal alien since your intent is to live in the United States full time without a green card or visa. Simply leaving the country for a short time every six months to renew your visitor status does not mean you are escaping the need for legal immigration status. When you leave the United States and attempt to re-enter as a visitor, the U.S. immigration official can simply refuse you entry for five years or more if he or she thinks you are living in the United States permanently without proper status. Because of the things you are trying to do, such as buying U.S. health insurance, a car and a house, you have all the makings of a resident, not a visitor, and effectively would have to mislead the immigration officials to gain entry as a visitor when you are in fact a resident. Purposely misleading an immigration official is considered more serious than being an illegal alien. You should speak to a good immigration attorney as soon as possible.

Problem 3: There is nothing preventing you from selling your car in Ontario and buying a new one registered in Florida. However, there are numerous regulatory hoops you need to jump through in Florida to import a Canadian car into that jurisdiction.

Problem 4: This depends on which insurance company you talk to, but most will require that you provide proof of a clean driving record and a valid Florida driver's licence.

Problem 5: If you wish to keep your half of the house separate from your friend's in the event of your demise, it would likely be best to register the property as Joint Owner as Tenants in Common. This will allow you to transfer by will your share of the residence separately to your respective heirs. You should also have a valid Florida will. Before you go into a Tenants in Common situation, you need to seek some professional advice so that you understand it fully and weigh it against other alternatives.

U.S. RESIDENCY HAS MANY OBLIGATIONS REQUIRING CAREFUL FINANCIAL PLANNING

I am writing to you on behalf of my aunt who is a citizen and resident of Canada. For a number of years she was a United States resident with a green card that was reissued to her. Is she eligible to stay in the United States for more than six months? Six months only is required by Canada, but will having a green card entitle her to a longer stay?

— R.J., Glendale, Arizona

If your aunt has a current, valid green card, she is able to stay in the United States for as long as she likes. The green card confers legal permanent residence status. There are many U.S. tax obligations of green card holders that your aunt needs to get in compliance with if she wishes to keep the green card. A good cross-border financial planner will be able to review her situation and make appropriate recommendations on taxes, medical coverage, investment and estate planning. She does need professional help, as there are some complex issues to address.

SICK RELATIVE IS NOT ENOUGH TO JUSTIFY U.S. VISITS

I am a Canadian citizen living in Toronto, but for the past three years have spent some months with my sister here in Ormond Beach, FL. Last year her husband passed away, and this year she has had a couple of bouts of illness which indicate that she should no longer live alone. She cannot afford a retirement centre. Three years ago we filed a petition for my immigration to the United States, but have been told that there is a 10- to 15-year wait for a visa to come through. I phoned USCIS recently and learned that their "six months in the United States" is six months per visit, so that theoretically I could go home for a few days every six months and stay here indefinitely otherwise. Actually I am going home February 11 to 28. So technically, I could stay to the end of August.

But the IRS is another matter. I worked in the United States for 26 years before returning to Canada to retire. Had I known then that I could get dual citizenship I would have done so. I now receive Social Security, income from small annuities from which 15% non-resident tax is deducted, and a little from an IRA. I also have U.S. Medicare Parts A and B. I file a T1 General in Canada and a 1040NR in the United States, which gives me a small refund. I have never filed a Closer Connection form, but will probably have to do so for this year. My Canadian income is limited to OAS and interest from about $120,000 in investments.

I talked with an IRS representative recently, and he suggested that I might be better off filing as a U.S. resident and staying on the six-month basis. But how does that affect my Canadian connections? Of course, OAS would be taxed, but Social Security would not. I won a condo in Canada and am buying a life-lease apartment there, so I do not want to stay here indefinitely. However, a few months more next year would be helpful. Can I do it without running afoul of the USCIS, IRS or Canadian authorities?

— F.R.B., Ormond Beach, Florida

Dealing first with the USCIS, you are technically correct that you can renew your six-month visitor's status by leaving the country and re-entering for another six months. However, every time you enter the United States, you must be prepared to justify why you are asking for a visitor status when in fact your intentions are other than those of a temporary visitor. Any entry to the United States when you tell the USCIS officials you are doing one thing and in fact are acting to the contrary is an illegal entry. Therefore, they can deny you entry if they have suspicions or evidence indicating otherwise.

In addition, if you enter as a visitor and stay longer than 183 days, you have technically overstayed your visa and have become an illegal alien. With the new USCIS requirements for checking in and out of the U.S. (which will be implemented over the next two or three years), overstaying a visa will be easily tracked and you could be denied re-entry by the USCIS for five years or more at that time.

With respect to the IRS, if you spend more than 183 days in a calendar year in the United States, you are considered a tax resident and are required to file a U.S. tax return on your world income. You then have to rely on the Canada/U.S. Tax Treaty to ensure you are not double-taxed on income sourced in one country but taxable by both countries. Canada will not recognize you as a resident of the United States until you are legally able to live there; therefore, you would likely have to file tax returns in both countries on a continuing basis.

There is some irony in the fact that complying with the IRS rules by filing required tax returns gives the USCIS clearly documented proof you are acting like a resident of the U.S. when you are not legally allowed to do so.

The Value of a Buck 2

HOW TO BEAT THE
EXCHANGE RATE BLUES

Regular visitors who plan an annual winter migration to the Sunbelt often exhibit symptoms of confusion, helplessness and insomnia just prior to leaving the country. This highly contagious phenomenon is known as the Exchange Rate Blues. A general feeling of malaise develops when the soon-to-be-departed snowbirds begin calling banks or poring over the financial pages of the newspaper. This is done in an often futile attempt to pick the best possible moment to convert their hard-earned Canadian dollars into American currency. Questions like "Should I wait until _____?" (fill in the blank with an appropriate response such as "tomorrow," "next week," "until the Bank of Canada sets its rate" or "until the exchange rate goes up another cent," etc.) feverishly run though the minds of travellers infected with the Exchange Rate Blues. Finally, the deal is struck and the currency exchanged, but the very next day the Exchange Rate Blues continue when new symptoms known as the "I should haves" appear. "I should have waited until _____" (again fill in the blank with the appropriate response, such as "when the exchange rate improved" if the dollar went up, or if it went the other way, "I should have changed more"). It's funny that when the dollar is trading around 65 cents U.S. we'd give our right arm to exchange at 85 cents, but when the dollar reaches that level we still want to hold off for a better rate.

I have spoken to thousands of Canadians in the United States, and every one of them, including myself, has suffered from the Exchange Rate Blues at one time or another. The vast majority usually start feeling the symptoms around August or just before a large amount of dollars needs to be exchanged.

Americans visiting Canada, for whatever reason, just don't seem get caught up in this exchange rate blues; it's as if they are inoculated against it.

ELIMINATING THE EXCHANGE RATE BLUES

Most people wouldn't dream of becoming currency speculators to earn money for their retirement because of the great risks involved in such activity. However, going through the ritual guessing game of which way the Canadian dollar is going is precisely that: currency speculation. In fact, currency speculation is the root cause of the Exchange Rate Blues. The Exchange Rate Blues, by the way, is very similar to the feeling that novice commodity traders have every time they make a trade, or gamblers when they place a bet.

How do you avoid currency speculation and cure the Exchange Rate Blues? The answer is very simple for those planning to winter in the United States in their retirement but most people will ignore it until it is too late. Place enough income-producing assets and savings in U.S.-dollar-generating investments long before retirement even begins. These savings, if accumulated faithfully, should produce income sufficient to safely cover expenses during your stays in the United States or to pay for travel to other parts of the world (see Chapter 6 for assistance for investing in the United States).

If all or most of your savings are wrapped up in your RRSPs, the new Canadian foreign content rules, which allow up to 100% of your RRSP to be invested in foreign investments, now provide you the opportunity to receive the U.S.-dollar income needed for your retirement from inside your RRSP. Don't ignore or put off this advice because it sounds so basic: simplicity is a key ingredient in a successful retirement plan. Over the 30 years of experience I have had in retirement planning, I have seen far too many people hurt and have their retirement goals fall short of expectations quite unnecessarily by failing to implement this very important strategy. Since the Canadian dollar has recently been trading at about 30-year highs, for those who have failed to implement this strategy to date in their investment plans, now might be a great time to do so. Protect yourself from a potential falling Canadian dollar while you have the opportunity to do so. There is little risk if the dollar continues to go up, but there is substantial risk if it heads south on you again.

What I am advising is simply a variation on the time-honoured tradition of not putting all your eggs in one basket. You will be diversified against currency risk and hedged against rapid fluctuations in either currency. You'll also save the many hundreds or even thousands of dollars in commissions that financial institutions build into their exchange rates. These commissions are particularly high when small sums are exchanged.

To determine the rate of commission, compare the rate listed in the financial sections of the newspaper with that posted at your bank or at the airport on the same day. It can be as high as 10% or more.

For those people making a permanent or temporary move to the United States for employment reasons, the Exchange Rate Blues can be avoided by simply biting the bullet and changing all your hard-earned Canadian dollars into one or two large lump sums and then never looking back. After you have been in the United States for a year or more, you will find that the extra quarter- or half-cent better rate you were thinking of holding out for will have absolutely no bearing on your financial success.

HEDGING YOUR BETS

Almost every corporation conducting cross-border commerce practises some form of currency hedging. A Canadian airline, for example, knows that next year it needs to pay for that new Boeing 787 they just ordered. They need to generate more U.S. income from their assets or purchase a currency futures contract locking in the current U.S. dollar rate — in effect an insurance policy that they will enjoy the current exchange rate or better when the jet has to be paid for. Failure to hedge or reduce their currency risk exposure in this situation might mean paying millions more for their 787, based solely on fluctuations in the Canadian dollar.

Canadians who spend any part of their retirement south of the border, or for that matter in most other parts of the world, will require U.S. funds. If you are currently age 65 and want to maximize your time in the sunny south, you'll need at least US$270,000 in today's dollars to fund 15 years of six-month stays at a spending level of just US$3,000 per month. If you do not protect yourself, or hedge your currency risk as the Canadian airline does, your retirement in the United States could end up costing you thousands of dollars more or, as in many cases through the 1980s and 1990s, end your retirement travel altogether. Figure 2.1 shows the year-end Canadian dollar values, as expressed in U.S. funds, since 1975.

Dollar speculation for the ten-year period of the 1990s has cost some Canadians most or all of their winter vacations, since the dollar was devalued more than 25% during that period. However, over short periods of time, the speculators sometimes looked as if they knew what they were doing, such as during the period from 1987 to 1991 or from 2002 to 2006. In fact, over the long term, they were losers. I have a true example in my planning practice of a couple who made a permanent move to the United States in 1992. They chose to speculate that the Canadian dollar would increase or at least stay the same in value and they left the majority of

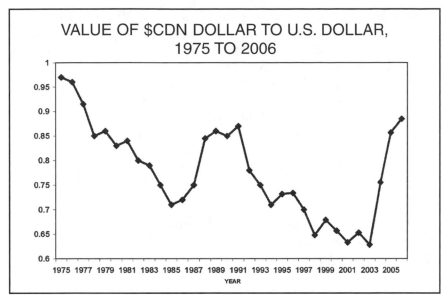

Figure 2.1

their large investment portfolio in Canadian investments. From that time to the year 2000 when they finally decided to change their strategy, they lost well over $1 million of their net worth, not to mention the lost opportunity costs of being able to invest the $1 million at normal portfolio rates of return. This lost opportunity cost probably cost them an additional $1 million. The sad thing about this case is that had the Canadian dollar increased in value and their speculation paid off, their lifestyle would have been affected only marginally; however, now they face cutting back to ensure they don't outlive their money. It is difficult for speculators to understand that the risk is not the Canadian dollar exchange rate going in their favour: protecting themselves if it goes down is the real risk. Speculating on the Canadian dollar can be profitable if you happen to get lucky. If you want to have a secure retirement, though, avoid the Exchange Rate Blues, and avoid becoming a currency speculator by diversifying away from the currency risk well in advance of your retirement.

NO EXCHANGE LOSS IF YOU CONVERT CANADIAN DOLLARS NOW

Investing all or a portion of your savings in the United States or in U.S.-dollar securities in Canada, depending on whether you are going to be a full-time or part-time U.S. resident, is a surefire way to avoid the Exchange Rate Blues and protect yourself from currency risk. Whenever we

23

recommend this strategy, nearly every client says, "How can I exchange my dollars now? I'll take too big a loss." Recently a well-educated multimillionaire from Vancouver told me (with full conviction, believing his mythical statement was, in fact, true) that he didn't want to move to the United States because he couldn't afford to take the hit to his net worth if he converted his assets into U.S. funds. The truth is there is no loss or gain at the time you convert Canadian dollars to U.S. dollars. It is very simply a fair market value exchange. Losses or gains occur prior to any conversion but only become visible or are realized when the actual conversion is made. To illustrate this point, Figure 2.2 shows that CDN$1,000 changed into foreign currency would net you $880 in U.S. dollars, $6,825 Hong Kong dollars, ¥101,486 Japanese Yen or 1.42 oz. of gold.

We'll assume that you paid no commissions and all exchanges transpired simultaneously.

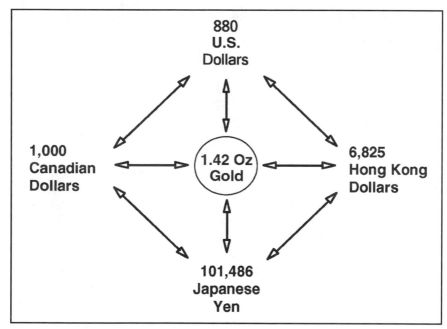

Figure 2.2

Would you consider it a gain because you changed CDN$1,000 to $6,825 Hong Kong dollars? Or would you consider yourself hitting a jackpot because your CDN$1,000 bought you more than ¥101,486 Japanese Yen? Of course not. Why should you think you have lost any money because your CDN$1,000 bought you only US$880? Yet it happens all the time, and because the idea is so firmly entrenched, it is really difficult to explain to Canadians they are not losing any value in such an exchange.

Figure 2.2 also illustrates that it doesn't matter what currency you are using, or whether it is denominated in dollars, yen or something else. It takes the same relative amount of each currency to purchase the same tangible object such as the 1.42 oz. of gold used in this chart. For gold, you could substitute a month's rental on a U.S. vacation property and the net result would be the same. To further illustrate that there is no loss or gain on currency exchange transactions, run through a full cycle of exchange from CDN$1,000 to ¥101,486 Japanese Yen to 1.42 oz. of gold, to US$880 and back to CDN$1,000. There is no loss at any time during the currency exchange, since in theory you could go back and forth from the CDN$1,000 to the US$880 as often as you like if you paid no commissions for the exchanges. Losses or gains occur only if you repeat part of this full cycle of exchange at some other point in time. The relative values of the four currencies and the gold will change, but guessing what those relative values will be is pure speculation and not for the risk-averse.

The only loss when exchanging Canadian dollars to U.S. funds is that which is perceived, not real. This misconception comes from Canada's proximity to the United States and the fact that both countries call their currency the dollar. At one time (approximately 35 years ago) one dollar Canadian was worth approximately one U.S. dollar. But there is no law or agreement that says a Canadian dollar must be worth one American dollar, just as there is no law that says one Canadian dollar must equal one Hong Kong dollar. The relationship between the Canadian dollar and the U.S. dollar is market-driven, based on worldwide demand, and is every bit as unrestrained as the relative values of the Canadian dollar and the Japanese yen. Had the United States called their currency something different, like *zlotnays*, this perception of loss would likely never have happened.

One final point on the issue of currency exchange and Canadians waiting "for the dollar to come back." Currencies should not be confused with stocks or bonds, which tend to be "mean reverting." Mean reverting is the tendency to come back to what might be considered a normal or average value. Large stocks such as IBM exhibit this tendency, so if IBM stock goes down it normally would come back in value if you waited long enough. However, currencies are not mean reverting and do not display this tendency to revert back to what could be considered a normal value; they are constantly setting new levels without regard to past history. A good example of this is the British pound. After the Second World War, one pound would buy more than five U.S. dollars, whereas now it will buy less than two dollars. Is there anyone out there who believes, British or not, that they should wait for the pound to come back to five before they do a currency exchange? The wait could be a lifetime or two — perhaps forever — but is that any different for a Canadian waiting for the loonie to go back to one U.S. dollar? Think about it: the real risk for most people is that the loonie goes down further against the U.S. dollar, whereas there is no risk if it goes up. So why are so many people waiting for it to go up regardless of what its current levels do to their exchanges? Even in late 2006, with the Canadian dollar reaching better than 30-year highs against the U.S. dollar, people who felt they needed to protect themselves from a falling Canadian dollar were still waiting for it to go higher before they made their exchanges. If that describes you, remember the earlier discussion regarding becoming a currency speculator: in the short term, you may come out okay, but longer term, you inevitably lose out.

WHAT CAN YOU EXPECT IF YOU INVEST IN THE UNITED STATES?

For most periods prior to 2004, interest rates on bank term deposits, GICs and government bonds in Canada were higher than the same respective rates in the United States. Consequently, Canadians tended to avoid investing in the United States because they felt they could get better returns in Canada. Canadian rates tend to be higher to compensate global investors for a greater risk factor perceived in Canadian currency investments. However, due to current convergent policies of the Bank of Canada and the U.S. Federal Reserve, Canadians can now take advantage of higher interest rates in the United States.

In today's global economy, investments need to be administered as if you were operating a business on a worldwide basis. Since Canada constitutes only approximately 2% to 3% of the world's economy, you're not only taking a greater risk, but missing out on growth opportunities by not investing outside Canada. If the business of your investments is astutely managed and diversified worldwide, you'll earn the same level of profit or income at the same relative risk whether your portfolio is in the United States or Canada, providing your portfolio expenses are the same.

For example, compare a mutual fund in Canada to one in the United States with the same objectives, restrictions, management and fee structure; over time, you will see that their returns will also be similar on a percentage basis. The only difference is that one generates Canadian-dollar funds, and the other generates U.S. funds. In fact, most brokerage firms and mutual fund companies in Canada have U.S.-dollar investments that you can use without even leaving Canada. As a result, you do not have to take any reduction in income and can maintain the same level of safety by directing some or all of your investments to the United States. This effectively avoids speculation on the Canadian dollar, and will cure the Exchange Rate Blues.

Please note that commissions paid to brokers and the management expense ratios — the fees you pay directly out of the mutual fund to the managers in Canada — are on average twice what they are in the United States and were increased more than 15% on average during the poor market years of 2000 to 2003. I have not been convinced by any Canadian brokerage firm or mutual fund company that they need to charge twice the rates of their U.S. counterparts when the cost of doing business in Canada is approximately the same or even less in some circumstances. Canadian consumers should be outraged at this and either demand their fund providers lower their rates or bypass them altogether and purchase Exchange Traded Funds (ETFs), which have become very popular with investors. ETFs not only give Canadians full access to the U.S. and other world markets but they can give the same diversified portfolios at a fraction of the cost of mutual funds.

Chapters 6 and 12 provide insight for non-residents and residents, respectively, who are investing in the U.S. Chapter 11 helps Americans who wish to invest in Canada.

AVOIDING U.S. INCOME TAX ON YOUR INVESTMENTS

Investing in the United States as a non-resident can be rewarding and worry-free if you follow the same investment principles you would use in Canada, and then stick with those investments that are exempt from both American income and estate tax. There is no substitute for diversification and good management, regardless of your investment objectives. Chapter 6 lists those investments that Canadians can use to produce a steady tax-free U.S. income for U.S. non-residents and non-citizens, while avoiding the non-residents' estate tax discussed in Chapter 4. The fact that these investments are exempt from tax and reporting requirements in the United States does not mean that you don't have to report the income to the Canada Revenue Agency (CRA). A Canadian resident is subject to tax on world income in Canada.

WHERE IS THE BEST PLACE TO EXCHANGE MONEY?

Experienced travellers will tell you that the rate of currency exchange can vary dramatically, depending on the form of your Canadian dollars — cash, cheque or traveller's cheques — and the facility you use to make the exchange — a bank, brokerage firm or airport. Whether you are in Canada or the United States will also be a factor in obtaining the best exchange rates. World currency markets dictate exchange rates based on numerous demand factors, but it is primarily commission rates, spreads or markups and other related charges that vary between exchange rate vendors.

There is no exact formula that will guarantee you the best rate of exchange each time, but the basic guidelines listed below have saved previous readers of *The Border Guide* hundreds and even thousands of dollars in exchange commissions.

- Exchange large sums at one time, whenever possible. The costs of exchanging $1,000 five separate times is roughly twice that of changing $5,000 once.

- When exchanging at a bank, ask for the "spot" rate. This is the special rate right from the market at that time. Generally this service is available only when exchanging amounts of $5,000 or more.

- Avoid using Canadian cash for the exchange. Commission rates on cash can go over 10%, particularly if you are outside Canada. Cheques and traveller's cheques generally attract the best rates. Personal cheques work fine only at a bank where you are known.

- Shop around to at least three institutions and give each vendor the exact amount you want to exchange, and the form of Canadian dollars used in the exchange. Exchange rates vary widely from institution to institution and change constantly throughout the day. If you are going to use a bank, include both U.S. and Canadian banks in your survey. You may get some pleasant surprises if you do. There are now several U.S. banks and brokerage firms in the United States, owned by parent Canadian banks, that exchange Canadian dollars at greatly reduced commission rates in order to attract new customers.

- Use foreign exchange brokers. Some even guarantee that they will beat the bank rate every time. We've found that some foreign exchange brokers exchange Canadian for U.S. dollars at far better rates than any bank or brokerage firm. They also won't try to sell you something else you may not want or need. The good ones are easy to work with regardless of where you are, including the United States, through their toll-free numbers. See "Dealing with Foreign Exchange Brokers" in the next section.

- If you have a relationship with a brokerage firm, you can generally exchange money there at no or very low commissions or price markups. They are, of course, hoping you will invest the money through them and will often attempt to sell investments to you whether you are looking or not!

- If you're in a major gambling centre such as Las Vegas, the casinos tend to offer excellent rates of exchange. They may frown upon it, however, if you do not stop to gamble with some of your newly acquired U.S. currency.

- Credit card companies may offer a preferred exchange rate when you use their cards to purchase foreign goods. However, these preferred exchange rates still may not be very good for the consumer's benefit. Credit card companies generally charge 2% to 3% currency exchange fees as well as transaction fees for some foreign purchases. They also charge exorbitant interest rates if you are not back in Canada or have not made other arrangements to pay the bill when it's due. Some banks, such as the Bank of Montreal, now issue U.S.-dollar VISA cards, which means you pay your bill in U.S. funds. You can negotiate a better rate through an exchange broker at the time you make payment. Using a U.S.-dollar charge card in conjunction with a currency exchange broker is a much better solution than being at the mercy of the issuing bank to set its own exchange rate for a Canadian-dollar charge card for U.S. purchases. Using a Canadian-dollar charge card in the U.S. means paying additional fees and getting hit with a poorer exchange rate on each transaction.

DEALING WITH FOREIGN EXCHANGE BROKERS

Foreign exchange brokers are a relatively new phenomenon in Canada. They have been made possible by deregulation, which took away the banks' near monopoly on currency exchange. Banks do not really like this competition since their currency exchange departments tend to be among their most profitable. So if you ask your local bank manager about dealing with these brokers, don't expect too many favourable comments.

Foreign exchange brokers have done much to eliminate the air of mystery and poor service associated with exchanging currency. They provide ordinary customers with the same level of service that banks usually reserve for very large clients and they do it at a much lower cost, even lower than special promotions and preferred rates for snowbirds. Foreign exchange brokers can give you real-time dollar (or other currencies) exchange quotes from world currency markets at any time, and once you've established a working relationship you can deal with them from anywhere in Canada or the United States using their toll-free numbers. You could be in Florida, your Canadian dollars in a bank account in Moose Jaw, and the currency broker in Vancouver. Yet you can exchange any amount and have the U.S. cash wired to your Florida bank on the same or very next business day. One valuable service exchange brokers provide that banks do not is allowing you to use standing orders. You can set the rate you want your money exchanged at, and when the exchange rate reaches your stated price, if it does at all, your transaction is processed automatically. For example, if the Canadian dollar was at US$0.85 and you had CDN$5,000 to exchange, your standing order might look like this: "Exchange my CDN$5,000 when the Canadian-dollar rate hits US$0.86." This standing order can be placed overnight or on weekends to be traded on other world exchanges such as the Tokyo Exchange. In certain circumstances you may wish to buy what is, in effect, an insurance policy to hedge against a falling Canadian dollar, when the funds you wish to exchange will not be available for a period of time because they may be locked in a GIC, you are waiting, for example, to close a house purchase. A good currency broker can help you through the ins and outs of this relatively complex transaction to ensure you understand how it works and the limitations of these hedging contracts.

The majority of foreign exchange companies in Canada are well capitalized and professionally managed. However, since this is a new financial industry and foreign exchange companies are not regulated like banks or stock brokerage firms, consumers planning to use them need to investigate who they are dealing with and what guidelines they should follow to protect themselves. The following guidelines will help *Border Guide* readers take advantage of the better exchange rates offered by foreign exchange brokers without being taken advantage of themselves:

- Know who you are dealing with by asking for referrals from other customers of the exchange brokers and their company. Ask for financial data on the company, get a banking report from the bank(s) the company uses to facilitate its transactions, and determine how long the company has been in business and how many offices and employees they have. Generally, the longer they have been in business and the larger they are, the safer they will likely be to use.

- When dealing directly over the counter at a local foreign exchange broker, request that the broker have a U.S.-dollar bank draft prepared in advance for you to exchange directly with your Canadian-dollar draft or cheque in the applicable amounts.

- When dealing over the phone with foreign exchange brokers and when they are wiring U.S. funds to a third party such as a bank or brokerage firm, have the brokers wire the U.S. funds in trust to the third party if possible, so you can confirm the funds have been released by the broker before you pay them for the U.S. funds.

- Don't forget to use some of the exchange techniques we have discussed in the previous section of this chapter, such as exchanging large amounts at one time and getting more than one quote.

Custom House Currency Exchange is a foreign exchange firm that my clients and I have used to successfully exchange millions of Canadian dollars over the past 15 years. This Victoria-based firm guarantees it will beat the bank exchange rates. Custom's toll-free number, good anywhere in Canada or the United States, is 1-800-345-0007. You can also visit their website at www.customhouse.com. Custom House has 75 offices in Canada, the U.S., the U.K., Australia and New Zealand and completes more than ten billion dollars of currency transactions per year. You do not need to be near one of their offices to transact business as phone, wires, fax and Internet can all be used to facilitate any currency transaction from almost any location.

The Taxman Cometh   3

CROSS-BORDER TAX PLANNING

I n Chapter 1, we alluded to the fact that cross-border financial planning can be very beneficial for all those who undertake it diligently, and very costly to those who choose to ignore it or try to do it without professional help. The key points, in order to provide the best return on your investment of time and money, come in the areas of income tax and non-resident estate tax planning. This chapter will deal with the income tax issues, while Chapter 4 will delve into the non-resident estate tax.

Figure 1.1 in Chapter 1 refers to the various categories of immigration status. Each category has different issues regarding income tax. The first category that we will examine is the typical winter visitor who spends less than six months a year in the United States and has no visa or other immigration status in the United States other than visitor. We will then look at U.S. citizens and green card holders living in Canada and Canadians potentially becoming U.S. residents under certain tax rules without having legal status there. Chapter 8 will deal in more detail with the tax issues of transitioning from being a Canadian resident to a U.S. resident, and Chapter 11 will assist Americans becoming residents of Canada.

TAXING NON-RESIDENT ALIENS

Non-residents, or non-resident aliens, as the U.S. tax and immigration publications like to refer to them, are generally taxed on their U.S. source income only. Income from U.S. sources includes interest on bonds, notes and other interest-bearing obligations, all wages for services performed in the United States, dividends, rents, royalties and the gains from sale of U.S. real property. The Canada/U.S. Tax Treaty sets forth the withholding rates, if any, on these sources of income (see Figure 8.9 in Chapter 8).

The treaty withholding rate is 10% on interest. The Internal Revenue Service has taken the position that it will not collect the treaty withholding tax on interest from all U.S. banks, Savings & Loans, and similar institutions, providing the non-resident has filed an IRS Form W-8BEN, Certificate of Foreign Status of Beneficial Owner for United States Tax Withholding (see Figure 3.4 later in this chapter), with the payer of the interest. Form W-8BEN entitles you to this withholding exemption. Persons filing any type of U.S. tax return or form with the exception of Form W-8BEN must use IRS Form W-7, Application for IRS Individual Taxpayer Identification Number (see Figure 3.3), to apply for an Individual Taxpayer Identification Number (ITIN). The ITIN is similar to a Social Insurance Number or Social Security Number and is used to track payer and payee income tax reporting, as well as expedite non-resident income tax filings. You are not required to have an ITIN for completing form W-8BEN but if you have one or a Social Security number they should be used when you complete this form. Most banks keep a good supply of W-7 and W-8BEN forms, and they can also be obtained from any IRS office or the IRS website, www.irs.gov.

Non-residents earning dividends in the United States will face a 15% withholding rate, reduced from 30% by the Canada/U.S. Tax Treaty. Canadians will have to file the IRS Form W-8BEN to ensure they get the treaty rate of withholding rather than the regular rate.

Gains on the sale of U.S. securities are exempt from U.S. capital gains tax, providing you have filed a Form W-8BEN with your broker.

By properly filing a Form W-8BEN with your bank and brokers *they* will be prevented from filing certain tax slips for which the IRS would normally require you to file U.S. tax returns if the tax slips had been issued.

Canadians collecting rent from the United States have two options: either pay a flat 30% withholding tax on the gross rent, or file a non-resident tax return, Form 1040NR. With the 1040NR you can elect to be taxed as a business in the United States and net expenses against the rent and then pay regular tax rates on the net rental income at the applicable rate. Most Canadians with rental income will find that they will pay less tax, and perhaps no tax at all, if they file a U.S. return. Even if you clearly made no profit from your rental property and paid no withholding tax, you must still file a Form 1040NR, unless you enjoy playing Russian roulette with the IRS. IRS regulations have been enacted that will disallow any rental expenses 16 months after the normal filing deadline of June 15 each year if there was no return filed. If the IRS catches up with you for failure to file, you will be forced to pay tax and penalties on the gross rent collected. When no returns have been filed on the rental income the IRS may go back indefinitely and ask for back taxes, penalties and interest for the entire period. In addition, failure to file and take mandatory depreciation could result in your paying substantially higher taxes when you eventually sell the property even if you have to sell it at a loss. In other words, it is best to file a timely 1040NR each year you have any rental income or expenses.

Canadians selling real estate will be exempt from withholding tax if they are selling a personal-use residence in the United States, if it is valued at less than $300,000 and the buyers are going to occupy the home for their own personal use. Otherwise, the withholding rate is 10%, whether or not there will be any profit on the sale. Application can be made to the IRS to reduce or eliminate the withholding tax, if there is only a small gain or a loss on the sale of the property. It important to note that an exemption from withholding tax should not be confused with exemption from tax as tax is often due even when withholding is not. The gross amount of the sale transaction is reported by the buyer or the buyer's agent to the IRS on Form 1099-S and the details of any net gains or losses must be reported to the IRS on Form 1040NR by the seller, for the year of the sale. If there is further tax to be paid on a gain, it will be paid with this return and, likewise, if there is a refund due of any withholding, this is the mechanism for applying for it. The Canada/U.S. Tax Treaty was revised in 1980. Canadians may use the treaty to exempt any gains before December 31, 1984, provided they owned their property prior to 1980.

Just as American visitors to Canada who purchase property in Canada do not qualify for the Canadian principal residence exemption, Canadian visitors with property in the U.S. do not qualify for the $250,000 per person or $500,000 per couple U.S. principal residence exemption.

Remember that exemptions from U.S. tax on any of the aforementioned income do not mean it is exempt from Canadian taxation. Canadian residents are taxable on their world income and must report all of these U.S. earnings annually to the Canada Revenue Agency whether exempt or not. You generally will receive a credit on your Canadian return for any taxes paid to the United States to the extent allowed by CRA and Canada/U.S. Tax Treaty rules. It is very important, though, to ensure any withholding is done according to the Canada/U.S. Tax Treaty. The CRA will only allow credits on a Canadian return to the amount specified by the treaty, so any excess withholding will not be credited and will be lost unless attempts are made to recover it from the U.S. withholder, a difficult job at best.

Most Canadians investing to produce U.S. income will have no U.S. withholding tax to pay or tax returns to file if they use the exempt investments first mentioned in Chapter 2 and explained in detail in Chapter 6. In the section Who Must File Tax Returns in the United States? later in this chapter, Canadian non-residents can find exactly under what circumstances and when they must or when they should file a non-resident tax return, Form 1040NR, with the IRS.

DUAL CITIZENS AND GREEN CARD HOLDERS RESIDENT IN CANADA

Canada taxes its citizens on their world income only when they are residents of Canada. The United States taxes its citizens and permanent resident aliens or green card holders on their world income, with certain exclusions, regardless of where they reside in the world.

Many Canadians obtained U.S. green cards over the years, when they were handed out much more liberally than they are today or when there were green card lotteries. Some never used these green cards, while others might have used them but moved back to Canada to set up principal residence there. Chapter 7 deals with the immigration implications of Canadians in this situation. From a tax standpoint, the IRS considers all green card holders legal permanent residents of the United States and subject to the same filing requirements as anyone else with resident status. That is, they must file annual tax returns in the United States on their world income. There can be numerous tax advantages to paying taxes in the United States rather than Canada, and these are covered later in this chapter and in Chapter 8. However, Canadians in this situation need to determine as soon as possible whether they should officially abandon their green cards or use them to their best advantage. In other words, they need to come out of the closet. The best means to make the final decision about what to do in this situation is to complete a full cross-border financial plan that addresses every issue from the perspective of getting the best of both the Canadian and U.S. systems. If you do nothing and continue to sit in the woods with your green card, you inevitably end up getting the worst of both systems, instead of the best. If you have had your green card for more than eight years, you may be subject to the same income tax and estate tax rules as expatriate U.S. citizens discussed later in this chapter.

Canadians who were born in the United States or obtained U.S. citizenship from another source (see Chapter 7, sections on Derivative Citizenship and Dual Citizenship) and who are also naturalized Canadian citizens are dual citizens of Canada and the United States. Dual citizens living in Canada are in a similar situation taxwise to the green card holders described above. They need to file annual tax returns in both countries on their world income. Similarly, Canadians who are dual citizens or reside in Canada need to determine, as soon as possible, whether they should officially abandon their U.S. citizenship or use it to their best advantage. Our advice here is also the same. Complete a cross-border financial plan and use it to position your dual citizenship to obtain the best advantages between Canada and the United States. This planning can easily save thousands or even hundreds of thousands of dollars in taxes. Chapters 8, 9 and 13 will show you what many of your options are.

VOLUNTARY DISCLOSURE

Canadian residents holding U.S. green cards, U.S. citizens, dual citizens and derivative U.S. citizens who have not been filing U.S. annual tax returns on their world income have one key option to come out of the closet and get back on the correct U.S. filing rolls without penalty. If the past six years' returns are filed under voluntary disclosure regulations, the IRS will normally waive basic penalties (but not interest) on tax due, if any, and reduce the normally unlimited statute of limitations for failure to file for the same six years by not asking any questions about what happened to any income or taxes due before the six years. We have completed many past-due tax returns with good success, seeking penalty relief under regular IRS voluntary disclosure regulations. If you wait for the IRS to come after you, this voluntary disclosure is not available to you and you will be nailed with the full tax, penalties and interest perhaps even further back than the six years. The Canada/U.S. Tax Treaty rules will also allow the IRS to seize assets and bank accounts with CRA's obliging assistance. This makes it extremely important that Canadian residents who are citizens or green card holders take action immediately to get right with the IRS before the IRS finds them, and to know what their liabilities are to avoid a possible financial disaster. The IRS has recently hired over a thousand additional auditors and have started coordinating records with the U.S. Citizenship and Immigration Service (USCIS) to bring as many expatriate filers into compliance as possible. Those who have ignored or were unaware of this IRS filing requirement will find one door slammed shut that might have once been open to them before February 6, 1995, with new expatriation legislation as explained in the next section.

Sitting in the woods as a green card holder or U.S. citizen living in Canada hoping no one will find out is clearly the worst of all possible strategies. By hiding, you are effectively giving the IRS control of your financial life or your final estate's future. The IRS may raise its ugly head unexpectedly at any time, as many in this situation have found out, much to their dismay, and huge taxes and penalties may be assessed well after there was opportunity to zero them out by forward-looking cross-border financial planning. Often, U.S. citizens or green card holders in Canada who were not in compliance with the IRS are found out only after their deaths, when their executors find they must either pay the tax and penalties or face perjury charges or other sanctions themselves. This is not a pleasant position for any executor to be put in, and beneficiaries get mightily upset when they see a good portion or even all of their inheritance evaporate before their eyes in favour of the IRS.

The requirement to file in the United States on world income does not necessarily mean that there would be taxes due to the United States on income earned in Canada. There are exemptions such as the earned income exclusion of US$82,400 and the ancillary housing costs exclusion of $11,536, providing the earned income was not U.S.-sourced. When one fails to file in a timely fashion the IRS can deny these exclusions entirely. In addition to this employment income exemption, the Canada/U.S. Tax Treaty allows for foreign tax credits for taxes paid in Canada on the U.S. return for the same income. Since Canadian tax rates have been significantly higher than U.S. rates in recent years, the foreign tax credits from taxes paid in Canada usually would cover any U.S. taxes due. However, there are certain circumstances under which U.S. taxes can be due on income that would not be taxed currently, if the taxpayer or U.S. citizen was filing only in Canada — for example, if a U.S. citizen in Canada had income from mutual funds in Canada inside an RRSP that, because it is inside the RRSP, is exempt from current tax in Canada. But since the IRS currently taxes RRSP income without the deferral allowed by CRA (see Chapter 8, "Withdraw Your RRSP Tax Free!" for more detailed information on how the U.S. taxes RRSPs), these people would pay tax to the United States at the standard U.S. tax rate with no offsetting Canadian credit available since no Canadian tax was owing on the RRSP income on a current basis unless there are actual withdrawals from the RRSP. A similar problem can arise when a Canadian resident or U.S. citizen takes advantage of the $500,000 small-business capital gains exemption, as there would be no Canadian tax due but the IRS would require taxes be paid on this $500,000 business sale. In addition, Canadian principal residence exemptions work differently than the U.S. principal residence exemption, so consequently sales of principal residences may be taxed on the Canadian return and not on the U.S., or vice versa.

U.S. citizens in Canada taking dividends from their closely held Canadian corporations in an attempt to zero out or reduce personal Canadian tax with the dividend tax credit could also find themselves paying U.S. taxes on the dividends received. Similarly, income earned and held inside the closely controlled private corporation in Canada can be taxed by the IRS as if the income was earned personally by the taxpayer with no tax credit for taxes paid by the corporation (this topic is discussed in more detail in Chapter 11). One can correctly surmise that the IRS regulations requiring U.S. citizens to file annual returns, in light of the differences in the applications of tax rules between Canada and the United States, is extremely complex and can provide for some very unpleasant surprises. Voluntary disclosure will be of great advantage to U.S. citizens who want to get back into the good graces of the IRS and avoid penalties. They may also want to prevent the IRS from scrutinizing financial transactions prior to the six years of required returns that may require the payment of large tax amounts. As noted earlier, the IRS is now tracking passport renewals and travel visa requests by U.S. citizens and is actively campaigning to ferret out and prosecute non-filers around the world. U.S. citizens living in Canada who have not been filing U.S. returns and who do not take advantage of the voluntary disclosure programs may find themselves facing severe penalties. Once the IRS catches up with them, they may also be forced to file U.S. tax returns for more than six years.

As a consequence, U.S. citizens and green card holders in Canada require constant cross-border tax advice to avoid unnecessary tax and should construct a plan that takes best advantage of the U.S. and Canadian tax systems while avoiding common pitfalls. Proper planning from a knowledgeable cross-border planner can turn these apparent tax problems into great tax-saving opportunities. In general, U.S. citizens and green card holders living in Canada are going to be hit with the worst of both the Canadian and U.S. tax systems if they remain full-time residents of Canada. If they have no intention of returning to the United States, serious consideration should be given to renouncing their U.S. citizenship, but only after taking into consideration the new Expatriation Rules explained in the next section. This step should be taken only after they have addressed all their options in a comprehensive cross-border financial plan. Green card holders living in Canada need to follow the same tax rules as U.S. citizens, but face the added burden of losing their green cards. Filing a U.S. tax return is one of the key indicators used to determine whether the residency rules required to maintain the green card are being followed.

U.S. TAX LEGISLATION CONCERNING EXPATRIATION FROM THE UNITED STATES

The American Jobs Creation Act of 2004 contains new provisions regarding expatriation. For the purposes of this Act expatriation means a person who deliberately relinquishes his or her U.S. citizenship and a person who renounces his or her permanent resident status or green card after holding it for at least eight of the last fifteen years. This new law eliminates the past requirement that the expatriate was giving up his or her U.S. citizenship or green card for tax reasons. Consequently, this new act applies regardless of whether a principal purpose of the expatriation was for U.S. tax avoidance purposes or for any other reason. Now an individual will be subject to an alternative tax regime (ATR) if he or she expatriates. The ATR applies if —

- the individual had an average annual income tax liability over the preceding five years greater than $131,000, adjusted for inflation;
- the individual's net worth is $2 million or more; or
- the individual fails to certify and provide evidence of compliance with U.S. federal tax obligations for the preceding five years.

No relinquishment of citizenship or termination of lawful permanent residency will be effective for federal tax purposes until such person gives notice of an expatriating act or termination of residency to the Secretary of State or the Secretary of Homeland Security and provides a statement by completing IRS Form 8854, Expatriation Information Statement.

The alternate tax regime applies to the expatriate for a period of ten years from the date of expatriation. The amount of tax the expatriate individual would have to pay it is the greater of —

- the amount of tax the expatriate individual would have paid as a non-resident alien; or
- the amount of tax that the expatriate would have paid on his or her U.S. source income as specifically defined for purposes of the expatriation provisions.

Under the ATR, U.S. source income is defined to include —

- income that is effectly connected to a U.S. trade or business;
- gain on the sale or exchange of stock or debt issued by a U.S. corporation, U.S. person or the United States or other government body; and

- gain from the exchange of certain property that generated U.S. source income for property that generates non-U.S. source income.

With certain exceptions, if the expatriate is present in United States for more than 30 days in a year during the ten-year period, for such year, the person will be subject to income tax as a U.S. person.

Similarly, under the ATR, expatriates are subject to an estate tax and gift tax for the ten-year period after expatriation on all U.S. situs (located in) property as applied to non-resident aliens. Situs property includes shares of U.S. corporations and U.S. real estate.

Currently there is no specifically designed tax form for the ATR, but the expatriate is required to do annual filings using Form 8854 with the nearest American Embassy or consulate. The filing must include information detailing the income, assets, and liabilities of the individual, the number days the individual was physically present in the U.S. during the taxable year and other basic taxpayer identification information. If the expatriate fails to file the statement described above by the due date, there is a potential penalty of $10,000 in addition to paying the tax due and accumulated interest and penalties.

There is a provision in U.S. immigration law referred to as the Reed Amendment that allows the federal government to deny an expatriate admission into the United States. This law has never been enforced, and many experts believe that it is unenforceable as currently enacted. However, the law may be amended and there is a risk the United States could deny an expatriate to right to re-enter the U.S.

NON-RESIDENT TO RESIDENT IN THE UNITED STATES

Canadians who regularly spend less than four cumulative months a year in the United States do not have to worry about becoming a resident of the United States for tax purposes. They will be free of any filing requirements other than the situations listed later in this chapter in the section Who Must File Tax Returns in the United States?

From Chapter 1, under How Long Can You Remain in the United States as a Visitor?, you may recall that different sets of rules apply to winter visitors, such as being considered a U.S. resident for tax purposes and yet having no right to remain in the United States as an immigrant. This section will examine the tax rules that make this apparent contradiction possible whether you have a U.S. visa or not.

THE SUBSTANTIAL PRESENCE TEST

Winter visitors are considered residents of the United States for tax purposes if they meet the Substantial Presence Test. Winter visitors satisfy this test if they have been present in the United States for at least 183 days during a three calendar year period that includes the "current year." The current year is the particular tax year for which the winter visitor is determining a resident status. For purposes of the Substantial Presence Test, a winter visitor will be treated as "present" in the United States on any day that he or she is physically present in the country at any time during the day. This would include any cross-border trip you make to the United States being counted as a full day, even if you were present in the country for only a few hours. Note that the days present in the United States need not be consecutive but are cumulative throughout each calendar year.

Each day of presence in the first preceding year is counted as one-third of a day, and each day of presence in the second preceding year is counted as one-sixth of a day. For example, Figure 3.1 illustrates the results of these calculations for a winter visitor who spends four months in the United States Sunbelt, plus a few shopping days in the adjoining border town. Even though this winter visitor never came close to spending six months in the United States in any one year, he can be deemed to have spent 187 days in the current year and is therefore a U.S. resident for tax purposes under the Substantial Presence Test.

THE SUBSTANTIAL PRESENCE TEST

Number of days present this year ....124 x 1 = 124

Number of days present last year....................................124 x $\frac{1}{3}$ = 42

Number of days present previous to last year................124 x $\frac{1}{6}$ = 21

Total days deemed present in the current year........................187

Figure 3.1

In computing the days of presence in the United States under the final rule, certain days are not considered days of presence. These include any day that an individual is prevented from leaving the United States because of a medical condition that arose while the visitor was in the country.

If an individual is not physically present for more than 30 days during the current year, the Substantial Presence Test will not apply even if the three-year total is 183 or more days.

As an example: John is physically present in the United States for 52 days in 2006, 300 days in 2005, and 186 days in 2004. John meets the 31-day requirement for the current year. He also meets the 183-day requirement ((186/6) + (300/3) + 52 = 183). As a result of this Substantial Presence Test formula, John is considered a resident of the U.S. for tax purposes by the Internal Revenue Service.

Another example: Barbara was physically present in the United States on 120 days in each of the years 2004, 2005 and 2006. The full 120 days count for 2006; for 2005, count 40 days (120/3); and, for 2004, count 20 days (120/6). Since the total for the three years (180) is less than 183, Barbara would not be considered a resident under the Substantial Presence Test for 2006.

THE CLOSER CONNECTION EXCEPTION

Winter visitors who meet the Substantial Presence Test may nevertheless be considered non-resident aliens for the current year if (1) they are present in the United States for fewer than 183 days during the current year; (2) they maintain a "tax home" in a foreign country during the year; and (3) during the current year they have a "closer connection" to the foreign country where they have a tax home than to the United States.

This Closer Connection exemption is available only to those winter visitors who file IRS Form 8840, The Closer Connection Exception Statement (see Figure 3.2) or Form 1040 NR, the non-resident Tax Return, by June 15 of each year for the previous calendar year. Filing Form 8840 is very important for anyone who may be considered resident of the United States under the Substantial Presence Test. Filing Form 8840 in a timely manner brings closure to a myriad of tax rules that could have quite adverse effects if they were applied to a Canadian retroactively without the protection afforded by the act of filing this basic form. Failure to file Form 8840 when required may result in fines of up to $1,000 for each source of income received — even if no tax would have been payable on your U.S. tax return.

The visitor's regular or principal place of business is considered the location of his tax home. If the individual has no regular place of business because of the nature of his business, or because he is not engaged in any business, the visitor's tax home is his regular place of abode "in a real and

Form **8840**

Department of the Treasury
Internal Revenue Service

Closer Connection Exception Statement for Aliens
▶ Attach to Form 1040NR or Form 1040NR-EZ.

For the year January 1—December 31, 2005, or other tax year
beginning   , 2005, and ending   , 20

OMB No. 1545-0074

20**05**

Attachment
Sequence No. **101**

Your first name and initial	Last name	Your U.S. taxpayer identification number, if any

Fill in your
addresses only if
you are filing this
form by itself and
not with your U.S.
tax return

Address in country of residence	Address in the United States

Part I   **General Information**

1   Type of U.S. visa (for example, F, J, M, etc.) and date you entered the United States ▶ ....
2   Of what country or countries were you a citizen during the tax year? ....
3   What country or countries issued you a passport? ....
4   Enter your passport number(s) ▶ ....
5   Enter the number of days you were present in the United States during:
    2005 _____   2004 _____   2003 _____ .
6   During 2005, did you apply for, or take other affirmative steps to apply for, lawful permanent resident
    status in the United States or have an application pending to change your status to that of a lawful
    permanent resident of the United States (see instructions)? . . . . ☐ **Yes** ☐ **No**

Part II   **Closer Connection to One Foreign Country**

7   Where was your tax home during 2005? ....
8   Enter the name of the foreign country to which you had a closer connection than to the United States during 2005
    ▶ ....
    Next, complete Part IV on the back.

Part III   **Closer Connection to Two Foreign Countries**

9   Where was your tax home on January 1, 2005? ....
10 After changing your tax home from its location on January 1, 2005, where was your tax home for the remainder of 2005?
    ....
    ....
    ....

11 Did you have a closer connection to each foreign country listed on lines 9 and 10 than to the United
    States for the period during which you maintained a tax home in that foreign country? . . . . . . ☐ **Yes** ☐ **No**
    If "No," attach an explanation.
12 Were you subject to tax as a resident under the internal laws of **(a)** either of the countries listed on lines
    9 and 10 during all of 2005 or **(b)** both of the countries listed on lines 9 and 10 for the period during
    which you maintained a tax home in each country? . . . . ☐ **Yes** ☐ **No**
13 Have you filed or will you file tax returns for 2005 in the countries listed on lines 9 and 10? . . . . ☐ **Yes** ☐ **No**
    If "Yes" to either line 12 or line 13, attach verification.
    If "No" to either line 12 or line 13, please explain ▶ ....
    ....

    Next, complete Part IV on the back.

For Paperwork Reduction Act Notice, see page 4.   Cat. No. 15829P   Form **8840** (2005)

Figure 3.2

Form 8840 (2005)   Page **2**

Part IV   Significant Contacts With Foreign Country or Countries in 2005

14 Where was your regular or principal permanent home located during 2005 (see instructions)? ....

15 If you had more than one permanent home available to you at all times during 2005, list the location of each and explain ► ....

16 Where was your family located? ....

17 Where was your automobile(s) located? ....

18 Where was your automobile(s) registered? ....

19 Where were your personal belongings, furniture, etc., located? ....

20 List social, cultural, religious, and political organizations you currently participate in and the location of each:

   a _____ **Location** _____

   b _____ **Location** _____

   c _____ **Location** _____

   d _____ **Location** _____

   e _____ **Location** _____

21 Where was the bank(s) with which you conducted your routine personal banking activities located?

   a _____ **c** _____

   b _____ **d** _____

22 Did you conduct business activities in a location other than your tax home? . . . . ☐ **Yes**   ☐ **No**
   If "Yes," where? ....

23a Where was your driver's license issued? ....

   b If you hold a second driver's license, where was it issued? ....

24 Where were you registered to vote? ....

25 When completing official documents, forms, etc., what country do you list as your residence? ....

26 Have you ever completed:

   a Form W-8 or Form W-8BEN (relating to foreign status)? . . . . ☐ **Yes**   ☐ **No**

   b Form W-9, Request for Taxpayer Identification Number and Certification? . . . . ☐ **Yes**   ☐ **No**

   c Form 1078, Certificate of Alien Claiming Residence in the United States? . . . . ☐ **Yes**   ☐ **No**

   d Any other U.S. official forms? If "Yes," indicate the form(s) ► .... ☐ **Yes**   ☐ **No**

27 In what country/countries did you keep your personal, financial, and legal documents? ....

28 From what country/countries did you derive the majority of your 2005 income? ....

29 Did you have any income from U.S. sources? . . . . ☐ **Yes**   ☐ **No**
   If "Yes," what type? ....

30 In what country/countries were your investments located (see instructions)? ....

31 List any charitable organizations to which you made contributions and their locations:

   a _____ **Location** _____

   b _____ **Location** _____

   c _____ **Location** _____

   d _____ **Location** _____

32 Did you qualify for any type of government-sponsored "national" health plan? . . . . ☐ **Yes**   ☐ **No**
   If "Yes," in what country? ....
   If "No," please explain ► ....
   If you have any other information to substantiate your closer connection to a country other than the United States or you wish to explain in more detail any of your responses to lines 14 through 32, attach a statement to this form.

Sign here only if you are filing this form by itself and not with your U.S. tax return

Under penalties of perjury, I declare that I have examined this form and the accompanying attachments, and to the best of my knowledge and belief, they are true, correct, and complete.

► _____   ► _____
           Your signature   Date

Form **8840** (2005)

Figure 3.2—continued

substantial sense." The tax home maintained must be in existence for the entire current year.

A visitor will be considered to have a closer connection to a foreign country if he or the IRS establishes that he has maintained more "significant contacts" with the other country than with the United States. Factors considered in determining this include the location of the visitor's home, family, personal belongings, routine banking activities and organizations to which he belongs. It is very important to note the closer connection exception, under a Form 8840 filing, is unavailable to a visitor who has taken steps to change his status to permanent U.S. residence during the current year or is a U.S. citizen or green card holder.

Persons who are high at risk for possibly being deemed a U.S. resident under this Substantial Presence Test may want to take an additional precaution and file Form 8840 together with a timely filed Form 1040NR, the non-resident tax return. If you have a high six-figure RRSP or larger, a large or complicated Canadian business structure, have done a Canadian estate freeze, use Canadian dividends as your chief source of income or any combination of these situations and regularly spend more than four months a year in the U.S., I would consider you to be at high risk of an IRS challenge to your being a non-resident of the U.S., but not necessarily at higher risk of audit. I would encourage the Form 1040NR filing even though it is not technically required. The reason for this is that the Form 8840 filing by itself does not trigger any statute of limitation protection, so in theory the IRS could challenge the veracity of the form even though you had filed it many years previously. However, if you file Form 1040NR, with Form 8840 attached, in a timely fashion and with the appropriate treaty election, the IRS has only three years to challenge the contents of the return and Form 8840 or be statute barred from doing so, unless they can prove fraud was involved.

TAX TREATY PROTECTION FOR U.S. NON-RESIDENTS AND RESIDENTS

One of the foremost roles of the Canada/U.S. Tax Treaty is its tiebreaker rules for determination of residency. These rules prevent a situation where an individual is taxed as a resident of Canada and the United States at the same time on their world income. By following these four tiebreaker rules and passing just one of the tests clearly in favour of one or the other country, the taxpayer will be protected from having to face two complete sets of tax rules at the same time. The tiebreaker rules in Article IV of the Canada/U.S. Tax Treaty are outlined here, along with comments to explain them:

1. The individual shall be deemed to be a resident of the country in which he has a permanent home available. If a permanent home is available in both countries, or neither, a individual is deemed to be resident in the country in which his or her personal and economic relations are closer (center of vital interests). Generally, a permanent home is any accommodation that is considered permanent. The home may be rented or owned. It is considered permanent where it is available for the individual's use throughout the year. A person's center of vital interests would be objectively determined and would be based upon their familial, social, occupational, political and cultural activities. Economic relations are also considered and are generally linked with the locality of the main source income.

2. If the country in which the individual has his center of vital interests cannot be determined, he shall be determined to be a resident of the country in which he has an habitual abode. What constitutes habitual abode requires an evaluation of the individual's lifestyle over a sufficient length of time. In most circumstances the length of time spent in one country over any other may be determinative. Also the transient nature of the stay may be examined, e.g. living at vacation property at the lake versus at a house in the city.

3. If the individual has an habitual abode in both countries or in neither country, he shall be deemed to be resident of the country of which he is a citizen. The immigration status is very important; for example, if one was to have a permanent residence status that would most definitely be considered. Ultimately though, citizenship is the final determination.

4. If the individual is a citizen of both countries or of neither of them, then competent authorities of the contracting countries shall settle the question by mutual agreement. The competent authorities are committees of individuals from both Canada and the United States who sit down and examine the facts and make a determination. This process should be avoided at all costs, as it is lengthy and heart-wrenching. It is difficult to determine in advance what the outcome may be.

The Canada/U.S. Tax Treaty affords all Canadian visitors a great deal of latitude from filing in the United States and paying taxes on income not sourced there. In addition, income that is effectively sourced in the United States is generally prevented from being double-taxed: once in the United States, and again in Canada. The treaty accomplishes this in three key ways:

1. **Foreign Tax Credits.** The treaty allows for a system of credits so that tax paid to one country on specified income will be allowed as a full credit against any tax due on that same income in the country of residence. For example, a non-resident who earns a taxable rental income in the United States files and pays tax as required by the IRS. The tax paid to the IRS after netting income and expenses on Form 1040 NR is converted to Canadian funds and is used on the Canadian return as a full credit. This reduces or eliminates Canadian taxes due to CRA on that same rental income, adjusted for Canadian depreciation and rental expense rules. (The CRA limits these credits to the amount of the stated Canada/U.S. Tax Treaty withholding rates on any specific taxable income source, regardless of what foreign tax was actually paid.

2. **Exemptions.** The Canada/U.S. Tax Treaty provides for certain exemptions from filing or reporting income of a non-resident in the United States that would otherwise be taxable by the IRS. The Substantial Presence Test, without any treaty protection, would apply to a large number of Canadian winter visitors who regularly spend four to six months each year in the American Sunbelt. Under the Canada/U.S. Tax Treaty, there is an exemption from the Substantial Presence Test for those Canadians who without the treaty protection would be required to report their world income in the United States under the terms of this test. IRS rules implemented in the 1992 tax year require Canadians who are using the Canada/U.S. Tax Treaty as protection from the Substantial Presence Test to file a Closer Connection Exception Statement, IRS Form 8840 (see Figure 3.2) and/or Form 1040NR declaring they are treaty-exempt.

3. **Withholding Rates.** Provisions in the treaty establish the amount of maximum withholding tax either country can take on various forms of income in that country from residents of the other country. These withholding tax rates are detailed in Chapter 8 in Figure 8.9. The provisions for maximum withholding rates prove very useful when doing cross-border financial planning, as you will see in Chapters 8, 9 and 13.

CANADA AND THE U.S. DO EXCHANGE TAXPAYER INFORMATION

The exchange-of-information capabilities between Canada and the United States, as provided for in the Canada/U.S. Tax Treaty, often trap those who do not report income earned in one country to the other, where applicable. Computer reporting of interest, dividends and real estate sales is done on what appears to be a routine basis between CRA and IRS in both directions. It is not uncommon for the IRS to take information from the CRA and convert it into a Form 1099 income reporting slip and issue it to a U.S. taxpayer or vice versa — the CRA takes information obtained from the IRS, converts it into a T5 slip or similar reporting slip for Canadian tax purposes. Canadian and U.S. tax authorities can at any time ask for and obtain a complete tax profile of anyone they choose who lives in the other country. The current Canada/U.S. Tax Treaty contains provisions to enforce the tax judgement from one country in the jurisdiction of the other through the facilities of the local taxing authorities. CRA will be able to exercise its collection authority in the United States and the IRS in Canada with nearly the same powers they already have in their own respective countries. This was not possible under the 1980 Canada/U.S. Treaty. Under the previous rules, if a taxpayer owed tax to one country but lived in the other, it was difficult for the country owed the tax to collect it unless the authorities could find assets within their country to seize.

WHO MUST FILE TAX RETURNS IN THE UNITED STATES?

This section is to make you aware of the situations and the types of income on which a non-resident is legally required to file a tax return of any form in the United States. A non-resident must file a return under the following circumstances:

- The sale of any U.S. real property requires that the seller file IRS Form 1040NR, the non-resident tax return, before June 15 following the year of the sale. If the property was held jointly, each of the joint owners must file separate Form 1040NRs reporting their respective share of the property sales. Form 1040NR must be filed whether or not there was any gain or withholding tax collected on the sale. There are no exceptions to this rule.

- Any non-resident who regularly spends four to six months per year in the United States and is deemed to be a resident under the Substantial Presence Test and who is claiming to be exempt under the Canada/U.S. Tax Treaty must file Form 1040NR or the Closer Connection Exception statement, Form 8840 (see Figure 3.2), by June 15 every year they are subject to the Substantial Presence Test. (See discussions about the Substantial Presence Test in previous sections of this chapter.) Many Canadians who regularly spend this amount of time in the United States are unaware of or are ignoring these filing requirements because they don't think the IRS will ever catch up with them. The potential penalties that can accumulate when these forms have not been filed and the IRS finds a person was a U.S. resident under the Substantial Presence Test are so mind-boggling that you would not believe it was possible for the IRS to legally assess them. The long and the short of it is, don't take any chances: file Form 8840 completely and accurately every year that you fall into this category. The 30 minutes you spend completing the form could save you many thousands of dollars in potential penalties, not to mention a great deal of costs and aggravation. As mentioned previously in this chapter, you may also want to file a Form 1040NR each year along with the Form 8840 for added protection against any potential taxes and penalties. In addition, because of the increasing scrutiny U.S. Customs and Immigration apply to those entering the United States, it wouldn't surprise me if they started asking to see a recently filed copy of Form 8840 before they let you into the country. It is recommended that you carry a copy of the most recently filed Form 8840 or Form 1040 NR with you as part of your Border Kit mentioned in Chapter 7 each time you enter the United States.

- A Canadian who spends more than 183 days in the United States is considered a resident for tax purposes and must file a U.S. tax return, Form 1040, declaring all world income. You are not eligible to file a 1040NR or Form 8840. The treaty will do little to prevent your world income from being taxed in the United States, but it will help to eliminate most, if not all, of the taxes due to the IRS. Canadians in this situation should review Chapter 7 on immigration, with a view to obtaining permanent residency in the United States, so that they may take full advantage of the lower U.S. tax rates as outlined in a later section of this chapter. When counting the days of residency, remember to include cross-border shopping days in the U.S., not just time spent vacationing in the Sunbelt.

- Any non-resident who collects rental income in the United States from any owned property, including his or her own personal-use home, must file Form 1040NR by the required deadline, unless the lessee is withholding the 30% non-resident withholding tax on the gross rental income.

- Any non-resident who carries on a business of any form in the United States must also file Form 1040NR regardless of whether that business is profitable. This filing requirement applies even though you may not have any legal immigration status to work in the United States.

- If a non-resident has had withholding tax withheld incorrectly or at an improper rate, he or she must file Form 1040NR for the year in which the error occurred to obtain a refund. Be sure to keep all the reporting slips that any withholding entity must provide you with. Generally, these would be 1042S, 1099 or 8288A slips, which are similar to Canadian T4s or T5s. Lottery and certain gambling winnings are considered taxable income in the United States and are subject to non-resident withholding tax. If you hit a jackpot in Las Vegas, this filing method could make you an even bigger winner by giving you some or all of your withholding tax back. Planning tip for gamblers: Keep detailed daily records of both winnings and losses. The losses can be useful when filing for a refund of withholding tax from a jackpot. Without good records, the IRS will not allow an offset of losses against winnings as is now allowed under the latest amendment to the Canada/U.S. Tax Treaty.

- The estate of a non-resident descendant who has a U.S. taxable estate of more than $60,000 must file IRS Form 706NA within nine months of the death of the descendant. See Chapter 4 to determine the taxable estate of a non-resident. Also, as noted in Chapter 4, if the estate is going to take a treaty benefit from the Canada/U.S. Tax Treaty then a regular Form 706, the U.S. Estate Tax Return, must be filed fully disclosing the treaty benefits requested.

- Any non-resident who makes a gift of taxable U.S. property of more than $12,000 total in one year to any single person, or $120,000 (inflation adjusted) to a spouse, is subject to U.S. gift tax and must file IRS Form 709, the gift tax return, to pay any taxes due by April 15 after the year end in which the gift was made. The gift tax rates are equal to the estate tax rates. Be aware of unintentional gifts such as putting a son or daughter or spouse on title to your residence located in the U.S. See Chapter 4 for a more complete discussion of gift taxes.

HOW AND WHEN TO APPLY FOR A U.S. SOCIAL SECURITY OR TAX ID NUMBER

Generally speaking, Canadians do not need a U.S. taxpayer identification number, commonly known as a Social Security Number (SSN) or Individual Taxpayer Identification Number (ITIN). However, you will be required to have at least an ITIN if you are going to sell a home or conduct any other financial transaction in the United States, including the filing of, or being claimed as an exemption on, U.S. tax returns/forms. SSNs and ITINs look alike, but ITINs are now for those non-U.S. persons who have no visa, green card or other employment-type immigration status in the United States.

Those who have obtained SSNs in the past may continue to use them, but it is quite incorrect for Canadians under any circumstances to provide the Canadian Social Insurance Number (SIN) to any U.S. entity for any reason. Doing so is not only illegal from the standpoint of providing a false SSN, but it throws the IRS computers for a loop. Your SIN may be the same as some innocent American's SSN, or there may be no record of it at all in IRS files! When you open a bank or brokerage account, ask for IRS Form W-8BEN, Certificate of Foreign Status (see Figure 3.4 later in this chapter), which will satisfy any legal tax reporting requirements. See Taxing Non-Resident Aliens at the beginning of this chapter.

There is no real disadvantage to having an American SSN/ITIN unless having another number to keep track of bothers you. An SSN/ITIN is required not only for the circumstances noted above, but it can be a convenience to you in certain financial transactions, such as filing tax returns, opening bank accounts or selling property. It may also be to a person's advantage to have a taxpayer identification number, to obtain increased assurance the IRS has properly recorded certain facts that could be helpful in the future, such as tax losses that are permitted to be offset against future profits. In fact, the IRS, with the new requirement to have an SSN/ITIN, will hold refunds or delay return processing for those who have failed to supply an SSN/ITIN.

To obtain your own permanent ITIN, you will need to complete and attach IRS Form W-7 (see Figure 3.3), with the required IDs, and your number will be provided in four to six weeks. The IRS has stopped issuing ITINs unless you can prove, via the tax return/form filing, you need one. Bank and brokerage firms, when you are opening accounts with them, will require you complete Form W-8BEN, Certificate of Foreign Status (see Figure 3.4) if you are a non-resident or Form W-9, Request for Taxpayer Identification Number and Certification, (see Figure 3.5), if you are a U.S. resident taxpayer, a U.S. citizen or green card holder. Even though these forms are not filed at any time with the IRS, the bank or brokerage companies cannot open accounts without them and must keep them on file as well as update them periodically.

If you have a U.S. visa or other legal immigration status to work in the United States, you can take your visa to the nearest Social Security Administration office and complete Form SS-5 and obtain an SSN. All residents of the United States are required to have an SSN or an ITIN if they don't have an employment-type visa.

CANADA AND UNITED STATES INCOME TAX COMPARISON

There are two main issues to consider when it comes to the actual amount of tax you pay: the tax rates, and the income on which those rates are applied, called your taxable income. No comparison between Canada and the United States would be complete without considering both these factors. Since there are fifty states and ten provinces, a detailed comparison of each state and each province is beyond the scope of this book. Appendix B includes the average maximum tax rates from all provinces and the key Sunbelt states. However, we will provide you with a guide to the major opportunities of cross-border financial planning as well as illuminating potential tax minefields that need to be avoided. We will also compare the tax rates of Ontario and Florida, the two locations that generate the most winter visitor and immigration traffic (Quebec also accounts for a similar number of visitors to Florida). Other provinces and state tax rates will vary somewhat from the Ontario and Florida numbers, but the trends will be the same. The states in the United States that have a personal income tax collect their tax on a separate return in the same manner as Quebec and the other provinces that now have decided to levy their taxes as tax on income rather than a percentage of the federal tax collected.

Figure 3.6 charts the tax rates and income brackets of Ontario and Florida. The rates shown are for the year 2006 and include all provincial and federal surtaxes; the Ontario brackets are in Canadian dollars and the Florida brackets are in U.S. dollars. For the purpose of our comparison, we assume that the Canadian is married to a spouse who has too much income to qualify for the married exemption in Ontario, and that the Florida person is also married and filing jointly with a spouse.

As you can see from Figure 3.6, a Florida taxpayer in the highest income bracket has a strong advantage over the Ontario taxpayer because the Florida tax rate is approximately 9% lower than Ontario's and it takes a much larger income to reach the highest bracket in the United States. On the same income stream, a high-income earner resident in Ontario would cut total taxes by 40% to 50% in the income range of CDN$65,000 to CDN$225,000 if he or she had the choice of paying taxes in Florida. Chapter 8 will show you some direct comparisons using actual cross-border

Form **W-7**
(Rev. January 2006)
Department of the Treasury
Internal Revenue Service

Application for IRS Individual Taxpayer Identification Number
► See instructions.
► For use by individuals who are not U.S. citizens or permanent residents.

OMB No. 1545-0074

An IRS individual taxpayer identification number (ITIN) is for federal tax purposes only.

FOR IRS USE ONLY

Before you begin:
● **Do not submit** this form if you have, or are eligible to obtain, a U.S. social security number (SSN).
● Getting an ITIN does not change your immigration status or your right to work in the United States and does not make you eligible for the earned income credit.

Reason you are submitting Form W-7. Read the instructions for the box you check. **Caution:** If you check box **b, c, d, e,** or **g, you must file a tax return with Form W-7 unless you meet one of the exceptions** (see instructions).

a ☐ Nonresident alien required to obtain ITIN to claim tax treaty benefit
b ☐ Nonresident alien filing a U.S. tax return
c ☐ U.S. resident alien **(based on days present in the United States)** filing a U.S. tax return
d ☐ Dependent of U.S. citizen/resident alien ⎫ Enter name and SSN/ITIN of U.S. citizen/resident alien (see instructions) ► ....
e ☐ Spouse of U.S. citizen/resident alien ⎭
f ☐ Nonresident alien student, professor, or researcher filing a U.S. tax return
g ☐ Dependent/spouse of a nonresident alien holding a U.S. visa
h ☐ Other (see instructions) ►
   Additional information for a and f: Enter treaty country ►   and treaty article number ►

Name (see instructions)	1a First name	Middle name	Last name
Name at birth if different , , ►	1b First name	Middle name	Last name

Applicant's mailing address	2 Street address, apartment number, or rural route number. **If you have a P.O. box, see page 4.**
	City or town, state or province, and country. Include ZIP code or postal code where appropriate.

Foreign address (if different from above) (see instructions)	3 Street address, apartment number, or rural route number. Do not use a P.O. box number.
	City or town, state or province, and country. Include ZIP code or postal code where appropriate.

Birth information	4 Date of birth (month / day / year) / /	Country of birth	City and state or province (optional)	5 ☐ Male ☐ Female

Other information

6a Country(ies) of citizenship | 6b Foreign tax I.D. number (if any) | 6c Type of U.S. visa (if any), number, and expiration date

6d Identification document(s) submitted (see instructions)
☐ Passport   ☐ Driver's license/State I.D.   ☐ USCIS documentation   ☐ Other ....
Issued by: No.:   Exp. date: / /   Entry date in U.S. / /

6e Have you previously received a U.S. temporary taxpayer identification number (TIN) or employer identification number (EIN)?
☐ No/Do not know. Skip line 6f.
☐ Yes. Complete line 6f. If more than one, list on a sheet and attach to this form (see instructions).

6f Enter: TIN or EIN ► .... and
Name under which it was issued ►

6g Name of college/university or company (see instructions) ....
City and state   Length of stay

Sign Here

Under penalties of perjury, I (applicant/delegate/acceptance agent) declare that I have examined this application, including accompanying documentation and statements, and to the best of my knowledge and belief, it is true, correct, and complete. I authorize the IRS to disclose to my acceptance agent returns or return information necessary to resolve matters regarding the assignment of my IRS individual taxpayer identification number (ITIN), including any previously assigned taxpayer identifying number.

Keep a copy for your records.

Signature of applicant (if delegate, see instructions)	Date (month / day / year) / /	Phone number ( )
Name of delegate, if applicable (type or print)	Delegate's relationship to applicant	☐ Parent ☐ Court-appointed guardian ☐ Power of Attorney

Acceptance Agent's Use ONLY

Signature	Date (month / day / year) / /	Phone ( ) Fax ( )
Name and title (type or print)	Name of company	EIN

For Paperwork Reduction Act Notice, see page 4.   Cat. No. 10229L   Form **W-7** (Rev. 1-2006)

Figure 3.3

Form **W-8BEN**	**Certificate of Foreign Status of Beneficial Owner**	
(Rev. February 2006)	**for United States Tax Withholding**	OMB No. 1545-1621
Department of the Treasury Internal Revenue Service	▶ Section references are to the Internal Revenue Code. ▶ See separate instructions. ▶ Give this form to the withholding agent or payer. Do not send to the IRS.	

Do not use this form for:	Instead, use Form:
• A U.S. citizen or other U.S. person, including a resident alien individual	. . . W-9
• A person claiming that income is effectively connected with the conduct of a trade or business in the United States	. . . W-8ECI
• A foreign partnership, a foreign simple trust, or a foreign grantor trust (see instructions for exceptions)	. W-8ECI or W-8IMY
• A foreign government, international organization, foreign central bank of issue, foreign tax-exempt organization, foreign private foundation, or government of a U.S. possession that received effectively connected income or that is claiming the applicability of section(s) 115(2), 501(c), 892, 895, or 1443(b) (see instructions)	. W-8ECI or W-8EXP

Note: *These entities should use Form W-8BEN if they are claiming treaty benefits or are providing the form only to claim they are a foreign person exempt from backup withholding.*

| • A person acting as an intermediary . . . . | . . . W-8IMY |

Note: *See instructions for additional exceptions.*

Part I   **Identification of Beneficial Owner** (See instructions.)

1 Name of individual or organization that is the beneficial owner	2 Country of incorporation or organization

3   Type of beneficial owner: ☐ Individual   ☐ Corporation   ☐ Disregarded entity   ☐ Partnership   ☐ Simple trust
      ☐ Grantor trust   ☐ Complex trust   ☐ Estate   ☐ Government   ☐ International organization
      ☐ Central bank of issue   ☐ Tax-exempt organization   ☐ Private foundation

4   Permanent residence address (street, apt. or suite no., or rural route). **Do not use a P.O. box or in-care-of address.**

City or town, state or province. Include postal code where appropriate.	Country (do not abbreviate)

5   Mailing address (if different from above)

City or town, state or province. Include postal code where appropriate.	Country (do not abbreviate)

6 U.S. taxpayer identification number, if required (see instructions) ☐ SSN or ITIN ☐ EIN	7 Foreign tax identifying number, if any (optional)

8   Reference number(s) (see instructions)

Part II   **Claim of Tax Treaty Benefits** (if applicable)

9   I certify that (check all that apply):

a ☐   The beneficial owner is a resident of .... within the meaning of the income tax treaty between the United States and that country.

b ☐   If required, the U.S. taxpayer identification number is stated on line 6 (see instructions).

c ☐   The beneficial owner is not an individual, derives the item (or items) of income for which the treaty benefits are claimed, and, if applicable, meets the requirements of the treaty provision dealing with limitation on benefits (see instructions).

d ☐   The beneficial owner is not an individual, is claiming treaty benefits for dividends received from a foreign corporation or interest from a U.S. trade or business of a foreign corporation, and meets qualified resident status (see instructions).

e ☐   The beneficial owner is related to the person obligated to pay the income within the meaning of section 267(b) or 707(b), and will file Form 8833 if the amount subject to withholding received during a calendar year exceeds, in the aggregate, $500,000.

10   **Special rates and conditions** (if applicable—see instructions): The beneficial owner is claiming the provisions of Article .... of the treaty identified on line 9a above to claim a .... % rate of withholding on (specify type of income): ....
      Explain the reasons the beneficial owner meets the terms of the treaty article: ....
      ....

Part III   **Notional Principal Contracts**

11 ☐   I have provided or will provide a statement that identifies those notional principal contracts from which the income is **not** effectively connected with the conduct of a trade or business in the United States. I agree to update this statement as required.

Part IV   **Certification**

Under penalties of perjury, I declare that I have examined the information on this form and to the best of my knowledge and belief it is true, correct, and complete. I further certify under penalties of perjury that:

1 I am the beneficial owner (or am authorized to sign for the beneficial owner) of all the income to which this form relates,
2 The beneficial owner is not a U.S. person,
3 The income to which this form relates is (a) not effectively connected with the conduct of a trade or business in the United States, (b) effectively connected but is not subject to tax under an income tax treaty, or (c) the partner's share of a partnership's effectively connected income, and
4 For broker transactions or barter exchanges, the beneficial owner is an exempt foreign person as defined in the instructions.

Furthermore, I authorize this form to be provided to any withholding agent that has control, receipt, or custody of the income of which I am the beneficial owner or any withholding agent that can disburse or make payments of the income of which I am the beneficial owner.

Sign Here ▶

Signature of beneficial owner (or individual authorized to sign for beneficial owner)	Date (MM-DD-YYYY)	Capacity in which acting

| For Paperwork Reduction Act Notice, see separate instructions. | Cat. No. 25047Z | Form **W-8BEN** (Rev. 2-2006) |

Figure 3.4

Form **W-9**
(Rev. November 2005)
Department of the Treasury
Internal Revenue Service

**Request for Taxpayer
Identification Number and Certification**

**Give form to the
requester. Do not
send to the IRS.**

Print or type
See Specific Instructions on page 2.

Name (as shown on your income tax return)

Business name, if different from above

Check appropriate box: ☐ Individual/ Sole proprietor ☐ Corporation ☐ Partnership ☐ Other ▶ .... ☐ Exempt from backup withholding

Address (number, street, and apt. or suite no.)

Requester's name and address (optional)

City, state, and ZIP code

List account number(s) here (optional)

Part I   Taxpayer Identification Number (TIN)

Enter your TIN in the appropriate box. The TIN provided must match the name given on Line 1 to avoid backup withholding. For individuals, this is your social security number (SSN). However, for a resident alien, sole proprietor, or disregarded entity, see the Part I instructions on page 3. For other entities, it is your employer identification number (EIN). If you do not have a number, see *How to get a TIN* on page 3.

Note. If the account is in more than one name, see the chart on page 4 for guidelines on whose number to enter.

Social security number

or

Employer identification number

Part II   Certification

Under penalties of perjury, I certify that:

1. The number shown on this form is my correct taxpayer identification number (or I am waiting for a number to be issued to me), and

2. I am not subject to backup withholding because: (a) I am exempt from backup withholding, or (b) I have not been notified by the Internal Revenue Service (IRS) that I am subject to backup withholding as a result of a failure to report all interest or dividends, or (c) the IRS has notified me that I am no longer subject to backup withholding, and

3. I am a U.S. person (including a U.S. resident alien).

Certification Instructions. You must cross out item 2 above if you have been notified by the IRS that you are currently subject to backup withholding because you have failed to report all interest and dividends on your tax return. For real estate transactions, item 2 does not apply. For mortgage interest paid, acquisition or abandonment of secured property, cancellation of debt, contributions to an individual retirement arrangement (IRA), and generally, payments other than interest and dividends, you are not required to sign the Certification, but you must provide your correct TIN. (See the instructions on page 4.)

Sign Here   Signature of U.S. person ▶   Date ▶

Cat. No. 10231X

Form **W-9** (Rev. 11-2005)

Figure 3.5

tax situations, to provide a more complete picture for those considering permanent residence in the United States. Florida has no personal state income tax, so the rates reflect the actual U.S. federal tax rates. Appendix B compares the provincial tax rates with those of popular Sunbelt states.

As I previously noted, you must look at taxable income as well as the tax rate to get a complete picture of the total taxes paid. Now we will look at the deductions that reduce your gross income to your taxable income. This list of deductions is by no means a complete summary of all the deductions available in both Canada and the United States, but it does cover major tax deductions that apply to a married couple at or near retirement age.

PERSONAL EXEMPTIONS

Canada has converted the basic personal exemption of $8,839 to a non-refundable federal tax credit of $1,500. The age exemption for those over

CANADIAN AND U.S. TAX RATES 2006

CANADA		UNITED STATES Married Filing Jointly	
Taxable Income	Tax Rate	Taxable Income	Tax Rate
$36,378 or less	21%	$15,100 or less	10%
$36,379–72,756	32%	$15,101–61,300	15%
$72,759–118,285	40%	$61,301–123,700	25%
$118,286 and over	46.4%	$123,701–188,450	28%
		$188,451–336,550	33%
		$336,551 and over	35%

Figure 3.6

65 has been reduced to a tax credit of $676 and, after the 1994 federal budget, has been eliminated for those with incomes exceeding approximately $29,619. For a spouse or a dependant with no income, there are non-refundable credits available of $1,275. The February 28, 2000, Canadian federal budget allows for the first indexing of these personal exemptions in ten years so inflation should no longer erode these basic personal exemptions. The benefits of credits are enhanced by the applicable provincial tax rates.

The United States has a standard deduction total of $10,300 (all numbers referring to U.S. deductions are in U.S. funds) for married taxpayers. If the taxpayer itemizes certain deductions, as outlined in the next several sections of this chapter, rather than taking the standard deduction, he may take a greater total deduction. Add $2,500 to the standard deduction if you and your spouse are older than age 65. Add another $3,300 for yourself and each dependant including your spouse, regardless of his or her income, for personal exemptions. The United States is more liberal with their dependant deductions. You may claim adult children, grandchildren, parents and other close relatives who live with you and for whom you supply over 50% of their financial support. The basic personal exemptions are phased out for married persons with incomes of between $225,750 and $348,260. Certain itemized deductions will also be reduced by 3% of adjusted gross income up to 80% for incomes starting at $150,500.

PENSIONS

Canada has converted the $2,000 pension deduction into a non-refundable federal tax credit of $340. Old Age Security is taxed up to 100% owing to a clawback on incomes exceeding $60,806.

The United States has no standard pension deduction and allows a tax-free return of contributions to contributory pension plans, making these pensions partially tax free. U.S. Social Security payments are totally tax free, until a married couple's income exceeds $32,000; they are taxed on 50% of the benefit over this income level up to $44,000, and then the tax is levied at the regular tax rates on 85% of these benefits if income exceeds the $44,000. Those in the top tax brackets will pay a 30% maximum tax on Social Security payments.

MORTGAGE INTEREST AND PROPERTY TAXES

In Canada, mortgage interest and property taxes are not generally deductible in any amount.

In the United States, mortgage interest on as many as two homes is fully deductible as an itemized deduction. The definition of a residence could also include an RV or a yacht. Total mortgages on these residences cannot exceed $1.1 million. Property taxes are deductible regardless of the number of homes involved even if they are located outside the United States.

PROVINCIAL AND STATE INCOME TAXES

In Canada, provincial taxes cannot be taken as a deduction from federal taxes paid. In the United States, state and municipal taxes are deductible as an itemized deduction. If, for example, Ontario residents were able to deduct their provincial income tax against the federal tax as the IRS allows within the U.S., the maximum effective tax rate in Ontario would drop from 46.4% to 41%.

EARNED INTEREST DEDUCTIONS OR DEFERMENT

In Canada, the $1,000 earned interest exclusion and the ability to defer interest on investment vehicles such as Canada Savings Bonds and annuities were eliminated for all Canadian taxpayers several years ago.

In the United States, any amount of interest earned on certain municipal bonds is tax free on the federal and, in most cases, the state level. Interest on U.S. Savings Bonds or other federal government securities is tax free at the state level. Any amount of interest, dividends or capital gains can be deferred as long as desired through the use of various forms of deferred annuities.

CAPITAL GAINS DEDUCTIONS

As of October 2000, only 50% of actual gains are taxable, making the maximum capital gains tax approximately 24%, depending on the province. Persons who own qualified small businesses may obtain $500,000 in capital gains exemptions on the sale of the shares of their companies. All capital gains on the sale of a principal residence in Canada are tax free. On the date of a taxpayer's death, all his or her capital assets are deemed as sold at fair market value and any capital gains are fully taxed. If there is a surviving spouse, the capital gains can be deferred to that spouse's death.

The United States taxes capital gains at a reduced rate, with a maximum federal rate of 15% (the maximum capital gains tax is 0% if you are in the first two income tax brackets, as noted in Figure 3.6). There is a capital gains exemption of $250,000 ($500,000 for a married couple) on the sale of a principal residence. In addition, any gains on the sale of investment real estate can be rolled tax free into a new property of equal or greater value. It should be noted here that these capital gains exemptions and tax-free rollover of real estate gains are not available to non-residents owning real property in the U.S. There is no capital gains tax on deemed dispositions at death. Beneficiaries will receive appreciated property with a stepped-up cost basis so they can sell the appreciated property without any income tax owing. However, some assets of larger estates may be subject to the estate tax. See Chapters 4 and 9 for more details.

MEDICAL EXPENSES

In Canada, medical expenses that exceed 3% of income are allowed by converting the deductible expenses into a non-refundable federal credit at the 17% computation.

In the United States, medical expenses that exceed 7.5% of adjusted gross income are deductible as an itemized deduction.

Premiums paid for health insurance are included as a deductible medical expense. U.S. persons who are on high deductible health insurance plans are able contribute up to $5,450 per year to a Health Savings Account. Contributions to the Health Savings Accounts are fully deductible against taxable income and are allowed to be invested on a tax-free basis. As long as withdrawals are used for qualified medical expenses, they are tax free.

REGISTERED RETIREMENT PLANS

Canadians with earned income can contribute 18% of their last year's earnings to a Registered Retirement Savings Plan (RRSP) each year, to a maximum of $18,000 (growing by $1,000 each year to 2010 and then indexed for inflation beyond that).

Americans with earned income can contribute up to the lesser amount of 100% of their income or $5,000 to their own and $5,000 to a spouse's Individual Retirement Account (IRA) for those over 50. Add $500 to each of contributions for those over 50. There is also a Roth IRA subject to the same contribution limits as a regular IRA but not deductible from taxable income. The Roth IRA allows U.S. savers not only to accumulate earnings tax free inside the plan but also to withdraw the full plan balance tax free regardless of how much the savings grew. There are numerous other related qualified plans that can allow contributions of up to 25% of income to a maximum of $44,000 per year or $49,000 if over 50, depending on your employment status and income levels.

CHARITABLE DONATIONS

In Canada, donations, not exceeding 75% of income, to qualified Canadian charities are allowed as a non-refundable federal credit at the 17% computation for the first $250, and 29% for the remainder. Highly appreciated assets donated to a charity, such as shares of privately owned companies or certain kinds of land, are deemed to be sold and capital gains tax is paid on 25% of the gain. After the May 2, 2006 Federal budget, capital gains for donations of public securities and ecologically sensitive land will be tax exempt.

In the United States, donations, not exceeding 50% of income, to qualified charities are allowed as an itemized deduction. Donations of highly appreciated assets provide the taxpayer a full charitable deduction on the fair market value of the asset without either the taxpayer or the charity paying any capital gains tax on the transaction.

EDUCATION PLANS

Canadians with children can contribute up to $4,000 for each child under age 18 to a Registered Education Savings Plan (RESP) each year. The income in an RESP is tax-deferred until it is paid to a beneficiary, when it is taxed at the full-time student's lower rates. In addition, the Canada Education Savings Grant (CESG) can add 20% per year to the RESP contribution with an annual limit of $400 and a lifetime limit of $7,200.

The U.S. has an Education IRA of up to $4,000 per child per year that accumulates on a tax-deferred basis as an RESP does but can be taken out tax free if used for qualified education expenses. There are several refundable tax credits for tuition to encourage low-income persons to attend colleges. Most states have programs called 529 College Savings Plans through which parents or grandparents can contribute up to $275,000, and all income earned in the plan is tax free if the proceeds are used for qualified college expenses. These 529 plans are considerably more flexible than RESPs.

STOCK OPTIONS

Canada allows for a $100,000-per-year deferment of tax on the exercise of stock options to the date of sale of the underlying shares. Amounts of more than $100,000 resulting from the exercise of stock options or when the shares from the exercised options are sold are taxed immediately as capital gains with half excluded from taxable income.

The United States has Incentive Stock Options (ISO), which allow unlimited deferral of tax upon the exercise of the stock options, providing the options meet all the IRS criteria to qualify as ISOs. The stocks purchased from the exercise of the ISOs must be held for a minimum of one year to receive the 15% long-term capital gains tax treatment. Non-qualified stock options are taxed upon exercise at ordinary tax rates.

MISCELLANEOUS DEDUCTIONS

In Canada, union and professional dues, safety deposit box fees, interest on funds borrowed for investment purposes and fees for investment advice are deductible expenses.

In the United States, tax preparation fees*, vehicle licences, property and casualty losses exceeding 10% of income, unreimbursed employment expenses, trustee fees*, safety deposit box fees*, interest on funds borrowed for investment purposes to the extent of portfolio income, IRA administration fees* and fees for financial planning or investment advice* are deductible expenses.

The net effect of the differentials in tax rates and deductions between Canada and the United States can be best illustrated by example, or by an exact calculation based on your personal situation. Chapter 8 shows some typical cross-border tax situations that will show you how the application of different tax rates to the same income source can result in substantial net tax differences between the two tax systems.

---

*denotes expense deductions which, in total, must exceed 2% of taxable income before they are deductible.

CROSS-BORDER Q&A

EDUCATION PLAN FOR A U.S. GRANDCHILD

I have been a subscriber to the MoneySaver *for a number of years, and I'm wondering if you or someone can help me with a current question. My daughter lives in Los Angeles and is expecting her first baby in October. She and her family expect to remain in the U.S. as American citizens, at least for the foreseeable future. As I would like to help with the baby's college education, I am looking for information as to whether there are any Education Plans to which I could contribute (similar to the RESPs). Or is there some other way to do this and obtain a tax deduction?*

Thank you for any help you can give.

— John B., Whitby, Ontario

Congratulations on your upcoming American grandchild.

There is an excellent college savings program in California to which you can contribute up to US$275,000. The program is called the Golden State Scholar Share plan, and it is the California version of the federal U.S. Section 529 College Savings Program. I use the California plan for my own children even though I am an Arizona resident, as it has more investment options and has lower fees than the AZ 529 Plan. This program is funded with after-tax dollars only, but all interest dividends and capital gains are tax free as long as the funds are used for education purposes in most U.S. colleges, or even in a majority of the key Canadian colleges. Your daughter can control the distribution of the funds, and if your new grandchild doesn't go to college, your daughter can transfer the funds to another grandchild or close relative to use, or even to her own grandchildren. Unless you have a U.S. Social Security number, your daughter will need to open the account. She can contact the plan toll free at 1-877-728-4338 or on the Web at www.scholarshare.com. It is important to note that just because your daughter is located in California, there is no requirement that you must use the California 529 plan. Most other states have 529 plans as well, some even better than California's. It is a competitive market, so it pays to shop around.

FILINGS FOR PART-TIME WORK IN THE U.S.

I am a Canadian MoneySaver *subscriber, and that is where I found your comments on Canada-U.S. matters. I need your help.*

If I may ask/present my situation: I am going to provide some computer programming services from Toronto for a U.S. client while residing in Canada and will probably make US$10K to 15K.

The client sent me IRS Form W-8BEN, Certificate of Foreign Status of Beneficial Owner. Is this the right form for me?

I inquired with IRS (and maybe I'll do it again) regarding how to fill in the form and my understanding is —

Part I: This part is straightforward, except for item 6 — do I have to get an ITIN?

Part II: It looks to me as if I have to fill in only 9a (Canada) and possibly 9b; but what about part 10? By IRS telephone instructions, I have to enter article 15 and 30% rate! Is that right?

If it is possible for you to respond, I thank you very much in advance.

— Tom R., Toronto, Ontario

If you agree that you are an independent contractor and not an employee of the U.S. company, you are exempt from withholding. However, you will need to provide the U.S. paying company with Form 8233, Exemption From Withholding on Compensation for Independent Personal Services of a Nonresident Alien Individual (all forms and instructions are available from the IRS website, www.irs.gov), rather than W-8BEN (see page 1 of Form W-8BEN instructions). The explanation lines of Form 8233 state that you are performing independent personal services from Canada with no fixed base in the U.S. and are exempt from withholding under Article XIV of the Canada/U.S. Tax Treaty. Note that Article XV is for employees or dependent service providers who are exempt from withholding only if payment is less than US$10,000. You do need to get a Individual Taxpayer Identification Number (ITIN) to claim treaty benefits by filing a W-7 Form, Application for ITIN.

CHOOSE TAX FILING WISELY

If you have any information on the following question, I would appreciate receiving it from you. I believe that if all of my income is from Canada, and Canadian income tax rates are higher than American rates, there is no point in filing a U.S. return. That's because a reciprocal agreement between the two countries allows one to deduct the amount paid in Canada from the amount payable in the United States, and the Canadian amount would always be more. I have read a variety of U.S. and Canadian publications on this subject and none of them covers this point.

— Margaret L., Satellite Beach, Florida

You did not state what country you are a resident of and whether you were a U.S. citizen or green card holder. If you are a Canadian resident and non-U.S. citizen or green card holder, you are correct that there is little point in filing a U.S. tax return, unless you had U.S.-sourced income. However, if you are a green card holder or U.S. citizen, there are several important points as to why you should look at filing U.S. tax returns:

1. You are required by law to file U.S. returns when your world income exceeds the total of your standard deduction ($10,300 for 2006) and personal exemptions for yourself and your spouse ($3,300 each for 2006).

2. You may be able to receive an overall reduction in taxes paid by using the Canada/U.S. Tax Treaty to your best advantage, thus getting the lowest tax rate available to you.

3. Proper foreign tax credit planning may help you recover some of the higher taxes paid to Canada on future U.S. returns, since unused foreign tax credits can be carried forward for up to ten years.

There is not a lot of literature that can help you on this matter but you should try both CRA and IRS publications included in Appendix A, as well as other chapters in this book.

REMARRIAGE LEGALITIES NEED ATTENTION

I am a Canadian citizen who winters in Florida. My income comes from my late husband's Canada Pension Plan (CPP), company pension and some investment income. I am going to be married this spring to an American and we plan to reside in Florida year-round.

I wish to maintain my Canadian citizenship. Do I need to apply for a green card in order to stay in the United States for more than six months each year or will my marriage qualify me for residency? Also, will I pay income tax in Canada or in the United States (my income is all from Canadian sources)? Are there other legal repercussions of which I should be informed? We plan to be married in Canada and will have a prenuptial contract drawn up by my Canadian attorney.

— Shirley L., Lakeland, Florida

For you to reside legally in the United States, your new husband will need to sponsor you for a green card. You do not have to give up your Canadian citizenship to do this, even if you apply later for U.S. citizenship.

If you no longer reside in Canada on a permanent basis, you do not have to file Canadian tax returns after you file a final exit return. You will report all your world income on your U.S. return only. You will have to notify the payers of all your Canadian pensions that you are a non-resident. They will then apply 15% non-resident withholding tax on your company pension and 0% on CPP and OAS. You will get a credit for the withholding tax paid to Canada when you file your U.S. returns, which will likely cover most if not all of any U.S. federal income tax you may have to pay.

There are some other issues, both good and bad, relating to Medicare and estate planning that you should discuss with a cross-border financial planner to make sure you maximize benefits and minimize pitfalls. You should also have your Canadian prenuptial agreement reviewed (or prepared) by a Florida attorney to ensure it will be effective there.

REMARRIAGE LIVING IN CANADA

I am a Canadian citizen living in Ontario. I married a U.S. citizen in May 2005. She lives in New York City. I have no ties to the U.S. and have submitted the paperwork to sponsor my wife to become a Canadian permanent resident.

My wife and I are both retired and live off our investment income. After my wife takes up Canadian residence we will have no ties to the U.S., other than a couple of Roth IRAs which my wife isn't sure how she is supposed to handle.

My wife has questions about how she is supposed to file her U.S. tax returns. Since I do not have (and don't want) an ITIN, does my wife choose Married Filing Separately or Single on her U.S. tax returns? How does she account for me (if needed) on her U.S. tax returns? Must she also file a Canadian tax return even though she does not yet live in Ontario with me or have any Canadian income?

— *Wayne B., Toronto, Ontario*

Your wife must now file her U.S. tax returns as Married Filing Separately if you do not get a U.S. ITIN (Individual Tax Identification Number). In this filing mode she can take an exemption for you *only* if you have the ITIN. She will almost always pay higher taxes on any income in the Married Filing Separate mode, and the Canada Revenue Agency will require your new wife to pay tax on any earnings from the Roth IRA every year, that is, these earnings will no longer be tax free.

If you get an ITIN she will be able to file Married Filing Jointly and would normally pay less income tax under this filing option. You may find the ITIN relatively easy to get; it has no negative consequences but many positive ones.

Your wife does not have to start filing Canadian returns until she has officially taken up Canadian residency. You should take a look at having her sponsor you for your U.S. permanent resident status/green card, as you both would need to file only one tax return in the U.S. This would likely save you both a tremendous amount of income tax.

JACKPOT WITHHOLDING

During our visit to the United States this past winter my wife won money on a slot machine in an Indian Casino and from her winnings an amount equal to 30% of the winnings was deducted for U.S. federal tax. Is there any way of recovering this amount as she is a Canadian citizen?

— Jack S., London, Ontario

The 30% withholding from your wife's winnings is routine for the casinos as it required by the IRS. However, if you have good records of how much your wife lost during the same year in which she had her win then you can file a U.S. non-resident tax return to offset her gambling winnings with her losses in the same year and she would be taxable only to the extent her winnings exceeded her losses, if at all. So if she spent more than she won in the year she should get a full refund of the 30% withholding. The proof of her losses that the IRS will normally want to see can be charge card records, casino records, chip/token purchase receipts, or just a very good log of money spent on the gambling. The tax form your wife needs to file is the IRS Form 1040NR, with a deadline of June 15 after the end of the year in which she had her big win. If she does not have a U.S. Social Security number she will need to apply for an Individual Tax Identification Number (ITIN) by completing a Form W-7 and attaching it to the return. Without this, the IRS will withhold her refund if she is entitled to one.

REAL ESTATE EXEMPTIONS

A friend of mine told me his tax accountant advised him that if he and his wife spent six months a year in the United States (they have a home in SunCity West, AZ), up to $300,000 would be exempt from capital gains tax on the sale of their home there. I was reading your seventh edition of The Border Guide *and note the response to a question to the effect that a U.S. taxpayer has an exemption of $250,000. Has this been increased to $300,000* *and could this be what my friend's accountant is referring to? I can see from the question and your response that an exception could apply but may not apply where the person has a home in both countries.*

— Henning H., Winnipeg, Manitoba

The $300,000 exemption mentioned by the accountant is only from withholding tax, not from the tax due for non-residents of the United States. You must file a return and report any gains in the year of sale for any property and pay capital gains taxes at both the state and federal levels whether or not you were or were not subject to withholding tax. The $250,000 exemption I mentioned in the seventh edition of *The Border Guide* is an actual exemption from tax, but it is only for U.S. resident taxpayers on their principal residence. It has no application to snowbirds or non-residents of the U.S. There are no exemptions for non-residents other than if they qualify for not being subject to withholding tax, but this does not affect tax on the sale of their U.S. residence.

TAX-FILING STRATEGY COULD SAVE MONEY

My wife (deceased in August 1999) and I bought a condo in Florida in 1986. We received our green cards as resident aliens in 1988, through my sister in L.A., who has been a U.S. citizen since 1946. Since then we have spent six months in Florida and six months in Canada. I elected to file Canadian income tax and also U.S. income tax relative to reciprocal tax laws. All taxes paid to Canada (federal and provincial) were used as a credit on U.S. tax forms, adjusting the income each year for the current exchange.

All of my income, investments, bank accounts and family are in Canada. We do not own property in Canada as my son has ample room in his residence, and we spend the six months with him. On the U.S. side, I own the condo, with about a $48,000 value.

A year ago a consultant advised me that I have dual resident status. Also, I have been given power of attorney by the State of California to look after my sister's affairs in Los Angeles. She is 98 years of age and ruled not competent to attend to same.

My questions: (1) What is the situation regarding capital gains? (2) Should I sell my condo? (3) In effect it is my principal residence for six months and the only property I own: Isn't your principal residence exempt from capital gains? (4) Dual residency in Florida calls for my will to be probated in Florida. I only have a Canadian will. Can that will be probated in both places?

— Howard S., Ft. Lauderdale, Florida

Your U.S. condo can be both your Canadian residence and U.S. principal residence for tax purposes. Consequently, any gain on the sale of this residence would not be reportable to CRA. In the United States you could use your principal residence exemption of up to $250,000 allowed to all U.S. taxpayers. Consequently, you should not have any tax to pay either country on the sale of your Florida residence. If you hold the condo at your death, it will be income tax free in both countries under current rules.

By filing returns both in Canada and the United States as you currently do, you may be paying more tax than necessary. You should look into this with a competent cross-border accountant or planner as there may be some substantial annual income tax savings if you arrange your affairs correctly and file only in the U.S. on your world income.

Your will, if it is a valid Canadian will, is generally usable to settle your Florida affairs. If you have both Canadian and U.S. property, it may be advantageous for you to put all your assets into a U.S. living trust so that your estate is not required to go through probate in either country, saving a great deal of cost and aggravation for your heirs.

BETTER LATE THAN NEVER

I read your informative article "Save on Currency Exchanges" in the newspaper. If possible, I would appreciate an answer to the following questions. A person born and living in the United States for 25 years moves to Canada 30 years ago, receives Canadian citizenship, still retains his U.S. citizenship, lives and works in Canada all those 30 years but now lives in the United States about five months each year.

If this person decides to purchase property in Arizona and builds a house on that property, are there rules and regulations that he should be aware of before he starts this project? Is this dual citizen required to file his Canadian income with the IRS even though he had no U.S. income? If so, what is the proper procedure for doing this? Thank you for your assistance.

— Ralph A., Apache Junction, Arizona

As a citizen of both Canada and the United States, you are subject to the tax rules of both countries at the same time. Canadian citizens pay tax on their world income only when they are residents of Canada, whereas U.S. citizens pay tax on their world income regardless of where they are resident. Consequently, you are subject to filing returns in both Canada and the United States unless you leave Canada to become a resident of the United States only.

The requirement to file in the United States is not negated based on the fact that all your income was Canadian-sourced. This requirement to file has always been there ever since you left the United States 30 years ago, so in effect you are quite overdue with your IRS filings. Please remember that just because you were required to file U.S. returns does not mean that you necessarily owe any tax to the IRS. There are certain exemptions and foreign tax credits from taxes paid to Canada for U.S. citizens living outside the United States that can greatly reduce or even eliminate U.S. taxes payable. However, the only way to find out whether you have taxes due is to go back and actually file returns. There is a voluntary disclosure program currently available from the IRS that can allow you to get back in their good graces without filing 30 years of returns. Take advantage of it before they catch up to you.

Getting square with the IRS needs to be your top priority regardless of whether or not you build a place in Arizona. There may be some tax savings in store for you in the future if you file in the United States and leave Canada for tax purposes. There are no particular issues you need to be concerned about in building your new place in the Sunbelt except that you might consider using a living trust to hold title to your property so it does not have to go through probate in Arizona or Canada.

Some of the issues you need to deal with are quite complex and I would recommend you seek out assistance from a qualified person knowledgeable in both the applicable Canadian and U.S. matters.

DOES A GREEN CARD HAVE AN EXPIRATION DATE?

My wife and I moved to Florida in 2005 on a permanent basis as retirees. My wife is a U.S. citizen and I have a green card issued in 1963. I do not intend to work. I returned to Canada in 1964, retaining my green card and filed Canadian income tax returns from 1964 to 2004. I will file a U.S. return for the year 2005, and subsequent years. I will not file a Canadian return. My questions are these:

1. *Is my green card still valid, or do I have to reapply for another one?*

2. *Do I apply in Tampa or do I have to go back to Toronto?*

3. *When I file my U.S. return, am I likely to be asked why I have not filed a return since 1964 and if so, how do I answer? And depending on the answer, will the Internal Revenue Service inform Immigration and Naturalization of my status?*

4. *Will I be able to apply for U.S. citizenship after three years?*

— Edward P., Venice, Florida

1. Since you did not surrender your green card, and it has no expiration date, it is technically still valid. However, you were supposed to surrender the green card in 1964 when you left the United States.

2. Your best bet is to tread softly with the U.S. Citizenship and Immigration Service for a while, and just start using the green card again each time you cross the border. According to new USCIS rules, you do need to file a USCIS Form I-90 to obtain a new green card with updated pictures and a ten-year expiration date. Since you have a permanent Florida home, the U.S. Citizenship and Immigration Service will likely not bother you.

3. The Internal Revenue Service may question you, though, about where all your tax returns were filed since 1964. If you hurry you can also take advantage of a voluntary disclosure program with the IRS that requires you to file the last six years' U.S. returns. You should end up paying no penalties but will have to pay the taxes due, if any, with interest for the six years. Since income taxes were higher in Canada than in the U.S. during this period, the credits from the Canadian tax paid should cover most, if not all, the U.S. taxes due for the six years. The IRS should forgive any taxes that may have been due before the six years.

4. You need three or more continuous years in which you spend over six months a year in the U.S. before applying for U.S. citizenship.

SELLING U.S. LAND

When selling undeveloped real estate in the United States, the titles company will hold back a portion of the proceeds for the IRS.

How can I claim this back? Can I claim it against the capital gains taxes on my Canadian T1 return?

— Tom J., Kingston, Ontario

The U.S. non-resident withholding tax should be 10% of the sale price of your property. If you have not yet actually sold the property, you can apply to the IRS for a clearance certificate, 6 to 8 weeks in advance of the sale, and they will authorize a lower withholding, closer to the actual tax due on the capital gains. Regardless of whether or not you get a clearance certificate, you must file a U.S. tax return, Form 1040NR, the non-resident tax return, to report the sale. Form 1040NR is due by June 15th in the year following the sale. It is by filing Form 1040NR that you obtain any refunds due to overwithholding at the time of sale. You will also need to apply for a U.S. ITIN (Individual Tax Identification Number) by filing a Form W-7 with the IRS. It is best that you get this number well in advance of the sale, as this will make things go a lot more smoothly.

Depending on which state the property is located in, there may be additional non-resident withholding tax and state tax returns to file.

The net tax that you pay to both the IRS and the applicable state will be a tax credit for Canadian taxes due on your T1 for the capital gains in the same tax year.

You can do all this on your own if you have the time and patience, but I do recommend you get professional help, particularly if the transaction is large, as mistakes can be very costly.

EFFECTS OF DUAL CITIZENSHIP

What effects does dual citizenship have on Canadian citizens regarding income tax, etc.?

— Candy O., Tampa, Florida

Although your question is a short one, there are no short answers. There are a large number of tax issues that will need to be addressed if a Canadian becomes a dual citizen, including your country of residence, the size of your estate and the types of income you are receiving.

Probably the first question you need to address is why become a dual citizen. Unless you intend to reside in the United States for more than six months a year and Canada for less than six months, you will not likely benefit taxwise by becoming a dual citizen. You may even expose yourself to some unnecessary tax complications.

Canada taxes its citizens only when they are actual residents of Canada. U.S. citizens are taxed wherever they live in the world, with tax credits allowed against foreign taxes paid by those U.S. citizens in other countries of residence. Consequently, if you become a dual citizen and still intend to reside in Canada, you will be required to file tax returns in both countries on world income. Filing in both countries affords you no tax advantages since you will pay the Canadian tax rate and take a credit for those taxes paid on the U.S. return. Your total tax paid between the two countries under most circumstances will not be any greater, but why complicate your life unnecessarily?

The real tax advantages of dual citizenship come when you become a non-resident of Canada and are no longer subject to Canadian tax rules.

Depending on your sources and amounts of income, you can realistically cut your annual income tax bill in half or more, with good cross-border financial planning.

Under the Canada/U.S. Tax Treaty, you can be a dual citizen and maintain a lifestyle of winters in the Sunbelt and summers in Canada without being subject to taxes in both countries. Consequently, dual citizens can arrange their financial affairs in such a way that they pay tax on their world income only in the United States. Once you have completed an exit tax return from Canada, your tax situation becomes much clearer. CPP/QPP and OAS are partially tax free in the United States and are not subject to non-resident withholding tax or OAS clawback by CRA. Taxes on RRSP and RRIF withdrawals drop to 15% or 25%, depending on whether they are periodic or lump-sum withdrawals. Canadian dividend and corporate pensions are subject to a non-resident withholding tax of 15%. Under the new treaty, interest withholding has been reduced to 10%. You can also take advantage of a large variety of tax-free, tax-deferred or tax-sheltered investment options in the United States to substantially reduce or eliminate any tax on investment income.

The tax advantages of becoming a dual citizen and paying your taxes in the United States need to be greater than the net cost of U.S. Medicare, approximately US$6,200. each per year, or less if you qualify for U.S. Social Security. There are many complex estate-planning issues that should be addressed before making the move to dual citizenship, particularly if your and your wife's total estate is over CDN$5 million. Over this amount, U.S. estate taxes will have to be taken into account.

Because of the complexity of the issues involved with becoming a dual citizen, I don't recommend you attempt such a move without a written plan completed by a knowledgeable cross-border financial planner. Talking to an attorney or accountant in either or both countries may give you only part of a much larger puzzle and can be confusing, especially if they lack knowledge of the other country's systems.

TORONTONIAN MARRYING NEW YORKER

I have just finished reading your very helpful book, The Border Guide, *in search of an answer regarding my situation: a Canadian citizen, age 72, I am in a new relationship with a partner living in New York. We were married in October this year. My new wife was 68 in July.*

I have low income. I almost have no savings left.

My questions are as follows:

1. *Health care: My wife works in a hospital and is also self-employed. She is covered by her workplace Medical Insurance. She was told I'll be covered by her insurance while we are married and she still works for the hospital. She will be covered by U.S. Medicare when she retires. I understand that I have to wait until after one year of marriage to apply and to be covered by U.S. Medicare. She plans to work another year so I am covered during the waiting period. Is this necessary and the only way to do it?*

2. *My stay in the U.S.: What first steps should I take now that we are married? I would like to apply for permanent residency. Do I have to give up Canadian citizenship to become an American citizen? Can I travel during the waiting period?*

3. *Income: I understand that I will always receive my CPP and OAS. But I will eventually lose my Guaranteed Income Supplement (GIS). You wrote me that I may receive half of my wife's Social Security. Can you confirm this and give me some details? Is this only if she predeceases me?*

— J. K., Toronto, Ontario

Since you have married a U.S. spouse who has qualified for Social Security under her own earnings, you will be eligible for both U.S. Medicare and a Social Security pension (approximately 50% of her pension) after one year of marriage. If she predeceases you, you would then be eligible for 100% of her Social Security pension which on average is US$1,000 per month. This would mean you would get a gift from the U.S. of about US$500 a month after your first year of marriage. I am sure you will agree this is a very generous wedding gift from U.S. Social Security. If you predecease her, she would be eligible for about 70% of your CPP as a widow's benefit. Even though your wife is still going to work for another year, she should apply for her Social Security now as she is over 65 and will not have her pension reduced although she has employment earnings. You also will get Medicare Part A at no cost (this is the major part of Medicare) and will have to pay for Part B, like other U.S. residents (about $90 per month). You likely will have to give up your Guaranteed Income Supplement (GIS).

You need to have your new wife sponsor your application for your permanent residence, more commonly called your green card. Since you are already in living in New York, you need to get this done as soon as possible and at the same time apply for advance parole, which will allow you to leave the U.S. and re-enter while the green card application is in process. The green card will take you over two years to get finalized. I would recommend you get some help from an immigration attorney to do this as, it can be a complex process. Once you have had your green card for three years, you can apply to become a dual U.S./Canadian citizen. You do not have to give up Canadian citizenship under current rules at any time during this process.

WITHHOLDING TAX COMPLIANCE ON U.S. RENTAL INCOME

What options are available to Canadian owners/renters in Florida who through ignorance have failed to comply with the 30% withholding tax, and who wish to square themselves immediately with the Internal Revenue Service?

— Ed F., Williamsburg, Ontario

Your question is a very good one, and a situation we run into quite often. Anyone who rents out his or her U.S. property for longer than two weeks per year is subject to taxation on this income in both the United States (under the Internal Revenue Code) and Canada (under the Income Tax Act).

First, you must decide which of the two methods explained below is appropriate for you. The first method has the renter withhold 30% of the gross rental income received and forward it to the IRS Service Center in Philadelphia, Pennsylvania. The onus is on the renter to withhold the tax if you are a non-resident landlord, but the IRS will come after both the renter and the landlord if the tax is not paid as required.

The second method is to make an election under Section 871 of the Internal Revenue Code to be taxed as effectively conducting business in the United States. You would then file a Form 1040NR tax return in the United States annually.

On this return, expenses incurred to earn the rent — such as property taxes, utilities, mortgage interest, travel, etc. and allowable personal exemptions — are subtracted as deductions to arrive at a net taxable income for tax purposes of a non-resident.

By filing Form 1040NR for both the current and past years, the non-resident taxpayer will generally pay less tax. In fact, most people in this situation make little or no profit after all expenses have been deducted, and therefore no tax is due. Even if you do have some net rental profit, the tax rate after deducting personal exemptions of $3,300 starts at only 10%.

A husband and wife can split this income on separate U.S. returns, and both take personal exemptions if the rental property was purchased jointly. It is important to get into compliance as soon as possible and file at least the last three years' returns before the IRS finds you.

The forms for filing a return — the Form 1040NR and the necessary rental income Schedule E may be found at any IRS office or may be requested by calling the IRS toll free at 1-800-829-3676, or they can be downloaded from www.irs.gov. If you do not already have a U.S. Social Security Number for tax purposes or an Individual Taxpayer Identification Number (ITIN), you need to apply for one by completing IRS Form W-7. You must attach it to the first U.S. tax return you file.

There is a statute of limitations (the period of time the IRS has to audit a return) of three years if you have filed a completed Form 1040NR. If you have not filed or you filed without reporting all income, the statute of limitations does not apply, and the IRS can go back as far as they like to collect earlier taxes.

Don't forget to report this income on your Canadian tax return as well; the penalties from the Canada Revenue Agency can be as bad or worse than those from the IRS. I recommend you find someone experienced in cross-border tax filings to assist you with these tax filings, as the process can be complex.

RESIDENCY FOR TAX PURPOSES

Do I need to have a green card or other visa before I am considered a U.S. resident for tax purposes? Are there other regulations that apply to becoming a resident for tax purposes without actually immigrating?

— Oscar G., Sun City, Arizona

Residency for tax purposes does not relate to permanent resident status, but rather to your physical presence within the United States. The following is the general explanation offered by the IRS in its Publication 927, "Tax Obligations of Legalized Aliens." If you are in the United States as a lawful permanent resident (have a green card) at any time during the year, you are considered a resident alien for tax purposes and are taxed just like a U.S. citizen. That is, you are taxed on your income from any source throughout the world.

Even if you do not have a green card, you are still treated as a resident alien if you are actually in the United States for enough days during the year. Generally, if you are in the United States for 183 days during that year, you are considered a resident for tax purposes for that year. But you may also be considered a resident for a year if you are in the United States for fewer than 183 days during that year, providing you were there for a certain minimum number of days over a three-year period. You do not count the days you were there under a diplomatic, student, or teacher visa. Under the Canada/U.S. Tax Treaty, most Canadian visitors to the United States who stay less than the 183 days would not be considered residents of the United States. Consult a tax advisor if you are in doubt about your status.

The more important question is whether you can be taxed in the United States and not in Canada if you do not have any legal immigration status in the United States. The answer to this question will be no in most circumstances as it is very difficult to convince CRA you are a non-resident of Canada when you are not a legal resident somewhere else.

SHARING THE WEALTH OF TAX INFORMATION

My wife, a Canadian citizen, sold a condominium in the United States in 2005 at a small loss from the original 2000 purchase price. She did not report the sale to CRA due to the loss, although she did report it to the IRS. I obtained an exemption from withholding tax because a loss was incurred. She has just received a letter from CRA requesting copies of the purchase and sale documents and the reason why the disposition was not reported on her 2005 tax return.

Is it necessary to report the sale of property in the United States (not principal residence) to CRA when no profit results? Also, if an "equity membership" in a golf club is sold for more than the original cost, is this deemed to be income or profit? Am I required to report it for Canadian tax purposes?

— Don R.C., Naples, Florida

You didn't tell me which country your wife is a resident of for tax purposes.

Judging by the tone of CRA's request, they still consider your wife a Canadian resident. If they are wrong and your wife is a non-resident, you need to provide them with information to prove she has left — such as a U.S. green card, sale of Canadian residence, etc. If she is still a resident of Canada, CRA is correct in their requests. Residents of Canada must report their world income to CRA, including both the sale of the condominium and the golf club membership. Tax could be owing to CRA on the net gain on the sale of these two items, adjusted for Canadian dollars on the difference in exchange rates between the purchase and sale, which could be substantial with the recent increases in the Canadian dollar.

This is a good example of CRA and the IRS sharing your tax information as allowed under the Canada/U.S. Tax Treaty.

You Still Can't Take It with You

4

NON-RESIDENT ESTATE PLANNING

C anadians have not had to deal with any true inheritance or estate taxes since the capital gains tax was introduced in 1972. The provinces that had an inheritance tax at the time opted out of their own tax programs in favour of collecting the provincial portion of the capital gains tax from the deemed disposition at the death of a taxpayer. However, Canadian citizens (or Americans) owning property in Canada need to be aware of the increasingly heavy hand of the taxman encroaching on their estates when transferred to heirs, regardless of which country they permanently reside in.

The first step in understanding cross-border estate planning is comprehending all the forces of Canadian law that come into play, and the need for estate planning in the first place.

Many Canadians are complacent and believe estate or inheritance taxes concern only Americans. However, on joint estates of less than CDN$5 million, the Canadian inheritance or estate tax can be much greater than it is in the United States. See Figure 9.1 in Chapter 9 for more details.

"What?" you say, "There is no inheritance tax in Canada." Look again. The deemed disposition at death of capital assets with capital gains and retirement programs such as RRSPs and RRIFs creates a substantial tax liability at death. In some cases, these hidden taxes can exceed 50% of the value of the estate. CRA and the provinces do not call these taxes inheritance taxes, but — if it looks like a duck, and walks like a duck ... The Ontario Fair Tax Commission has made the following recommendation to the federal government on a Canadian estate tax:

> *Ontario should seek the agreement of the federal government and other provinces to establish a national wealth transfer tax. This tax should be fully comprehensive and should apply to gifts as well as transfers at death. The tax should exempt spousal transfers.*

It should have a generous exemption but should contain no credit for capital gains taxes on deemed dispositions.

The current government in Ontario and other provincial governments have shown little support for this initiative, buoyed as they are by balanced budgets for the first time in decades, so let's hope the commission will drop the initiative altogether. If you think the federal government is not seriously considering this or similar proposals, think again. A wealth transfer tax is one of the last "politically correct" taxes it has not imposed on the Canadian taxpayer, and it would love to get a piece of the action as baby boomers begin to inherit an estimated $1 trillion from their aging parents. It is to be hoped that the federal budget surpluses of the last few years will push thoughts of an inheritance tax well into the background until the federal government scraps them completely. If an NDP government were elected tomorrow, this inheritance tax would almost certainly be part of the first budget. With the 2006 minority Conservative government, the NDP may be able to negotiate this tax or remove their support for the minority government.

The province of residence of the deceased collects approximately half of this deemed disposition tax at death. However, several provinces don't seem to be happy with their share of the tax and have implemented new taxes disguised as user fees.

British Columbia led the way by implementing a probate fee, with many other provinces quickly getting into line. The probate fee is a cleverly disguised inheritance tax, since the majority of one's assets go through probate either at time of death, a spouse's death or both times, hitting the estate twice. The Supreme Court of Canada declared Ontario's probate fees unconstitutional in October 1998. Consequently, all the provinces have had or are having their fees adjusted to turn them into taxes. Here is a brief summary of the fees:

- **Newfoundland and Labrador:** $60 for the first $1,000 and $5 per $1,000 thereafter with no maximum fee.
- **Nova Scotia:** $75 for the first $10,000, progressing to $800 for estates of $200,000 and $5 per $1,000 thereafter with no maximum fee.
- **Prince Edward Island:** $50 for the first $10,000, progressing to $400 for estates of $100,000 and $4 per $1,000 thereafter with no maximum fee.
- **New Brunswick:** $5 per $1,000 with no maximum.

- **Quebec:** This province has a different legal system with no probate or probate fees.

- **Ontario:** $5 per $1,000 for the first $50,000 and $15 per $1,000 thereafter with no maximum.

- **Manitoba:** $6 per $1,000 with no maximum.

- **Saskatchewan:** $12 for the first $1,000, and $7 per $1,000 thereafter with no maximum fee.

- **Alberta:** $25 for the first $10,000, progressing to a maximum of $6,000 for estates of $1 million or more.

- **British Columbia:** $200 for estates of less than $25,000. For estates between $25,000 and $50,000, there is a fee of $200 and $6 per $1,000. On more than $50,000, there is a flat fee of $350 and $14 per $1,000 thereafter with no maximum fee.

Canadians or Americans who live in one country and own property in the other face additional tax rules, which can leave them exposed to double tax. The double tax arises from Canada's deemed disposition tax stacked on top of the U.S. resident/non-resident estate tax, if applicable. This multiple death tax can total up to 70% of the property value in the other country. The 1996 amendment to the Canada/U.S. Tax Treaty goes a long way toward eliminating most of this potential double tax for Canadians and Americans in this situation. See "The Double Taxation Issue" later in this chapter.

Canadians, particularly those who own property in both the United States and Canada, are setting their estates up for trouble in the form of high taxes, liquidity problems and high legal fees if they ignore current or future inheritance taxes. Use the examples in Figure 4.1 to see what happened to the estates of some well-known people, as measured by estate shrinkage. Estate shrinkage, as the name implies, is simply the amount of the estate consumed by probate fees, legal fees, accounting fees, and estate taxes before the beneficiaries actually inherit it.

From Figure 4.1, you can also see that there is a great deal of difference in estate shrinkage between these wealthy deceased persons. Why did Elvis Presley have 73% shrinkage while Henry Kaiser, with a much larger estate, had only 2%? The answer is simple: proper estate-planning techniques.

There are a number of planning techniques you can use to reduce or eliminate inheritance taxes — regardless of your residency and whether you have property in both Canada and the United States. This chapter

ESTATE SHRINKAGE			
Name	**Gross Estate**	**Net Estate**	**Shrinkage**
John Rockefeller	$26,905,182	$9,780,194	64%
Elvis Presley	$10,165,434	$2,790,799	73%
Walt Disney	$23,004,851	$16,192,908	30%
Henry J. Kaiser, Jr.	$55,910,973	$54,879,958	2%

Figure 4.1

provides you with some basic guidelines and directs you to some of the most appropriate estate-planning techniques for your situation. Remember that attempting to implement an estate plan without the assistance of a financial planning professional who is familiar with both U.S. and Canadian estate-planning techniques is analogous to reading up on removing your gall bladder, and then carrying out the procedure by yourself.

THE U.S. NON-RESIDENT ESTATE TAX

On November 11, 1988, President Ronald Reagan, in his last major formal announcement, signed the Technical and Miscellaneous Revenue Act (TAMRA) of 1988, making adjustments to the Tax Reform Act of 1986. There are two major provisions in TAMRA that affect Canadians who own U.S. property such as real estate, stocks, bonds or businesses. The first provision is a dramatic increase in estate or death taxes for non-residents on their U.S. property.

The second provision is the loss of the unlimited marital deduction by Canadians or non-U.S. citizens who are residents of the United States. They can no longer transfer assets, estates or gifts tax free to a Canadian citizen spouse during their lifetimes or upon death. For gifts made after July 14, 1988, only the first $120,000 (inflation indexed) of gifts per year to a non-citizen spouse will not be taxed under this new provision. Before this revision in TAMRA, there were no tax disadvantages for Canadians who resided in the United States and chose not to become U.S. citizens.

This dramatic increase in U.S. estate taxes, which took effect after November 11, 1988, affects Canadian and other foreign owners of U.S. real estate, company shares, debt securities and other property. Under this reform, estate tax rates on these investments jumped from between 6% and 30% to between 18% and 45% (depending on the taxable estate value).

Estate tax can be analogous to income tax, depending on the means by which it is calculated. There are two main factors that determine the amount of tax paid: first, the tax rate in any given bracket; second, the amount of the estate that the tax rate applies to. We will deal with each of these issues and then illustrate how they apply with some examples.

THE TAXABLE ESTATE

Estate tax in the United States is technically a transfer tax on property owned at death. If the property is transferred during one's lifetime, it is subject to a gift tax at the same rates as the estate tax, with some minor exceptions noted later in this chapter in the section What Is a Gift Tax? U.S. citizens and residents of the United States are subject to estate taxes on their worldwide assets, while non-resident Canadians are subject only to tax on their property deemed to be situated in the United States. The Income Tax Rules and Estate Tax Rules covered in Chapter 1 detail the situations in which Canadians may be considered residents of the United States for estate tax purposes. Estate tax is based on the fair market value (not just the appreciation) of all assets either on or exactly six months after the date of death. The property subject to estate tax for a Canadian who is a non-resident of the United States includes real property located in the United States; personal property normally located in the United States, such as autos, jewellery, boats, RVs, furniture and artwork; shares of U.S. corporations, regardless of where they were purchased or where they are physically held; and certain bonds and notes issued by U.S. residents and corporations.

Assets normally excluded from the estate of a non-resident include U.S. bank deposits; government and corporate bonds issued after July 18, 1984; and shares or notes of non-U.S. corporations. Chapter 6 provides more specific details, under "Exempt Investments," about which investments are exempt from both income tax and estate tax for non-residents.

The total of all taxable assets noted above, less any of the exempt assets and minus certain deductions for estate settlement costs and non-recourse mortgages, equals the taxable estate.

U.S. FEDERAL ESTATE TAX

Once the taxable estate has been totalled, the estate tax applies at the graduated rates, with the lowest rate being 18% and the highest 45% on taxable estates of more than $3 million. Refer to Figure 4.2, which illustrates the tax for some sample estates, and Figure 4.3, which illustrates the estate-tax exemptions and maximum tax rates.

U.S. ESTATE TAX RATES
(All figures in U.S. dollars)

Taxable Estate	Tax (before Credit)
$10,000	$1,800
$20,000	$3,800
$40,000	$8,200
$60,000	$13,000
$80,000	$18,200
$100,000	$23,800
$150,000	$38,800
$250,000	$70,800
$500,000	$155,800
$1,000,000	$345,800
$1,500,000	$555,800
$2,000,000	$780,800

Figure 4.2

U.S. ESTATE TAX AND EXEMPTIONS

YEAR	EQUIVALENT EXEMPTION	MAXIMUM TAX RATE
2006	$2,000,000	46%
2007	$2,000,000	45%
2008	$2,000,000	45%
2009	$3,500,000	45%
2010	Tax Repealed	0%
2011	$1,000,000	55%

Figure 4.3

UNIFIED CREDIT

Non-residents and non-U.S. citizens are allowed an estate tax credit of $13,000 to offset any estate tax payable. This credit effectively exempts the first $60,000 of the estate from attracting taxation, as illustrated by the example in Figure 4.4.

NON-RESIDENT ESTATE TAX AT CURRENT U.S. DOMESTIC RATES

Dorothy, a Canadian non-resident of the United States, owns a villa in Hawaii her deceased husband had purchased for her more than fifteen years ago. The villa is valued at $300,000, fully furnished, with a small mortgage of $50,000 remaining at a local bank. This property is all she owns in the United States.

Dorothy's taxable estate is $250,000 (the $300,000 value of the villa less the $50,000 non-recourse mortgage).

Her estate tax from Figure 4.2 would be $70,800 less her unified credit of $13,000 for a net tax of US$57,800 before Canada/U.S. Tax Treaty benefits are applied. (See Figure 4.5.)

Figure 4.4

Residents or citizens of the United States are subject to the same tax rates, but there is one significant difference. They are allowed a unified estate tax credit of $780,600, effectively equal to an applicable exclusion exemption of the first $2 million of assets. (Refer again to Figure 4.3, which indicates how, under current U.S. rules, this applicable exclusion/equivalent exemption amount and the maximum estate tax rate will change over time under current U.S. rules.)

THE CANADA/U.S. TAX TREATY ESTATE TAX PROVISIONS

The Canada/U.S. Tax Treaty as amended in 1996 (after six years of negotiations) brings some good news for Canadians owning property in the United States. The new treaty agreement corrects an oversight in 1988, when the United States increased non-resident estate taxes to the level paid by U.S. residents but did not increase corresponding exemptions. Thus, many Canadian non-residents saw their taxes double or even triple after the 1988 tax package took effect.

The new treaty amendment increases the non-resident exemption, according to a specified formula, from US$60,000 or US$2 million per person.

This means that most Canadians, those with total worldwide estates valued at US$2 million or $4 million for husband and wife (about CDN$5 million) or less, won't be hit with the non-resident estate tax. In simple terms, the new treaty rules and the new and larger U.S. equivalent exemptions from estate tax by the IRS mean that only the top 1% to 2% of the population wealthwise, if they follow the correct procedures and file the correct estate tax returns, need concern themselves with U.S. estate taxes at this time.

DETERMINING EXEMPTIONS

When calculating the portion of U.S. non-resident exemption under the treaty rules, compare your total world estate to your U.S. estate. You will get the same percentage of the $2 million maximum exemption as the ratio of value of U.S. assets relative to the value of your world assets. As you may have already surmised, to get this higher exemption under this new formula, you must reveal your worldwide assets to the IRS by filling in a full Form 706, U.S. Estate Tax return, and be subject to an IRS audit. Since nearly 100% of all large estate tax returns in the United States are audited, executors will have this added burden, which could prove to be time-consuming and expensive.

Here's how it would work for non-resident Canadians who own U.S. property with a fair market value of US$200,000 and a total net worth including the U.S. property of US$1 million. Under the amended treaty, they would receive 20% or $400,000 of the $200,000 exemption (calculated by ($200,000 / $1,000,000) X $2,000,000 = $400,000). They would not be subject to any U.S. non-resident estate tax since their US$200,000 property is valued at less than the allowed exemption of $400,000 under the treaty formula. They might still be subject to the Canadian deemed disposition tax at death if the property appreciated in value during the term of ownership before death.

While most Canadians will benefit from the larger estate tax exemption, those with larger estates could actually face a higher tax burden because the ratio of U.S.-to-world assets results in an exemption of less than $60,000. For example, a person with a worldwide estate of US$8 million with the same US$200,000 property would receive an exemption of only $50,000 (calculated by ($200,000 / $8,000,000) X $2,000,000 = $50,000). In this circumstance, the higher-net-worth individual could bypass the treaty and revert to the domestic rules for the non-resident estate tax mentioned in the preceding sections of this chapter and receive the $60,000 exemption since it is higher. It's important that you consult a financial planner who is up to speed on cross-border issues to determine your best options.

When determining the value of your world estate, you must follow U.S. reporting rules, which can be very different from Canadian rules. A U.S. taxable estate includes such things as the value of life insurance policies that you own on which you are the insured, the full value of Canadian-controlled private corporations which you control, and the present value of all the future payments you might leave a spouse under the spousal benefit of your pensions. Since most Canadians do own life insurance on their own lives and do have some form of government and private pensions, the value of their world estates for the purposes of figuring the size of their U.S. exemptions under the new treaty can be greatly affected. Note that the treaty does not give Canadian residents with appreciated U.S. property any break from the Canadian deemed disposition tax (Canada's estate tax equivalent) at death. The sole exception is a credit that will now be allowed to offset this tax if any U.S. non-resident estate tax is paid. (See The Double Taxation Issue in the next section.)

The treaty has some other positive changes. For example, it adds U.S. stocks to the list of investments that Canadians can make that will be exempt from the non-resident estate tax. This applies only to Canadians whose world estates are less than US$1.2 million. (See Chapter 6 for a complete list of exempt investments, in addition to this specific U.S. stock exemption.)

NON-RESIDENT ESTATE TAX ACCORDING TO THE TREATY RULES

Dorothy's taxable estate would remain the same as in Figure 4.4 at $250,000 and tax before the equivalent exemption of $70,800. Her new exemption would be:

($250,000 ÷ 1,000,000) x $1,500,000 = $375,000

Unified credit from Figure 4.2 for $375,000 exemption is $113,300.

Therefore, the net U.S. estate tax due is $70,800 – $113,300 = $0.

Figure 4.5

Previously, exempt investments included only bonds and treasury bills issued by the U.S. government, bank deposits, life insurance and corporate bonds issued after July 18, 1984. The inclusion of U.S. stocks will enable most Canadians who are non-residents of the United States to freely hold a very diversified portfolio of U.S. stocks, bonds and mutual funds without being exposed to any non-resident estate tax. Figure 4.5 shows the effects of the new Canada/U.S. Tax Treaty. Compare it with Figure 4.4, which was calculated under the current U.S. domestic rules. I am assuming Dorothy has a worldwide estate of US$1 million, including her Hawaiian villa.

Another important change in the treaty for those Canadian citizens who are either dual citizens or U.S. residents is the ability to waive the right to roll their estates over to their spouses to defer any estate tax to the second spouse's death. This waiver allows the deceased's estate to take a double exemption equivalent to US$4 million. Consequently, estates of that size can benefit greatly if they are structured correctly to take advantage of this double exemption.

In summary, the new articles regarding non-resident estate tax in the Canada/U.S. Tax Treaty provide some relief for Canadians owning U.S. property, but at the expense of complexity. The estate may incur legal and accounting fees that can be, in some instances, greater than the tax itself. The treaty will be of little relief to the double taxation status of U.S. citizens in Canada who own Canadian appreciated property or for Canadians living in the United States as dual residents with U.S. property.

THE DOUBLE TAXATION ISSUE

Earlier in this chapter, we discussed the Canadian equivalent to estate tax, the deemed disposition tax on appreciated assets, including foreign assets, at death. This tax is, in effect, an income tax on capital gains. By its own definition, the U.S. estate tax is not an income tax. Consequently, under domestic rules CRA does not allow a foreign tax credit on estate taxes paid to the United States to offset the deemed disposition capital gains tax on foreign assets. In other words, there is no foreign income tax credit available from CRA since an estate tax cannot offset an income tax. Conversely, the IRS will not allow the capital gains tax paid to CRA as a credit or deduction against U.S. estate taxes payable, for exactly the same reason. The 1996 Canada/U.S. Tax Treaty now allows for a credit of these two taxes and all but eliminates this double tax in this specific area.

Canadians who own appreciated U.S real estate and other taxable U.S. assets should no longer face two separate taxes on the same assets at the same time, without any means of obtaining offsetting credit.

Figure 4.6 illustrates this double tax more clearly. Let's use the examples of Figures 4.4 and 4.5, and assume that the owner of the Hawaiian villa dies this year, both under the old treaty and under the new treaty. As you can see from Figure 4.6, Dorothy's husband's estate, according to the new Canada/U.S. Tax Treaty rules, would pay the equivalent total of the higher of either the Canadian deemed disposition tax or the U.S. non-resident estate tax. In Dorothy's case, her equivalent estate tax exemption was higher than the value of her U.S. property, so she had a zero non-resident estate tax due in the U.S., leaving her husband's estate with the Canadian deemed disposition tax only. Even if she had U.S. estate taxes to pay, she would not pay both taxes, since the executor would take a credit for U.S. taxes paid against the Canadian deemed disposition tax. Note that if the U.S non-resident estate tax is equal to or larger than the Canadian deemed disposition tax, no tax should be due to CRA.

There are a number of estate-planning techniques designed to assist Canadians to avoid or reduce the effect of this non-resident estate tax. These techniques will be discussed in the next section.

HOW TO AVOID THE U.S. NON-RESIDENT ESTATE TAX

Each of the following techniques has its individual merits and drawbacks in dealing with the non-resident estate tax. There is no silver bullet solution for all people in all situations. I will briefly cover the circumstances under which each technique works best and what to watch out for with each option. These options are given as a guide only and any attempt to apply these methods to your own situation should be accomplished with the assistance of a qualified cross-border estate-planning professional. The new Canada/U.S. Tax Treaty with its articles on estate tax may make the following strategies less necessary than in the past, since those Canadians with estates of less than US$2 million would likely always qualify for larger non-resident exemptions than the $60,000 under existing U.S. domestic rules.

BECOME A U.S. RESIDENT

In a previous section in this chapter, "The U.S. Non-Resident Estate Tax," I mentioned the fact that residents of the United States receive an estate tax equivalent exemption of $2 million (see Figure 4.3, which outlines the future changes for this exemption) compared to the non-resident exemption of $60,000 (unless the 1996 Canada/U.S. Tax Treaty allows for a greater exemption — see the earlier sections of this chapter). A husband and wife who become U.S. residents would be eligible for a total husband and wife exemption of US$4 million (increasing to $7 million by 2009) or about CDN$5 million, which is enough for many Canadians to be fully exempt from paying any estate taxes. Without further estate planning, persons with larger estates could still be subject to tax.

COMPARATIVE ESTATE TAXES
UNDER OLD AND NEW TAX TREATIES

Dorothy's deceased husband paid $100,000 for the Hawaiian villa when he bought it fifteen years ago. At his death, it is valued at $300,000:

DOUBLE ESTATE TAX — OLD TREATY

Canadian Tax		U.S. Non-Resident Estate Tax	
$300,000	Deemed sale	$300,000	Value
– 100,000	Cost	– $50,000	Mortgage
$200,000	Capital gain	– 60,000	Exemption
$46,500	Tax payable	$190,000	Taxable estate
		$57,800	Tax payable

Total tax payable ($46,500 + $57,800) = **$104,300**

ESTATE TAX — NEW TREATY

Canadian Tax		U.S. Non-Resident Estate Tax	
$300,000	Deemed sale	$300,000	Value
– 100,000	Cost	– 50,000	Mortgage
$200,000	Capital gain	– 375,000	Exemption
– 0	Credit for U.S. tax paid	$0	Taxable estate
$46,500	Tax payable	$0	Tax payable

Total tax payable ($46,500 + $0) = **$46,500**

Figure 4.6

There are many other implications in becoming a U.S. resident besides estate tax reduction. These ramifications will be covered in greater detail in Chapters 7, 8 and 9.

MORTGAGE YOUR U.S. PROPERTY

Examples given in Figures 4.4, 4.5 and 4.6 illustrate that non-recourse mortgages can be deducted from the taxable estate and only the net equity will be taxable. A non-recourse mortgage is from a lender whose only security is the property itself. In case of a default, the lender cannot go after the borrower's other assets if there is insufficient collateral in the property.

One side benefit of taking out a mortgage is that you may be able to deduct the mortgage interest on your Canadian tax return. If you invested the mortgage proceeds in income-producing investments outlined in Chapter 6, Exempt Investments, you would be able to deduct the interest as interest paid to produce investment income. This could go a long way toward producing U.S. investment income that could protect you from a falling Canadian dollar. For this to work most effectively, the return on your investments must provide a return greater than the cost of your mortgage.

You should also be aware of potential currency risks if you mortgage your property and then take the proceeds back to Canada, since your loan obligation is in U.S. funds. In this situation, a falling Canadian dollar would require larger Canadian-dollar conversions with each payment; conversely a rising Canadian dollar could produce taxable capital gains.

Mortgages advanced through traditional Canadian banks in Canada, or non-arm's-length lenders such as controlled Canadian corporations, will not work for this strategy, since the debt would not be non-recourse.

JOINT PROPERTY OWNERSHIP WITH CHILDREN

Since each individual non-resident has a $60,000 estate tax exemption, and possibly more under the Canada/U.S. Tax Treaty, it sometimes makes sense to place all family members on the title of an existing U.S. property or when purchasing a new one. A family of five, for example, could combine their exemptions and own a vacation home worth $300,000, and none of them would be subject to a non-resident estate tax. On the surface, although this strategy appears to be very simple and basic, it can be wrought with pitfalls.

Much as we may not care to admit it, our children are only human, and they will experience some of the not-so-pleasant things in life such as divorce and bankruptcy. Many unsuspecting parents have had to pay off an ex-spouse or a child's creditors so they could keep their own winter vacation home. Serious family discord can sometimes result in a battle over control of a family-owned property.

Once you have considered the drawbacks carefully and still feel this is a suitable technique for you, you should consider several things concerning the actual placement of adult children's names on the property title. If you already own this property and want to place one or more children on title, there are both Canadian and U.S. tax implications to be mindful of. First, CRA will consider this transfer subject to capital gains tax on the portion of the property being transferred. From a U.S. standpoint, the IRS will consider the transfer of the American property a gift and subject to gift tax. A more detailed description of the gift tax appears later in this chapter under "What Is a Gift Tax?" If both you and your spouse are not already on title, you can run into some of the same U.S. gift tax problems when adding a spouse to the title.

Sometimes the best method to complete this type of a transfer may be to sell a portion of the property to your children, even if you have to loan them the money in Canada at no interest. You can avoid the U.S. gift tax, but not the Canadian capital gains tax if the property has appreciated in value. The capital gains tax, if any, could be paid by the recipient children, who are likely getting a pretty good deal anyway.

When using joint with right of survivorship to own your U.S. property, it is important that you be aware of the fact that the first to die of the joint owners is assumed by the IRS to have contributed the entire capital for the purchase of that particular property. That means the entire property would be included in taxable U.S. estate of the first to die unless the executor could provide proof to the IRS that the other joint owners actually contributed to the property purchase.

If you are about to purchase U.S. property, this arrangement is much easier to make at the time of purchase than after the sale is completed. One additional benefit of this technique is that the estate will likely avoid probate at the time of both parents' deaths since a Joint Ownership with Right of Survivorship titling of the property with the children will allow the property to pass directly to them without probate by order of law after both parents have died.

HAVE AN INSURANCE COMPANY PAY THE TAX

Life insurance benefits from a non-resident insured person are not included in their taxable estates. The recent development of no-load life insurance has made this planning option more practical than ever. Most people who buy life insurance are unaware that an average of 150% of their first year's premiums, and 20% of the next nine years' premiums go toward agent's commissions, manager overrides, marketing costs, sales trips to Hawaii and other related costs. No-load life insurance strips out all these unnecessary costs so you enjoy both lower premiums, and cash values equal to your paid premiums, plus interest at fair market rates. No-load life insurance works a lot like a term deposit, yielding slightly higher rates, but has the added benefit of a life insurance death benefit. It can be purchased only through some fee-only financial planners or directly from certain life insurance companies in the United States. You pay a fee for the service of the financial planner, much as you would for hiring any professional, such as an accountant or an attorney, to do a specific job for you.

No commissioned agent should be involved. If you sell your property later, you can generally cash in your policy and walk away with all the premiums, plus a good rate of return.

This method is simple and can be very cost-effective for most couples. Used in combination with the method of establishing appropriate trusts outlined in the next section, it provides a worry-free, easy-to-maintain U.S. estate plan. Most insurance companies would require Canadians to have both a U.S. address and a U.S. Social Security Number or Individual Tax Identification Number for the purchase of the life insurance policy.

There are no negative tax or legal complications with this method, other than that the interest earned on your policy, under certain situations when you cash in your policy, must be reported to CRA, just the same as if you had earned the interest at a U.S. bank.

ESTABLISH APPROPRIATE TRUSTS

The Canadian spousal trust allows the deemed disposition capital gains tax, ordinarily due at the death of the first spouse, to be deferred until the second spouse's death. In a similar manner, there is the opportunity to defer U.S. estate tax until the death of the surviving spouse.

The U.S. estate tax deferment is accomplished through the use of a qualified domestic trust (QDOT). This is a very simple trust created either during one's lifetime through a living trust with the QDOT language, through a will, or by the executor of the estate. At the death of the first spouse, the QDOT holds the descendant's share of the U.S. property in trust, under certain IRS guidelines, for the benefit of the surviving spouse for his or her lifetime. (A further discussion of living trusts is included later in this chapter under Living Trusts — A Simple Solution to Problems with Wills.)

If the QDOT is created under a living trust arrangement, you will achieve the added benefit of avoiding U.S. probate of your estate at either spouse's death, if you have the trust hold all your U.S. property. If you are transferring property into the living trust, you may face a deemed disposition tax by CRA if it is not done correctly; check with your cross-border advisor.

A living trust/QDOT, along with a joint and last survivorship no-load life insurance policy, may easily be the best solution for coping with the non-resident estate tax. It is simple, flexible, economical, easy to maintain, and does not operate in any untested or controversial areas of tax law. According to CRA rules, you will need to disclose annually on your Canadian tax return (using Form T1135) that you own foreign property, unless it is used for your personal use only, whether or not it is owned by the trust.

USE EXEMPT U.S. INVESTMENTS

Chapter 6 provides the details of U.S. investments you can use to generate income that is free from both U.S. income and estate tax. Use of these investments will go a long way toward simplifying your estate plan.

Unfortunately, real estate does not fall under the category of exempt investments, so it must be dealt with under some of the other estate-planning techniques. Remember, exempt investments, unless held in a living trust, could be subject to probate in the United States, and all foreign investment and property ownership must be reported each year to CRA on your tax return.

USE A CANADIAN HOLDING COMPANY

Many Canadians hold U.S. winter homes or similar property by purchasing or transferring the property through a single-purpose Canadian holding company. This is by far the most complex strategy and, coincidentally, was the one most often recommended by lawyers and accountants on both sides of the border.

However, in 2005 the CRA changed its rules and will no longer allow this practice. Those with winter residences already in single-purpose holding companies are grandfathered but no new arrangements of this type will be allowed. From an IRS perspective, owning personal-use real estate inside a corporation was never a good idea and is still not. Corporations must pay capital gains tax at the rate of 35% instead of the 15% personal capital gains rate. In addition, both the IRS and the CRA may infer taxable benefits to the shareholders for the personal use of the residence.

SELL YOUR PROPERTY AND RENT

Selling your property and renting each year may seem a bit drastic but it can be a very good alternative for some people. It is a simple solution and the only tax consideration may be capital gains tax on the sale of your property. Capital gains taxes in both Canada and U.S. are at record lows in recent history, and with the run-up in prices that most areas of the Sunbelt have had over the past decade, triggering real estate gains now is a good strategy. Review Chapter 3 for the tax rates and filing requirements for non-residents selling real property in the U.S.

Proceeds from the sale of the home should be put into U.S. tax-exempt investments, to generate U.S. dollar income to finance future winter stays.

If the death of the property owner is anticipated in the near future, a quick sale to a family member in Canada is a very smart estate tax-saving move.

ESTATE TAX CONCERNS IN INDIVIDUAL STATES

In June 2001, the U.S. federal government brought in a sweeping new set of estate tax rules that were designed to phase out, by 2010, the estate taxes at the federal level. (See Figure 4.3, which shows the scheduled reduction to 2010.) This federal program has deprived individual states (already hurting for more sources of revenue) of a key source of income, as most states had piggy-backed on the federal program to collect estate tax. Prior to June 2001, the IRS had allowed each state to levy against their residents a maximum credit of state estate taxes. Therefore, each state would just charge the maximum credit, more commonly called the "pick-up tax," allowed by the IRS, and the taxpayer paid the same total tax. The credit system in effect allowed individual states to share in the estate-tax pie without any taxpayer concerns, as taxpayers paid the same amount but split it between the federal and state governments rather than paying it all to the federal government through the IRS.

With this phase-out of the estate tax by the IRS, the credit through the pick-up tax rule to the states was also phased out in 2005. To counter this loss of revenue, many states that had the constitutional option to do so legislated their own separate estate tax. Since states are not party to the Canada/U.S. Tax Treaty, non-resident Canadians are facing a new source of potential taxes at a state level, with no treaty protection against double taxation or access to other treaty benefits.

Consequently, Canadians and U.S. citizens living in Canada will need to be aware of what the states where they own property are doing to replace the pick-up tax, if anything, and perhaps plan around them using some of the techniques to eliminate the federal estate tax discussed above. For example, Washington state has implemented its own estate tax in an extremely high rate of nearly 20% on estates over standard federal exemptions. Arizona, California and Florida, because their constitutions do not allow a new estate tax without bringing it to a full vote of the state residents, now have no state estate tax. About one-third of the other states have plans to or have already implemented their own estate tax system.

The bottom line here is that after years of negotiating with the federal government to include estate tax relief in the Canada/U.S. Tax Treaty, individual states may bring Canadian non-residents right back to the equivalent of pre-1996 days with the old treaty and potential double tax on estates for Canadian residents owning property in the U.S., particularly in states such as Washington.

In recent years, several Canadian provinces have separated their provincial income tax systems from the federal system, the way Quebec has for many years, and residents of those provinces must file a separate provincial tax return. As noted above, neither provinces nor states are party to the Canada/U.S. Tax Treaty. Provinces such as British Columbia and Ontario have wording in their provincial income tax acts that does not allow for foreign tax credits for estate tax purposes. This means that residents in these provinces would not get any foreign tax credits at the provincial level for U.S. estate taxes paid on the death of the taxpayer. The result would in effect be a double tax. This situation would not have been anticipated in the Canada/U.S. Tax Treaty negotiations that created the new estate tax rules in 1995. Consequently, Canadians and Americans who own property on a cross-border basis need to be acutely aware of the provincial and state estate tax rules where they own property, as well as of the Canadian federal and U.S. federal rules.

IS YOUR CANADIAN WILL VALID IN THE UNITED STATES?

There are plenty of legitimate concerns among Canadians owning property in the United States about whether their Canadian wills will be valid in the United States at the time of their deaths.

Generally speaking, if your Canadian will has been drafted correctly and is valid in Canada, it will also be valid in the United States. There is no real need to have separately drafted wills for American and Canadian property. There is some merit to having a separate U.S. will drafted in the state you normally reside in to simplify the probate process, but having two wills can also create problems, such as trying to convince the courts which one is valid. You will also have to pay for and keep track of two separate wills when it is usually unnecessary.

If you do not have a valid will in either country, your estate will be subject to the intestate laws in your place of residence. This creates double work for your appointed executor when there are assets in two separate jurisdictions, such as a Canadian province and a U.S. state. Many people ignore the need for a will or do not look at alternative estate-planning vehicles because they are under one or more misconceptions about wills, joint ownership and the probate process.

Probate comes from the Latin word meaning "to prove." After a person dies, probate is the process of proving how the deceased person wanted his or her property distributed. This "proof" is accomplished by presenting the will to court for probate.

Unfortunately, it isn't always that easy. You may know someone who has been through the frustration and the expense of probate. To help you better understand wills and the alternatives now available, here are twelve costly misconceptions that apply whether your assets are in Canada or the U.S. or both:

- **Misconception 1. Probate costs are low.** Wrong! Most personal representatives hire an attorney to help with the paperwork of probate. Here's why: The laws relating to probate and estate administration are extremely complex for a layperson. So while provincial and state laws do allow a personal representative to go through the probate without a lawyer's help, most personal representatives do not want to face this challenge alone. So they hire a lawyer. Legal fees for even a simple probate taking less than one year can reach $5,000 to $10,000. Provincial probate fees, depending on the province involved, can add 1.5% of the value of the probate estate to the total costs.

  Total legal fees and other estate administration costs can average from 3% to 10% of the total estate value, depending on the complexity of the probate, the state or province of residence of the deceased, and the property location. Owning property in both the United States and Canada definitely increases the complexity of the probate.

- **Misconception 2. Your will and your assets remain private.** Sorry! Probate is a matter of public record, so all of your assets and liabilities will be spelled out to the penny in court records. Names of beneficiaries and the amounts of their inheritances are all open to the public. Anyone can go to the court and ask to see your probate file. If you valued your privacy in life, you'd probably find probate uncomfortable.

- **Misconception 3. A will can be probated in just a few weeks.** No way! Even with a simple estate, probate can take from ten months to two years. During that time, the deceased person's property must be inventoried and appraised. Relatives and beneficiaries must be notified. Creditors must be notified and paid. Income taxes must be paid. Any contested claims and contested inheritances must be settled. Only then is the property distributed to the beneficiaries.

- **Misconception 4. A will helps you avoid taxes.** Dead wrong! A standard will does nothing to lower your taxes. A properly drafted will may take advantage of certain estate-planning options such as setting up trusts that can save or defer estates taxes. A standard will simply indicates how you want your property distributed and who you want to care for your children.

- **Misconception 5. A will or a testamentary trust (a trust set up by your will) avoids probate.** Not true! By law all property governed by a will must go through the probate process, before it passes to beneficiaries. The law does not allow minor children to inherit bank accounts, stocks and bonds or real estate. That is why parents often set up a testamentary trust for their children, which holds the property until the children reach the age of majority. But since the testamentary trust is part of the person's will, it still must be probated by the court.

- **Misconception 6. Joint tenancy is the safest way to own property.** Not so! Joint tenancy with right of survivorship exposes each party to the debts of the other. For example, assume you own a home in joint tenancy with your child. Your child starts a business that goes broke. His creditors are chasing him trying to collect their money. The home you own with your child could now be taken away from you to satisfy your child's debts.

  Also, joint tenancy property must go through probate when the second person dies, or in the event that both people die in a common accident. As noted earlier in this chapter, for non-residents owning property jointly in the U.S., the IRS presumes that the first joint owner to die has the entire property included in his or her taxable estate unless the executor can prove contributions by the other joint owner or owners.

- **Misconception 7. Your permanent home and your vacation home can be handled through the same probate.** Yes, but only if they are located in the same province or state. If you own a home or property in another province, or in the United States, you'll need to open a second probate, which means you'll hire another lawyer. This usually doubles the probate expense. And, if you own real estate in a third location, you'll need to open a third probate and hire a third lawyer.

- **Misconception 8. A will prevents quarrels over assets.** Not on your life! Wills are the subject of more lawsuits than any other document. Today, it is common for unhappy friends or relatives to contest a will, resulting in higher legal fees and added delays. This is one more reason why the average probate takes from ten months to two years.

- **Misconception 9. Family members can sell property in the estate to raise money.** A fatal mistake! The court freezes the estate's assets until the probate has ended. The court may allow the personal representative to give family members small living allowances, but only up to the amounts allowed by provincial or state law. Permission to pay beneficiaries out of the estate must be granted by the court. Regardless of the outcome, asking the court's permission to sell property increases the legal fees and can take a great deal of time.

- **Misconception 10. A will from one province is not legal in another or in the United States.** Untrue! If the will is legal in one province, it is also legal in another, and in the United States. However, if your will contains certain legal language, it can go through probate more quickly and smoothly. If you want to avoid delays in probate, you might want to have your will that must go through probate reviewed by a lawyer in each province or state in which you own property.

- **Misconception 11. The cost of planning your estate is only the cost of drawing up your will.** Not quite accurate! The cost of any estate plan is both the cost of drawing up the documents and the cost of carrying out the plan. If your will costs $150 in legal fees and the probate costs $5,000, the cost of your estate plan is $5,150. This is a lot more than merely the cost of the will. This will is not only the most common document in our legal system, it is also one of the most expensive.

- **Misconception 12. You must name your lawyer as your personal representative.** No. When you name your lawyer as your personal representative, you are in effect giving him or her your permission to get paid twice — once for acting as your personal representative, and again when he or she acts as your lawyer. You can select anyone you wish to be your personal representative. For convenience's sake, you may want to choose someone who lives in your province or state.

LIVING TRUSTS — A SIMPLE SOLUTION TO PROBLEMS WITH WILLS

A living trust is a legal entity formed to hold your property for your benefit while you are alive. After an estate-planning lawyer drafts your living trust, she helps transfer your assets into the trust. Property held by a living trust does not go through probate after death.

Here's why: the law says that any property owned when you die must go through probate, with a few exceptions such as joint tenancy property with right of survivorship. When you set up a living trust, property is transferred into the trust and retitled in the name of the trust. So after your death, the property doesn't have to go through probate, because the property is no longer in your name — it's owned by the trust.

If you want to manage the trust, name yourself as trust manager, or "trustee." A trust company's involvement is not needed at all. As trustee, you can (1) put property into or take it out of the trust, (2) change the trust and even (3) revoke the trust — any time you wish. If you want someone to manage the trust for you, you can select a relative, friend, lawyer, bank or trust company. Normally, both husband and wife are trustees while either is still living. In the case of death or disability, a successor trustee is named in the trust document, usually the same person who would be your personal representative in your will. While you are living, the operation of the trust provides you with all the same rights to your property, and your personal affairs operate pretty much the same as before.

When you form a living trust you accomplish the following:

- Save your family thousands of dollars in legal fees.
- Save your family months of lengthy court proceedings.
- Keep your family's legal affairs out of court records.
- Protect your family from the dangers of joint tenancy.
- Reduce the likelihood that your wishes will be challenged by unhappy friends and relatives.
- Give your family complete control over the property, because the trust assets are not frozen by the court.
- Avoid added probates for property you own in other provinces or states.
- Provide more efficient management of your estate in the event of death or disability.

As you can see, a living trust can be a very useful tool in cross-border financial planning, particularly when it has the qualified domestic trust provisions mentioned earlier in this chapter for deferring non-resident estate taxes. Living trusts are a very common estate-planning vehicle in the United States and are routinely recommended by estate planners at all levels. In fact, Canadians wintering in the United States see a continual barrage of advertisements for living trust seminars put on by banks, attorneys, brokerage firms and financial planners. Some use the living trust as a loss leader to sell other products or services.

A small number of Canadian lawyers and financial planners have started to recognize the benefits of living trusts. For Canadians over age 65, the CRA is now allowing "alter ego" trusts. These trusts are very similar in both use and design to U.S. living trusts, and they can help people avoid the additional tax reporting that standard Canadian trusts require. Trusts should not be reserved for Americans only. Canadian trusts, like wills, are generally valid in the United States and vice versa. However, if you are going to use your trust to hold property in both Canada and the United States simultaneously, I highly recommend that you use a cross-border financial planner to help coordinate legal services such as drafting the documents and the transfer of the assets in both your Canadian home province and U.S. state. There may be Canadian tax implications, including land transfer tax, when transferring assets to a trust.

POWER OF ATTORNEY — SHOULD YOU HAVE ONE?

One of the simplest and most useful documents you can add to your estate plan is a power of attorney (POA). This will be of great assistance to you in almost all U.S. states and Canadian provinces.

POAs are very basic documents that give some other person(s), whom you trust, the right to transact business or make medical decisions on your behalf if you are physically or mentally unable to do so for yourself. Anyone who has had a spouse or a loved one in this situation may have discovered the long, costly and frustrating process of going to court to get authorization for a conservatorship or guardianship, so you can pay for and implement this person's care. Correctly drafted, a power of attorney should eliminate the need for the conservatorship or guardianship.

To be effective, the POA must be a durable or enduring power of attorney. A durable or enduring POA means that it will be valid even after you become incapacitated, the point at which a non-durable POA would lapse.

Many lawyers in Canada and the United States recommend two separate durable POAs, one for general financial needs and one for medical needs. Good estate lawyers will routinely include the proper POAs with the wills and trusts they draft at no extra cost. Have the POAs reviewed and updated regularly every two to three years by a lawyer in each of the jurisdictions that they are most likely to be used in, to ensure they will be valid there. If you have property in more than one province or state, you may have multiple powers of attorney.

Durable POAs are the kind of documents you hope you never have to use, but when you need them they are invaluable.

WHAT HAPPENS IF YOU DIE IN THE UNITED STATES?

We've covered a lot of ground in this chapter on cross-border estate planning, but what actually happens when a death occurs? How does the IRS find out whether the deceased owned property in the United States?

Whether physical death occurs in Canada or the United States, there is technically no difference with respect to taxes or any other obligations. At the time of your death, either your personal representative or, if there is a living trust, your successor trustee has certain responsibilities. This person must do the following:

- Make a separate list of assets in both Canada and the United States and arrange for appraisals of the property.

- If the descendant did not have a living trust holding his assets, probates in the province(s) or state(s) where he owned property would have to be initiated.

- Determine what, if any, estate tax or probate fees are due to the IRS and to the state(s) or the province(s) where the property is located.

- Arrange for the filing of the final tax returns in Canada and, if necessary, in the United States by the appropriate deadlines.

- Arrange for the filing of the federal and state estate tax returns in the United States if the taxable estate, as defined earlier in this chapter, exceeds $60,000.

- If property in the United States is to be sold, obtain estate tax clearances for both the IRS and the appropriate state department of revenues.

- Hire and coordinate the professionals needed to execute all these responsibilities.

- Notify beneficiaries of their rights under the will or trust.

The IRS will normally learn about a death during one or more of the above procedures. The Canadian executor, personal representative or successor trustee becomes personally liable for any estate tax due if it is not paid correctly from the estate. If there is no specified executor, the tax code states that any person in receipt of a deceased person's property is considered that person's executor, known as a statutory executor.

There is an automatic estate tax lien attached by the IRS to all U.S. property of the deceased. These liens, even though they may not appear as being attached directly to the property title, must be satisfied before they are released. If a personal representative wants to sell the property before the estate is finalized, he or she will be required to obtain federal estate tax clearance and may face withholding taxes of up to 60%. The withholding tax may be refunded after the estate is settled by filing the appropriate returns.

CRA gives the personal representative six months from the date of death or to April 30 in the year following the date of death, whichever is sooner, to file the final Canadian return of the deceased and pay any tax due. The IRS requires that the non-resident estate tax return Form 706NA be filed within nine months of the date of death. Incidentally, estate tax returns are audited at least ten times more often than regular tax returns. The IRS routinely audits nearly 100% of all larger estate tax returns because collecting the extra taxes can be very lucrative.

WHAT IS A GIFT TAX?

Throughout this chapter we have referred to gift taxes. This terminology is not familiar to most Canadians, but they hear it mentioned frequently in the United States. Gift taxes are paid by the giver/donor, not the recipient/donee.

The U.S. gift taxes were unified with U.S. estate tax until 2004. In 2004, the lifetime gift tax exemption was frozen at $1 million, while the estate tax exemption has been raised to $2 million. Gift tax applies to a transfer of property during one's lifetime, while estate tax applies to the transfer of property at one's death. The rates for gift taxes are identical to the estate tax rates provided in Figure 4.2 earlier in this chapter until 2010, when the estate tax is scheduled to be totally repealed and the gift tax rate falls to a maximum of 35%. The lifetime exemption or any portion thereof, if used up through gifting, is not available for use as an estate tax exemption after death.There is no lifetime gift tax exemption for non-residents of the U.S. through the Canada/U.S. Tax Treaty as there is for estate tax.

In addition to the lifetime exemption, there is an annual gift tax exemption of $12,000 of U.S. property per donor whether resident or non-resident of the United States, to any recipient the giver chooses. For example, a married couple with one child could give $12,000 each to the child tax-free each year and not reduce their lifetime estate or gift tax exemption. Non-U.S. residents, non-citizens and citizens alike are allowed an annual tax-free gift of US$120,000 in property to a non-U.S. citizen spouse. U.S. citizens and residents can gift unlimited amounts of cash or property to a citizen spouse at any time.

Canadians are subject to gift tax rules whenever they give or transfer any U.S.-located property. You should be careful and plan transfers of U.S. property accordingly. As noted earlier, adding children's or spouse's names to the title of U.S. property would be treated as if the property were given as a gift. There are severe penalties for failure to pay this tax, and ignorance of the law will be of no help to you should you get caught.

CREATING OR RECEIVING A CROSS-BORDER INHERITANCE OR GIFT

Every year I receive numerous inquiries from parents who live in Canada and their children or other beneficiaries live in the U.S. or vice versa, and they want to know what are the tax implications of this situation. Conversely, I hear from the children or the beneficiaries as to what tax obligations they may have if they receive a gift or an inheritance from Canada while they are living in the U.S. or from the U.S. if they are living in Canada.

Generally speaking, once an estate is settled and all taxes have been paid by the estate representative, the remaining estate can be dispersed to beneficiaries whether they live in Canada or the U.S. without any further tax obligations to either the CRA for the IRS from the beneficiary. This general rule also applies to cross-border gifts in either direction as long as the donor has complied with U.S. gift tax rules in the case of a U.S. donor and with respect to the CRA deemed disposition rules for a Canadian donor. Only if the donor in the case of the gift or the executor in the case of an inheritance has not complied with the gift tax or estate rules of their particular country are there any tax obligations conferred to recipients or donees. Both the CRA and the IRS have rules that may require recipients or donees of gifts or inheritances to pay the tax obligations of the donor or the estate, respectively, if the taxes were not paid correctly before the gift or the inheritance was received.

U.S. resident beneficiaries of Canadian estates or recipients of Canadian gifts in excess of $100,000 are required to file IRS Form 3520, Annual Return to Report Transactions with Foreign Trusts and Receipt of Certain Foreign Gifts, due by the normal filing date, including extensions, of your U.S. tax return for the year the inheritance or gift was received.

Although Form 3520 is strictly a reporting form and no tax is due by filing the form, failure to file Form 3520 comes with substantial penalties ranging from 5% of the amount of the gift to 35% of the amount of the inheritance. Consequently prompt filing should not be ignored under any circumstances.

CROSS-BORDER Q&A

SEPARATE POWER OF ATTORNEY IN THE UNITED STATES

I have a will and a power of attorney for property in Ontario, Canada. Will these be acceptable in Florida if needed? My property is a condo and a bank account in the United States.

— J.W., Fort Pierce, Florida

Your will, if a valid will in Ontario, would normally be accepted as valid in the state of Florida. Your power of attorney may or may not work in Florida depending on what you want to do with it and what the requirements are at the condo and the bank. I strongly recommend you draft an additional Florida power of attorney prepared or reviewed by a Florida attorney for use in that state. You should also show the new power of attorney to the condo association and the bank to see if they would act on it if necessary. It is not worth taking the risk that your Ontario power of attorney would not work in Florida when it is needed.

DOES A LIVING TRUST SATISFY CANADA REVENUE AGENCY?

What will happen to my property, in terms of taxation, when I die? According to information I have gathered from attending estate-planning workshops, I could have a living trust. However, I need to know if this would satisfy CRA or the Ontario government. These questions could not be answered by the American financial planners I have asked.

My house and property are located in Arizona, where I would like to live for eight months of the year instead of the usual six months less a day. How would I apply for resident alien status? My efforts to reach U.S. Immigration by telephone have been thwarted by their computer answering system.

— Morris C., Lake Havasu, Arizona

You are correct in thinking that you should have a living trust as part of your estate plan. You can use this trust to hold both Canadian and U.S. assets. However, you need to be aware of some tax implications that CRA may catch you on. CRA considers most transfers into a living trust a deemed disposition unless you are over 65 and use a Canadian alter ego trust. Consequently, if you have any potential capital gains in the property you are transferring into a non-alter ego trust, you will be subject to Canadian tax when you complete the transfer. If you are transferring your personal residence, you will have no Canadian tax to pay. Items such as term deposits, GICs and bank accounts can be transferred in without tax consequences and the tax on income earned after the transfer into the trust can be either paid by the trust or passed through to you individually.

If your trust is set up correctly, it will allow your estate to avoid probate in both Canada and the United States, which is a desirable goal for most people.

Since you are likely to be trustee of your own trust, the trust will be a resident of the same country that you are. This means that if you are earning income from assets in a non-alter ego trust, you will be subject to different sets of reporting requirements depending on your residency and that of the trust. For example, if you have Canadian bank term deposits in the trust and you are a resident of Canada, your trust will file Canadian tax returns to report the interest earned. If you passed this interest through to yourself personally, the trust would issue you a T3 slip and you would ultimately pay the tax on your personal return. The trust would pay no tax by offsetting the interest earned on the term deposit with a deduction for the interest paid through to you, but it would still have to file its own return. Alter ego trusts are not considered separate taxpayers by the CRA, and all income flows through to the trustor as if he or she earned it directly. No tax returns need to be filed with the CRA on them.

It is much simpler if you are a U.S. resident with a U.S. bank deposit. The Internal Revenue Service does not require the trust to report interest earned if you report it on your own personal tax return, which cuts out any unnecessary duplicate reporting. Also, transfers of property into a living trust are not considered deemed dispositions and are allowed without tax consequences.

As far as your chances of immigrating to the United States, you will likely need either a business or family sponsor to give you a realistic chance at a green card. There are no green card lotteries in the near future that I am aware of that Canadians will be able to participate in.

WHERE THERE'S A WILL, THERE'S A WAY

I am a Canadian citizen, and I own property in Florida. May I legally bequeath this property and money to a relative who lives in Europe? If so, is a will appropriate or is there another way to accomplish this?

— *Arne I., St. Petersburg, Florida*

You certainly may bequeath your Florida property to a relative in Europe. You can pass on the property via your will, or by forming a simple trust. From the information you've provided, the only real advantage of the trust would be to avoid the expenses of probating your will in Florida. Keep in mind that your executor or personal representative will have to file a U.S. Estate Tax IRS Form 706NA and pay any U.S. non-resident estate tax if your U.S. property exceeds the $60,000 exemption (unless the Canada/U.S. Tax Treaty allows for a greater exemption). The tax, if any, would have to be paid before the property passed to your European beneficiary. If you did not make provision in your will to pay any U.S. estate tax and/or Canadian deemed disposition tax on this property from other funds in your state, the Florida property would likely have to be sold to pay the taxes.

CALCULATING THE NEW TREATY EXEMPTION

We are Canadian citizens who are permanent residents of Ontario but spend about six months in Naples, Florida; we own a condo there.

Could you please advise me to what the actual exemption for estate taxes now applies? You referred to US$60,000 in the seventh edition of The Border Guide, *but implied that this could end up higher for non-resident aliens.*

— A.E.B., Naples, Florida

Under the 1996 amendment to the Canada/U.S. Tax Treaty, Canadians can now get two major benefits to help them reduce their U.S. non-resident estate tax. The first benefit is they get a crack at a higher estate tax exemption than the $60,000 you mention in your letter. However, to determine whether you can get a higher exemption you must use a basic formula: U.S. taxable estate divided by worldwide estate multiplied by the current U.S. estate tax exemption of $2 million equals your non-resident estate tax exemption.

For example, if your condo is worth US$250,000 (and it is your only U.S. estate taxable property) and your worldwide estate value is the equivalent of US$1 million, your non-resident exemption would be $250,000 (taxable estate) divided by $1,000,000, (worldwide estate) times the U.S. estate tax exemption of $2,000,000 = US$500,000. This exemption is available to both spouses, so if you can prove that you each paid for half of the condo (not just putting it in joint names), you can each calculate and use your own individual exemptions to reduce or eliminate any U.S. non-resident estate taxes. In general, as you can conclude from the formula, those Canadians with larger worldwide estates have diminishing benefits and could likely get only the $60,000 minimum exemption whereas those Canadians with estates of less than $2 million could get the full exemption and pay no U.S. non-resident estate taxes. In certain circumstances, transfers between spouses can qualify as the equivalent of a double exemption.

The second benefit from the 1996 treaty amendment is that if you do have to pay U.S. non-resident estate tax, you will get a credit for it against a Canadian deemed disposition of your U.S. property at death. The treaty gives you relief from paying the Canadian deemed disposition tax, which can reach 25% of the appreciation on your U.S. property if you are fortunate enough to have bought when property values were low and/or the Canadian dollar higher than its current value.

Be careful with the formula noted above; it is deceptively simple. There are items that you could never expect to include in your worldwide estate — for example, death benefits from life insurance you own for which you are the insured — and you have to file a very oncrous U.S. estate tax return, Form 706, Estate Tax Return, to get the exemption over the $60,000 limit with the treaty formula, which would subject your entire worldwide estate to IRS audit. To get the basic $60,000 non-resident estate tax exemption under domestic rules, the non-resident is required to file the much simpler IRS Form 706NA, Non-Resident Estate Tax Form.

CHANGING TITLE AND U.S. TAX OBLIGATIONS ON FLORIDA PROPERTY

I am a Canadian who lives seven months per year in Ontario and five months in Sarasota. I owned our house in Florida jointly with my husband, who passed away recently. How do I remove his name from any ownership documents? Also, I think my house would sell for $225,000 to $250,000. Please tell me the Florida laws that apply to Canadians.

— Doreen A., Sarasota, Florida

Since you owned your Florida property jointly with right of survivorship and are now the sole owner, you can simply have the title changed at your local county recorder's office. They will require a copy of your deceased husband's death certificate and have you complete a basic form that varies from county to county.

You didn't say whether you had filed IRS Form 706NA, Non-Resident Estate Tax Return, and paid the U.S. non-resident estate taxes. This form needs to be filed within nine months of a death unless you received an extension. You would need to prove to the IRS that you paid for your half of the jointly owned property with your own cash. Otherwise the entire value of the property will be included in your deceased husband's estate.

Form 706NA details how to calculate the non-resident estate tax due.

You would be wise to get an appraisal of the Florida property, including the contents, as of the date of your husband's death. If the value of your deceased husband's share of the U.S. assets exceeds the non-resident estate tax exemption of $60,000 (as it appears it does), you will have to pay tax starting at 26% of the amount that exceeds $60,000. Although your filing will be quite simple, I recommend seeking professional help to complete Form 706NA, as it can be rather intimidating. Remember, if you have taxes due, interest and penalties for late filing will keep accruing, so you should get started as soon as possible. The Canada/U.S. Tax Treaty should allow your deceased husband's estate a greater exemption than the current $60,000. Ask a professional for an assessment as to whether or not the treaty will be of benefit to you in this situation. Don't forget about the Canadian deemed disposition tax if your property accrued any capital gains before your husband's death.

CANADIAN TAX OBLIGATIONS WHEN SELLING FLORIDA PROPERTY

As a recent widow, I plan on selling my Florida home in the near future, if the real estate market improves. I could use up-to-date information regarding the sale of real estate concerning Florida sales taxes and Canadian capital gains (or loss) taxes. What is the advisability of changing the deed from joint ownership to a family member to avoid paying estate taxes? Is this change made through a Florida lawyer or my lawyer in Ontario?

— *Veruca S., Chatham, Ontario*

This question is similar to the previous one with respect to U.S. tax obligations and filing requirements for a widow with Florida property. In addition to U.S. obligations, you may have to pay Canadian tax on the deemed disposition at your husband's death. This would be the capital gains tax on the appreciation of your Florida property on your deceased husband's share, since the time it was purchased. If your husband died in 2006, this tax would be due to CRA no later than six months from the date of death or April 30, 2007, whichever comes first.

Changing the joint ownership with right of survivorship from your deceased spouse to another family member could cost you a hefty U.S. gift tax if you do it all at once. If you are transferring U.S. property either while you are alive or through your will, you are subject to transfer tax in the form of a U.S. gift tax or estate tax, respectively. These taxes are levied at the same rates, with the gift tax having a $12,000 annual exclusion and the estate tax a $60,000 once-in-a-lifetime exemption for a non-resident (unless the Canada/U.S. Tax Treaty allows for a greater exemption). Consequently, if you transferred the property worth say $200,000 to a family member, a gift of $200,000 would attract tax on $188,000 (the fair market value of the property of $200,000 minus the $12,000 annual exclusion). The tax starts at 26% and must be paid by filing IRS Form 706NA.

You would probably be much better off selling a share of the residence to the family member and avoiding this potential problem. If the family member has no money, you can loan him or her the funds in Canada and take back a promissory note.

As always, we recommend you seek professional advice before you make any changes. A good U.S. estate planning attorney in Florida should be able to advise you on your best course of action.

PROBLEMATIC TRANSFER OF U.S. PROPERTY TO DAUGHTER

I acquired a Florida condominium from my mother that cost her $30,000 in 1986 and is now worth $150,000. I am often told that the condo should also be in someone else's name to avoid any complications should I pass away. This practice seems to be commonplace. What are the possible complications? Are the Canadian taxes equivalent to what I would pay on a second home in Canada? Do I have to pay taxes in the U.S. if I pay them in Canada? I look forward to your response.

Clarifications:

1. *I acquired the condo from my mother. At first, she transferred it to me, and in return she retained the right of usufruct. Last year, she gave up this right.*

2. *The condo is in my name.*

I think this information would be helpful to many Quebeckers who own a home in Florida. Thank you in advance.

— Lise A., Montreal, Quebec

When you acquired the property from your mother, there were tax implications that appear to have been overlooked. Since your mother gifted the property to you, that would be considered a deemed disposition for Canadian purposes and she would pay Canadian income taxes on the gain in the property since she originally purchased it. In the U.S. there would have been no income tax on this transfer to you but your mother would have to pay U.S. gift taxes, which can be as high as or higher than income tax on the gift of real U.S. property.

The Canadian income taxes need to be calculated based on the difference between what your mother purchased the property for and the fair market value at the time of the transfer to you. The U.S. gift taxes are based on the full, fair market value at the time of transfer less the present value of her right to live on the property. When your mother gave up the right to use the property there is also a Canadian taxable deemed disposition and a U.S. gift based on the fair market value of her right to use the property. If the Canadian and/or U.S. tax and gift tax returns, respectively, have not been filed, you are leaving an open back door for the Canada Revenue Agency or the Internal Revenue Service to come after you and/or your mother for the tax and penalties, which could be substantial.

I recommend you get some professional help to voluntarily get into compliance with the CRA and IRS rules as soon as possible. I realize this isn't good news but is better you know now rather than much later as the longer you leave it the worse it may become. You are correct in noting that it is common practice to complete these sorts of transfers for various perceived benefits, but as you can see it is a virtual minefield when one is not familiar with all the Canadian and U.S. rules that apply.

Now that the condo is in your name it is likely best you leave it as such as trying to just put it someone else's name creates all the same issues as noted above.

Yes, you are somewhat correct that owning a U.S. property has much the same tax consequences as owning a second property in Canada. However, the IRS gets first swing at the income taxes on a sale or rent of U.S. property and any tax you pay to the U.S. is normally a full credit against any Canadian tax on the same property income.

CANADIAN LEAVING INHERITANCE TO U.S. BENEFICIARY

We have some questions on inheritance. If you leave money to a member of the family in the U.S. when you die, how is that taxed? Is there a set sum for all of the U.S. or is it governed by state rules? Is there any way of making this easier? I would appreciate it if you have any knowledge on this and could help me.

— Charles H., Regina, Saskatchewan

There is no U.S. tax for the U.S. beneficiary on any funds regardless of the amounts that you leave or the U.S. state that your family member is located in. However, before the funds leave Canada for the U.S., your executor will need to ensure all the Canadian tax on your estate has been paid to the Canada Revenue Agency and the province(s) in question.

You may want to consider the formation of a testamentary trust through your will for your family member in the U.S. Without a correctly drafted trust, if this person were to die, be sued or get divorced the day after he or she received the funds from your estate, all or part of the money could go to a creditor. This kind of trust is very practical on amounts over $500,000. Depending on the trustee you choose for the trust, a trust below that amount tends to be a bit expensive to maintain.

Your family member in the U.S. will have to file IRS Form 3520 in the year in which he or she receives the inheritance from you. There is no tax due when submitting Form 3520 but failure to complete it could result in a 35% tax penalty on the amount of the inheritance.

IDAHO PROPERTY INADVERTENT GIFT

My husband and I purchased recreational property in Idaho in 1979. In 1992 we added the names of our three adult children to the title of the property. The adjusted cost basis (ACB) was CDN$26,000 at that time. Market value was US$35,000 to $40,000. Since that time we have made improvements of CDN$54,000 (total ACB $80,000), of which 75% has been paid by my husband and me. Market value today is estimated US$200,000 to $225,000.

If either my husband or I were to die, what would be the tax consequences in Canada and the U.S.?

If we were to gift our share of this asset to our children, what would be the tax consequences? Is there a gift exemption in the U.S.? Would there be a Canadian deemed disposition along with the U.S. gift tax and carry-over basis?

If we sold the property how would the taxes be handled? Could my husband and I claim this as our personal residence?

— Joan M., Calgary, Alberta

I suspect your situation is much more complicated than you may have imagined, as you have several issues that you have not dealt with, probably primarily because you were not aware of them. I am sure you know, though, that tax departments in Canada and the U.S. don't have any sympathy for those who don't know the rules.

First, you made U.S. taxable gifts to your children at least twice, once when you put their names on the title in 1992 and once when you made improvements without them contributing to the cost of the improvements in proportion to their ownership shares. If the value of these respective gifts at the time when they occurred was less than US$12,000 to each child from both you and your husband, then you have no U.S. gift tax to pay but you should have filed U.S. gift tax returns to confirm and document all this with the IRS. For U.S. tax purposes the children carry over your cost basis to themselves and so at the time of sale they will pay the capital gains tax in proportion to their percentage of ownership, or in your case on 20% of the gain of what you paid for the property plus the cost of the improvements. In other words, all five owners would have exactly the same U.S. capital gain to pay tax on when the property is sold. If you still owned the property at the time of your and your husband's respective deaths, for U.S. tax purposes, the children would get a free step up in basis to fair market value at the time of death on the one-fifth share that each you and your husband own. If either or both of your worldwide estates are less than US$2 million, your children would have no U.S. non-resident estate tax to pay at death.

From a Canadian tax perspective you should have paid deemed disposition taxes when you made the gifts to the children, based on the difference between your original cost and the fair market value at the times of the gifts. The children then get a new basis for Canadian tax purposes equal to the fair market value at the time they received the gifts. Consequently, you and your husband have a different tax basis for Canada Revenue Agency purposes than your children. CRA may want to collect the possible deemed disposition tax due back at the time of both of the inadvertent gifts, and you may be charged interest and penalties. At the time of your and your husband's respective deaths, each of your one-fifth share goes through a deemed disposition and capital gains tax is due to the Canada Revenue Agency on the date of death based on the difference between your cost and the fair market value at death.

If you wish to gift the remaining two-fifths of the property you and your husband still own now to your children, you go through all the same U.S. and Canadian tax issues as I have noted above when you made the original gifts.

My recommendations would depend on whether your children are likely or unlikely to use the property after you and your husband are gone or no longer able to travel. If they are unlikely to use it, it would likely be best to sell the property before your deaths and take credits under the Canada/U.S. Tax Treaty for taxes paid to the U.S. on each of your five respective Canadian tax returns.

As you can see, this all gets very complicated and I strongly recommend you get professional help when putting children on your U.S. property title or when you are going to sell. This is not a do-it-yourself procedure.

One final complication that I have not mentioned but which must be considered is that the State of Idaho may also tax the gifts, the estate and/or the gains on any sale.

Doctor in the House 5

GETTING THE MOST FROM
OUT-OF-COUNTRY MEDICAL COVERAGE

One of the most perplexing questions confronting Canadians wintering or taking up permanent residence in the United States is medical insurance. Americans moving to Canada can, after a 90-day wait (in most provinces), simply join the provincial medicare system. There appears to be an endless squeeze in both Canada and the U.S. between medical services provided and the costs of those services. This squeeze guarantees that the areas of travel insurance and medical insurance plans in general are complex and constantly changing.

The last thing people need to worry about when they travel is becoming ill or suffering an accident. Unfortunately, sickness and accidents respect neither your travel itinerary nor your socioeconomic status. A medical emergency can happen anywhere, at any time and to anyone!

Any unforeseen expense is important to today's traveller and you will want to be protected, no matter how great or small the potential loss. Minor problems, such as the loss of luggage, can be a traumatic experience for many travellers, ruining their holidays or business trips. A catastrophic illness or an accident outside Canada can turn a relaxing trip into a financial nightmare.

The decline in out-of-country coverage by the provincial health care programs in the late 1980s and early '90s greatly increased the demand for private health insurance to fill the widening gaps in coverage. This demand lured many insurers into the travel health insurance market. The competition made it difficult for consumers because they had nearly 100 plans from 30 companies to choose. They did, however, benefit from the competitive pricing that drove premiums down significantly. Many of these new insurers lacked the specialized experience and resources to effectively manage claims and lost huge sums of money very quickly. The health insurance industry has now consolidated into about a dozen committed and professional companies offering 20 to 30 plans. Current

111

provincial out-of-Canada medical benefit coverage is listed in Figure 5.1 along with phone numbers to call or websites to visit for more recent updates and changes.

Many travellers are unaware of the need for adequate travel insurance. While provincial health and hospital programs may provide adequate benefits at home, a Canadian who finds himself or herself in trouble outside the country may discover the provincial plan covers only a small portion of the actual medical expenses. As illustrated in Figure 5.1, provincial plans vary considerably with respect to the amounts paid outside Canada. Prince Edward Island pays the most for out-of-country medical services and is the only province to date that reimburses travellers at provincial rates of reimbursement. British Columbia, at $75 per day for a hospital bed, currently pays the least. This is only a small fraction of what hospitalization actually costs, especially in the United States, where medical expenses may easily exceed $2,000 per day. In most U.S. hospitals, $75 a day would barely get you a parking spot, a bed pan or a couple of aspirins. Canadians should be aware that in many parts of the world, physicians and hospitals do not follow the Canadian system of billing, where the daily room charge is all-inclusive and covers most services and treatments. Many hospitals outside Canada charge a fee for room and board, and then charge for every procedure and bandage they use. In the past the Ontario Health Insurance Plan and other provincial plans have not only reduced their portion of these costs but have made it more difficult to collect them. More people had to rely on their travel insurance for the entire medical bill. It remains to be seen whether this trend will reverse itself in the near future.

Travellers who purchase token medical insurance plans may discover that the plans they purchased are inadequate or do not cover them when they need hospital and medical treatment. Your bargain medical insurance may be instead a simple trip cancellation or flight accident insurance policy. Many of you have heard stories of Canadians who were forced to mortgage their property in order to pay for U.S. medical expenses. The purchase of proper travel insurance not only reduces financial risk but provides peace of mind as well.

Many people purchase travel protection as a supplement to their provincial medical plans, before heading south for the winter. The typical insurance plan has an expiration date of less than six months. If travellers covered by these plans wish to stay longer than six months, they either go without coverage or have to return to Canada to trick their insurance carriers into giving them extended coverage. Premiums have become quite

---

PROVINCIAL HEALTH INSURANCE PLANS
HOSPITAL BENEFITS OUTSIDE CANADA

- **British Columbia** 800-663-7867; www.health.gov.bc.ca: $75/day as well as a small payment by the B.C. Medical Services Plan for services rendered in the emergency room before admission.

- **Alberta** (780) 427-1452; www.health.gov.ab.ca: $100/day.

- **Saskatchewan** (306) 787-3475; www.health.gov.sk.ca: $100/day, outpatient — $50/day.

- **Manitoba** (800) 392-1207, ext. 7303; www.gov.mb.ca/health/: 1 to 100 beds — $280/day; 101 to 500 beds — $356/day; 501 or more beds — $570/day; pays the greater of 75% or per diem in the case of referrals only.

- **Ontario** 800-268-1154; www.health.gov.on.ca: $400/day for "high level" care; $200/day for outpatient care.

- **Quebec** 800-561-9749; www.ramq.gouv.qc.ca: $498/day, including surgery in a day hospital.

- **Prince Edward Island** 800-241-6970; www.gov.pe.ca/hss/: $570/day regardless of bed capacity.

- **New Brunswick** (506) 453-2536; www.gnb.ca/0051/: $100/day; higher rate possible but requires prior approval.

- **Nova Scotia** 800-563-8880; www.gov.ns.ca/health/: $525/day for hospital bill and 50% for ancillary charges such as X-ray and lab bills.

- **Newfoundland and Labrador** 800-563-2163; www.gov.nf.ca/health/: $350/day maximum.

All provinces cover medical expenses outside Canada to 100% of the provincial level.

Figure 5.1

costly, and a typical married couple aged 65 can expect to pay between $2,500 and $5,000 for a six-month policy, depending on the company and the deductible chosen. Numerous travel insurance plans are available through travel agencies, insurance companies, the Canadian Automobile Association, the Canadian Snowbird Association and premium credit cards. The types of coverage and premiums can also vary widely.

Most plans have benefit limits of $1 million to $5 million for covered medical expenses, although some plans have no dollar limitations on benefits. Terms may range from twenty-four hours to a maximum of one year. Premiums are based on the age of travellers — usually with categories for those over age 65 and those age 65 or younger — and may also depend on the number of people in a party. Nearly all carriers require you to purchase your coverage before you leave Canada. Don't automatically assume that the association in which you are a member has the best medical plan for you. More often than not, you will get better coverage through a travel insurance broker, who can give you quotes from many companies as well as provide you with information on the claims-paying experience. Many associations change underwriters every year, so claims paying can vary greatly from year to year. Several associations tend to make the sale of travel insurance a key source of annual income, so they may tend to pressure members into thinking they must get the travel insurance from them even when they know there are better policies elsewhere.

A very positive development in the travel insurance industry with all this new competition has been a much better choice of plans with deductibles ranging from $50 to $10,000. Choosing a high-deductible policy can reduce annual travel insurance costs by 50% or more without a significant increase in risk. (See Appendix F for a listing of the names, addresses, websites and phone numbers of the major Canadian travel insurance providers.)

All policies are not alike, and you often need to work through a maze of costly options to ensure coverage for all major travel hazards. Here are some pointers to help you through that maze:

- In general, you get what you pay for. Buying the lowest premium may get you inadequate coverage. However, just because a plan is expensive doesn't mean it won't have gaps in its coverage. Premium alone should not be the sole criterion for purchasing travel insurance.

- Check with your credit card company: some gold or premium cards will provide limited medical coverage for travel stays between two weeks and sixty days. These are sometimes included in the annual credit card fee. We must caution you to check out this type of coverage carefully, since many plans are inadequate. All major Canadian banks have cut back the maximum age for any travel coverage to 65, and below age 65, they continue to add restrictions.

- Look for a policy that covers all expenses that your provincial plan does not, with no limitations on standard doctors' fees or daily hospital expenses.

- Check the upper limit of the policy. Many policies have total benefit limitations as low as $25,000, so you'll have to pay any costs beyond that amount that your provincial plan doesn't cover. Even a brief emergency stay in a U.S. hospital can exceed this limit. Claims paid recently by travel insurance companies for the U.S. have been over $600,000 for claims such as heart bypass operations with complications. So as long as your upper coverage limit is higher than this amount, you should be okay.

- Choose the highest deductible available from an insurance carrier. Canadians are conditioned to think they must have no out-of-pocket expenses regardless of how small the claim. Since small claims are relatively expensive to process, you'll pay through the nose for a low or no-deductible policy. You'll pocket big savings by sharing a small amount of risk, while limiting your exposure to smaller bills. If an insurer offered you a six-month, maximum $4,750-of-expenses-covered medical policy for $392 you'd think it was outrageous, yet at least one major insurance carrier will offer you a $392 reduction from an $873 premium if you take a $5,000 deductible rather than a $250 deductible. A difference of only $4,750 more in total coverage costs you $392! Other insurance plans provide similar savings if they offer a choice of deductibles.

- Review the "exclusions" clause of your policy very carefully. Many policies will exclude coverage for any prior medical condition, or pre-existing condition, as insurance companies like to call them, that has been treated by a doctor within the past year, or some other specified time period. If you had a bypass operation several years ago and have an annual checkup by your doctor, any hospital stays that are even remotely related to your heart may not be covered.

- If you have a pre-existing medical condition, look for a policy that will at least provide you with emergency coverage for that illness up to a specified dollar amount. If you are uncertain how your pre-existing condition will be covered, pick up the telephone and call the underwriting department of the company in question and ask to be medically underwritten so that your conditions and the coverage for them will be spelled out in advance, eliminating surprises. Be absolutely clear and honest about any conditions or treatment you've had or are currently having, and do not be tempted not to mention a pre-existing condition when signing up for travel insurance. A five-minute telephone call may save you thousands of dollars. Be very leery of insurance companies that don't complete some form of medical underwriting using detailed questioning in their applications. These companies are the most likely to decline claims related to pre-existing conditions, as they try to do their underwriting after a claim is made. On the surface such plans may appear to be easy to qualify for, but you may be denied coverage later. There is definitely an inverse relation between the difficulty and detail required in the application form and the number of claims paid — the harder it is to get through the detailed application, the more likely your claim will be paid.

- Talk with friends and other travellers who have made a claim through the insurance carrier you are considering, to see whether they were treated fairly and their claims paid on time.

- Don't expect miracles from insurance companies when submitting claims. Most companies will pay only according to the letter of the policy and they have highly structured claims systems to prevent fraud. Some companies pay only after the provincial plans have paid their portion of the claim. Only British Columbia, Ontario and Quebec allow insurers to bill them directly on your behalf. With payments from Ontario and some other provinces running many months behind, payment from private carriers will, as a consequence, also be slow. The better travel insurance carriers will pay your claims quickly, without waiting for provincial plans to pay up.

- Look for a few of the better travel insurance carriers that have set up claims-paying offices and have negotiated payment schedules with hospitals in the more heavily populated winter visitor areas in the United States. This will often mean much faster claims processing. Instead of you paying the hospital and waiting months for reimbursement, you pay nothing and the carrier pays the hospital directly. This valuable service is worth asking for when shopping for travel insurance.

- Some provinces have reduced the repatriation allowance for Canadians returning to Canada for further medical treatment. It currently costs about $15,000 to fly a patient back to his or her home province from the Sunbelt. Check your policy to see whether you are covered for the portion your provincial plan won't pick up.

- Look for a plan that has a toll-free or collect emergency assistance telephone number manned by the insurance carrier itself, not by a third party. It can be very reassuring to have a 24-hour hotline that you can call if you need assistance or wish to verify coverages. Often hospitals will call this line for you and establish any necessary liaison between you and your insurance provider.

- Most companies have early-bird rates if you purchase your insurance well in advance of travel. For example, major carriers will give you last year's rates before the new season's rate increases if you purchase before mid-August for upcoming winter travel. Rate increases for many years have been in the 10%-plus range, so these early-bird savings can be significant.

REMAINING IN THE UNITED STATES MORE THAN SIX MONTHS

There are currently no Canadian provinces that allow you to remain covered by provincial medicare plans after absences of longer than six months, except Ontario and Newfoundland. Ontario allows seven months and Newfoundland allows eight months of out-of-province travel. This is a real dilemma for those who want to remain in the United States for an extra month or two. Most travel insurance policies will cover you up to a maximum of six months (for Ontario residents up to seven months and for Newfoundland and Labrador eight months) and will pay only if the provincial plan pays. There are several options for someone in this situation:

- Do nothing and hope the province will not find out that you were out of the province longer than you should have been. In the past this option would have been much less of a gamble, but with hungry provincial medical administrators looking to cut costs we do not recommend this strategy.

- If you have a group insurance plan with your employer or even with your own corporation, the group insurance can normally be expanded to include coverage on a limited basis in the U.S. A U.S. citizen or green card holder could possibly get on a group plan through a U.S. employer.

- Find an insurance carrier that will cover you when medicare may not cover you, and for longer than six months at a time, or make a trip back to Canada to get an extended policy, keeping in mind that most travel insurance companies require you to have current valid provincial medicare coverage before they will pay claims.

There are some international company policies available through brokers in Canada that offer such a policy, but with OHIP allowing seven months of travel now it is expected that other carriers will come out with extended coverage. See the next section of this chapter for information on a broker to call.

- Purchase year-round insurance coverage that will cover you anywhere in the world for both emergency and non-emergency medical services. These high-deductible plans are discussed in the next section of this chapter. If you are in good health, these policies are very reasonably priced and give you access to any medical facility in the world you may choose to use if there is a waiting list in the province or city where you are living in Canada.

- Become a resident of the United States if you are eligible (see Chapter 7) and enrol in an American health care plan. This will be discussed in the next section.

INSURANCE FOR CANADIANS MOVING TO THE UNITED STATES

There are a great many myths about Canadians finding effective and affordable medical insurance when they take up permanent residence in the United States. I have prepared plans for Canadians, both winter visitors and permanent residents, for a good number of years and have successfully discredited most of these myths. We have been able to develop a variety of alternatives that ensure Canadians receive the best of both medical systems.

Canadians and Americans like to constantly debate which country's medical system is the best. My nearly 30 years' experience in this area has taught me that you can never answer this question in advance unless you can determine when, where and what medical assistance you will need in advance. Of course, this is the million-dollar question, because if you knew when, where and what illness you were going to have, you could shop the medical purveyors in either country to get the best care. However, this is equivalent to trying to plan your spending in retirement so that the last cheque you write on the day you die bounces. By combining the best benefits from both countries and planning it so you can easily access either the Canadian or the U.S. medical systems, you can obtain the best protection with maximum flexibility. (See the next section Have Your Cake and Eat It Too!)

Canadians over 65 who have resided in the United States legally for at least five years, or are U.S. citizens, are eligible for complete U.S.

Medicare regardless of any pre-existing conditions. The cost is approximately US$500 per month each, or US$90 per month if you or your spouse has contributed at least the minimum amount to U.S. Social Security programs on U.S. employment earnings. (See Chapter 13 for more information about qualifying for U.S. Social Security.) There are also numerous private insurance carriers that provide Medicare supplements to fill any gaps in U.S. Medicare coverage. If you do not qualify or are waiting to qualify for U.S. Medicare and are over 65, there is limited but quite adequate choice of coverage available for you from among some private insurance carriers, most of whom originate outside the United States. Be sure to secure this coverage before becoming a U.S. resident so that it is effective when you leave Canada and there are no gaps in coverage.

Those under the age of 65 have a wide variety of health insurance options. Health insurance works much like car insurance in the United States. If you want zero deductible, with your auto insurance company paying for the slightest scratch, you will pay a substantially higher premium than someone with a $1,000 deductible. With health insurance in the United States, you can choose your coverage and your deductible. For example, a healthy person aged 60 can get a health policy with a $2,500 deductible and a $2-million coverage limit from an A.M. Best A-rated company for less than $350 per month.

A good health insurance broker knowledgable about both U.S. and Canadian health issues can be of great assistance to those who are considering living in the U.S. In addition, those who are tired of having only travel insurance and want full medical coverage and complete year-round access to the U.S. medical system should talk to a health insurance broker. The cost of this insurance, particularly if you use a high-deductible plan, can be very reasonable when compared to your standard travel insurance policy. Unlike travel insurance, these policies will cover you for non-emergency medical assistance in the U.S. as well as for emergency help 12 months a year, regardless of where you travel. With this year-round access, if you needed what your provincial plan classified as non-emergency heart surgery and you were in a waiting queue in Canada, you could get almost immediate surgery in the U.S. for only the cost of your deductible. You should also note that if you have one of these year-round full-coverage policies and develop a serious medical condition, you cannot be dropped from your plan; whereas if you have travel insurance only, when your current six-month policy expires, you might never be able to get coverage again and would be limited to travel within Canada for the rest of your life, unless you are prepared to risk travel without insurance.

We have used a very good broker for the past 17 years who has helped clients in even the most difficult of situations get full U.S. medical coverage. Through working with us to solve cross-border health insurance issues, he has become as close to an expert as you will be able to find in this unique area. His name is Bill Norgaard, of Norgaard Insurance Services, and you can reach him toll free from Canada and the U.S. at 1-877-679-7900, or e-mail bknorgaard@qwest.net.

Those heading to the United States for employment will generally have excellent medical coverage available from most large employers' group plans.

If you are under 65 and have a pre-existing condition, expect to pay higher premiums and/or have some conditions excluded from coverage or be denied coverage altogether. When choosing a health insurance carrier in the United States, stick to an A.M. Best-rated company with an A2 to A1 rating that has been providing health insurance for at least ten years. Read over any policy and the company's sales literature very carefully.

There is much debate in the United States as to whether the current medical system should be changed to make it more accessible to more people. The major concern is how the new system will work, what it will cost and who will pay for it. Revamping the American medical system would have the likely outcome of giving Canadians who become residents of the United States better access to the U.S. medical system. Some recent U.S. legislation now in effect improves the chances of someone under 65 with a pre-existing condition obtaining new health insurance or maintaining existing coverage until he or she can get on Medicare at 65. In addition, there are several U.S. states that will make special provision for persons with pre-existing conditions. For example, I had a client, aged 55, with a serious pre-existing condition who normally would have been refused health coverage by any health insurance company in the United States. The client took up residence in Washington state and because of the state laws, she was able to obtain adequate medical coverage at a reasonable cost in spite of her medical condition until she would reach age 65 and be eligible for U.S. Medicare.

HAVE YOUR CAKE AND EAT IT TOO!

By extending its out-of-province travel coverage to seven months or 212 days, the Ontario Health Insurance Plan has provided a great opportunity for those who can take advantage of it. For the first time it is now practical for those who can get legal immigration status in the United States to leave Canada for tax purposes yet maintain OHIP without breaking any rules. OHIP eligibility rules on their website state "Coverage is based on citizenship and Ontario residency and is not determined by whether you have a job or are unemployed, or whether or where you pay your income tax." In order for this to work, a retired person would need to exit Canada for tax purposes and return to his or her Ontario residence or cottage for five months each year. For most Ontario snowbirds, this would be a perfect setup — seven months in the Sunbelt in the winter and five months in Ontario in the summer. CRA, in the February 1998 federal budget, unknowingly put a very necessary tax rule in place that makes this setup possible. The new rule brought in was intended to prevent Canadians exiting Canada to avoid the Bronfman rules (the deemed disposition of assets upon exit from Canada). The 1998 budget rule states that if a taxpayer is a resident of the United States or another treaty country under the applicable treaty residency rules, he or she is automatically a non-resident of Canada for tax purposes. Under CRA rules before February 1998, having OHIP coverage regardless of other factors, including the Canada/U.S. Tax Treaty tiebreaker rules (see Chapter 3 for the treaty tiebreaker rules), would be an indication of Canadian residence and you would have been taxed on your world income in Canada at full Canadian rates if you exited Canada with that OHIP coverage still in place. Now, those who can obtain legal resident status in the United States, then complete a comprehensive cross-border plan and execute it with professional help, may have the best of both worlds, access to both the Canadian and U.S. medical systems at low cost and paying income taxes in the United States at substantially lower rates. Chapters 7, 8 and 13 should be read closely before making a decision to look into this setup that allows you to "have your cake and eat it too." The plans and procedures needed to make this work are very complex and difficult to maintain, and should not be attempted without professional help from an experienced cross-border planner.

Many Canadian residents have worked in the U.S. for extended periods and paid into the U.S. Social Security system, and these people as well as U.S. citizens in Canada can get full access to U.S. Medicare at age 65, even though they don't live in the U.S. Having U.S. Medicare not only gives these people full access to the U.S. medical system at low or no cost, but, if they like to winter in the U.S. Sunbelt, U.S. Medicare can also provide very good travel insurance coverage that is not limited to emergency treatment only as are most travel policies. As long as these people continue to follow their provincial medicare rules, they will maintain continuing Canadian coverage while being on U.S. Medicare. Therefore, these people will also have the best of both worlds. (The exception is that unless they are from Ontario, as discussed above, they will likely still be paying Canadian taxes on their world income as Canadian tax residents.)

WHAT HAPPENS IF YOU GET SICK IN THE UNITED STATES?

Contrary to what you might have been led to believe by some Canadian media, you will not be left to die in the streets because you do not have large buckets of cash with you when you arrive in the emergency room of a U.S. hospital. It is the law in every state that you cannot be turned away from an emergency medical facility because of your ability, or lack thereof, to pay for your emergency treatment.

If you are using a travel insurance company with an emergency assistance line, your first call should be to them as soon as possible after entering the hospital.

If you are unable to make the call, instruct someone else to do it for you. Usually the hospital will have trained personnel to deal directly with the insurance company for you since they have a vested interest in getting paid. The travel insurance company can be invaluable in providing you with reassurance, finding medical specialists, or just getting you home in the shortest possible time.

If you do not have travel insurance, contact your provincial medicare office during business hours at the first possible moment. It won't be quite as easy as contacting a private insurance provider with a 24-hour hotline, but you should receive some valuable assistance nonetheless.

Be careful not to overdo it with medical treatment that can be deferred until you return to Canada, unless you have purchased one of the year-round full-coverage policies discussed earlier in this chapter. Out-of-province medical travel insurance will not cover elective procedures, so you could be doing it at your own expense. Once again, if you are not sure what is or isn't covered, call the emergency assistance line and confirm the treatments that will be covered.

If your condition has been stabilized and your doctors agree that you are well enough to travel, your insurance company and/or the provincial medicare services will make the necessary arrangements to have you flown back to Canada for follow-up treatment. The insurance company will normally make arrangements for loved ones and your automobile to return to Canada.

Generally, you are exempt from any adverse consequences from the IRS or United States Immigration if your stay in the United States has to be extended beyond normal limits for medical reasons.

CROSS-BORDER Q&A

SOME CAN MAKE USE OF BOTH OHIP AND U.S. MEDICARE

My wife and I are U.S. citizens by birth and have resided in Ontario for 18 years, with landed immigrant status. By virtue of our residency and my working prior to retirement, we enjoy full benefits of several senior programs, including OHIP and the Ontario Drug Benefit Plan.

Since retirement, we have been spending our winters in Florida. Each year we purchased out-of-country supplemental health insurance. Two years ago, as these premiums began escalating, we reinstated our U.S. Medicare insurance, both Parts A and B. My reasoning at that time was that while in the States, Medicare would be our primary insurance provider, with OHIP as the supplemental coverage. I then confirmed that this was a valid approach, first by asking Medicare (Social Security office), followed by the questions to OHIP.

Medicare advised that primary coverage would be forthcoming at the time of need, the same as for any U.S. citizen with the same coverage; however, they could not respond to the supplemental coverage from OHIP.

The OHIP office I spoke to advised that, indeed, it is a valid plan. The routine would be to obtain duplicate originals of all bills, so that after submitting them to Medicare and receiving reimbursement, the second set of originals, along with documentation showing Medicare reimbursement, would be submitted to OHIP. OHIP would then determine their allowable share of the costs and reimburse accordingly.

My question is this: Have you had any information from correspondents that would indicate problems with this arrangement? If not, it might be helpful for others in like circumstances to look into. We do pay a small penalty for not having taken Part B at age 65, but it's negligible compared to buying supplemental insurance on the Ontario market!

— Lee F., Port Huron, Michigan

Your Medicare strategy is a sound one that gives you full access to both the U.S. and Canadian medical systems any time you have a need. Since U.S. Medicare has no rules requiring that you must be present in the United States for a certain time period each year, you only have to ensure you follow OHIP rules and are residents of Ontario without being out of province more than seven months each year. The economics of using U.S.

Medicare instead of travel insurance supplements to OHIP also makes sense since twelve months at $90 per month for U.S. Medicare is a lot less than six months of travel insurance regardless of which company you're comparing and provides you much better coverage.

HEALTH COSTS OFTEN RAISE U.S. COST OF LIVING

In a recent Canadian newspaper article you invited readers to forward their queries about cross-border living. My concern is whether it is affordable for dual citizens to live here year-round. As you know, medical costs are covered in Ontario by OHIP. I have never paid toward medical coverage in the United States.

My understanding from your recent article in the paper on this matter is that our cost would be $6,000 per year, plus an HMO or such supplement, which could easily double that figure — all in U.S. funds.

I would much appreciate obtaining additional information and clarification if what you indicate is possible.

— L.M.A., Lauderhill, Florida

U.S. Medicare, available to all U.S. citizens and legal permanent residents (of at least five years) after the age of 65, does cost approximately $500 per month if you have never paid into the U.S. Social Security system. With the required 40 quarters of U.S. Social Security credits, the cost of U.S. Medicare drops to $90 per month for Part B only with Part A provided at no cost. However, HMOs (Health Maintenance Organizations) usually do not charge extra and are contracted to provide you with complete medical coverage for only the Medicare premium you are paying to Medicare plus small fees for doctor visits and drugs. U.S. Medicare does not provide for long-term care beyond 100 days, so private insurance should be obtained for this, which can add $200 to $400 per month more in premiums. Long-term care insurance should be purchased regardless of whether you are a Canadian or U.S. resident, so this cost is not really an extra expense of U.S. residence. Insurance premiums can be a deductible expense for those U.S. filers who itemize their deductions.

Even though OHIP appears to be free, it is not. It is paid for by income tax, employer health tax and other tax revenues. Those looking to live in the United States need to understand exactly what they are paying for in Canada and just how much it is costing them. You should calculate whether the U.S. taxes you'd pay at your income level would drop sufficiently to produce a net savings, after accounting for increased U.S. medical expenses. Generally speaking, if you have not paid enough U.S. Social

Security to receive Medicare Part A at no additional cost, lower U.S. income taxes will not be sufficient to cover the medical costs, unless your annual income is more than $70,000 for husband and wife. With Medicare Part A paid for, the income tax advantage falls to those couples with about $50,000 total taxable income per year.

RESIDENT ALIENS MAY FIND MEDICARE PROBLEMS

I am a Canadian citizen, 72 years of age, with resident alien status and a Social Security Number in the United States. I have tried and failed to get Medicare. I pay my taxes in Canada and return to Ontario for the mandatory period to retain OHIP. My son is a U.S. citizen, and for what it is worth, a commander in the U.S. Navy. I have no family or relatives in Canada; he was the one who sponsored me. I am in good health, but the problem could arise that I would become incapacitated. There is no one to care for me in Canada, and my family worries about this. Is there any point in discussing this with OHIP? I am prepared to continue paying my taxes in Canada and fulfill any criteria that may be necessary.

— P.M.S., St. Augustine, Florida

You didn't say how long you have held your resident alien status, more commonly called a green card. If you've had your green card for at least five years and since you are over age 65, you are entitled to apply for and receive U.S. Medicare. Assuming you qualify for U.S. Medicare, you would have to pay the full premium of approximately $500 per month. You didn't say whether you were ever employed in the United States, or have a spouse who was employed there. Those who contributed to Social Security through wage deductions, or whose spouse contributed, pay only $90 per month for both parts of U.S. Medicare. A Medicare supplement is generally also recommended, which can cost you another $100 to $200 per month, depending on the company and extent of coverage taken. A Health Maintenance Organization (HMO) that contracts with Medicare can provide the supplemental coverage at no additional monthly cost.

U.S. Medicare does not cover long-term nursing care so if you are going to give up OHIP, you should purchase insurance from a wide choice of private insurance companies to cover this potential risk. You can buy this now whether or not you have U.S. Medicare.

If the cost of U.S. Medicare with supplemental and long-term care insurance is less than the savings in income tax and annual travel insurance premiums, you will come out ahead financially by moving to the United States. Aside from not having to file returns in Ontario, you will also achieve your goal of being close to your family in the United States.

There is no provision in OHIP to allow for persons in your situation.

If you haven't had your green card for five years, there are at least two or three insurers who will cover you for an annual premium comparable to that of U.S. Medicare and a supplement until you do have the qualifying time.

RESIDENT ALIENS MAY NEED HOSPITAL INDEMNITY INSURANCE

I have attended a couple of your seminars. I am under the impression that in order to use your advice, the planning has to start sometime before the actual date of leaving Canada. Is this correct?

My wife and I are quite happy with our present situation of living six months each in the United States and Canada. If for financial or medical reasons, however, we had to choose one place, it would be Florida. But we want to be prepared.

I can get fairly good medical-only coverage through my former place of employment. Is it possible to obtain hospital-only coverage down here? Our ages are 73 and 72.

— *John W., Fort Pierce, Florida*

Yes, there are several good companies with hospital indemnity-type policies for anywhere from $100 per day to several thousand dollars per day for hospital stays. Also, check with the American Association of Retired Persons (AARP), 1-800-424-3410 or on the Net at www.aarp.com. Most policies of this kind cannot be applied for after age 75, so don't wait much longer to start your planning with a knowledgeable cross-border financial planner before you leave Canada. If you need some help locating an insurance company for this coverage, give us a call and we can put you in touch with a broker.

SNOWBIRD MUST QUALIFY FOR U.S. SOCIAL SECURITY, MEDICARE

I am a Canadian, age 56, spending my first year as a "Snowbird." I hope to spend five to six months in Florida each winter. I would appreciate your answers to the following:

1. *In the 1960s and '70s, I worked in the United States and have earned 35 credits of Social Security benefits. I understand 40 credits are required to receive retirement and Medicare benefits. Can my work life in Canada contribute to my U.S. credits? Can I receive Social Security benefits from the United States and also from Canada? I worked full time in Canada from 1974 to 1996.*

2. *If I need to work longer in the United States to qualify for benefits, I hope to be able to do so. I no longer have a green card, but for the Social Security benefits it may be worth the effort to apply. Can you comment? My son (age 25), born in Canada, has an American father. Will his dual citizenship make my application for a green card any easier?*

I appreciate any information you can give me.

— *J.L., Cocoa Beach, Florida*

1. In response to the questions you raised in your letter, since you already have 35 quarters of credit for U.S. Social Security, you may, as early as age 62, use the Canada-U.S. Social Security totalization agreement (a Social Security treaty between the two countries) to apply for a reduced Social Security pension. However, the totalization agreement does not cover U.S. Medicare, so you would be required to obtain the full 40 quarters of credit to qualify for free Part A Medicare at age 65. However, since you do have more than 30 quarters of credits, you do qualify for a one-third reduction in the standard Part A premium of $400.

2. In order to get your final five quarters for a full Social Security pension and Medicare, you could work in the United States for a year plus one quarter. However, to work, you will need to get another green card. Your son, as a dual citizen, can sponsor you for one without a long waiting period.

You may have another angle for a full Social Security pension and Medicare. If you were married to your ex-husband for more than ten years and he qualified for Social Security, you can get a benefit of half of the amount he is entitled to receive plus Medicare. This benefit would not affect the amount he would receive, so you should have no problem getting it if he qualifies. Also, 50% of his benefit could actually be more than 100% of your reduced benefit.

DOES A CANADIAN SPOUSE RECEIVE MEDICARE?

I live on the Maine-New Brunswick border. My fiancée lives on the New Brunswick side. We spend most of our time together and winter in Florida. We would like to get married and live in the United States.

However, my fiancée has MS and depends on the New Brunswick government for medication and medical services. Would she receive Medicare help here in the United States if we were to get married? Could she use the same hospital and doctors if Medicare were to help? I'm 59, disabled and on Medicare.

— *Joe C., St. Agatha, Maine*

Your fiancée can become eligible for U.S. Medicare. However, the following steps need to take place first: (1) she must be age 65, and (2) you should have celebrated at least your first year's wedding anniversary together. This assumes you would also be over 65 and on U.S. Medicare at the time you apply for your fiancée's coverage. Your fiancée would need a good Medicare supplement to ensure complete coverage of hospital, doctors and medicine. It is unlikely she will be able to use the same doctors she has now if she is on Medicare. Except in the case of an emergency, this coverage is generally only for the United States, so she would need to establish new relationships with U.S. doctors near your Florida home.

Take the Money and Run $\boxed{6}$

AN INVESTOR'S GUIDE TO
THE UNITED STATES

The Canadian dollar has been fraught with uncertainty for most of the past three decades. In recent years, it has declined to record low levels against its U.S. counterpart, and then in early 2003 decided to rocket over 50% to the high 91 cent range by 2006. Few experts had predicted such a significant increase in the value of the Canadian dollar in so few months. The major reasons for the dollar's comeback are as varied as the number of economists you can find to talk about it, but common themes are that Canada's enormous national debt was finally wrestled under control, the U.S. dollar weakened against other major currencies, there was an increase in the price of oil and other commodities and the Quebec separatist question was pushed to the background. Fortunately, the federal government and most Canadian provinces have balanced budgets and are actively paying down their debts.

The weakness in the U.S. dollar and the U.S.'s policy of stimulating the economy by keeping interest rates low has allowed Canada to keep its Bank of Canada rates relatively high to keep inflation at bay. This situation creates downward pressure on Canadian exports, as they have rapidly become more expensive, which in turn may slow the Canadian economy and start a reversal of the current upward pressure on the Canadian dollar.

Since the Canadian economy relies heavily on exports of commodities, in particular oil and gas, the Canadian dollar has recently been dubbed the "Petro" dollar. Consequently, the Canadian dollar is subject to a great deal of volatility. The real truth of the matter is that no one really knows which way the Canadian dollar will head. At best, experts can only somewhat consistently predict the general direction of short-term trends.

If the Canadian dollar continues to be subject to wide swings in relative value against the U.S. dollar, you may want to take a good hard look at investment opportunities across the border, particularly if you are moving there for work or retirement. With the Canadian dollar at near

30-year highs, this may be the time to "make hay while the sun is shining" and use the Canadian dollar to shore up your U.S. dollar investments before it falls again.

THE INVESTMENT OPTIONS

Canadians often lack the confidence to invest across the border. They may opt for putting available U.S. funds into U.S. currency savings accounts at their local Canadian banks, where they'll earn a meager 1% to 3% interest. By doing this they also give up the security of Canadian Deposit Insurance Corporation (CDIC) insurance. Contrary to what some bank employees may tell you, no Canadian bank or trust company offers CDIC insurance on any U.S. dollar account.

This chapter is intended to help Canadians take advantage of U.S. investment opportunities, while minimizing or eliminating any adverse income tax and non-resident estate tax consequences. Chapter 2 discussed the need to protect yourself against a fluctuating Canadian dollar and how to obtain the fairest rate of exchange. Now I will focus directly on the major investment options in the United States, in the context of the income and estate tax implications for Canadians who reside there part time (these tax consequences were discussed in Chapters 3 and 4). Chapter 12 helps Canadians who become residents of the U.S. with many of the investment options that are available to them on the U.S. side of the border.

CERTIFICATES OF DEPOSIT

Term deposits, or guaranteed investment certificates (GICs), as they are known in Canada, are called Certificates of Deposit (CDs) in the United States. CDs are issued by most U.S. banks, credit unions or by Savings and Loans (S&Ls).

Interest on CDs is guaranteed, and rates currently range from 4% to 6%, depending on the term selected. CDs are insured in the United States by an agency of the U.S. government, the Federal Deposit Insurance Corporation (FDIC), for up to US$100,000 per bank, and per account holder. The FDIC is similar to the CDIC. However, the CDIC's insurance limit is CDN$60,000.

By filing an Internal Revenue Service (IRS) Form W-8BEN (provided by the bank, see Figure 3.4), Canadian non-residents who invest in CDs or other similar accounts are totally exempt from paying U.S. income and non-resident estate taxes.

Unlike most Canadian GICs, funds invested in CDs are not normally locked in and are fairly liquid. However, if you withdraw principal before a CD matures, you may be penalized and could lose one to six months' interest earnings. Currently, with the higher rates available in the U.S., it is a great time for Canadians to obtain an additional 1% or 2% interest on their fixed deposits by investing in U.S. CDs.

MUTUAL FUNDS

Mutual funds are diversified portfolios of professionally managed investments of any variety or mix of stocks and bonds. Also known as investment funds, these funds are very similar in both Canada and the United States. However, the mutual fund investor in the United States has a much broader choice, with more than 11,000 funds currently available. That should be more than adequate to suit any investment objectives with any level of risk.

Some U.S.-dollar mutual funds are available through your Canadian broker or advisor, provided you do not mind paying higher commissions and higher annual expenses on the U.S.-dollar funds available in Canada.

Many mutual funds in the United States have reduced commission levels from around 8% to 4% or less, and many are available to the investor at no sales cost on either purchase or on early liquidation. These are known as no-load funds. True U.S. no-load funds will not have any brokerage commission at all, either on the sale or after the sale in the form of trail commissions paid annually to a broker. The Canadian definition of no-load funds is much more liberal than what the U.S. Securities and Exchange Commission permits; Canada allows for very large commissions, very high expense ratios and trail commissions paid to brokers and agents. When investing in mutual funds, read the detailed version of the prospectus before you invest and be aware of all the fees payable at the time of purchase, upon withdrawal and on an annual ongoing basis. There is a great diversity in how individual funds charge their fees, so careful shopping can save you a great deal of money. Canadian mutual funds on average charge management and administration fees typically in the 2% to 3% range per year while U.S. funds are typically half that with some good index funds available for less than 0.10% per year.

It is important not to ignore the extent of the drag the higher fees on the mutual funds in Canada creates on your investment portfolio. For example, if you are able to choose a good index fund that reduces your annual expenses by 2% on a $100,000 portfolio, assuming a 10% annual return, your money will double in roughly seven years or about three years earlier on the lower-cost portfolio. With compounding, this gives you about a 30% greater return on your investments. In the lower return environment we have been in for the last several years, the drag of the higher fees on mutual funds is magnified even more.

There is also the relatively new form of popular investments called exchange traded funds (ETFs). ETFs are portfolios of stocks or bonds that primarily follow popular indexes such as the Toronto Stock Exchange Index or the Dow Jones Industrial Index. For this reason, they are similar to mutual funds; however, ETFs trade like individual stocks and have several cost and tax advantages over mutual funds. ETFs in Canada are primarily called I-units, whereas in the U.S. they are primarily called I-shares, but because they trade like stocks, they can be bought at any stock exchange in either Canada or the U.S. This is not possible with mutual funds, as Canadian mutual funds can only be purchased in Canada and U.S. mutual funds can only be purchased in the U.S.

Some U.S. ETFs have management expense fees as low as 0.08% per year, while most Canadian ETFs have fees ranging around 0.6%. Still, this is a great cost saving over mutual funds, particularly if Canadians purchase U.S. ETFs. These lower costs may spur you on to add some U.S.-domiciled funds to your investment portfolio. In a flat or down market, paying the higher Canadian management fees can absorb most or even all of your total return available from that particular market.

If you are considering investing in mutual funds in the United States as a non-resident, you'll find that without a U.S. address and Social Security Number (SSN) or Individual Taxpayer Identification Number (ITIN) you will have difficulty at almost all brokerage firms. For this and other regulatory reasons, we recommend non-residents buy ETFs through a Canadian brokerage or online brokerage firm.

Returns from mutual funds or ETFs are not guaranteed and will fluctuate accordingly. Many growth funds averaged 10% to 15% on an annual basis during the 1990s and into the new millennium. It should be noted that the 1990s was a very unusual period in history for investors, with returns well above long-term averages, so investors of all types should reduce their expectations going forward. Returns on equity funds will generally have one negative year for every two positive years, so they should be considered long-term investments not to be dropped at the slightest downturn. These returns are a result of the type of fund managed and economic conditions.

Interest and dividend distribution from U.S. mutual funds and exchange traded funds earned by non-resident investors are subject to a 15% U.S. withholding tax that can be taken as a full tax credit on your Canadian tax return. Capital gains and capitals gains distibutions are tax free in the U.S. for non-resident Canadians from an IRS perspective, but they must be reported to the CRA as any other capital gain for Canadian purposes would be. Mutual fund and ETF investments in the United States — whether purchased in Canada or the United States — are also subject to non-resident estate tax on amounts totalling over US$60,000, including all other U.S. property. The Canada/U.S. Tax Treaty has added U.S. stocks, including mutual funds and exchange traded funds, to the list of investments that Canadians can make that are exempt from non-resident estate tax. This applies only to Canadians whose world estates are less than US$1.2 million. I will take a closer look at exempt investments in a later section of this chapter.

MONEY MARKET FUNDS

Money market funds are offered by both banks and mutual fund companies. When purchased through a U.S. bank or a Savings and Loan company, these accounts are merely daily-interest savings/chequing accounts. They are currently paying 3% to 4% interest and are insured by the FDIC if purchased through a bank.

Money market mutual funds generally yield 0.5% to 1% higher than bank money market accounts, but hold various types of short-term government and corporate securities directly. There is no FDIC insurance on money market mutual funds, but if you select a portfolio of strictly U.S. government securities you have the same government guarantee without the FDIC's $100,000 limit.

Money market mutual funds are fully liquid and impose no sales charges to get in or out of a fund. Many also provide free cheque-writing services. For non-residents, it is much easier to open a U.S. bank money market account than one at a brokerage firm.

LIMITED PARTNERSHIPS

U.S. limited partnerships (LPs) are similar to Canadian LPs. They offer an opportunity to participate directly, with limited liability, in various businesses and investments, while providing professional management.

A non-resident investing in American LPs will be required to file a U.S. non-resident tax return, whether or not any taxes are due. Taxes paid in the United States will give Canadian taxpayers a corresponding credit on their Canadian tax returns.

Rates of return and safety factors for the LP investor will vary as much as the types of LPs available. Great caution is advised when choosing an LP, and professional advice from a qualified investment advisor or Certified Financial Planner is highly recommended.

LPs are considered long-term investments and generally require you to commit your investment until the LP matures, normally five to seven years or beyond. They are more suited to resident investors, but a large number of them will accept non-residents. The fair market value of an LP is subject to non-resident estate tax on estates of more than $60,000 unless the underlying securities in the LP are exempt investments (or if the Canada/U.S. Tax Treaty allows for a larger exemption, as noted in Chapter 4).

INCOME TRUSTS

Income trusts have become very popular in Canada for those who derive income from Canadian businesses. This new structure allows businesses to operate as a trust under special rules of the Canada Revenue Agency. Income trusts can pass through their income directly to the owners of the trust without paying any corporate income tax. This special tax treatment in effect eliminates the double tax created at the corporate level and passes on the benefit to the individual. In Canada, many different kinds of businesses can form income trusts; the most popular income trusts are in the oil and gas industry. In the U.S. the only income trusts to receive the special tax treatment are Real Estate Investment Trusts (REITs). REITs, which have been used for many decades, can pass through the business income directly to trust owners. Because income trusts are traded on stock exchanges, much like stocks, many U.S. investors have invested in Canadian income trusts to produce income for their investment portfolios. The Canada/U.S. Tax Treaty treats income trusts like dividends, charging a non-resident withholding tax of 15% whether a Canadian purchases a U.S. trust or an American purchases a Canadian trust.

REAL ESTATE

Real estate investments in Canada and the United States depend on the same three principles: location, location, location! Investors must do their homework in order to be successful.

Canadians choosing to invest in the United States will find much more paperwork than they may be accustomed to because of the many consumer protection regulations that Canada has not yet adopted. They may also encounter some unfamiliar terminology.

For instance, rather than using an attorney to complete the paperwork, most U.S. investors are required to use the services of a title insurance company. These title companies complete the necessary paperwork and provide trust services for the equitable exchange of funds between buyer and seller. They also provide the mandatory title insurance required to ensure there is clear title to the property. The buyer typically pays for this insurance, which can range from $500 to $1,000 or more on an average residence.

Marriage involves much less paperwork than divorce, and real estate is much easier to purchase than to sell. When a non-resident sells or is deemed to have sold property in the United States, he or she is required to file a non-resident U.S. income tax return, Form 1040NR, reconciling any capital gains or losses in the year of sale. Without proper clearance certificates from the IRS, the non-resident may be subject to federal and state withholding taxes.

If you are placing a mortgage on your property, you should find an institution familiar with the unique requirements of U.S. non-residents and resident aliens. You will likely be confronted with additional mortgage costs known as "points or closing fees." Points and closing fees are the institution's way of covering the upfront costs of handling the mortgage, and they may reduce or discount your mortgage interest rate.

The equity value of your real estate, together with your other U.S. assets, is subject to estate taxes over the $60,000 exemption on property held by non-residents. The Canada/U.S. Tax Treaty exemption formula may provide some Canadians with an exemption greater than $60,000, so please review Chapter 3.

SPECIALTY FUNDS

A handful of mutual fund families have recently created a variety of investments aimed specifically at the non-resident U.S. investor. With these funds, which are registered outside the United States, Canadian investors can enjoy the advantages of U.S.-dollar investments and investment advice while avoiding any adverse tax consequences. They are fully exempt from any U.S. income or estate tax; as well, there is no need for IRS Form W-8BEN and no income tax-reporting requirement to the IRS.

Because these funds are managed in the same way as standard mutual funds, they give you access to professionally managed portfolios corresponding to various asset classes. For example, there are funds specializing in U.S. government bonds, Japanese stocks, Canadian stocks, German government bonds, and so on. The mix of funds you choose will depend on your investment objectives. Once you have opened an account, deposits and withdrawals can be made easily, and periodic dividend cheques can be mailed to you anywhere or deposited in your local bank account.

Specialty funds are available only to non-residents and/or non-citizens of the United States, and cannot be purchased while you are in the United States. If you want to maintain their exempt status, you must open your account while outside the United States. Purchases must be directed through U.S. stockbrokers. Commissions can be substantial, with front-end sales loads as high as 5%, and redemption fees of up to 4%. Many of these funds sport high annual expense ratios of up to 3%! Selling brokers are compensated from one or more of these expense categories. There are some good no-load funds now available in the specialty fund area but you need to find a fee-only planner to get them for you or go directly to the company.

SPECIALTY PORTFOLIOS

Specialty portfolios are professionally managed portfolios made up solely of the exempt investments listed below and tailored to each investor's personal objectives and preferences. Investors with US$500,000 to invest, who want international diversification, quick access to funds, and managers who work on a fee basis rather than commissions, should consider this alternative. These portfolios are managed only for non-residents. Only a limited number of investment firms manage specialty portfolios. Finding the right firm may be time-consuming, but the increased flexibility, safety and cost savings can be well worth the effort.

EXEMPT INVESTMENTS

Throughout this book, I have periodically referred to exempt investments, meaning U.S. investments that are exempt from both income and estate tax for non-residents. You should already be familiar with the fact that exposure to U.S. taxes can be a direct function of the type of investment you make in the United States. The list of the exempt investments detailed below can be your guide to eliminating those investments that can create unnecessary tax burdens for non-residents, while at the same time allowing them a number of choices to develop a safe, income-producing portfolio of U.S. investments. Exempt investments include:

- Banking and Savings & Loan deposits, including CDs, savings accounts, chequing accounts and money market funds, in general any kind of deposit at these institutions. A completed Form W-8BEN must be filed with the savings institution.

- U.S. Treasury bonds, notes, bills and agency issues if issued after July 18, 1984.

- U.S. corporate bonds if issued after July 18, 1984. A completed Form W-8BEN must be filed with the company issuing the bond or the brokerage account where you purchased and hold the bond.

- Specially structured mutual funds. These are the specialty funds explained in detail in the preceding section Specialty Funds.

- Some investment companies or brokerage houses offer money market funds where the securities in the portfolio consist of only government and corporate bonds that have been noted above as exempt securities. A completed Form W-8BEN must be filed with the brokerage firm.

- Life insurance death benefits regardless of the amount.

- Canadians whose world estates are less than US$1.2 million. ($2.4 million for husband and wife with joint property) under the current Canada/U.S. Tax Treaty will be allowed to add U.S. stocks, including mutual funds shares and ETFs, to this list of exempt investments for estate tax purposes only. The U.S. stocks or U.S. mutual funds will still be subject to the treaty withholding on dividends of 15% unless they are purchased through your Canadian broker inside your RRSP.

UNDERSTANDING INVESTMENT RISK

Investors think of risk in two erroneous ways. The first is that investment risk reflects only potential downward movement in the value of an investment. In reality, risk is a measure of market volatility. Therefore risk reflects both the probability of upward and downward price fluctuations.

The second assumption is that "market" risk is the only kind of risk that exists in today's investment marketplace. Market risk is the degree an investment's price behaviour correlates with the general market for that investment. A good example of this is stock, whose value will generally reflect upward or downward movements in the stock market as a whole.

This section will outline at least seven types of investment risk and place special emphasis on those types of risk that can most affect retirees or persons planning for their retirement regardless of their country of residence:

- Specific risk reflects risks inherent to one investment in particular. A purchaser of GM stock would be concerned about problems peculiar to GM, such as the amount of debt, potential labour problems, effective management, and so on. This type of risk might be eliminated by properly diversifying a portfolio.

- Market risk is best exemplified by the stock or real estate markets. Market values of individual stocks or parcels of real estate tend to follow movement in the stock market or regional real estate markets in general. Market risk can pose a substantial short-term risk to investment principal. If your investment horizon is longer than three years, market risk in the stock market decreases rapidly and tends to decrease the longer the time period of your investment.

- Inflation risk is the most insidious and harmful risk to retirees, largely because its effects are not immediately obvious. Inflation reflects a loss of purchasing power, and it primarily affects fixed investments such as bonds, term deposits, GICs, CDs and fixed annuities. If an investor had $10,000 in Canada Savings Bonds that yielded 10% per year in income, and inflation averaged 5% that year, what would happen to the value of the bonds? The bonds would still be worth $10,000 on the investor's annual statements, but would the investor still be able to purchase $10,000 worth of goods and services? No, because of the 5% annual inflation, the investor's $10,000 is worth 5% less, or $9,500! Income from the bonds is also worth 5% less, compounded for each year of inflation! If the investor held these bonds for ten years, and inflation averaged 5% per year, he would get a cheque from the Canadian government for $10,000, but the bonds would purchase only $6,139 worth of goods and services. This type of risk may be reduced by adding inflation hedges to a portfolio.

- Interest rate risk reflects how movements in interest rates affect the value of investments. Anyone whose income depends primarily on interest rates has seen their income plummet from 2003 to 2004. Term deposits that came due for renewal during those years also renewed at very low rates. Interest rate volatility over the last 20 years has made bonds and term deposits much riskier to hold, particularly in a portfolio that has little or no diversification.

- Currency risk is similar to inflation risk in the way that it affects investments. This type of risk is especially important to Canadian retirees and was discussed in Chapter 2. Changes in the value of currencies can affect purchasing power the same way inflation does. For instance, if the Canadian dollar were to depreciate 5% in a year in relation to the American dollar, Canadians could purchase

5% less in American goods. More than $1 trillion of currency is traded each day all over the world, up from almost nothing in the 1970s. This type of risk may be eliminated by diversifying a portfolio in the global sense.

- Economic risk affects investments much as market risk does. Stocks and real estate tend to do well when the economy is brisk. Gold and utilities are examples of "counter cyclical" investments, which perform well when the economy is down. Gold has always been the traditional investment that provides insurance against any potential form of severe economic collapse.

- Government risk affects both Canadian and American residents. This type of risk results from both governments' frequent changes to the tax laws — often with negative effects for the investor. A major recent example was the Tax Reform Act of 1986 in the United States. A current example of this type of risk is government regulation that supports income trusts. If the government suddenly decides to pull its support and change the tax rules, thousands of investors would be left out in the cold.

By knowing all of the risks inherent in investing and prudently diversifying investments, the informed investor can enjoy a high, tax-favoured income at low levels of risk. The effects of inflation and wide currency swings can be minimized.

THE REWARDS OF GLOBAL INVESTING

In 1990, Merton Miller, William Sharpe and Harry Markowitz won the Nobel Prize in economics for their pioneering work in quantifying returns and risk from a portfolio perspective. Their research turned up some rather surprising results. It turns out your grandmother was right after all; don't put all your eggs in one basket. The market may not compensate you for the additional risk with higher returns. There is also no such thing as a free lunch. Decrease your overall risk and you also decrease returns over the long run.

Most surprising were the results attained by combining two assets that behave differently. Take a stock that performs well during economic downturns, and take a cyclical stock (a stock that tends to vary in value according to certain economic cycles). Both are expected to return 11% over the long run. If you buy equal portions of both stocks, the long-run return will be 11%. But year-to-year volatility will decrease, because one stock will do well when the other does poorly. In fact, adding an asset that may be considered risky by itself may actually reduce the total risk of the overall portfolio!

What does this have to do with international investing? International stock and bond markets do not move in lockstep with the U.S. and Canadian stock markets. For example, there were numerous periods in the 1990s when European markets outperformed North American markets and vice versa, Far Eastern markets both skyrocketed and declined largely out of sync with North America or Europe markets. By combining foreign stocks and bonds with U.S. and Canadian investments, we lower risk and enhance returns over the long run.

Invest in foreign securities and you attain diversification through exposure to different economies. Over the last twenty years, many markets have grown faster than the U.S. or Canadian stock markets. This means added profits for investors. Opportunities are also emerging with the opening of Eastern European countries and former republics of the Soviet Union.

Currency risks are also hedged. Canadian investors in foreign securities would have benefited greatly from currency gains when the Canadian dollar dropped from US$0.89 to US$0.83 in less than six months from late 1991 to early 1992 and then from $0.83 in 1992 to below $0.71 in 1994 and again from $0.72 to $0.63 in 1998. However, Canadians who invested strictly in U.S. investments between 2003 and 2006, when the Canadian dollar went from US$0.63 back up to US$0.91, would have suffered nearly a 50% loss of return. In a global economy, diversifying currency risk is very important.

More aggressive investors may find excellent opportunities in "emerging markets." Some of these markets have boomed during the last few years. Many Latin American countries freed up their economies with skyrocketing stock markets as a result. Mexico, Chile, Argentina and Brazil are recent examples. Indian and Israeli markets have also exploded. While we don't recommend that a portfolio contain only emerging market stocks, an exposure of 10% or so may aid returns and lower portfolio risk.

How do you select and purchase shares of stock or bonds in these markets? By using a mutual fund or exchange traded fund, stock selection is left to experts who focus on the country in question. This expertise can be crucial since financial disclosure and accounting standards are rarely as investor-oriented as they are in the United States and Canada. Information on foreign companies is also difficult to come by. Funds buy large blocks of stocks or bonds and transaction costs are reduced. Shares of mutual funds and exchanged traded funds can be bought and sold quickly and inexpensively and offer instant diversification.

CHOOSING AN INTERNATIONAL INVESTMENT MANAGER

The key to successful investing is formulating a long-term, internationally diversified portfolio policy based on your own objectives and preferences. The first words out of a potential investment manager's mouth should be questions related to your personal investment objectives. These objectives should contain concise information regarding the returns you expect, and the level of risk or volatility you are willing to assume in exchange for these returns. Be leery of investment advisors who will simply take your money with no questions asked and just throw it in a big investment pool without any customization to your individual needs. It is very important that they understand you and your needs before even a nickel is invested.

It is also important to consider present and future income needs from the portfolio, investment time horizon, liquidity requirements, income and estate tax information, and your current estate plan. You should be active in these early stages when portfolio policy is being formulated, and again when your individual situation changes. Charles D. Ellis's book *Investment Policy*, second edition, published in 1993 by Business One Irwin, is considered a classic in this area.

Unfortunately, in the real world, most financial advisors may be little more than salespeople enjoying upfront commissions based solely on sales volume. Clearly, there is little or no incentive for an advisor to monitor a client's account after a commission is received. In the U.S., less than one-third of advisors operate on a fee-only basis instead of on commission. In Canada it is even worse: over 90% of financial advisors operate solely or largely on a commission basis. It is primarily this pressure to sell more at higher prices that allows financial scandals such as Nortel in Canada and Enron in the U.S. to go unchecked for such a long period of time, because so many people are making so much money on all transactions.

Moreover, advisors working on a commission basis earn more by selling or shifting existing investments. This latter procedure, if done excessively, is called "churning" and is illegal.

The key to successful investment performance is active, professional portfolio management, with the most important considerations being the client's goals and best interest, closely matched to the manager's investment philosophy.

Why is formulation of a long-term portfolio policy emphasized here? Because some recent studies from the *Financial Analysts Journal* (Gary Brinson, L. Randolph Hood and Gilbert L. Beebower, "Determinants of Portfolio Performance," July–August 1986, and Gary P. Brinson, Brian D. Singer and Gilbert L. Beebower, "Revisiting Determinants of Portfolio Performance: An Update," May–June 1991) show that more than 90% of investment returns generated by large pension plans result from following a long-term investment policy. Less than 10% of portfolio returns were attributed to "stock picking," or market timing (switching funds between investments or asset classes in response to perceived changes in the economy). The successful investment advisor will pay close attention to those decisions that will generate 90% of their portfolios' returns.

There seems to be an inherently unfair bias in the way the investment marketplace treats "retail," or individual investors versus "wholesale," or institutional investors. What are these differences, and how can investors overcome them? How can you ensure equal treatment?

First, let's examine some of the differences. The retail marketplace is largely transaction-based. Stockbrokers, commissioned financial planners and insurance salespeople are compensated according to the number and size of financial transactions they effect. Put another way, the more they sell you, the more they make. The focus is not always on managing an investor's funds for the long term, but on switching from investment to investment.

Even banks collect commissions indirectly. Term deposits or bank CDs return an interest rate plus a guarantee of principal for a specified period of time. The banks invest the funds in government and corporate debt securities, mortgages and leases, and other investments. The return is often significantly higher than what is paid out to bank depositors.

The institutional marketplace, which includes pension funds, insurance companies and mutual funds, is performance-based. Portfolios are often managed by one or more managers, whose compensation is based on how big the portfolio gets. They are paid for performance rather than buying or selling investments. Here, the incentive is to reduce commission costs, since commissions reduce the size of the portfolios they manage.

Individual investors are constantly bombarded by the media and salespeople with information about the latest investment guru, the hottest stocks or the best market pundit. This is also known as "investor pornography" because lots of excitement is promised but very little of substance ever happens. Investors often buy on the premise that the broker, salesperson, or financial planner can pick "hot stocks" or other investments (why is life insurance so often the hot investment?) and can time favourable moments to switch between stocks, bonds or cash, depending on market conditions. If market timing and security selection contribute less than 10% of a typical portfolio's return, why do the media and retail investment marketplace focus so much time and energy promoting these advisors who claim to have exceptional abilities in these areas? Because strategies that lean heavily on security selection and market timing generate many, many more transactions (read: commissions) than establishing and sticking to a long-term investment policy.

Although many institutional investors use stock picking and some form of market timing, more have become asset allocators. This involves diversifying investments between cash equivalents, stocks, bonds, real estate and other asset classes. Asset allocators do not try to forecast the markets, the economy or interest rates, since they believe these markets and indicators are unpredictable over the long run. They also diversify their holdings and use a buy-and-hold strategy to minimize transaction costs and income taxes.

How can you level the playing field? Find an investment advisor who focuses on formulating a long-term investment policy based on your needs and preferences, which is 90% of the ball game. In choosing an investment manager, you should consider the following:

- Choose a manager compensated on the basis of performance or a flat fee, not commissions.

- All things being equal, choose the manager with lower management fees.

- Make sure the manager cannot make "big bets" with your portfolio. Choose a fund or firm whose management philosophy requires the manager to be diversified to some degree.

- Choose a manager who will manage the portfolio on a tax efficient basis.

- Choose a manager who uses no-load mutual funds, exchange traded funds and/or a discount brokerage arrangement to transact securities trades, thus minimizing your investment costs.

CROSS-BORDER Q&A

DOES U.S. LAW FORBID NON-RESIDENT BROKERAGE ACCOUNTS?

I have searched in vain for a way out of my dilemma; the Florida broker I had dealt with for about a year was forced to close my account. Apparently, regulations prohibit a non-U.S. resident brokerage account, with or without a W-8BEN, no matter which address I use. Please explain how I can resolve this.

— Edward S., North York, Ontario

Your dilemma can be solved by contacting either Vanguard Investments or Charles Schwab Global. Vanguard is the largest mutual fund and exchange traded funds investment company in the U.S. Charles Schwab is the largest discount brokerage firm in the United States. Both of these companies are excellent to deal with and have mechanisms for non-residents of the U.S. to open full brokerage accounts. Vanguard can be found on the Internet at http://vanguard-international.vanguard.com and Schwab at www.schwab-global.com. There is a little more paperwork involved to set up these accounts, but they give you full access to trade in your account as you require. You may have luck with other brokerage firms for these non-resident alien (NRA) accounts as well.

I believe your stockbroker was confusing his company's policy and procedures with those of the regulatory bodies, as there are no laws, that I am aware of, prohibiting non-resident accounts if they are done properly.

HOLDING SECURITIES IN STREET FORM AND U.S. TREASURY NOTES

If I hold U.S. Securities in street form in my Canadian account, are they still subject to the $60,000 limit for estate tax? Technically, the answer is probably yes, but are there reporting procedures between the two countries? Finally, I have read about U.S. Treasury notes. Are these available to Canadians? If so, where and how?

— Ronald Z., Corunna, Ontario

Holding securities in street form, as you already guessed, does not exempt them from non-resident estate tax. Any U.S. securities, unless they are specifically exempt, add to the taxable estate of non-residents. Tax exempt securities that would likely be purchased through a brokerage firm include Certificates of Deposit from U.S. banks, U.S. government Treasury bills, Treasury notes and Treasury bonds issued after July 1984. U.S. securities are taxable for non-resident estate tax purposes, whether the securities are held in Canada, the United States or elsewhere in the world. Canadians whose world estates are less than US$1.2 million can, under the current Canada/U.S. Tax Treaty, hold U.S. stocks and similar securities as exempt from the non-resident estate tax.

There are no automatic formal reporting procedures between Canada and the United States with respect to brokerage accounts. However, the

Canada/U.S. Tax Treaty allows for the exchange of tax information in either country at any time. The Internal Revenue Service and the Canada Revenue Agency have been using this treaty clause quite frequently to catch taxpayers for not reporting income. The answer to your final question about purchasing U.S. Treasury notes is that you can hold as many as you desire, and if you use an online broker such as Charles Schwab Global, www.schwab-global.com, you can purchase them there at a very reasonable cost.

SPECIALTY FUNDS FOR NON-RESIDENTS

I am semi-retired and like to devote time to my business and leisure. I spend five months of each year in the United States, so I need U.S.-dollar income. I am afraid that the Canadian dollar will decline from its recent highs in value against the U.S. dollar. Are there investment advisors in the United States who manage accounts especially for non-residents?

— *Tom C., Phoenix, Arizona*

A number of U.S.-based mutual fund companies have started specialty mutual funds for non-residents. These funds are registered offshore in places like the Cayman Islands or Guernsey. They may only be purchased by non-residents of the United States while outside the country. Most of the funds we have examined are load funds, with the exception of Vanguard Investments, and the load funds exact their pound of flesh in one or more of the following ways:

- upfront commissions
- commissions incurred when fund shares are sold
- high annual costs, some of which are passed through to brokers

Vanguard is truly a no-load company whose funds can be purchased without any of the above commissions or other fees. They can be contacted on the Internet at http://vanguard-international.vanguard.com.

Another alternative is to choose an investment advisor who can manage a diversified, international portfolio specifically tailored to each investor's needs and preferences. This type of professionally managed portfolio generally requires that $500,000 or more be invested. These accounts can be specifically tailored for each individual, but should invest only in exempt investments, such as U.S. Treasury securities and corporate bonds issued after July 18, 1984, bank certificates of deposit, exempt money market funds and specialty mutual funds. Accordingly, specialty portfolios should be exempt from U.S. income tax reporting and withholding, and not included in the non-resident's U.S. estate. Funds should be invested only in marketable assets that can be turned into cash within a week or two.

Specialty portfolios are appropriate for investors who desire:

- a custom-tailored, long-term investment policy
- personal, one-on-one attention
- prudent, professional management of their investments
- privacy
- increased safety and returns of international diversification
- quick access to funds
- minimal commissions
- exemption from U.S. income tax reporting
- exemption from U.S. income tax withholding
- exemption from the U.S. non-resident estate tax

Investors typically pay management fees of 0.5% to 1.5% per year, depending on the manager and the size of the account.

KEEPING A CANADIAN BROKERAGE ACCOUNT AS A U.S. RESIDENT

I am a retired Canadian and a recent green card resident of Florida. My income (except for U.S. Social Security) is all Canadian and I have an investment portfolio with a Toronto brokerage firm. This account consists of bonds and mortgage-backed securities. Trading in this account is infrequent and usually only to replace investments that have matured.

My broker has recently advised me that SEC (Securities and Exchange Commission) regulations prohibit him from making Canadian trades for a U.S. resident! Is this a unique situation? There must be a great many Canadians in the United States who own Canadian securities. This creates a very serious situation for me and I would appreciate your comments and your advice as to what steps I might take. Are there Toronto firms that could do trades for me if necessary?

— *Darwin M., Sarasota, Florida*

Your broker is correct; in order for him to legally deal with a U.S. resident both he and his company must be licensed in your state of residence. Many Canadians in the United States have received similar notices from their brokers. Negotiations between Canadian and U.S. securities regulators did partially solve this problem, at least with respect to RRSPs. From a simplification standpoint, life would be easier for you financially if you just moved your assets south. U.S. brokerage firms can do everything Canadian brokerage firms can do, including holding Canadian securities, and they can normally do it at lower costs, particularly if you deal with Charles Schwab or Fidelity Investments, both of which offer great discounted brokerage services.

This can be solved easily by setting up a U.S. brokerage account and transferring the cash and securities into it through a broker-to-broker transfer. U.S. brokerage firms can and do hold just about any listed Canadian bonds and stocks that would normally be traded on any of the Canadian exchanges. Those they can't accept, such as Canadian mutual funds, should be converted to cash before the transfer. Generally you will be able to do everything you are currently doing in your Canadian account at far less cost.

CAN CANADIAN BROKERS ACT FOR U.S. RESIDENTS?

I am retired with no employment income. I do, however, trade commodity futures through a U.S.-based broker, using a computerized system. The net results are reported to Canada Revenue Agency.

I intend to carry on this activity during the winter months from my temporary U.S. address and would like to know if the results (hopefully good) might be considered income earned in the United States and therefore liable to be reported to the IRS.

A complicating factor is that the income might never be actually received in the United States since a trade could be initiated in one country but come to fruition in another. Would appreciate your insight into this.

— *Gordon C., St. Catharines, Ontario*

You pose an interesting and unusual set of questions. If you are able to ensure that your trading is simply a capital transaction and is subject to tax as capital gains (or losses), then you have no worries about being taxed in the United States, providing you don't spend more than 183 days a year there and you file the Closer Connection Form 8840 with the IRS annually by June 15. If you follow these two requirements, the Canada/U.S. Tax Treaty clearly states that your capital gains are taxable only in Canada, regardless of the fact that you may be in the United States for part of the year.

If this trading is regular enough that it might be considered your only job, there is a possibility any income could be classified as business income. You would be considered to be doing business in the United States, meaning that the business income would be taxable there and included as part of your world income in Canada. If you have no immigration status or authorization to work in the U.S., you are an illegal alien.

I suggest you check to see if your U.S. broker is licensed to do business in Ontario by the Ontario Securities Commission. If not, they could be trading for you against U.S. Securities and Exchange Commission regulations, and you could have little or no consumer protection for inappropriate advice or someone's running off with your funds.

TRANSFERRING ACCOUNTS AND FINDING A U.S.-BASED BROKER

My family and I became U.S. residents in 2006 on an L-1 visa. For stocks and securities trading we dealt with TD Waterhouse investor services while in Canada, but they insist that they can no longer trade on our behalf. They blame U.S. SEC rules, but I have seen conflicting information about this.

TD Waterhouse in Canada does offer a U.S. division that will carry my accounts in Canadian dollars, but I am not certain that I should go through the necessary exercise or that all the downside has been made clear.

Are there any alternatives for someone in my position? Is there any significant risk or loss of flexibility in transferring my accounts? Can you recommend anyone in the Detroit area to provide financial advice?

— Murray K., Farmington Hills, Michigan

Your brokerage firm is correct. They cannot legally trade accounts for U.S. residents unless both the broker and the firm are licensed in your particular state in the United States. Also, there are generally some state securities requirements that could make it illegal for them to deal with you. Canada and the United States have negotiated a securities agreement that may alleviate this trading problem, at least for RRSPs. Trading in RRSP investments while you are a U.S. resident can now be done in most of the U.S. states, providing you and your Canadian brokerage firm meet specified criteria.

Your alternatives depend on your personal goals regarding the kind of investor you are, whether the accounts are RRSPs, and whether you plan to be a permanent U.S. resident. Generally, it would simplify your financial life immensely if your account were in the United States. It would be much easier for you to manage and administer, particularly for income tax reporting. You should also be able to reduce your brokerage costs as competition in the United States tends to keep transaction costs very low. My colleagues and I like to recommend Charles Schwab, Fidelity Investments or TD Ameritrade as the best all-around discount brokers in the United States. You can provide Charles Schwab, Fidelity or Ameritrade with a list of your securities and they should be able to tell you which ones can be held in the United States. They can also initiate the transfer of your account. Generally, most listed Canadian stocks and bonds can be held in your U.S. account. Mutual funds would have to be liquidated and turned into cash to transfer to the United States.

Coming to America 7

MOVING TO THE UNITED STATES

Many Canadians would never dream of moving to the United States, while others spend thousands of dollars attempting to obtain legal status as U.S. residents. There are other Canadians who live in the United States illegally year-round, or who stay longer than U.S. Citizenship and Immigration Service (USCIS, formerly the Immigration and Naturalization Service — INS) rules allow for a winter visitor. With the relative ease of crossing the border, and the ability to remain in the United States for extended periods of time, why should someone consider becoming a legal resident of the United States?

For some people, U.S. residency means a new business opportunity. Others have had enough of paying more than half of their earnings in high Canadian taxes, while others just prefer the warmer climate. Whatever your motives, this chapter is designed to assist those people who have thought that at some stage in their lives they might like to emigrate from Canada to the United States. Chapters 8, 9, 13 and 14 will help you determine whether U.S. residency would be a good move for you financially, after taking into consideration the key cross-border issues of income tax, estate tax and medicare. For those seriously contemplating a move, all the issues in this and the next three chapters need to be addressed simultaneously for maximum benefit.

This chapter offers a general discussion of American immigration rules and policies. Individual factors can greatly influence the course of any immigration undertaking. Immigration can be a complex and lengthy procedure under current law and should not be attempted without the services of a good U.S. immigration attorney.

HOW TO BECOME A LEGAL RESIDENT OF THE UNITED STATES

There are normally two legal ways to immigrate to the United States. The first is through a business or a professional relationship. The second is through the sponsorship of a close family member. This is about as simple an explanation as it gets about who is entitled to immigrate to the United States. After that, the whole process becomes complex and contradictory. Figure 7.1 provides a chart of the basic business categories under which you may acquire either a permanent or something-less-than-permanent resident status.

You can see from Figure 7.1 that there are numerous opportunities for U.S. immigration for persons with business contacts. Business and professional immigration categories will be explained in greater detail in the next section. Where does this leave the retired person who wants to immigrate and retire to the U.S. Sunbelt? That's where some advance planning can pay big dividends. Those who have recently retired or are about to retire should consider keeping open any business or professional relationships long enough to assist them in getting permanent immigration status. For those of you who are retired, investing in a small U.S. business with a full-time manager or just a USCIS specially authorized investment can be a suitable means of obtaining a visa or legal permanent resident/green card that allows you to legally live in the United States year-round.

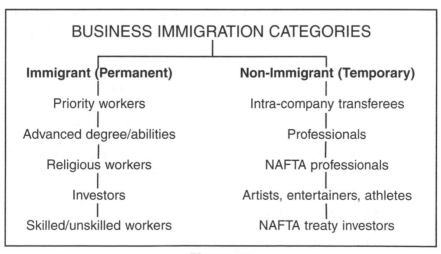

Figure 7.1

Those with no applicable business or professional means may wish to look for any possible close family connections that can give them legal status in the United States. Figure 7.2, shown later in this chapter, addresses the key family relationships that can prove useful for immigration purposes. For most purposes "close" family relationships to the USCIS means U.S. citizens who are parents, children or siblings.

IMMIGRATION CATEGORIES

This section lists some of the basic qualifications for each of the business and family immigration categories outlined in Figures 7.1 and 7.2.

Immigrant or Lawful Permanent Resident (LPR) status is also known as a "green card." This is similar to Permanent Resident status in Canada. The green card is no longer even green. Every so often, the green card is given a new look to impede fraudulent reproduction. Current versions of the green card now include an expiration date, holograms and soon one of the biometric IDs discussed in Chapter 1. This means the card is now like a driver's licence and must be renewed before the expiration date, but unlike a driver's licence you don't lose your status just because your card expires.

GREEN CARD OR EMPLOYMENT-BASED IMMIGRANT CATEGORIES

FIRST PREFERENCE — EB-1

Priority Workers. There are three priority worker classes, known to the U.S. Citizenship and Immigration Service (USCIS) as EB1-A, 1-B and 1-C categories:

1-A: Extraordinary-ability immigrants in the sciences, arts, education, business and athletics. The regulations define extraordinary ability as a level of expertise indicating that the individual is one of that small percentage who have risen to the very top of a particular field of endeavour. No employer sponsorship or labour certification is required for a person in this category. A Wayne Gretzsky, the CEO of a large company or a Nobel Prize winner would be examples for this category.

1-B: Outstanding professors and researchers. Applicants in this category must be coming to the United States to conduct research for a private firm in full-time research activities or for a university. They must display documented achievements in their field. The university or the private research company applies to the USCIS for this visa.

1-C: Executives and managers. An executive or manager employed for at least one of the three years preceding the application by the U.S. employer's Canadian affiliate, parent, subsidiary or branch office qualifies for this category. This is a good opportunity for obtaining a green card for those business people who have a business in both countries. This category is very similar to the L-1 intra-company transferee visa in the non-immigrant petitions.

SECOND PREFERENCE — EB-2

Professionals. Holding Advanced Degrees, 2-A, or Exceptional Ability Immigrants, 2-B.

2-A: Advanced Degree. This category includes people with PhDs and Master's degrees. Five years or more experience of progressive work may be accepted in lieu of the advanced degree, providing a Bachelor's degree has been acquired. Unless they qualify for the national interest waiver discussed below, applicants for this category must have an employer (1) petition on their behalf for a position that requires this advanced education and (2) obtain a labour certification from the U.S. Department of Labor. To obtain labour certification, the employer must demonstrate that there are no U.S. workers who are qualified and available to fill the position.

2-B: Exceptional Ability Immigrants. USCIS provides for admission of a person with exceptional ability in the arts, sciences or business. If you can convince USCIS that it is in the U.S. national interest (because of your significant positive contribution to the U.S. economy) to waive the employment and labour certification requirement, this petition can be submitted directly without an employer sponsor. Like many aspects of immigration rules, the term "exceptional ability" has not been clearly defined. It is a lower standard than "extraordinary ability" but still requires a degree of expertise significantly above the ordinary. As for the 2-A category, 2-B applicants must have an employer petition for them and they must obtain a labour certification unless they are granted the national interest waiver of those requirements.

THIRD PREFERENCE — EB-3

Skilled and Unskilled Workers. This catch-all category is for immigrants with offers of employment. This category is further subdivided into the following:

3-A: Professionals with Bachelor's degrees and labour certifications.

3-B: Skilled workers performing a job requiring at least two years of higher education, training or experience.

3-C: "Other workers." This subcategory is for positions that require less than two years of higher education, training or experience.

FOURTH PREFERENCE — EB-4

Religious Workers. Must have been a member of and worked for a denomination for at least two years and seek entry as (1) a minister (needs a baccalaureate degree); (2) professionals working in a religious capacity; or (3) other religious organization workers.

FIFTH PREFERENCE — EB-5

Immigrant Investors. This is sometimes referred to as the "gold card." It is similar to the program Canada has used for years for attracting foreign business entrepreneurs. Because of the large investment, job creation requirement and other restrictions, the EB-5 green card category has been greatly underutilized since its inception in the early '90s. However, in 2002 the USCIS introduced a second option, the Regional Center program, which is ideal for the retiree or inactive investor who wishes to immigrate to the U.S. Both these EB-5 programs (discussed in more detail below) provide for a Conditional Lawful Permanent Residence (in other words, a conditional green card) for two years until all the requirements listed below are met; then full green card or LPR status is granted.

- **Regular Program:** Establish a new or expand an existing commercial enterprise with an investment of $500,000 (in rural or special high unemployment areas) or $1 million in other areas that will benefit the U.S. economy and create at least ten full-time jobs for U.S. authorized workers. Direct involvement of the investor in the day-to-day operations or at least active management of the business is expected, including living near the location of the business investment.

- **Regional Center Program:** The investment amounts for these EB-5 programs generally require only the lower $500,000 amounts because the investments are deliberately created in the targeted areas of high unemployment or areas of desired economic expansion. The ten employee requirement of the Regular program is replaced with a less restrictive "indirect employment creation" which allows the investor to qualify for a EB-5 green card without hiring ten people directly in the company that the investor has invested in. Consequently, the investor can qualify by presenting evidence that ten jobs will be created throughout the Regional Center economy, a much easier hurdle to face. The EB-5 management requirement is minimal in that the investor can be a limited partner and still qualify, making this program much more acceptable for those are not interested in day-to-day management or actively running a business. The investor is not required to live where the investment is made; he or she can, for example, live in Florida and invest in Washington state.

There are generally three or four Regional Center programs for the investor to choose from. Thus the only major concern an investor has is to choose the right investment, the program managers do the rest, and in approximately ten months the investor has his or her conditional two-year green card. At the end of the two years, the green card becomes permanent with full rights of permanent residency and a path to U.S. citizenship. The investment can be sold at any time after the permanent green card has been obtained; in fact, most of these investments self-liquidate in five to seven years after inception. Choosing the right investment cannot be overemphasized, as the program should give investors a fair return on their investment, and the green card should be considered a secondary benefit or just the icing on the cake. Under mandate by Congress, Regional Center EB-5 petitions are given priority by USCIS which, among other benefits, often results in a quicker path to approval.

The procedure for obtaining an EB-5 investor green card is relatively straightforward. The investor must produce five years of tax returns to substantiate the legal source of investment funds. The source of the funds can also be in the form of a loan or gift from a friend or relative. The investor must also present evidence that traces the capital, through bank transfers and other documentation, from the investor directly to the enterprise being invested in.

If the investor is already in the U.S., he or she then applies for a green card through USCIS. Customarily no interview is required, and approval has been taking approximately ten months. If the investor still lives in Canada, an application for the green card is generally made at a U.S. consulate; however, for consular processing purposes, an interview is necessary. Approval of the green card in this case takes on average about ten or eleven months, approximately the same as through USCIS.

EMPLOYMENT-BASED NON-IMMIGRANT CATEGORIES

For all the non-immigrant visas noted below, a spouse and dependent children are allowed to accompany the visa holder for the same amount of time in the United States and are themselves issued special visas. However, it should be noted that the spouse of an L or E visa holder may obtain employment authorization. The spouses of all the other visa applicants and all children of the original visa applicant are not allowed to work legally in the United States unless they in turn can get their own non-immigrant working visas based on their own qualifications. This is a particularly important consideration for young families in which one of the spouses receives a U.S. job offer in one of these non-immigrant categories. If little planning is done to develop a long-term immigration strategy so that all the children and the non-working spouse are not prevented from working and are put in the position that they may forced to move back to Canada at the end of visa, the family will be at a great disadvantage. It is therefore very important that when negotiating a job offer the employee gets a firm commitment from the employer to sponsor them and their family members for green cards as soon as it is practical.

1. **Intra-Company Transferees.** This category is classified as the L-1 non-immigrant status and can last, with renewals, up to seven years. This visa requires an ongoing relationship between a Canadian company and a U.S. parent subsidiary, branch office or affiliate. The visa applicant must be an executive, manager or a person with specialized knowledge or training needed for the U.S. company, and the applicant must have worked for the Canadian affiliate for at least one year out of the three years preceding the transfer to the United States.

2. **Professionals and Other Temporary Workers.** This category is divided into four categories and can last, with renewals, up to six years. The four categories of this visa are as follows:

   H-1B — Professionals in special occupations requiring a college degree or equivalent in work experience

   H-2A — Temporary agricultural workers in short supply

   H-2B — Temporary non-agricultural workers that are in short supply

   H-3 — Trainees

   The H-1B category can be granted for an initial three-year period, extendable to a six-year maximum. The H-2A, H-2B and H-3 categories can be granted for up to one year initially, extendable to three years for H-2A and H-1B or two years for the H-3. There is a cap on the numbers of these visas granted each year.

3. **Artists, Entertainers and Athletes.** There are two non-immigrant categories available for these emigrants from Canada. These are known as the P and O statuses and both are limited to the period of (a) particular event(s). The O visa is for extraordinary artists, entertainers, business people and athletes and can last for three years initially, then is renewable yearly thereafter or for the time period of the event(s), whichever is less. The P non-immigrant status can last for up to five years, extendable to a ten-year maximum. There is a cap on the number of these visas.

4. **North American Free Trade Agreement (NAFTA) Treaty Traders and Investors.** The Canadian Free Trade Agreement with the United States became effective January 1, 1989, and was superseded by NAFTA, which came into effect January 1, 1994. The Immigration section of NAFTA provides for the temporary entry of business visitors, eliminates barriers to trade, facilitates across-the-border investment, provides for joint administration and dispute resolution and emphasizes trade and the movement of people.

   This means that Canadian citizens under NAFTA can now obtain the E-1 Trader visa or the E-2 Investor visas, which are usually renewable indefinitely as long as the qualifying investment remains ongoing, and is considered the next best thing to permanent residency. Requirements for an E-2 visa are the following:

   • The applicant must be a Canadian citizen.

   • A substantial investment in a bona fide U.S. enterprise must be made. A substantial investment is not clearly defined but the State Department has issued a sliding scale guideline. If the value of the enterprise is less than $500,000, the applicant must provide 75% of the investment. The amount of the investment must be an amount normally considered appropriate to establish a viable enterprise of the nature contemplated. Most viable applications investing $50,000 to $100,000 or more with other capital readily available are accepted. A good business plan is essential, particularly if the applicant has limited capital to sink into the new enterprise.

   • The investor must be in a position to "develop and direct" the entity in which he has invested. Generally, that means the investor must have at least 50% ownership or control interest.

   • Certain "essential employees" of the investor may also be eligible for E-2 status. Essential employees must be employed in a supervisory or executive capacity or have special skills needed by the employer. Often a business partner spouse could obtain his or her own E-2 visa under this option.

- There is no requirement for a minimum number of employees to be hired, but the number of employees needed to operate the business in addition to the E-2 investor must be sufficient to make the enterprise successful. The investment must do more than support the investor and his or her family, so the more employees, the better the chances the visa will be granted.

- The company or employer of the visa applicant must be at least 51% Canadian owned and controlled.

NAFTA PROFESSIONALS

This category is a unique one and is called the TN status. It permits people to come in as non-immigrants on the basis of their being a "professional" as listed on a schedule to NAFTA. The Trade NAFTA (TN) visa is valid for one year and may be renewed annually for an unlimited duration as long as the visa holder maintains his non-immigrant intent (recently the USCIS has started to turn down TN visa holders who are renewing three or more times in certain professions and circumstances).

The list of professionals includes accountants, engineers, scientists, research assistants, medical and allied professionals, scientific technicians, disaster-relief insurance claims adjusters, architects, lawyers, economists, computer systems analysts, management consultants and others. It includes professors but omits teachers at the high school level. The professionals require at least a Bachelor's degree. Work experience will be allowed to replace education requirements for management consultants only.

FAMILY-BASED IMMIGRANT CATEGORIES

Family-based immigration is predicated on the fact that a close family member who is already a U.S. citizen or green card holder can sponsor other family members for permanent residence in the United States. There is also the possibility that a person looking to immigrate to the United States may already be a derivative citizen through family history. Derivative citizenship will be covered in detail in the next section. There are five main categories for family-sponsored immigration.

The immediate relative category is separate from other family-based immigration because it is not numerically restricted. This category is for spouses, unmarried minor children and parents of U.S. citizens. New spouses obtaining green cards by marrying U.S. citizens will receive two-year temporary green cards and must go through an interview process after the two years before permanent cards are issued. The purpose of this process is to thwart marriages of convenience whose purpose is to obtain legal immigration status fraudulently. Those who saw the movie *Green Card* will better understand what this process entails with its detailed questioning of the spouses to ensure they are truly married.

In all but one of the other four categories, the family member sponsoring the green card LPR of another family member must be a U.S. citizen (see Applying for U.S Citizenship later in this chapter). These categories are subject to quotas and waiting lists of a few months to several years. They work on a priority or preference system:

- **First Preference.** Parents, spouses, minor unmarried sons and daughters of U.S. citizens. At the present time there is a processing time of about six months in this category if filing is done at the U.S. consulate in Canada closest to the residence of the applicant. If the filing is done from the U.S. side of the border through an adjustment of status, expect a processing time of 12 to 20 months depending on the USCIS processing center used. Usually those processing their applications in the U.S. can request work permits and advance parole and be granted these in about six to eight weeks from the date of application. Advance parole is just a special permission document which allows applicants to stay legally in the U.S. and also allows them to leave and re-enter the U.S. while they are waiting for permanent green cards. For adult (over the age of 21) unmarried children of U.S. citizens, the processing time is currently about five years.

- **Second Preference.** This category is broken down into two subcategories:

  a. Spouses and minor children of lawful permanent residents or green card holders. There is currently a wait of about five years in this category.

  b. Adult unmarried sons and daughters of lawful permanent residents or green card holders. There is a waiting period of more than seven years in this category.

- **Third Preference.** Married children of U.S. citizens. There is a waiting period in this category of more than seven years.

- **Fourth Preference.** Siblings of U.S. citizens. There is a waiting period in this category of nearly 13 years. Even though the waiting list may be quite long, it is worthwhile getting on this list as a change in legislation could either reduce the waiting period and/or increase quotas, and people already on the list could move much more quickly. There have been recent proposals before Congress to eliminate the Fourth Preference altogether.

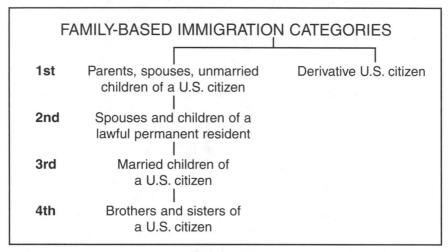

Figure 7.2

DERIVATIVE CITIZENSHIP — ARE YOU A U.S. CITIZEN?

With Canada and the United States so closely related in geography and history, there has been a substantial migration of residents across the 49th parallel. As a result, many Canadians, although they might never have lived in the United States, might be U.S. citizens solely on the basis of their ancestry. This is known as derivative citizenship — obtaining U.S. citizenship by inheritance or derivation.

Derivative citizenship was first established in law by the United States Congress in the late 1700s. Since then, Congress has amended the rules as to who is eligible for derivative citizenship status at least a dozen times. Consequently, the rules to determine derivative citizenship can be quite complex.

Figure 7.3 illustrates a possible flow chart regarding how to determine whether you are a U.S. citizen. The "Yes" notations indicate possible derivative citizenship if all other qualifications are met as outlined in the figure.

The flow chart gives you some idea about who may qualify as a derivative citizen, but with the twelve or more congressional amendments to the citizenship rules, it becomes a very complicated issue. For example, it is conceivable that one member of a family acquired U.S. citizenship on

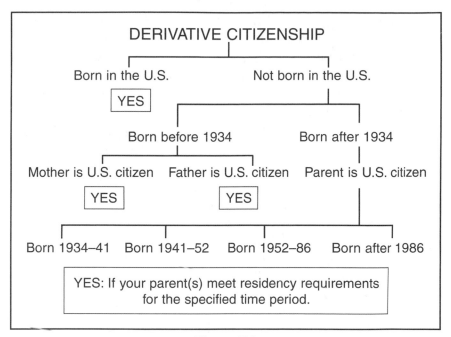

Figure 7.3

the day of his or her birth, while a sibling born later is out of luck. After May 24, 1934, U.S. residency of the U.S. citizen ancestor became a vital ingredient in establishing a person's American citizenship entitlement. In addition, during certain periods of time, Congress required the potential derivative citizen's parent(s) to meet some residency requirements. Figure 7.3 is further explained in the following summary:

Born in the U.S. If you were born in the United States, you have likely retained your U.S. citizenship, unless you have actively done something to renounce it. Before 1990, United States born people taking up citizenship, or even just voting in another country, were considered to have renounced their U.S. citizenship. Since then, the State Department has published new guidelines to determine retention of U.S. citizenship: they now presume a person intends to retain U.S. citizenship, even though that person obtains naturalization in or declares allegiance to another country. This new policy is retroactive. This means that it applies to people who think they might have lost their U.S. citizenship, even if the U.S. State Department has already made a negative finding by telling the person he or she has lost his or her citizenship. A recent client was told 30 years ago by the State Department that he had lost his citizenship. He wrote to the State Department after visiting the U.S. Consulate in

Vancouver and they revoked their past Loss of Citizenship declaration and the client had his citizenship back in less than eight weeks.

Both Parents Are U.S. Citizens. If both your parents were U.S. citizens at the time of your birth, you will generally have a claim to U.S. citizenship if one or both of your parents ever "resided" in the United States. This applies even if you have never lived in the United States yourself.

One Parent Is a U.S. Citizen. If only one of your parents was a U.S. citizen, you may be a U.S. citizen, if you and your parent have resided in the United States for the requisite time periods as summarized below.

- **Born on or before May 24, 1934:** If you were born before this date and your father was a U.S. citizen, you are eligible for U.S. citizenship. The law was changed effective October 6, 1994, to give mothers the same rights as fathers in conferring citizenship on their children. This is particularly important to persons and descendants of persons born to U.S. citizen mothers before May 24, 1934.

- **Born May 25, 1934, to January 13, 1941:** Canadians born in this period are subject to two conditions. First, the U.S. citizen parent must have had a prior U.S. residency. Second, the would-be derivative citizen must retain his citizenship through a two-year continuous presence (although not necessarily an uninterrupted stay) in the United States. The terms "residency" and "presence" have no clear definition, but are interpreted through facts and circumstances and previous case law.

- **Born January 14, 1941, to December 24, 1952:** Similar to those Canadians in the preceding category, the prospective derivative citizen and the U.S. parent are subject to residency requirements. Here, the U.S. parent must have ten years' U.S. residency, at least five of which were after age 16. The two-year continuous presence requirement for the potential derivative citizen was also in force.

- **Born December 25, 1952, to November 13, 1986:** If you were born in this period, your U.S. parent must have been physically present in the United States for ten years, at least five of which were after age 14. After October 10, 1978, the retention through residency requirement for the potential derivative citizen was abolished.

- **Born After November 13, 1986:** The U.S. parent must have five years of previous physical presence in the United States, at least two of which were after age 14 in order to transmit citizenship. No residency is required of the prospective derivative citizen.

- **As of October 1994,** a new law allows a person who was a citizen at birth but who lost that citizenship by failing to meet the physical presence requirements of the time to reapply to regain U.S. citizenship.

Once you've established that you're eligible for derivative citizenship, the biggest and most rewarding challenge comes from documenting the facts of the U.S. parent's relationship and residency. Prospective derivative citizens often need to become ancestral detectives, searching through old family and government records to shed new light on their pasts. Family bibles, voter registrations, census records, sworn statements of family members: all have been used successfully to establish entitlement for U.S. citizenship status.

APPLYING FOR U.S. CITIZENSHIP

United States citizenship is acquired through three methods:

- Birth
- Derivation
- Naturalization

Obtaining citizenship derivation was explained in the previous section on derivative citizenship. In general, any person born in the U.S. is considered a U.S. citizen even though his or her parents may have been just passing through the U.S. at the time of birth. You may apply for or confirm your citizenship status by either completing a Form N-600 with the USCIS or simply submitting an application for a passport to the U.S. State Department. Most people will find the passport route the quickest and most hassle-free method. The State Department is not nearly as bogged down as the USCIS in other immigration issues, and if you are turned down you will know about it much earlier, so you can begin the appeals process that much sooner, if you feel you have a legitimate claim.

Acquiring U.S. citizenship by naturalization is available to those who have a five-year continuous legal permanent residence in the United States. In other words, you must have had a green card and have been physically present in the United States without any interruptions of longer than six months over a period of five years. There are a few exceptions. Those married to U.S. citizens have only a three-year continuous residency requirement. For naturalization, one needs to demonstrate physical presence for the required amount of time; good moral character; and a minimum knowledge of English, U.S. history and government.

Naturalization is a relatively simple process that begins with submitting application Form N-400 to the USCIS, along with a specified fee (usually several hundred dollars including a fingerprint fee), two colour photographs and proof of some of the information requested in the application. Visit the U.S. Citizenship and Immigration Service's website to get copies of forms and latest fees at www.uscis.gov. The most difficult question on Form N-400 requests the details of every trip you have taken outside the United States since you received your green card. An oral examination is required after filing the N-400 to prove U.S. and English knowledge and verify eligibility for U.S. citizenship. After a successful examination, a U.S. District Court judge or an immigration officer will confer citizenship on you at a swearing-in ceremony. This entire citizenship process, depending on your county of residence, has been taking seven to twelve months to complete.

Whether American citizenship is acquired through birth, naturalization or derivation, it can provide the ease of U.S. access that many Canadians seek. We remind those who are considering U.S. citizenship (or any U.S. immigration, for that matter) to use the services of a competent cross-border financial planner to address the tax consequences of such a move *before* they attempt to obtain or reinstate U.S. citizenship. Those who fail to heed this advice could face seriously adverse tax consequences once they obtain citizenship.

DUAL CITIZENSHIP — IS IT POSSIBLE?

There are few issues — besides which way the Canadian dollar is going — that are more hotly debated by Canadians in the United States than whether one is or can become a dual citizen of the United States and Canada.

To begin with, there is such a thing as dual citizenship, even though you will have a difficult time finding an immigration official in either Canada or the United States who will admit that it exists, let alone tell you anything about it. There is no formal procedure to apply for dual citizenship. You basically acquire it by applying for U.S. citizenship and by not relinquishing your Canadian citizenship or vice versa.

Dual citizenship exists for Canadian citizens under two basic premises. First, there is the case of a Canadian green card holder and lawful permanent resident of the United States becoming a naturalized U.S. citizen. Since February 15, 1977, when Prime Minister Trudeau made his famous statement "once a Canadian, always a Canadian," Canada has not revoked its citizenship upon the U.S. naturalization of its citizens. Consequently, the Canadian holds citizenship status in both countries. Second, Canadian-born persons who meet the criteria for U.S. derivative citizenship status as outlined earlier in this chapter can hold both a Canadian and a U.S. passport at the same time. As a result, they are dual citizens as well.

Dual citizenship does not come from any formal application for "dual citizenship" but by default. Consequently, individuals contacting the U.S. Citizenship and Immigration Service offices, or even Canadian consulates in the United States, inquiring about how they can apply for dual citizenship get a series of blank stares and/or negative responses.

Currently you can hold dual citizenship if you are a Canadian citizen who qualifies for U.S. citizenship by simply applying for U.S. citizenship and not formally renouncing your Canadian citizenship. Your new Canadian passport will indicate your dual status inside the passport. The U.S. basically ignores the fact that someone applying for American citizenship would want to remain the citizen of another country at the same time and does nothing to formally recognize or deny this dual-status situation. The reluctance of the USCIS to accept dual citizenship may stem from fear of divided loyalties and citizenship by convenience.

Canadian/U.S. dual citizens are envied for having the best of both worlds and are in no way restricted from living, working or vacationing in either country for any reason for their entire lives. In addition, these dual citizens can pass this status on to their children by assisting them to obtain green cards in the categories noted earlier in this chapter. Also, children born directly to dual citizens can also become dual citizens providing they take action to do so prior to the age of 28.

THE GREEN CARD LOTTERY

From time to time, the U.S. Congress allows for an immigrant visa lottery. This is a free lottery, which offers a large number of visas on a random determinant basis with no employment or family-based qualifications required. Congress decides from which countries it will take entries, based on which countries they feel have not received a fair shake in the immigrant categories through the normal visa process and for other political reasons.

Congress holds two separate lotteries of 50,000 applicants each generally once or twice a year. Canadians were eligible for these bulk lotteries but have been excluded from subsequent lotteries since 1993. However, if you are a citizen of some other country but are living in Canada, you may be eligible for the lottery under the non-Canadian citizenship lottery quota. Typically, the entry process is made public several months before the draws are made in the fall and each person is allowed only one application. Spouses, however, if also eligible, may each file separate entries.

The entries are very simple to complete, and contrary to advertisements from immigration services you do not need to pay, nor do you gain any advantage from having someone prepare and submit your application.

Those who are interested in future lotteries should keep their ears to the ground or contact USCIS periodically. Check the USCIS website for the lottery dates and to find out which countries are eligible for submission, at www.uscis.gov. The most recent lottery accepted only electronic applications, greatly simplifying the process.

LEGAL RETIREMENT IN THE UNITED STATES

Even though statistics show large numbers of Canadians spending much of their retirements in the U.S. Sunbelt, there is no such thing as a retiree's visa. A separate visa category for retirees did exist once, but it was closed down in the mid-1970s, due to some changes in U.S. immigration rules. There was a move afoot to bring back this retirement visa, because of the obvious economic benefits to the Sunbelt states. However, all immigration policy is a political football, particularly after the 9/11 terrorist attacks, and it is difficult to predict how soon, if at all, any form of retirement visa will again be available. This surprises many Canadians who do not intend to become any burden whatsoever on the U.S. economy.

Canadians who retire in the United States find not only a bit of sunshine for themselves but they also help brighten the lives and economies in the communities where they make their home. That's why *The Border Guide* supports the passage of a retiree immigration visa status. Making this kind of farsighted legislation happen, however, needs support from readers like you.

If you agree that the United States needs a retiree immigration visa status, share your thoughts with Uncle Sam. Write to your favourite Congress person or any of the representatives in any state you winter or travel in.

Although immigration is now a hot issue, you can help diffuse some of the controversy by sharing some of your positive contributions. Remind Congress that Canadians support the U.S. economy with real estate purchases, retail sales, taxes and just by being nice folks! Each time an immigrant is bashed by some opportunistic politician, the chances of the retiree visa diminish. Make your voice count now! Even though you may not be able to vote, the people who work at the businesses you support certainly do. In 1998 and 2000, separate bills for a retirement visa were introduced in the House of Representatives, but they both failed to get to a vote, as regularly scheduled elections in those respective years changed the House make up and priorities. No new bills have since been introduced. Consequently, we need to find a new member of Congress to take up this cause.

Since there is no retirement visa yet, how, then, can you legally retire in the United States? In this chapter we have covered many immigration options, all of which apply to anyone, officially retired or not. In spite of this, most Canadian retirees or business people probably travel to the United States as temporary visitors. Because of the relationship between Canada and the United States, entering each other's country as a visitor is free of any formalities, at least for the time being, even though there are certain requirements that must be followed.

There are really two types of non-immigrant status for these people: visitors for business and visitors for pleasure. Visitors for business are B-1 visitors. Visitors for pleasure are B-2 visitors. The USCIS normally allows Canadians six months when they enter on this temporary visitor status. The B-1 and B-2 visas for Canadians require no formal application or documentation. All that's required to be allowed into the United States on this status is a simple statement with respect to the time and purpose of your visit. Although B-1 and B-2 visas allow you to remain in the United States for only six months, there is no prohibition against leaving the country and re-entering, even if it's only a day trip to Mexico. However, if you are entering the United States with the sole intention of remaining there as a resident, you would be entering under false pretenses. You will be considered an illegal alien, so leaving and re-entering would do you little good. The new U.S. restrictions requiring visitors to check in and out of the U.S. with full biometric identification, regardless of their mode of travel, by June 1, 2009 (this may be delayed further) mean that the amount of time a visitor spends in the U.S. will be tracked very closely.

In Chapter 1, we discussed the differences between being a legal resident of the United States for tax purposes and being one for immigration purposes. Consequently, leaving the United States after six months as a visitor and then re-entering may work on a limited basis for immigration purposes, but it will also subject you to a whole new set of tax-rules as you become a U.S. taxpayer on your world income. Refer back to Chapter 3 for more on the tax implications of remaining in the United States for more than six months a year.

THE BORDER KIT

As a temporary visitor, the retiree or business visitor must maintain a residence in Canada, because he or she cannot intend to reside permanently in the United States. This has been made critically important, given the new powers granted U.S. border officials in 1997 to ban anyone from entering the United States for five years, without appeal, whom they suspect is an illegal resident of the United States rather than a legal visitor. To avoid problems in being refused entry when you enter as a visitor, carry The Border Kit to prove you have a residence in Canada and are intending to return there. Include the following items in your Border Kit:

- most recent phone and other utility bills
- most recent property tax notice if you own, or rental agreement if you rent
- most recent Canadian tax return and non-resident IRS forms filed, such as Form 8840 or 1040NR (see Chapter 3)
- valid provincial driver's licence and medicare card
- proof of employment if still employed (e.g., latest pay stub)
- Canadian vehicle registrations if driving, or return plane tickets if flying

Don't carry any items that may indicate U.S. residency, such as a U.S. driver's licence, U.S. mail, anything relating to U.S. property you might own, U.S. bank credit cards, etc.

Although carrying this Border Kit may be a pain, Murphy's Law means that if you have the kit in your possession when you enter the United States, you likely won't be asked to produce proof of Canadian residence, but the first time you travel without it you may be refused entry until you can provide the proof.

RED FLAGS WHEN CROSSING THE BORDER

In addition to carrying the Border Kit, you can make cross-border travel in either direction much less stressful if you avoid the red flags that immigrations and customs officers are constantly on the lookout for. Some of these red flags are —

- travelling without a valid passport
- travelling on a one-way ticket
- travelling on a ticket that was purchased for cash and/or immediately before a flight

- travelling with U.S. residency documents ready for filing
- travelling in a vehicle that is not registered to you or any other person in the vehicle
- travelling in a vehicle registered to you in a country in which you have no legal immigration status — for example, a Canadian winter visitor in the U.S. attempting to drive a Florida-registered car into Canada
- travelling with a spouse or other companion who has a different immigration status than you do in the country you are attempting to enter — for example, a U.S. citizen or green card holder traveling to the U.S. with a Canadian companion who has no legal status in the U.S. and is attempting to enter the U.S. as a visitor
- attempting to cross the border under the influence of alcohol or drugs
- having a common name. Although having a common name is not your fault, your identity may be confused with many others whose names are similar and who are on a terrorist watch list, for example. You may mitigate this concern by having your passport or other forms of identification spelling out your entire name. For example, use John Albert Smith rather than John A. Smith and be very diligent in avoiding any other of the red flags noted above.
- having different names or variations of your name on your plane ticket and passport
- travelling with someone who has potentially one or more of the red flags noted above

CANADIAN RESIDENTS HOLDING GREEN CARDS

It is estimated that thousands of Canadians who currently reside in Canada also hold green cards — legal permanent resident (LPR) status — in the United States, because of previous employment, former more open immigration policies or the immigrant lottery. Often, these people are not sure what they should do with their green cards — whether they should leave them in the drawer, move to the United States, throw them away or get in touch with the USCIS for direction.

Anyone holding a green card under these circumstances needs to carefully consider his options before deciding whether to use it or lose it.

In strict technical terms, when green card holders take up permanent residency outside the United States, they have abandoned their LPR green card status. Actually, they still are in possession of the green card and could use it to take up full-time residency in the United States as long as they appeared in all respects to be U.S. residents. Some Canadians have had their cards seized when entering the United States because they gave immigration officials reason to believe that they were no longer permanent residents of the United States.

Keeping your green card active entitles you to all its privileges, such as being able to live and work year-round in the United States. On the other hand, a green card comes with corresponding responsibilities, such as filing tax returns and maintaining a presence in the United States. The tax consequences of holding a green card are discussed in Chapter 3 and the tax advantages are given in Chapter 8, 9 and 14. Since it is very difficult for most people to obtain green cards, Canadian residents who have them should carefully consider all their options before making any decision. There is no real middle ground here, as the USCIS allows no lengthy stays outside the United States without having to meet admission criteria for re-entry. The only way to keep your green card is to use it. The following guidelines should help those who wish to maintain their green card LPR:

- Use your green card every time you enter the United States.

- Maintain clear evidence of residence. For example, file U.S. Income Tax Returns, use a U.S. driver's licence and vehicle registration, keep U.S. bank and investment accounts — all with a U.S. address that belongs to you and you return to very frequently.

- Keep your Alien Resident Card information current. You can update by filing Form I-90 if your name changes or Form AR-11 for change of address.

- Ensure trips to Canada or abroad don't exceed one year from your last U.S. entry date. (If you anticipate an absence from the United States for longer than one year, obtain a Re-entry Permit (USCIS Form I-131) before leaving. Re-entry Permits are valid for a maximum of two years and cannot be renewed.)

If, after weighing all the factors, you are certain there will be no advantages to your keeping your green card, you should mail it to any U.S. Consulate office or surrender it next time you cross the border. As noted in U.S. Tax Legislation Concerning Expatriation from the United States in Chapter 3, long-term green card holders may be subject to some specific U.S. tax rules when they give up their green cards. Extreme caution and professional advice from a cross-border financial planner are recommended before you give up a green card or U.S. citizenship.

MARRIAGE TO A U.S. CITIZEN

Every year, probably thousands of Canadians marry American citizens. Many of these are second marriages, where the respective spouses have been widowed by their previous partners. Many others are couples who met at U.S. colleges or workplaces.

These marriages will trigger several important decisions that cannot be ignored without some major tax problems or missed opportunities. Some of the issues facing these cross-border couples are the following:

- Where do they as a couple actually reside?

- Where and how do they file tax returns for their maximum advantage?

- How do they revise their estate plan to fit a cross-border situation that avoids double estate taxation, takes advantage of all available deductions and in addition is fair to children from former marriages?

- How do they maximize government benefits such as CPP/QPP, OAS, Social Security and U.S. or Canadian medicare?

- How do they merge the two separate families in the two countries into their own personal goals, financial or otherwise?

All these issues are covered indirectly through discussions in other chapters. This section will attempt to put them all into focus. Cross-border marriages may be a common occurrence, but there is little assistance available and a great need for cross-border financial planning.

The first area of concern is which country to call home. For a retired married couple, this becomes largely a matter of choice; for those who are still working, where their skills will be most effectively employed and where the jobs are available will be important factors. A Canadian citizen spouse can sponsor a U.S. citizen spouse for permanent resident status in Canada, or a U.S. citizen spouse can sponsor a Canadian citizen spouse for a green card into the United States. (It should be noted here that it can be much easier to cross the border together if you can explain to the border officials that you both are legal residents in the same country — whichever country you may choose. Otherwise, many red flags come up with immigration officials, and it can be very stressful trying to explain your situation every time you cross.) The third option is for each spouse to remain a resident of his or her original country and a non-resident of the spouse's country. This third option presents some unique tax and border-crossing difficulties as noted above and is recommended only in unusual circumstances, and then only on a short-term basis.

Many couples in similar situations make their decisions based on the economic realities of where they can get the best results from their combined financial resources. The major issues to consider here are income and estate taxes, medical coverage and the cost of living.

The cost of living, especially when you include income tax and the Goods and Services Tax (GST), is generally accepted to be lower in the United States. Depending on lifestyle, large savings can be achieved by a couple spending the majority of their time in the U.S.

Income taxes are covered in detail in both Chapters 3 and 8. Estate tax issues are discussed in Chapters 4, 9 and 14. Chapters 5 and 13 cover medicare, medical insurance and the entitlements to government-sponsored programs such as U.S. Social Security, the Canada Pension Plan/Quebec Pension Plan and Old Age Security. A complete review of these chapters, preferably before the marriage takes place, will go a long way toward making your marriage a more fruitful and happy one.

Even after reviewing all the issues in the previous chapters and making the appropriate calculations, it should be abundantly clear that there is no easy answer as to where a Canadian-American couple should reside. It really depends on personal preference, along with a combination of all the other factors applied to your personal situation. A complete cross-border financial planning analysis can help you determine the financial implications of either move. The assistance of a cross-border financial planner is recommended for couples in this situation and his or her guidance should result in a good return on the investment of time and money. Ideally, both spouses should attempt to become dual citizens to maximize flexibility for themselves and their families for the rest of their lives.

WHAT TO DO IF YOU ARE REFUSED ENTRY TO THE UNITED STATES

A traveller's greatest fear when crossing an international border is being hassled by some overly officious immigration officer. Many of you have heard stories about friends or relatives being detained or turned away for no apparent reason. Perhaps their vacation plans were ruined because an immigration officer misinterpreted an innocent remark. Some of you may have even had this happen to you. Are you really defenceless against the onslaught of a border guard who is just having a bad day? Absolutely not! Here are some things you can do to ease your exits and entries to and from the United States, and eliminate some of the stresses involved with dealing with immigration:

- Have proper personal identification. We recommend Canadians always carry a valid passport.

- If you are a frequent border crosser, consider one of the new Nexus programs that are, in effect, a pre-screening to allow for more rapid border crossing. With these programs you normally won't speak to a customs and immigration official at all when crossing the border in either direction.

- Complete honesty is a must when being questioned by an immigration official.

- Produce a green card or other U.S. visa to the immigration official if you have these documents.

- Be prepared to provide proof that you intend to return to Canada if you are a visitor to the United States. You should always keep a Border Kit as noted in this chapter.

- If you are refused entry to the United States and can't see any quick resolution, ask for a deferred ruling to the USCIS office nearest to where you will be staying. You may be allowed to enter the United States until a hearing is set up, and you will get to present your case in a more favourable environment. You may also ask for "parole," which will also allow you to enter the U.S. and give you enough time to straighten out the particular concern in question. You will also have the time to engage an immigration attorney. These deferred hearings are extremely difficult to arrange based on new powers granted in 1997 to border officials that allow them to act more like an on-the-spot judge and jury. Deferred hearings and parole require additional paperwork and effort on the part of the immigration official. So if you don't know to ask for them, officials are very unlikely to offer you these options.

CROSS-BORDER Q&A

PROFESSIONAL CANADIAN WANTS TO WORK IN THE U.S.

I am a Canadian Certified General Accountant with a Bachelor of Commerce undergraduate degree. I am currently employed in the public education K–12 sector as a Chief Financial Officer in a large school district in British Columbia, Canada.

I am very interested in relocating to California with my spouse and child to work in my professional capacity. To date, I have made application to several opportunities that I have found on the Internet in the K–12 and college sectors.

How should I respond to employers with respect to eligibility to work in the States (i.e., what is involved and how long will it take for me to be eligible to work in California)?

I appreciate whatever advice you may provide. Thank you.

— Phil T., Maple Ridge, British Columbia

You should tell your respective employers that you have the qualifications to get an H1B visa for full-time employment, which can be obtained on an accelerated basis in about three weeks, provided you pay a $1,000 fee with the application by the potential employer. Then, once you start work, you could have them sponsor you for a green card, as the H1B is good for only six years, maximum. You should also have a good immigration attorney. Let me know if you need a referral.

PLAN AHEAD FOR CROSS-BORDER MARRIAGE

My fiancé and I are engaged to be married. We are both 65 plus and retired. This is a new and different venture for us because I am a citizen of the United States and she is a Canadian. We have so many unanswerable questions we would hope you can help us:

1. *Would it be beneficial for each of us to apply for American and Canadian citizenship? I understand that I would have to sponsor her application to the USCIS for permanent resident alien status. Is the acceptance of this application a green card? And if you keep this green card for three years, does this entitle you to U.S. citizenship? What is the procedure? To apply for the green card, is it acceptable to live six months in Canada and six months in the United States?*

2. *How do I apply for Canadian citizenship?*

3. *Would it be advisable to apply for dual citizenship?*

4. *When we are married, will we continue to submit our income tax forms to our individual countries? Or because we will be married, does that mean we will both have to submit to both countries? My income is approximately $30,000; hers is about $21,000.*

5. *I own two condos in Florida; she owns one. If we rent two of these, the rent about covers the cost of ownership. Would it be advisable to sell two of these condos and invest the money received? I presently have investments worth $25,000 in the United States. She has about $85,000 invested in mutual funds in Canada. She owns a condo in Ontario and currently we plan to spend six months there and six months in Florida. However, there may come a time when we might prefer to spend eight months in Florida and four months in Canada; hence the need for dual citizenship.*

6. *Is a living trust a good thing? My will has been prepared in Florida and hers in Ontario. Are these acceptable in each other's residence or must they be prepared in both places?*

7. *Upon death, will our estates be treated by Canadian, U.S. or both laws?*

8. *If there is anything else you can suggest to us, we would appreciate hearing from you.*

— *J.T., Sanibel, Florida*

Your questions are very good and very relevant for anyone in your situation. However, most of the questions require lengthy detailed analysis and answers to put you in a position to take the correct action. I will give you the key issues you need to resolve to obtain the answers to your questions.

There are several steps you need to go through before or immediately after you are married to determine the best course to take. The first step is to determine which country you are going to call your tax home. That should be the country where you are married and start the immigration process for the immigrating spouse. Once you are married, you should remain in that country until the immigrating spouse has legal documentation not only to legally remain there but to leave and re-enter the country. This will in turn determine what tax filings, estate-planning documents, immigration requirements, medical coverage and other forms of insurance you will require. If you attempt to be residents of both countries or if one spouse is to be a resident of Canada and the other a resident of the United States, you will have an endless state of confusion about which tax, estate and immigration requirements apply and which don't. Generally speaking, you want to be in a position to have to file the least number of returns and pay the least amount of taxes, but residency and/or U.S. citizenship all affect what returns you file.

A cross-border financial plan is definitely in order to determine which country you should call your tax home. This plan will determine such things as the amount of income tax you would pay according to which country and which scenario you are looking at and net out any potential increases or decreases in other costs such as medical coverage and estate taxes. The plan should show which country is best for you from a financial standpoint. Then it becomes easier to determine whether to become a dual citizen, what tax returns you should file, what changes have to be made to your wills or trusts, what changes have to be made to your investments and what medicare and other government benefits you can obtain.

Just because you call one country or the other your tax home does not prohibit you from spending time in both countries. Just remember to spend the most time in the country you are calling your tax home.

I realize I have not answered your questions directly but the issues go much deeper than you have anticipated and are not easily addressed until some cross-border financial planning is completed. A financial plan through an experienced cross-border financial planner is in order.

DERIVATIVE CITIZEN WANTS TO SPONSOR SONS

I am 53 and an only child. My father passed away ten years ago. He was born in Vancouver and moved to L.A. with his mother in about 1930. He was married twice to American citizens and was also in the U.S. Navy. His last divorce was in about 1942, and both his divorces were done in the U.S. His Navy records indicate naturalization in 1942 (he used to be British). I have no documentation to show he was a U.S. citizen other than Navy papers, marriage and divorce papers, birth certificate, etc. He stayed in the U.S. for over 12 years and I have records of all previous addresses. He married my mother in 1948 and lived in B.C. for the rest of his life. He never voted in Canada because he claimed he was a U.S. citizen. He also collected U.S. Social Security in 1990 and a portion of that was left to my mother when he died (mother later died in 1998). In 1992 I became her U.S. trustee to look after her Social Security, and she and I were both given Social Security cards.

I have two sons who want me to become a dual citizen so that eventually they can also have the option of working in the U.S. I have been working on this for two years for proof of him being U.S. citizen. Even though I have lots of paperwork on his personal history, I don't have documents to show that he was legally a U.S. citizen. I contacted the U.S. Navy six months ago for a search and have not yet heard from them. What do you suggest?

— Gail L., Vancouver, British Columbia

You should be gathering documentation for the purpose of applying for a U.S. passport rather than a Certificate of U.S. Citizenship. You are probably a U.S. citizen already by birth, either through your father or your mother or both. However, with all of the concerns regarding security these days, it is possible that the passport office will ask you to go back and apply for a Certificate of Citizenship first; this may happen if the quality of your documentation is poor. In spite of this, applying for a passport is your quickest and easiest route to determine if you are U.S. citizen. Passport application is normally processed in only four to eight weeks so you'll know very quickly an answer to your dual citizenship status.

The U.S. Navy may or may not have a copy of your father's naturalization certificate. U.S. Citizenship and Immigration Services, formerly INS, is the agency most likely to have a copy. It may take six months or longer to get copies of records from either the Navy or USCIS. What about your mother's U.S. citizenship documentation, as that too can be used to prove you are a U.S. citizen.

Once you have proof, such as a U.S. passport or U.S. Certificate of Citizenship, that you are a U.S. citizen and that you are living in the U.S. or have the intention of living in the U.S., you can sponsor your sons for green cards. Once they've lived in the U.S. for five years, they can apply for U.S. citizenship and therefore become dual citizens of Canada and the U.S. as well.

U.S. CITIZENSHIP IS A MATERNAL MATTER

I am interested in finding out about becoming an American resident. I retired eight years ago from a career in the Canadian Armed Forces and the federal government. My wife and I own a condominium in Canada where we live during the summer months. We also own a home in Florida near Tampa where we spend up to six months per year.

I am particularly interested in knowing more about derivative citizenship. I was born in Ontario in 1931. My father was Canadian but my mother is American, born in Chicago, Illinois. I understand there is some U.S. legislation pending that would allow me to claim U.S. citizenship. I believe it is known as the "Equity in Citizenship Act." I have not been able to track any progress in this legislation and fear it may not be passed before the current session of U.S. Congress ends. Perhaps you could inform me of its current and future status.

On the pessimistic assumption that there is no future for this legislation, I wonder what other avenues are available to me. Is there any possibility that a claim in court for American citizenship based on the inequities of the present legislation would prove successful?

— D.W., Mount Hope, Ontario

I have great news for those people in your position. The Immigration Technical Corrections Bill was passed October 6, 1994. This means that those born before 1934 to U.S. citizen mothers have derived U.S. citizenship from their mothers. Before this Technical Corrections Bill, citizenship could be derived only through a U.S. citizen father. Your best bet is to apply for a U.S. passport to affirm your U.S. citizenship status. A strong note of caution: Complete a comprehensive cross-border financial plan to ensure you are aware of the tax implications of being a U.S. citizen.

KNOW U.S. RULES FOR RESIDENCY CHANGE

My husband and I are thinking about residing in Florida on a permanent basis about five years from now. We will be 75 and 76 respectively at that time and feel that the 1,300-mile trip from northern Ontario will become too difficult. We need to know the following:

1. *Health insurance — how will it affect us?*

2. *What do we need to do to achieve resident status but keep our Canadian citizenship?*

We both have government pensions and pensions set up by ourselves. There would be no income from the United States except small amounts of interest income from bank accounts.

— A.C., Clearwater, Florida

1. Health insurance in most U.S. states is difficult to obtain when you are over 65 since most U.S. residents are covered by U.S. Medicare starting at 65. U.S. insurance carriers generally provide only supplemental coverage to Medicare. Your retirement medical package included with your government pensions may provide you some limited coverage in the U.S. You can buy into U.S. Medicare if you have been a legal permanent resident for five years, are a U.S. citizen or have worked in that country for a minimum of ten years. There is limited coverage from insurance carriers outside the United States for those over 65. Lloyd's of London or the Danish company Danmark or other similar companies from a good international insurance broker may be useful for your health insurance coverage in the United States. Don't forget about long-term nursing care insurance since U.S. Medicare and other health insurance policies don't cover extended care for long-term disabilities or incapacities. This coverage can be obtained at any age up to around 85 from numerous U.S. insurance companies.

2. To achieve residency you need either a family or a business to sponsor you for a visa or a green card (legal permanent resident) status. This may be difficult under current law as there are few options available for retired persons.

Once you have legal immigration status in the U.S., income tax would not likely be a problem for you since rates in Florida are much lower than they are in any Canadian province. You would have to file a return on your world income in the United States and you would cease to file any returns in Canada if you became a U.S. resident. CRA would withhold a non-resident withholding tax of 15% on all your non-CPP/QPP or OAS pensions and 10% on interest earned in Canada, and you would receive credit for this tax when you filed your returns in the United States. CRA will not withhold any tax on CPP/QPP and OAS payments for non-residents. You need to calculate the difference between your reduction in tax, food, clothing and housing costs and the cost of your health insurance to see if you'll come out ahead. For more information on these topics I suggest you obtain advice from a cross-border financial planning professional.

RECLAIMING CANADIAN CITIZENSHIP IS A COMPLICATED, LENGTHY PROCESS

I became a U.S. citizen in 1974, three years before the new Canadian citizenship law in 1977. I would like to reclaim my Canadian citizenship without jeopardizing my U.S. citizenship. Is that feasible without resorting to an application to a citizenship court? Are you aware of any challenges to claim dual citizenship on any basis for a case similar to mine?

— Brian M., Kanata, Ontario

Under the current set of rules, the only way you could reclaim your Canadian citizenship is to become a landed immigrant in Canada. This would require having a family member in Canada sponsor you; then once you have immigrated to Canada, you must reside there for at least five years. As a landed immigrant in Canada, you can apply for Canadian citizenship; the U.S. will not require you to give up citizenship just because you have taken this step. Although it may be a lengthy process, you can become a dual citizen. Those Canadians who became U.S. citizens after 1977 did not lose their Canadian citizenship and are therefore dual citizens who don't need to go through this complicated process.

GREEN CARD GONE? START OVER AGAIN

My spouse and I are in good health and financially independent. We are aware that since the mid-1970s, there has been no separate visa category for us due to changes in the U.S. immigration rules. You state in your book that those who have had a five-year continuous legal permanent residence in the United States and have not had any interruptions over six months for five years are eligible for U.S. citizenship by naturalization.

Both of us had green cards from the 1950s, until we surrendered them to U.S. immigration in 1969 for family reasons. I would appreciate your comments on the following questions:

1. *Since we had a green card and were physically present in the United States without any interruptions over six months for five years, are we eligible for naturalization via application form N-400?*

2. *Regarding taxation, is the criteria residency or citizenship?*

3. *Where does dual citizenship fit into this situation?*

— Hollis and Anne G., Gravenhurst, Ontario

Sorry — when you turned in your green cards in 1969, you gave up the qualifications you had to become naturalized U.S. citizens. You could have become naturalized U.S. citizens at that time in 1969, but since you are no longer legal permanent residents of the United States, you cannot use the USCIS Form N-400. In effect, you have to start over and get another green card each for legal permanent residence and have them for five years before you apply again. If you had any children while you lived in the United States who are U.S. citizens, they can sponsor you for the new green cards.

BORN IN THE UNITED STATES, DUAL CITIZENSHIP NOT LOST

I believe our situation is just the reverse of one you covered in a newspaper article. My husband and I had three children, all born in the United States and U.S. citizens until they became Canadian citizens in 1972. We had always assumed that by doing this we lost U.S. citizenship. Is this true?

— Ethel M., Indian Harbour Beach, Florida

When your children became Canadian citizens in 1972, they did not lose their U.S. citizenships. Under new U.S. immigration rules introduced in 1992, they would not be considered to have given up their U.S. citizenship in 1972, unless it was specifically their intention to do so. If it was not their intent or they are not sure whether it was their intent, they can likely reinstate their U.S. citizenship by contacting the U.S. State Department for a passport or the U.S. Immigration and Naturalization Service for an N-600 form.

OBTAINING A GREEN CARD

We are retired and financially independent Canadians and we want to retire in Arizona. What are our chances of immigrating to the United States? What is a "green card" and how do we get one? Does it help that I have a brother who is a green card holder and living in Florida?

— Axel R., Phoenix, Arizona

There are two basic ways of immigrating to the United States. One is to achieve permanent resident status through a job, and the other is through a relative. There are other ways as well, but these can involve lengthy immigration proceedings. In your case, since your brother already has a green card, immigration through a relative seems like the better possibility. However, a lawful permanent resident (or green card holder) cannot petition for his siblings. He must become a U.S. citizen to do so. Citizenship normally requires five years of permanent residence, unless the permanent residence was acquired through a U.S. citizen spouse, in which case the permanent resident need only wait three years before filing his application for U.S. citizenship.

Once sworn in as a U.S. citizen, your brother may immediately file a visa petition for you in the category of "fourth preference." The date of filing becomes your priority date as far as the wait associated with most preference visa categories. At the current time, the "quota wait" for fourth preference for Canada is 13 years. If this seems out of the question, you could try the business routes to immigration. If you have $500,000 to invest, you may be able to obtain a green card in a matter of months.

DERIVATIVE CITIZENSHIP

My parents were both U.S. citizens, but I was born in Canada and have lived there all my life. I am now 69. Could I obtain U.S. citizenship easily if I wanted to? Similarly, my wife, who is 66, also had U.S. citizens as parents. Would it be any easier for her to get U.S. citizenship?

— Donald E., Scottsdale, Arizona

One or both of you may already be U.S. citizens. You must prove your derivative citizenship by filing Form N-600, Application for Certificate of Citizenship, along with supporting documentation with the U.S. Citizenship and Immigration Service (USCIS) or apply for a U.S. passport from the State Department.

Based on your ages, citizenship could only have been transmitted through either or both of your respective parents. You must discover whether your parents ever knowingly abandoned their U.S. citizenships before your birth, by taking an oath of allegiance to the government of Canada and forswearing allegiances to all other nations.

In the event that documentary evidence is lacking for one of your derivative citizenship claims, all is not lost. It would only be necessary for one of you to prove U.S. citizenship. The other could immigrate as the immediate relative of the U.S. citizen, a category for which there is no quota or wait.

HIRING AN IMMIGRATION ATTORNEY

When should I use an attorney to help me immigrate to the United States? What would it cost relative to my status? How long does it take?

— Alice C., Tucson, Arizona

There is no law that says immigration documents may not be filed by an individual. However, there may be alternatives available to you that you may find out about only through a consultation with an attorney. Certainly, if you have a problem with the Immigration Service, you would be well advised to get professional assistance immediately. Most immigration attorneys work on an hourly basis.

IMMIGRATION STRATEGIES AND THE NEED FOR FINANCIAL PLANNING

My husband and I wish to immigrate to the United States. My husband is a civil technologist currently employed by a road construction firm. I run my own advertising and promotions firm, registered as an Ontario corporation.

1. *How can we immigrate with a minimum of fuss and expense? (I have heard rumours about bringing in $100,000 and hiring one employee.) What are the costs involved? Also, my husband's sister has lived and worked in Michigan for the last 15 years. If she becomes an American citizen, could she sponsor us and could we both get jobs and work? How long would it take for her to get U.S. citizenship and sponsor us?*

2. *Would it be to our greater advantage to procure jobs in order to immigrate? Or is it a disadvantage to me, especially since I have an existing corporation?*

3. *If we are no longer Canadian residents, I assume there are tax advantages, but does this lack of residency affect our current investments, such as our family home (must we sell?), our RRSPs held in a Canadian brokerage house, our life insurance held by Canadian firms, etc?*

— Laura P., Toronto, Ontario

1. From what you have told me, the best alternative for you to immigrate to the United States would likely be through your business. By forming a similar business in the United States, you have created the means for you to qualify for a visa under Treaty Investor Route (E-2) or a regular intra-company transfer (L-1), or even the new green card category (E-1C) for established businesses, similar to the L-1.

    The E-2 is likely the quickest and easiest to achieve. Many good immigration attorneys recommend you invest $100,000 or more in the U.S. business to qualify for this type of visa. However, Arizona immigration attorneys working for our clients in non-capital intensive service industries similar to your business have received E-2 visas for investments of less than $100,000. Even though there is no requirement to hire U.S. workers, the more employment you can create and the more capital you have to back up your business, the better off you will be.

The best long-term route, if you can swing it, is the green card route through a transfer from your established Canadian company to the U.S.-affiliated company you would set up. The green card confers permanent residency status, whereas all the other visas may be subject to continuing requirements and/or have expiration dates.

Your husband's sister can become a naturalized U.S. citizen if she has had her green card for five years or longer. It is currently taking seven to twelve months, from date of application, to complete this process. Once she is a citizen she can sponsor your husband for permanent resident status (or green card). However, there is a waiting list in this category of nearly 15 years. It wouldn't hurt to get on this waiting list as sometimes quotas are changed, and the waiting list can disappear, or at least be shortened.

As you can see, the maze of rules and regulations can be overwhelming, and I recommend you use a good immigration attorney in the area where you are likely to relocate. Be prepared to spend $3,000 to $5,000 on legal fees to get the job done for you and your husband. If you are well organized and can do a lot of the necessary work yourself, the legal fees could be lower, but they will increase if you do not have a concrete plan of action that you can outline to the attorney.

2. You will not be able to procure legal employment in the United States unless you have a visa or have some special skills or education that allows you a work visa, based on these exceptional qualifications. If you have a Ph.D. or other post-secondary degree(s) or equivalent experience, your immigration attorney will direct you to these special categories.

3. As far as taxes and other financial matters are concerned, there are some good planning opportunities and there are some pitfalls. These are difficult to condense and require a great deal of factual analysis. To ensure you maximize the opportunities and avoid the pitfalls, I recommend you complete a comprehensive financial plan, with the assistance of a professional planner who is knowledgeable in both Canadian and U.S. tax, investment, estate and insurance requirements.

IS U.S. CITIZENSHIP REQUIRED FOR ESTATE TAX EXEMPTIONS?

You mentioned in a previous article that dual citizenship exists, and that Canada does not revoke citizenship if one chooses to become a United States citizen. Does the United States also allow a U.S. citizen to remain a citizen of Canada?

My husband and I are both Canadian citizens by birth who became permanent U.S. residents and green card holders in 1977. We live permanently in Florida. Our problem is whether to become U.S. citizens to take advantage of the $2 million exemption from estate tax, since you mentioned that only U.S. citizens can take full advantage of this exemption.

— **M.S., North Miami, Florida**

It is Canada's choice whether you keep your Canadian citizenship. Only the country conferring citizenship can require that person to relinquish prior citizenship. For the time being Canada allows individuals to retain Canadian citizenship after becoming U.S. citizens.

Since you are a green card holder domiciled in the United States, you already qualify for the $2 million estate tax exemption and so does your husband. You do not have to become U.S. citizens to qualify for these exemptions.

As a U.S. citizen you gain the ability to defer estate tax on estates over $2 million to the second spouse's death by using the unlimited marital deduction. You may use a qualified domestic trust to take advantage of the unlimited marital deduction as an alternative to becoming a citizen.

If your or your husband's estate(s) are worth more than $2 million, you need to consider your options with the help of a professional estate planner. If you still have assets in Canada you'll need a cross-border estate planner.

THE REAL DEAL ON DUAL CITIZENSHIP

I am confused about dual citizenship. I have it on good authority that dual citizenship is only possible under some very unusual circumstances in the United States. Would you kindly tell me the real facts on this issue.

— **Ray Y., Venice, Florida**

To start off, dual citizenship does exist. I am a Canadian citizen myself and have become a U.S. citizen. Since Canada does not require that I give up my Canadian citizenship, I am a dual citizen. In my practice, I have recommended and assisted many clients to become dual citizens and personally know many others.

Dual citizenship comes not from any formal application for "dual citizenship" but by default. Consequently, individuals calling the U.S. Citizenship and Immigration Service offices in particular, or even Canadian consulates in the United States, inquiring about how they can qualify for or apply for dual citizenship get a series of blank stares and/or negative responses.

Since 1977, Canada has stopped demanding that Canadians who emigrate and who take up foreign citizenship give up their Canadian citizenship. Although there are only a few other countries in the world that have the same policy, such as the United Kingdom and Israel, the United States also now allows its citizens to hold U.S. citizenship if they become citizens of another country.

So currently you can achieve dual citizenship if you are a Canadian citizen by simply applying for U.S. citizenship and not formally doing anything to renounce your Canadian citizenship. Your new Canadian passport will indicate your dual status. The United States does nothing to formally recognize a dual status situation and ignores the fact that someone applying for U.S. citizenship is retaining the citizenship of the other country.

STAYING ON BOTH SIDES OF THE BORDER

My husband and I have lived and worked in Canada since 1975. I retired in 2003 but my husband is still working and would like to continue until he is eligible for Canadian Pension. We are both 57 years old.

We applied for and received our U.S. resident alien status in February 2003, sooner than we expected, and are not ready to move to the United States yet. We plan on moving permanently when my husband retires. In June 2005, we bought a retirement home in Florida.

I have been living in Florida for six months and six months in Canada since we received our green cards in May 2003, thinking I was within the bounds of immigration laws of both countries this way. We file both U.S. and Canadian income taxes and opted out of the Homestead tax deduction offered for first-time home buyers in Florida.

On my recent trip to the United States, I was questioned at length by U.S. immigration officials in Toronto. I was told I should give up either my green card or my OHIP card. My questions are the following:

1. Can U.S. Immigration confiscate either my green card or OHIP card? Is there a law that entitles them to do this?

2. *Does six months in the United States constitute legal permanent resident status? Does it have to be six consecutive months and only in one particular state?*

3. *If I were to give up my green card, would U.S. Immigration issue me one easily later on when my husband retires? Would it take very long?*

4. *I am covered by my husband's company health plan. If I move earlier and live permanently in Florida, will I still get free medical health coverage without my OHIP card?*

5. *We own properties in Canada and all our investments are there. In light of the continuing decline of the Canadian dollar, the increasing high cost of health care in the United States and the new non-resident tax deduction in effect on CPP and OAS, would we be better off to forget about residing permanently in the United States and just spend six months in Canada and go for six months to Florida in the winter as Canadian tourists?*

— Elaine F., Toronto, Ontario

1. U.S. Immigration has authority to take your green card if they can determine you are not living permanently in the United States, a requirement in order to keep your green card. They cannot take your OHIP card; only OHIP can do that and they may do just that once they discover an OHIP member has a green card.

2. You should not reside outside the United States longer than six months at any stretch and maintain full U.S. residency ties at all times to maintain your green card.

3. Whether you can get another green card depends on how you got it. If you got it in the lottery, you would have to wait for another lottery and hope you are lucky. If some close family member sponsored you, then you would have to reapply, a process that is taking anywhere from six months to five years, depending on preference status.

4. You would have to check with your husband's company benefits department; they should be able to answer this easily. Most plans require you to be a member of OHIP to get full health insurance coverage. OHIP requires you to live at least seven months a year in Ontario. I recommend you shop for U.S. coverage as soon as possible.

5. These kinds of questions require you to have a knowledgeable cross-border financial planner do a detailed cross-border financial analysis. Your planner can compare all the tax, immigration and insurance issues

and provide you with the information you need to make an educated choice. Only you can decide which country will be best for you.

Please note that your husband does not have to work until age 60 to receive CPP. He only needs to wait until age 60 (the earliest age at which he can apply) to start receiving CPP payments.

REASONS FOR BEING REFUSED ENTRY AT THE BORDER

An immigration officer refused us entry into the United States last November because we rented our house in Canada for six months while we were away. Why? When I mentioned I was born in North Dakota, he said if I hadn't renounced my U.S. citizenship, I could hold dual citizenship. Can I do this?

— E.W., Arizona City, Arizona

It sounds like the immigration official at the border was being a bit overzealous, but if he was concerned you were living in the United States permanently he had every right to refuse you entry as a visitor. Remember that whenever you enter the United States you are presumed to be entering permanently unless you can prove otherwise. It is this proof you must supply, if asked. Carry a border-crossing kit showing property tax notices, recent utility bills, proof of Canadian medicare, vehicle and driver's registration, pay stubs, bank and investment account records to prove you are remaining as residents of Canada.

It is relatively easy for you to confirm if you are still a U.S. citizen by applying for your U.S. passport at the nearest passport office. However, with U.S. citizenship may come tax obligations that you will need to address before you proceed any further. I suggest you contact a knowledgeable cross-border financial planner to analyze your specific situation.

BANNED FROM THE UNITED STATES

My husband and I are Canadian citizens, with a winter home in the United States. We overstayed the six-month limit, and when my husband returned to Canada he was told by U.S. officials he could not come back into the United States for five years or face fines and jail time. I am still in the States (and past my deadline as well). Do you have any advice?

— M.C., Fort Myers, Florida

There is not much you can do, except to get legal with the U.S. Immigration as soon as possible by leaving the United States. When you return to the United States as a visitor, make sure you have clear proof with you that you have not become a resident of the United States. You should carry such items as a copy of your current Canadian tax return, latest utilities paid in Canada, a copy of your home title or lease agreement if you rent, provincial medicare card, Canadian driver's licence, return-trip air fares purchased in Canada if flying, or if travelling by car a Canadian provincial plate on the car. This border kit should always be kept current and be available every time you enter the United States — it probably would have saved your husband all this trouble. You should never stay in the United States longer than six months at a time without returning to Canada unless you have proper immigration status.

As far as your husband's situation, he will have difficulty overcoming the five-year ban. He needs to hire a good U.S. immigration attorney who will go through the very limited procedures to get this ban overturned if he has a good reason for his overstay.

The Grass Is Always Greener 8

CANADIAN VERSUS
U.S. TAXATION POLICIES

O ne of the major considerations for people considering a move to
the United States is how much income tax they may be able to
save. Many Canadians are frustrated by the seemingly endless
spiral of federal and provincial taxes, PST, GST and property taxes. Most
Canadians accept higher taxes as the price of Canada's superior social
welfare system, but recently the higher taxes seem to have come with
commensurate decreases in government services. Have Canadians lost
confidence in the politicians who have created this monster and who now
seem incapable of stopping it? Some Canadians have voted with their feet
by moving to the United States and reaping a major tax cut.

This chapter will address those tax-saving opportunities and will provide good guidance for Canadians who may be derivative citizens of the
United States or have other immigration possibilities. It is for those who
may be looking for some financial advantage by becoming residents of the
United States for tax purposes. Chapters 12 and 13 will discuss the opportunities in investments, medical coverage, insurance and U.S. Social
Security benefits.

In Chapter 3, in the section Canada and United States Income Tax
Comparison, I outlined some of the basic tax rates and tax deduction comparisons between the United States and Canada. These comparisons can
now be incorporated into a cross-border financial plan from the perspective of someone who is actually moving to or contemplating a move to
the United States. I will use real-life examples showing how some Canadians have effectively used cross-border financial planning to maximize
the benefits while minimizing the pitfalls of moving south. Taxpayers in
both Canada and the United States have seen major tax relief. With the
regular federal budget of February 2000 and the mini budget of October
2000, Canadians saw the largest tax decreases in several decades. The
Conservative minority government elected in Canada in 2006 has reduced
the GST by 1% and increased the dividend tax credit. For Canadians who

have experienced nothing but increases annually for most of the 1990s, this is welcome relief indeed. A U.S. Republican-controlled Congress passed sweeping income tax and estate tax cuts in 2001 and 2003, currently scheduled to last to 2011, in an attempt to stimulate the economy by reducing the burden on its taxpayers. Because of constant changes to taxes in both countries, it is important to understand that the tax comparisons in this chapter are a moving target and you will need to incorporate any changes after the printing of this edition of *The Border Guide* to get the latest information. Since 1992, each edition of *The Border Guide* has seen a gradual widening of the gap, in favour of the U.S., with respect to income taxes paid by Canadian and American residents.

First, our discussion looks at a line-by-line analysis of each type of taxable income and deduction, and then I tie it all together using full comprehensive case studies of Canadians who have gone through professional cross-border financial planning.

KEEP MORE OF YOUR CPP/QPP AND OAS

A popular misconception among Canadians is that they lose CPP/QPP and/or OAS benefits after exiting Canada. In fact, the opposite is true and they will actually receive more of their benefits on an after-tax basis. The Canada/U.S. Tax Treaty amendment, effective in 1997 but retroactive to January 1, 1996, provides for some very interesting tax advantages for those Canadians who are collecting or are eligible for CPP/QPP and Old Age Security.

Because of provisions contained in the treaty, both your CPP/QPP and OAS are, for U.S. residents, no longer taxable at all by CRA for U.S. residents and are totally free from non-resident withholding tax. When you file tax returns in the United States as a resident, CPP/QPP and OAS are reported and taxed in a manner similar to U.S. Social Security. That means married couples with incomes of less than US$32,000 (including the CPP/QPP and OAS) or single persons with less than US$25,000 of income do not pay any U.S. tax on this income. Consequently, CPP/QPP and OAS are completely free from both Canadian and U.S. taxes for people in this income bracket. For those at the higher income levels, 85% of the total CPP/QPP and OAS is added to income and taxed at the standard U.S. tax rates; the other 15% is tax free. This means that the maximum federal U.S. tax rate on this income as U.S. residents is 30% even if your income exceeds the highest tax bracket as noted in Figure 3.6.

Since January 1996, Canadian residents in the United States have no longer been subject to the OAS 100% clawback rules as they would be as residents of Canada. This means Canadians moving to the United States who have been subject to the OAS clawback on income of more than $62,144 would be entirely exempt from the clawback regardless of the size of their income once they become U.S. residents. For a high-income married couple, getting out from under the OAS clawback can mean an immediate tax saving on their OAS alone of up to $12,000, depending on their U.S. tax brackets. This is one of the most ironic situations in cross-border planning: you have to leave Canada to get a benefit that it takes 40 years living in Canada to qualify for.

The March 1996 budget lowered the age at which RRSP withdrawals must begin to 69. This will move many more Canadian residents into the OAS clawback range much sooner. We expect CRA to lower this age for the start of RRSP withdrawal in steps from 69 to 65, the age at which OAS kicks in, next time the government is looking for more tax dollars.

Let's look at a real example of what this one item can mean. George and Susan moved from Ottawa to the United States, each with $10,150 of CPP and $6,000 of OAS benefits. This couple is retired and in the highest Canadian tax bracket (Ontario 46.4%) and both are subject to the OAS clawback; the applicable U.S. tax bracket in Florida is 25%. (See Figure 8.7 later in this chapter for details of their incomes. All dollar amounts in Figures 8.1 through 8.8 are in Canadian funds, and I have used the tax rates from Figure 3.6.)

As you can see from Figure 8.1, with the treaty and exemption from OAS clawback rules for non-residents, George would see a drop in his average tax rate (it goes from 65% to a maximum of 21%). This is on his combined CPP and OAS income. The resulting tax saving of $7,034 is significant, especially when you consider that George's wife is in a similar situation. Their combined savings would double that to $14,068. So before George and Susan even consider any potential tax reductions on investment and other pension income, they are in line for a raise of nearly $1,200 a month! Figure 8.7 shows George and Susan's complete sources of income. It is important to note here that although George and Susan are in approximately the top 5% of all income earners in North America, they are only in the middle U.S. income tax brackets.

INTEREST INCOME — TAX FREE, IF YOU WISH

In the United States, municipal bonds are a form of local government bond that pays interest without attracting income tax at either the federal or state levels. These are the bonds cities use to fund public buildings, roads, airports and hospitals. As a result, someone earning a great deal of

CANADIAN AND U.S. TAX RATES ON
CPP AND OAS INCOME, 2006

Income	
CPP	$10,150
OAS	$6,000

	Canadian resident	U.S. resident
Taxable income	$16,150	$13,728
Tax due	$10,466	$3,124
Effective tax rate	65%	21%
Total savings		$7,034

Figure 8.1

interest income can in effect zero out the tax liability on any amount of interest they earn by holding these municipal bonds. Some types of these bonds may be subject to U.S. alternative minimum tax. When you consider that interest in Canada is taxed at rates of up to 49% in some provinces, a zero tax rate looks pretty attractive. From the investment planning aspect (see Chapter 12), it's not wise to place most of your investment portfolio into municipal bonds or any other asset class, for that matter. Municipal bonds are currently paying rates of interest higher than those of most Canadian bank deposits — around 5% compared to about 4% on Canadian term deposits or GICs. If you're in a top Canadian income tax bracket, you will keep only approximately half of the 4% you earn on a GIC. A 5% rate on a tax-free bond would still yield 150% more after taxes if you are a U.S. resident. That is an incredible increase in income on an investment that provides a fixed income with a relatively low level of risk. In fact, at maximum Canadian tax rates, you would have to earn nearly 10% or better on a GIC to net the same amount on an after-tax basis that a 5% tax-free municipal bond does. When was the last time anyone saw 10% paid on a GIC?

In various federal budgets over the past couple of decades, Canada's parliament has gradually eliminated the ability to defer income taxes on Canada Savings Bonds, annuities and long-term GICs. This means that all interest earned on any investment must be paid on a current accrued annual basis and cannot be deferred to a later date when the interest is actually received. For anyone saving for retirement, the ability to defer income tax to a future date, particularly when he or she may be in a lower tax bracket, can dramatically increase total return. For example, if you had $100,000 earning 10% interest over 15 years and were in a 50% tax bracket, you could net $158,850 of earnings after tax if you could defer paying all the tax until the fifteenth year. You would net only $107,900 if you paid the tax on a current or accrual basis under present Canadian tax rules. This amounts to more than a 47% increase in income from a basic investment. That's why RRSPs — with their ability to defer taxes on current income — work so well over the long haul. In addition to receiving a deduction for your RRSP contribution, the interest and other income accumulate tax free. In the United States, the ability to defer tax on interest is not limited to RRSP-like investments. Taxpayers can deposit unlimited sums into investment vehicles, called deferred or variable annuities, that allow for tax-free compounding and deferral of interest, dividends and capital gains for any number of years. Tax is paid on the income only when it is taken out of the annuity at a time of your choice and the withdrawals can be spread over any number of years. Even so, it's still not prudent to place all your investments into tax-free or tax-deferred investments from an investment or an estate-planning standpoint.

Let's call on George and Susan again, to look at the interest income portion of their tax picture, and then compare this with their tax savings potential of moving to the United States. In the example used in Figure 8.2, we assume they have $450,000 of investments in interest-bearing vehicles such as bonds and GICs, earning an average rate of interest of 7%, for a total of $31,500. After moving to the United States, they split their portfolio into one-third tax-free municipal bonds earning 6% or $9,000, one-third tax-deferred annuities earning 7% or $10,500 and leave the remaining one-third in investments similar to those in their Canadian portfolio earning 7% or $10,500. Amounts in Figure 8.2 (and through Figure 8.8) are shown in Canadian funds.

In Figure 8.2, George and Susan's interest income, after taxes are paid, is more than 62% higher. It should be noted that one-third of the investment portfolio is in a tax-deferred annuity and will be subject to tax if withdrawn at some future date. But as we have mentioned, tax deferred can be tax saved. In the 25% tax bracket that George and Susan are in in the United States, you only have to defer the tax for approximately six years before you can save the entire amount.

There is a common misconception that moving to the United States means accepting lower rates of interest on savings. In fact, U.S. interest

CANADA		UNITED STATES	
	Interest income		
$31,500		$9,000	Tax Free
		$10,500	Tax Deferred
		$10,500	Taxable
		$30,000	Total
	Tax due		
$14,616		$2,625	
	Amount left after tax		
$16,884		$27,375	
	Tax saved		
		$14,259	

Figure 8.2

rates are now higher in most cases than they are in Canada, depending on where the Bank of Canada is setting its rates. If you move to the U.S., you can always earn exactly the same rate of interest by leaving your GICs and term deposits in Canada, but own them as a non-resident. This may not be the best alternative from an investment strategy or estate-planning perspective, but it is possible to have and hold Canadian certificates and bank accounts while you are a non-resident. (See Chapters 6 and 12 for more details on investment strategies that reduce risk and increase income.)

PENSIONS — PARTIALLY TAX FREE

There are major differences between the U.S. and Canada in the way pensions are taxed. CRA taxes all pensions by including 100% as taxable income, minus an equivalent exemption of $2,000 each year. The IRS allows pensioners to receive the portion of the pension resulting from the taxpayer contribution tax free. If an individual made 50% of the annual contributions to her company pension, roughly half of her pension at retirement would be tax free. The actual amount received tax free depends on current interest rates and the life expectancy of the employee at the time she starts receiving the pension. The IRS, for example, considers a pension annuity created from an RRSP (which would be fully taxable in Canada) as just a regular annuity. Only the annual interest earned is considered taxable. Thus a significant portion of the monthly payments from your RRSP-created pension would be tax free.

Finally, for those Canadians who have worked in the U.S. during their career and qualify for U.S. Social Security, the IRS provides more tax-favoured treatment, depending on total current income from all sources; anywhere from 100% of U.S. Social Security to a minimum of 15% can be received free from tax.

Let's look at George again. He receives $55,000 a year from a company pension that he contributed to over his 30-year employment. His numbers work out so that the IRS will consider 30% of his pension as excluded from taxation in the United States. Susan did not have a company pension but purchased a 20-year RRSP term annuity. She receives $25,000 a year from this and her return of principal from the annuity would be approximately $10,000 per year. In her case approximately 40% of her annuity would be excluded from U.S. taxes. Figure 8.3 shows the net effect on taxes on George and Susan's pensions by moving to the United States.

George and Susan would effectively cut their tax on the pension portion of their income by 52%. Obviously, this would represent a major raise for them, allowing them to keep $66,625 of their pension after tax, instead of only keeping $43,810 as Canadian residents.

EMPLOYMENT INCOME

Earned income in the U.S. is taxed similarly to the way that same type of income is taxed in Canada — it is added to taxable income. Earned income is taxed at your marginal tax rates in both countries. This makes tax comparisons between Canada and the U.S. very simple.

Although Susan is retired, she still does some management consulting for her former employer. She receives a fee of $30,000 a year. Figure 8.4 compares the taxation on this income between the two countries.

Susan is entitled to a whopping 46% tax reduction if she becomes a U.S. resident. This amounts to an effective 40% after-tax pay raise without her even having to talk to her boss. The tax savings result from the fact that the maximum tax rate is 46.4% for Ontario and 25% in Florida on this amount of income. Other provincial or state tax comparisons would, of course, be different. (See Figure 8.8 for another province and state comparison.)

Although I have not illustrated it here, Susan could have placed $5,600 into an RRSP and deducted this amount from her $30,000

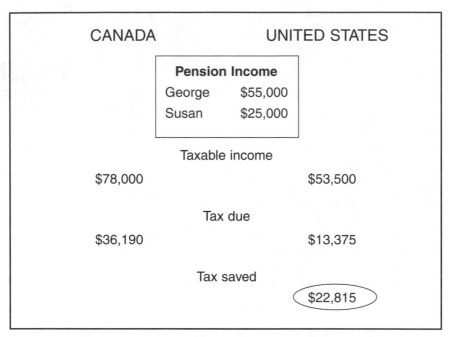

Figure 8.3

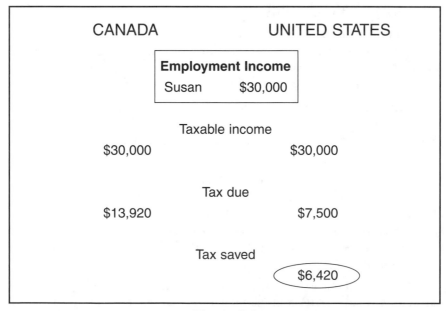

Figure 8.4

employment income in Canada. In the U.S. however, she could have placed up to $11,000 — roughly twice the RRSP deductible amount — into one of several deductible individual retirement account (IRA) options available to her.

CAPITAL GAINS

Capital gains receive some favourable treatment in both Canada and the United States. Since October 2000, Canadians have been allowed to exclude 50% of any capital gains from their taxable income. Consequently, Canadian capital gains are taxed at a maximum of 25%, depending on your province of residence. In the U.S., the maximum federal tax rate on long-term capital gains, those held longer than one year, is 15% in the highest income brackets and 0% in the lowest bracket. Since there is generally considerable risk in the types of investments that produce capital gains, most prudent people do not have a large percentage of their assets tied up in this area of investment. Consequently, the tax savings on capital gains are generally not enough to create any significant advantages either way when contemplating a move to the U.S., unless you have a small or closely held business that is highly appreciated (see Chapter 14).

Those who buy and sell real estate for investment purposes, or as their occupation, will find the ability to roll the gain tax-free from the sale of one property to another purchase of equal or higher value in the U.S. an excellent tax-saving device in those instances where it is applicable. There is also no deemed disposition tax at death on appreciated assets in the U.S., as there is in Canada. In fact, the beneficiary gets a free step-up in cost basis upon the death of the owner of the property. The step-up in cost basis means it is as if the beneficiaries purchased the property on the date of death of the owner at its fair market value. Consequently, a surviving spouse or other beneficiaries who inherit highly appreciated property can sell it free from capital gains tax. Some U.S. estate tax may apply for non-spousal beneficiaries for estates of more than US$2 million.

George and Susan would like to sell some growth mutual funds and real estate. For the current year, they have received capital gains distributions and other trading profits from their mutual funds of $8,000. They also sold a piece of property they had for ten years, which netted them a gain of $22,000. Figure 8.5 displays the results.

The tax reduction on capital gains is over 35% in the U.S., even though only 50% of the gain is taxable in Canada. In the U.S., George and Susan may realize greater tax savings on their capital gains by setting up

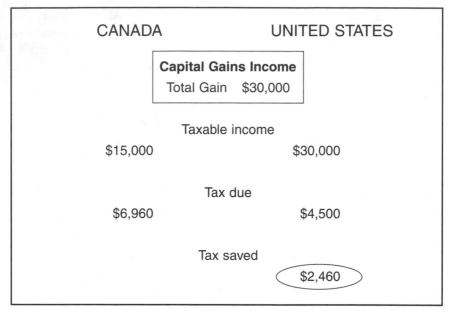

CANADA   UNITED STATES

Capital Gains Income
Total Gain $30,000

Taxable income
$15,000 $30,000

Tax due
$6,960 $4,500

Tax saved
$2,460

Figure 8.5

the mutual funds as a variable annuity. These funds provide for the unlimited deferral of capital gains, interest and dividend income until the deferred income is actually withdrawn.

DIVIDENDS

Dividends are taxed very differently in Canada than they are in the United States. In the United States they are taxed the same way as capital gains, at a maximum rate of 15%. In Canada dividends are multiplied or grossed up by 145% when calculating taxable income. An off-setting tax credit equal to 19% on the federal tax calculation of the grossed-up amount is allowed. This grossed-up amount and offsetting tax credit is new for 2006. As a result of the 2006 federal government budget, Canadians see the tax on dividends cut to roughly half of the pre-2006 rates. This makes the maximum tax rate of 23% on dividends in Ontario comparable to 15% in Florida.

George and Susan have $10,000 of dividend income. Figure 8.6 compares the net result of their earning dividends in each country. As a result of the 2006 budget, George and Susan get a 36% tax reduction dividend income by moving to the U.S. As noted in the section Capital Gains in this chapter, they can use mutual funds in the form of variable annuities to defer income on dividends in the United States and pay no current tax.

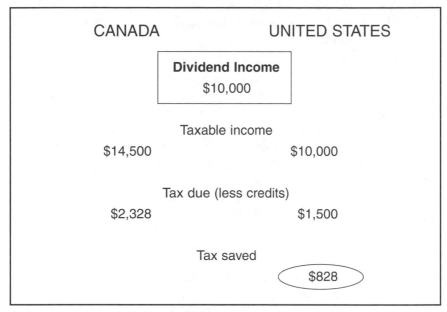

Figure 8.6

In both United States and Canada, dividends are taxed twice, once at the corporate level and again at the individual shareholder's level. As noted in Chapter 6, elimination of this double tax on corporations is the main reason why income trusts have become so popular and why the 2006 federal budget changed tax rules on dividends of public corporations. If you own a dividend-paying corporation, both levels of tax must be considered to do a fair comparison. For someone with a Canadian-controlled small business that qualifies for the small-business tax rate on active business income, the total tax paid on dividends at both the corporate and individual shareholder levels could be less on the Canadian side of the border on corporate income of less than $400,000, depending on the province and other factors. In the United States, it is generally better to pay salaries and bonuses to owner shareholders or use flow-through company structures that pay no tax at the corporate level than it is to pay corporate taxes and dividends. Salaries can be taxed only once, at a maximum federal individual rate of 35% for salaries of more than US$336,551 or about CDN$400,000.

ALIMONY

Alimony is taxed very similarly in both the U.S. and Canada: it is fully taxable to the recipient and fully deductible by the payer. Consequently, someone receiving alimony who is also moving to the U.S. will normally enjoy keeping more of his or her alimony by paying less tax.

However, there is one important cross-border planning tip you should know if you are currently undergoing a divorce and if your spouse is a U.S. citizen or a green card holder (or can get a U.S. visa of any type) and wishes to move back to the U.S. By including in the separation agreement certain legal language regarding spousal support, as specified by the IRS, the Canadian payer spouse can continue to deduct the payment on his or her Canadian tax return, while the U.S. resident spouse is not taxed on the payments for U.S. purposes. The IRS specifications to make this work are complex but are pursuant to Internal Revenue Code Section 71 (b)(1)(B) and Regulation 1.71-IT. Essentially, the alimony payer needs to make a declaration in the agreement that he or she will not deduct any alimony payments for U.S. tax purposes, but since the payer in this case is a Canadian resident and not required to file a U.S. return, it makes no difference. Appropriate cross-border legal help is necessary to make this strategy work, but it can make an enormous difference to the recipient spouse to have the income tax free, while the paying spouse is unaffected.

TOTAL INCOME — THE REAL COMPARISON

The examples used in Figures 8.1 through 8.6 are a good way to compare taxes on major income sources on a line-by-line basis. It does not, however, provide the complete picture, as it does not take into consideration personal deductions, the progressive tax rates and the different filing options available in the two countries. The best way to do a realistic tax comparison is to take the total world income with deductions and simultaneously calculate the Canadian and U.S. tax as if the individuals were residents of either country and then net out the final tax figures.

Since we are already somewhat familiar with George and Susan, we will do their total tax comparison in Figure 8.7 first. George and Susan are both retired, so we will also look at Bill and Mary, who are medical doctors, still working, with dependent children in college, in Figure 8.8. These tax comparisons are based on the estimated 2006 tax rates as available at time of publishing in the United States and Canada so they may produce small differences from similar returns that could be filed based on actual rates.

INCOME

	George	Susan	Combined
CPP	$10,150	$10,150	$20,300
OAS	$6,000	$6,000	$12,000
Pension	$55,000	$25,000	$80,000
Interest	$15,750	$15,750	$31,500
Dividends	$5,000	$5,000	$10,000
Employment	$0	$30,000	$30,000
Capital gains	$15,000	$15,000	$30,000
Total income	$106,900	$106,900	$213,800

CANADA   UNITED STATES

Adjustments to Total Income

CANADA		UNITED STATES	
Dividends	+$4,500	Tax-free interest	−$9,000
Capital gains	−$15,000	Tax-deferred interest	−$10,500
OAS repayment	−$12,000	George's pension	−$16,500
		Susan's pension	−$10,000
		Pers. exemptions	−$10,225
		Standard deductions	−$11,575
		OAS and CPP	−$4,845

Taxable income

$191,900 $141,155

Federal tax credits

$6,428

Net tax due

$64,652 $19,561

Tax savings

$45,089

Figure 8.7

George and Susan are both over 65 and own a summer cottage near Ottawa and a single-family dwelling in Naples, Florida. They pay property taxes, have no mortgages and made no donations for this year so they take the standard deductions for their age rather than itemizing these expenses. They have no sources of income other than those detailed in Figures 8.1 to 8.7.

George and Susan have cut their tax bill by 70% by moving to the United States and have increased their after-tax income by nearly $3,800 per month. If we were to assume that their joint life expectancy is twenty years and that they could invest these annual tax savings to earn an after-tax return of 6%, they would accumulate a total of $1,658,625 in additional net worth over their lifetimes or just enjoy the extra income with more travel, golf or other retirement activities.

The tax reduction enjoyed by George and Susan is quite typical of someone who retires in the Sunbelt. Larger savings can be achieved with more comprehensive cross-border planning. People whose income comes primarily from RRSPs or RRIFs and other investments can realize even greater savings than George and Susan did if they do proper planning. It is important to note that the amount of tax George and Susan actually pay in the U.S. is $0; this is discussed later in this chapter and illustrated in Figure 8.10.

MOVING TO THE U.S. TO CHANGE EMPLOYMENT

Now let's take a look at Bill and Mary, in their late 40s, with two children in college. Bill is an anesthesiologist who earns $250,000 net annually from his practice. Mary is also a doctor who works in a medical clinic as a general practitioner, with a salary of $100,000. They have a large mortgage on their home in Winnipeg with payments of $4,500 per month, interest only, and both make the maximum contribution to their RRSPs each year. Their property taxes are $5,000, vehicle licence is $1,000 and their two children still live at home. They have some joint term deposits that earn about $10,000 per year in interest, making their total income $360,000. Both have job offers in Arizona, at the same income level, adjusted for current exchange rates, and want to compare after-tax income between Manitoba and Arizona. Figure 8.8 shows the results of that comparison.

Even though their circumstances are quite different from George and Susan's, Bill and Mary achieve an even greater level of tax reduction, about 69%, more than a two-third reduction. They would realize an after-tax raise in monthly income of more than $6,920, or $83,044 per year.

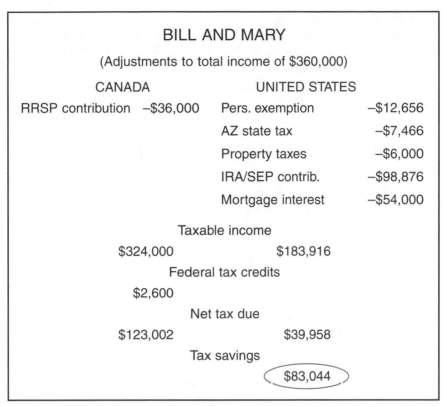

BILL AND MARY

(Adjustments to total income of $360,000)

CANADA	UNITED STATES	
RRSP contribution –$36,000	Pers. exemption	–$12,656
	AZ state tax	–$7,466
	Property taxes	–$6,000
	IRA/SEP contrib.	–$98,876
	Mortgage interest	–$54,000

Taxable income

$324,000 $183,916

Federal tax credits

$2,600

Net tax due

$123,002 $39,958

Tax savings

$83,044

Figure 8.8

This tax saving is partly due to lower U.S. federal and Arizona tax rates, but also because they deduct their large mortgage interest payments, property tax and state income tax. They make their maximum contribution to their Simplified Employee Pension (SEP), rather than an RRSP. Bill and Mary would also have to pay Social Security taxes in the United States. Although Social Security benefits are larger than those from CPP, so are their contributions. To keep the tax comparisons simple, we have not included any CPP, EI or Social Security payments in the net taxes due. Also not taken into consideration for either couple would be the savings in the United States because of no Goods and Services Tax (GST). The GST savings could amount to several more thousands of dollars a year, depending on their spending habits as U.S. residents. Sales taxes for Arizona are about the same as the Manitoba provincial sales tax, while property taxes are much lower for an equivalent house in Arizona.

Our two couples, George and Susan and Bill and Mary, both have high incomes. Those in lower income brackets will generally experience proportionate tax cuts ranging from a one-third to two-thirds reduction in overall tax on the same amount of income in both countries. If you and your spouse are paying a total of $10,000 or less in Canadian taxes, a move to the United States will not likely benefit you much in net savings unless you have access to low-cost medical coverage from U.S. Medicare, your employer's group retirement health plan or a bridge insurance carrier until you can get on U.S. Medicare at age 65.

CANADIAN NON-RESIDENT WITHHOLDING TAX

Canadians who leave Canada but still receive Canadian income have to look at the Canada/U.S. Tax Treaty for the rules governing taxation of the income sourced in Canada. The treaty, as described in Chapter 1, was created to prevent citizens and residents from being taxed twice on the same income, while at the same time allowing both countries some limited power of taxation according to the income source and type.

In Figures 8.1 to 8.7, George and Susan provide us with a typical example of a situation where the treaty comes into play. They have a number of income sources that cannot be changed, their CPP, OAS and pensions. This means that the Canada Revenue Agency (CRA), under the Tax Treaty, may be able to levy some tax on this income as that of non-residents, since it is sourced in Canada. At the same time, the IRS will have taxation rights on the income, because they are U.S. residents. The treaty, however, ensures that George and Susan will not be double-taxed on any of this income, by specifying how the income will be taxed and allowing for tax credits in one country for taxes paid to the other. The table in Figure 8.9 lists the withholding tax rates of Canadian-sourced income that a Canadian is likely to encounter on major forms of income when moving to the United States.

The non-resident tax rates indicated in Figure 8.9 are withheld at the source, such as they are at the bank that pays the interest or the company that pays the pension. It is the responsibility of the payer to withhold the correct treaty rate from the non-resident's income and forward that amount to CRA. It is the responsibility of the non-resident to notify any applicable payer that the recipient is, or is becoming, a resident of the United States. If the improper amount has been withheld, CRA will send a bill to the non-resident and expect payment. If CRA cannot locate the non-resident and the payer was at fault for withholding too little, the payer can be held liable for any taxes due.

If the correct withholding has been done, the non-resident is not required to file a tax return with CRA and the non-resident tax slip issued

CANADIAN NON-RESIDENT WITHHOLDING RATES, 2006

Interest 10%

Gov't bonds 0%

Dividends...15%

CPP/QPP and OAS..0%

Pensions/annuities 15%

Lump-sum RRSPs..25%

Rental income 25%

Management fees 15%

Capital gains ....Variable %

Royalties 0–15%

Income trusts...15%

Figure 8.9

by the payer, usually an NR4 slip, is considered the complete tax filing necessary. However, there are special filing options for those non-residents with rental income or pension income, if the withholding rate is higher than the actual tax would have been had that person been a resident of Canada. For example, if a non-resident has rental property that earns no net profit, he or she could elect to file a non-resident return under Section 216 of the Income Tax Act, netting out income and expenses and paying no tax rather than a 25% withholding on the gross rental receipts. Similarly, under Section 217 of the Income Tax Act, someone receiving a Canadian pension whose tax rate would have been less than the 15% withholding had she been a Canadian resident with that pension income only can file a special return and claim a refund (see restrictions for a Section 217 later in this chapter, under Withdraw Your RRSP Tax Free! In addition, she could apply to CRA for a reduced withholding rate on future payments on CRA Form NR5.

On capital gains income from the sale of Canadian real estate, non-residents must either face withholding rates of up to 25% of the full value of the property or file for a clearance certificate, Form T2062, from CRA prior to the sale of the capital property. When CRA issues the clearance certificate, it will determine what portion of the gain is taxable and will authorize the buyer to withhold at a rate that ensures total tax payment.

The seller must file a Canadian non-resident return as a final reconciliation of the transaction in the year in which the sale occurred.

Payments from RRSPs and RRIFs are considered pension payments subject to the 15% withholding rate as long as they are periodic. Periodic means the RRSP must be in the form of an annuity with payments to the pensioner until at least age 90 or ten years, whichever is less. Periodic payments from a RRIF must not exceed 10% of the value or twice the annual minimum payment as calculated using your age, the value of your account and CRA tables to qualify for the 15% withholding rate, rather than the lump sum rate of 25%. (See Withdraw Your RRSP Tax Free! later in this chapter.)

To illustrate more clearly how this system of withholding taxes and credits works, let's go back to George and Susan again, and see what actually happened when they left Canada for the United States. For this example, we assume that they converted all of their interest-bearing bank deposits in Canada to the United States, just as their cross-border financial planner recommended. CRA agreed that a 25% withholding tax on their capital gains on their Canadian real property of $30,000 was suitable and equal to the actual total tax due. You can refer back to Figure 8.7 if you wish to review George and Susan's income sources and taxes due, as Figure 8.10 only summarizes these numbers.

Figure 8.10 indicates that George and Susan would owe no additional taxes to the United States, because Canadian non-resident withholding tax was allowed as a foreign tax credit on their U.S. returns. The credit from the Canadian withholding tax, in fact, wiped out all of the tax they would have paid to the IRS, had the income been generated in the United States. If there was more Canadian withholding than U.S. taxes due, the excess unused credits of $5,939 could be carried forward for up to ten years to be used in a year when the withholding tax would be insufficient to provide a full credit against the U.S. taxes due on the foreign income earned.

The foreign tax credits in the United States are subject to some special rules which can affect the amount of credit actually allowed by the IRS. George and Susan's case has been simplified somewhat in Figure 8.10 to show the overall effect of the withholding and credit system under the Canada/U.S. Tax Treaty. On a real return, their results would likely be slightly different. Had the IRS under any of its own rules disallowed any of the Canadian tax withheld as a foreign tax credit, it could have been carried forward for up to ten years, to be used against future foreign income earned.

Income	George	Susan	Withholding Tax
CPP	$10,150	$10,150	$0
OAS	$6,000	$6,000	$0
Pension	$55,000	$25,000	$12,000
Interest	$15,750	$15,750	$0
Dividends	$5,000	$5,000	$1,500
Employment	$0	$30,000	$4,500
Capital gains	$15,000	$15,000	$7,500
Total non-resident withholding tax			$25,500
Total U.S. tax due (see Figure 8.7)			$19,561
Credit for Canadian withholding tax			−$19,561
Net tax payable to the United States			**$0**
Foreign tax credit carry forward $25,500 − 19,561 = $5,939			

Figure 8.10

WITHDRAW YOUR RRSP TAX FREE!

Many Canadians have small fortunes sitting in their RRSPs or RRIFs but are reluctant to withdraw any money from them because they face such high rates of taxation on the withdrawals. This section will deal with some of the cross-border financial planning techniques that can help you withdraw even large sums from your RRSP and effectively pay a greatly reduced tax or, with the right circumstances and planning, pay no net taxes at all. In many cases, these cross-border financial planning techniques can provide a major incentive for becoming a U.S. resident, as the savings, especially on the larger accounts, can be tens or hundreds of thousands of dollars!

The issue of what to do with RRSPs when Canadians leave Canada to take up residency in the United States is more often than not overlooked, especially for those who fail to complete a cross-border financial plan. When taking up residency in the United States, Canadians can find their RRSPs a great source of tax savings if they plan for them correctly. Without proper planning, RRSPs can create unnecessary U.S. taxes and can potentially be double-taxed by both the United States and Canada. Most people ignore planning for their RRSPs, think there is nothing they need to do, or have even been advised to leave their RRSPs in Canada by un-knowledgeable or self-serving advisors. They let their RRSPs sit and ac-cumulate interest or other investment income, as if they were still residents of Canada.

How Canadian RRSPs are viewed by the IRS will help explain some of the problems surrounding them and illustrate how you can take ad-vantage of the differences in the rules. I touched briefly on this issue ear-lier in this chapter, in Figure 8.3, with respect to Susan's RRSP annuity pension. The IRS considers your RRSP an ordinary investment by look-ing right through the RRSP trusteeship and CRA's deferment of income tax rules. The IRS looks at Registered Retirement Income Funds (RRIFs), Locked-In Retirement Accounts (LIRAs), Life Income Funds (LIFs), Locked-In Retirement Income Funds (LRIFs), Retirement Com-pensation Arrangements (RCAs) and other similar Canadian registered accounts the same way as it looks at RRSPs, so when we talk about RRSPs here, they are a proxy for the other plans as well. The IRS deems an RRSP to be a simple grantor trust, under U.S. rules, in which the grantor or con-tributor pays tax on all the income as it is earned or realized.

When you are a resident of the United States, the IRS will consider an RRSP the same way it would treat the underlying investments of the RRSP had the RRSP not been a registered investment. For example, if you as a U.S. resident earned bank interest during the year in your RRSP, the IRS would want you to report and pay tax on that interest as if you had earned it in a regular bank account. The IRS will consider the contri-butions you made to the RRSP and the accumulated interest, realized gains or dividends in it, before you became a U.S. resident, as tax-paid principal under the grantor trust rules. (Note that this IRS tax-paid treat-ment for interest and dividends does not apply to unrealized capital gains at your entrance date into the United States, nor does it apply to U.S. cit-izens or green card holders who have been residents in Canada.) Once you are a U.S. resident, citizen or green card holder, the IRS will tax the interest earned and paid during the year inside the RRSP. Similarly, divi-dends and capital gains on your RRSP account are subject to U.S. tax, as they are paid or realized each and every year, without the deferral of tax provided for by CRA. At first glance, this seems like a major problem, but knowing how the IRS taxes RRSPs and similar plans gives cross-border planners a great tool to help Canadians get their RRSPs out of Canada at low or even no net taxes.

If you were to leave your RRSPs in Canada, or if you are a U.S. citi-zen or green card holder with RRSPs, regardless of where you live, the IRS will tax you, as a U.S. resident, on all interest, dividends and capital gains earned on your account, even though you may not have actually received these funds. Income that you do not actually receive but are taxed on is called "phantom income." Many Canadians with RRSPs have been in the United States for years and never realized that they have a United States tax liability on this phantom income. The Canada/U.S. Tax Treaty protocol that came into effect in 1996 allows you to make an election annually on your U.S. return to defer the payment of U.S. tax on the RRSP phantom income until such time as it is actually withdrawn. In order for the deferment of tax on the income to be effective, a form requesting this deferment must be attached to your U.S. tax return every year. For tax years after 2004, the IRS has created Form 8891, which must be completed for each RRSP for each year to take advantage of the tax deferment. This "election" to defer taxes must follow an IRS procedure (specifically, Rev. Proc 2002 – 23) that details what information must be included on the tax return. Note that if you live in a state that has an income tax, state income tax may be due on the phantom income every year, regardless of whether you have filed the election with your federal tax return, as states are not party to the treaty or its elections. In fact, California, in 2003, put RRSP holders on notice that it did not allow any deferral of Canadian RRSP and similar plan income, and furthermore would come after them if they didn't report the income annually and pay full California state income tax on it. Many Canadians were caught off guard by these state rules and paid dearly for it. Withdrawals of your principal contributions to the RRSP are not taxed by the Internal Revenue Service or by the states at any time.

TEN KEY REASONS TO REMOVE YOUR RRSP FROM CANADA

What, then, is the best thing to do with your RRSPs or RRIFs after leaving Canada? There are no provisions between Canada and the United States for a direct transfer of your RRSP to the U.S. equivalent, an Individual Retirement Account (IRA). Consequently, you have only three options: withdraw the RRSPs; report the realized income each year and pay the tax on the phantom income; or make the annual elections under the treaty to defer federal tax on the income. If you are intending to reside permanently or at least for many years in the United States, I recommend the first solution, complete or staged withdrawal, for ten key reasons:

1. If you leave your RRSP in Canada, not only are you subject to the tax rules of both Canada and the U.S. simultaneously, but you are subject to any future Canadian tax legislation that could restrict future withdrawals more than current laws do now. For example, on December

20, 1991, CRA made several changes to the Income Tax Conventions Interpretation Act, restricting the definition of what qualifies as a periodic RRIF withdrawal, forcing RRIF holders to pay a 25% withholding rate instead of a 15% rate on withdrawals larger than twice the annual minimum. The March 1996, Canadian federal budget reduced the age at which RRSP withdrawals must start from 71 to 69. In 2004, the IRS brought in substantial new rules affecting foreign pensions, which can spill over into RRSP planning.

In addition to these tax complications, expect CRA to continue tightening their restrictions or increasing the withholding rates on RRSPs, as they are constantly looking for more revenue. Just like the old sayings "Make hay while the sun shines" and "Get out while the getting is good," you can cash in your RRSPs now and pay as little as zero net tax, as noted above, once you leave Canada. Why wait for future legislation to come along that will restrict your options or increase your tax due?

2. People with estates of more than US$2 million or who live in a state which has its own estate tax may face double taxation. The double tax arises because Canada will withhold 25% from your RRSP at your death, and this amount may not be allowed as a credit against U.S. estate tax due. The most recent Canada/U.S. Tax Treaty does not provide for a credit of the RRSP withholding at death against the estate taxes in the United States, so a double tax will likely be levied on any larger U.S. estates with Canadian RRSPs. A recent decision by a Canada/U.S. Tax Treaty Competent Authority hearing determined that a U.S. federal estate tax credit is available for Canadian taxes stemming from deemed disposition of RRSPs at death. Consequently, if you are in the position of having an RRSP as a U.S. resident, and the Competent Authority doesn't change its mind or isn't challenged in court by the IRS, you have only one level of estate tax to pay instead of two.

    As mentioned in Chapter 4 in the section Estate Tax Concerns in Individual States, the recent reductions in federal estate taxes have caused may states to opt out of the federal "pick-up tax" and levy their own estate tax. If you live in one of those states you most certainly will face double taxation since the treaty does not apply at the state level. In addition, many Canadian provinces now require residents to file separate provincial tax returns. Why pay any tax, even on one level, when you can get rid of the tax entirely by getting your RRSP out of Canada? Similarly, regardless of the size of your taxable U.S. estate, having significant assets in a foreign country locked into the special rules that apply to RRSPs makes it very difficult to use standard estate-tax reduction planning techniques available to most U.S. residents. In my more than 23 years in the U.S., I have yet to see even the most competent of U.S. estate attorneys properly design estate documents to deal adequately with RRSPs back in Canada.

3. Another reason to cash in your RRSPs after becoming a U.S. resident is to avoid currency speculation. (In Chapter 2, I have already covered the hazards of unknowingly becoming a currency speculator.) Keeping an RRSP in Canadian dollars when you are likely to need U.S. dollars for retirement is exposing yourself to unnecessary risk, as you are not properly matching your retirement income with the expenses of retirement. This difference could reduce retirement income in U.S. dollars to such an extent that you find yourself forced to work longer than planned or part time in retirement. Why take this risk? If the exchange rate on the Canadian dollar improves, you have still protected yourself. Since most Canadians in the U.S. will continue to have CPP and OAS or other sources of Canadian income, they will still benefit from the improved exchange rate.

4. As noted earlier in this section, the individual U.S. states are not party to federal treaties such as the Canada/U.S. Tax Treaty, although many states do voluntarily provide their residents the income tax benefits of a treaty. In those states with a state income tax and that do not voluntarily follow the treaty, an additional level of tax may apply each year even though you may have elected to defer the IRS tax under the treaty. For example, if you are a Canadian with RRSPs who takes up residence in the state of California and have elected to take the deferral of the RRSP income at the federal level, you will pay up to 9.3% state tax annually on the RRSP phantom income. This tax would not be recoverable in the United States under California state tax rules, so it would in effect be an unnecessary or a double tax.

5. At the death of a U.S. resident who has deferred tax on RRSPs under the treaty, the U.S. rules of Income in Respect to the Decedent (IRD) apply. Most Canadians are aware that when they die owning an RRSP or a RRIF they are taxed on the plan balance as if they cashed the entire plan on the day before they died, and consequently they are taxed at the highest Canadian rates on the entire amount of the plan. In the U.S., the IRD rules transfer the tax liability to the beneficiary, and he or she pays the tax each year just on the income received for that year, at his or her personal rate. In addition, the beneficiary is allowed a tax deduction for the tax paid on the IRD if the decedent had paid U.S. estate tax. Since the CRA taxes the decedent and the IRS taxes the

beneficiary, there is an automatic double tax because tax credits cannot be transferred between separate taxpayers. IRD results in double tax generally whenever it occurs, particularly where there are non-resident beneficiaries. Under IRD rules, at the death of a U.S. resident who had elected to defer tax on RRSP income, the maximum tax rate goes from zero (if the RRSP had been removed from Canada) to as high as 60% or more, including state taxes. This is not a tax to be ignored.

6. From an investment standpoint, getting your RRSP out of Canada early in your U.S. residency can be to your advantage for two key reasons: cost and investment selection. In a practical investment sense, competition favours an investor in the United States through lower commissions on securities, transactions and lower management fees on mutual funds. Mutual fund management fees and expense ratios are generally 2% to 3% in Canada, while in the United States they average 1% to 1.5% — generally half the cost for a similar mutual fund. In addition, the larger selection of U.S. mutual funds allows you to choose no-load index funds with expense ratios as low as 0.2%, or one-twentieth the Canadian cost. Compared to leaving your mutual funds in Canada, this cost savings over a number of years can be substantial, amounting to many thousands of dollars in your pocket instead of someone else's. Over approximately ten years, this extra cost on your RRSP investments can by itself be greater than the 25% non-resident tax you would pay to get your RRSPs out of Canada.

7. The U.S. Security Exchange Commission requires that your Canadian broker and the Canadian brokerage firm holding your RRSP funds be licensed in your state of residence and the securities they sell you must be U.S. registered before they can legally transact security trades for you as a resident in the United States. As a result, you may be stuck with all the stocks, bonds and mutual funds you own in your RRSP without being able to change investments to react to changing market conditions after you leave Canada — not a good situation. On June 23, 2000, the U.S. SEC and various provincial securities divisions in Canada came to an agreement on a partial solution to this problem of trading inside RRSPs for U.S. residents. The SEC offered an exemption to Canadian brokers trading on behalf of U.S. resident RRSP/RRIF holders with certain restrictions. Some of the restrictions eliminate many people from taking advantage of this exemption; as well, some U.S. states did not follow the SEC's lead and will not give Canadian brokers any legal trading rights for their residents. Consequently, after years of waiting for this SEC exemption, few people with RRSPs in Canada will be able to take advantage of it.

Why bother with this hassle with the Canadian brokers when you can deal with U.S. brokers at a much reduced cost once you have withdrawn the funds from Canada?

8. Those RRSP investors who invest in appreciating assets such as stocks or growth-type mutual funds will almost certainly face a double tax on all their capital gains. This double tax results from the manner in which the Canada/U.S. Tax Treaty sources the capital gains. The treaty states that gains on securities are sourced to the country of residence of the taxpayer. Consequently, U.S. residents with Canadian RRSPs will have all their gains classified as U.S.-sourced. This means that any foreign tax credits generated on the withholding upon cashing the RRSP cannot be used to offset the U.S. tax owing on the gains since tax credits are allowed against foreign income only, and since the capital gains are no longer considered foreign because of these treaty sourcing rules, a double tax results. In short, the minimum tax on capital gains from an RRSP for a U.S. resident, not including any state taxes, is 40% (the 25% withholding plus the 15% U.S. tax on capital gains) rather than just the 25% withholding tax on principal, interest and dividends.

    This double tax on capital gains is the reason it is strongly recommended that, before entering the United States all RRSP holders sell their appreciated stocks, bonds and mutual funds to get a stepped-up cost basis for U.S. purposes. A stepped-up cost basis is the term for when someone sells a security and buys it back at the same price in order to move the cost for tax purposes from the original purchase price to the current price. This step-up in basis will eliminate the double tax on any gains accumulated before you become subject to U.S. taxes under the treaty sourcing rules, but will not help you with the tax on the capital gains after you become a U.S. resident even if you make the treaty election to defer the tax each year.

9. There is something to be said for simplicity in one's financial life. Leaving your RRSP in Canada when you are a U.S. resident complicates your tax and investment management life substantially. You constantly need to find U.S. tax and investment advisors who understand RRSP reporting procedures, a difficult job at the best of times, for most of them are struggling just to keep current on the usual IRS rules and regulations. You will be lucky just to find a U.S. advisor who knows where Canada is let alone deal with it in complicated tax matters. The cost of qualified advisors and all the reporting they must do

on your behalf, particularly if you get the wrong advice, can often outweigh the benefits of any tax deferral you might obtain by leaving the RRSP in Canada and electing the treaty deferral. Even if you have only one RRSP, as a U.S. resident you face up to four relatively complex forms and elections that your tax preparer must include with each year's filings at the federal level. The following IRS forms are required when you have an RRSP in Canada: Form 8891, Form 8833, Form 3520, Form 3520A, Form TD F 90-22.1, Form 1116, Form 1116AMT. Most of these forms are required each and every year; others are only required when you make a withdrawal or an election. Even if you can find someone who knows how to complete these forms, it is expensive to get them filed and your tax return could be an inch thick. Even worse, if you fail to file the correct forms in a timely manner, the penalties could be prohibitive and cost you the value of your RRSP and more. For example, if you fail to file Form TD F 90-22.1, the penalty is a fine up to $500,000 or five years in jail. If you have more than one RRSP, many of these forms must be prepared separately for each RRSP, and if you have a state tax return to file, additional forms and taxes could be required each year.

10. In a recent Tax Court of Canada case, McFadyen v. The Queen, the judge cited as evidence of a residential tie with Canada the fact that Mr. McFayden, a non-resident of Canada, had maintained an RRSP in Canada, and subsequently assessed him with Canadian taxes on his world income for three years. If you want to ensure the CRA doesn't attempt to tax you as a Canadian resident, do not leave RRSPs in Canada: they might become a target following this Tax Court of Canada ruling.

In spite of all these reasons to get your RRSP out of Canada once you become a U.S. resident, there is a tendency for most Canadian advisors to continue to recommend that Canadians moving to the United States leave their RRSPs in Canada. The key reasons for this advice are believed to be a lack of understanding of the above noted complications and double-tax problems and how far-reaching the adverse consequences of holding RRSPs can be for U.S. residents. In addition, because of the way most Canadian advisors are compensated on RRSPs, it is in their own self-interest to keep the RRSPs in Canada where they can continue to collect commissions and other fees, so they have a bias against doing any research that could indicate it is in the client's best interest to get the RRSPs out of Canada when moving to the United States. However, there are certain circumstances in which I recommend leaving some or all of your or your spouse's RRSPs in Canada for limited periods to obtain maximum tax or investment advantage.

Making withdrawals from your RRSP that maximize benefits and minimize taxes is no simple task and should not be done without the supervision of a qualified cross-border financial planner. This is one area of cross-border planning where a simple error can be costly and irreversible. Using a knowledgeable professional may be expensive, but it can pay big dividends.

The timing of the withdrawals is critical. You need to match Canadian withholding taxes with U.S. taxability of foreign income. This correct matching of taxes paid to Canada and available foreign tax credits in the United States can mean the difference between paying 25% (40% on capital gains as noted above) or 0% tax on a net basis on your RRSP balance. When calculating the usable foreign tax credits on a U.S. tax return, all sources of foreign income must be considered, not just the RRSP income.

I have been inundated with hundreds of requests from *Border Guide* readers asking me to include more specific examples on withdrawing RRSPs at the lowest possible rate. Many would like to attempt withdrawing their RRSPs tax free on a net basis on their own and I would strongly advise them to use a knowledgeable professional. I am reluctant to provide these examples because this is one area that is far too complex and dependent on too many factors for me to even attempt to present it in any condensed written form. Any RRSP withdrawal planning for non-residents of Canada is affected by this partial list of factors:

- your age, health and marital status
- your spouse's age and health
- your and your spouse's life goals and objectives
- whether you have children and where they live
- type, amounts and sources of your current and future income
- type, amounts and sources of your spouse's current and future income
- amounts of past, current and future non-resident tax paid or to be paid to CRA by you and your spouse
- your need for current or future cash flow
- your and your spouse's net worth
- location and tax basis of non-RRSP assets
- size of your and your spouse's RRSPs

- the types of investments in your RRSPs
- whether any of your RRSPs are "locked in" by provincial legislation
- whether you are still a Canadian resident for tax purposes
- how long you've been a resident in the United States
- your immigration status in the United States
- whether you have previous U.S. tax returns in which you reported RRSP income correctly
- your state of residence in the United States
- the province in which the RRSPs are located
- the type of registered account — that is, RRSP, LIRA, RCA, etc.

As you can see, the many factors affecting RRSP withdrawal planning can be mind-boggling, particularly when you consider the number of combinations and permutations so many factors create. Trying to deal with all these factors is like reading how to remove someone's appendix and then setting out to do it: you may be lucky but the odds are stacked strongly against you. You need to consider the interest rates on RRSPs, foreign income, amounts withdrawn and available U.S. tax credits in order to withdraw your RRSP from Canada in the shortest time and at the lowest possible tax rate. Consequently, if you are not careful or fail to use competent professional advice on your RRSP withdrawals, as a non-resident of Canada you can miss opportunities to reduce taxes significantly. Worse yet, taxes and penalties can wipe out your savings entirely.

For smaller RRSPs, namely those of less than $100,000 in value, staged withdrawals can be controlled to match the foreign tax credits available. Section 217 of the Income Tax Act allows people who withdraw up to between $9,000 and $25,000 from their RRSPs and who have little or no other taxable income to file a return and obtain either a full or partial refund of the withholding tax. CRA amended its Section 217 filing requirements in 1996, including other world taxable income in a formula that provides tax relief only on a proportionate basis of Canadian-sourced income that qualifies for the Section 217 treatment in relation to total world income. Consequently, this option is no longer viable for those with substantial U.S. or world income. Section 217 filings work well for the RRSP belonging to a non-working spouse with no investment income.

Other than the correct non-resident withholding tax on withdrawal as a U.S. resident, you have no further Canadian obligations with respect to your RRSPs, and no need to file a return when making withdrawals, unless you qualify for a refund under Section 217 or incorrect withholding was done at source, as is all too often the case. If you are a Canadian non-resident, make certain that on all lump-sum RRSP withdrawals the payer takes exactly 25% non-resident withholding tax. If the payer takes more than 25%, you have a great hassle trying to get a refund of the overcharge from CRA, and if the payer takes anything less than 25% on the RRSP, you will need to file and pay the shortfall, often with interest and penalties.

BREAKING THE LOCK ON LOCKED-IN RRSPs

Canadians who have worked for employers within Canada find, much to their disappointment, that a good portion of their pension benefit is "locked in" when they leave the company before retirement age. This lock-in is a result of employment pension plan regulation at the provincial level. All ten provinces and the three territories have such legislation, designed to prevent employees from spending their accrued pension benefits before retirement age. In effect, the provinces feel the employees aren't responsible enough to roll their pension benefits into an RRSP and leave it there only for their eventual retirement, so they force the employees to roll the vested company contributions of their pensions into a Locked-In Retirement Account (LIRA).

Funds cannot be withdrawn from a LIRA, except in special emergency situations as defined by the applicable provincial legislation. At the normal retirement age set by the original company plan in which the employee was a member, the LIRA owners, if they wish to make withdrawals, can convert their LIRAs to Life Income Funds (LIFs) or Locked-In Retirement Income Funds (LRIFs). These both operate like Registered Retirement Income Funds (RRIFs) except that the start date at which withdrawals can be made for most provinces is age 55 and there is a maximum withdrawal rate each year, as well as the usual RRIF minimum. One additional option for LIRA holders is to use the LIRA funds to purchase a life annuity.

Until the year 2000, LIRA holders who became non-residents of Canada had no options other than the two mentioned above. This subjected U.S.-resident LIRA holders to numerous reporting requirements annually to the IRS and state tax authorities, potential double income and/or estate taxes, estate-planning issues, and investment planning issues, not to mention currency risks. Review the previous section of this chapter for more details of the concerns of U.S. resident RRSP/LIRA holders. In other words, being locked in with your RRSPs (in the form of a LIRA, LIF, or RRIF) as a U.S. resident is somewhat punitive!

After much lobbying of provincial governments to provide relief for non-resident owners of LIRAs, Alberta and British Columbia finally came through with legislation, effective March 1, 2000, and July 1, 1999, respectively. As of these dates, Alberta and B.C. LIRA owners can break the locks on their LIRAs if they can get written confirmation from Canada Revenue Agency (CRA) that they are indeed non-residents. If the LIRA owner is married, a spousal waiver of any benefits from the LIRA is also required. The CRA written confirmation can be obtained by an appropriately completed Form NR73, Determination of Residency Status. An answer should be received approximately eight weeks after submitting the NR73 to the CRA. In 2005, Manitoba introduced provisions into its Pension Act that allow those over the age of 55 to unlock up to 50% of a Locked-In Retirement Account.

The very good news here is that this new Alberta and B.C. legislation appears to treat all non-residents equally. So, for example, you may have been a resident of Ontario, holding a LIRA there, and are now living in the United States. If you happen to move your LIRA to Alberta, it appears you could break the lock on your (formerly held) Ontario LIRA by jumping through the same hoops noted above as an owner of an Alberta employment-related LIRA. Some of the Alberta and B.C. LIRA trustees, particularly the ones that operate in all provinces, may refuse to break the lock on LIRAS from other provinces. We have managed over the past few years to assist several clients in moving some substantial LIRAs to Alberta from other provinces and then breaking the lock and moving the funds to the U.S.

Employees of federally regulated industries, such as airlines, railroads and communication companies, regardless of their provinces of residence, can also qualify to break the lock-in on their LIRAs obtained from these companies. To qualify they must currently be and have been non-residents of Canada for at least two years. By providing proof of non-residency to the LIRA trustee he or she can break the lock-in and forward the funds to you, less the 25% non-resident withholding tax. In the past couple of years, some overzealous trustees of the LIRAs created from these federal regulated plans have been refusing to break the lock because the LIRA funds were no longer actually in the plan. This is a ridiculous interpretation of the rule because the only option the employee had when they left that federally regulated industry was to transfer the registered funds to a LIRA. You may need to fight for your rights if you are in this situation.

Dealing with RRSPs and LIRAs as a non-resident of Canada can be a tricky business. We recommend, at all times, that you seek the advice of an experienced and qualified cross-border financial planner.

REGISTERED EDUCATION SAVINGS PLANS (RESPs)

People residing in the United States and owning RESPs for their children, grandchildren or other relatives will be taxed on the annual realized income earned in their accounts in the same manner as explained for RRSPs/RRIFs/LIRAs in the previous two sections. However, there are no corresponding Canada/U.S. Tax Treaty elections to defer the income buildup inside of these plans to avoid the annual tax, and IRS Form 3520 needs to be completed and filed each year on an RESP. The Canadian tax deferrals and other benefits remain the same for U.S. resident holders of RESPs. However, there is one key problem with account withdrawals unique to non-resident RESP owners: they cannot withdraw any earnings from the account, even if they want to pay the taxes on it, unless it is used strictly for qualified education assistance payments. This presents a real problem for RESP holders who no longer have any eligible relatives left to be able to use the RESP income built up or they are nearing the end of the 25-year lifespan of the RESP. It is believed this is an oversight on CRA's part because this RESP income can be stranded in Canada indefinitely with nobody being able to benefit from it at all. Consequently, RESP owners who are moving to the United States need to consider withdrawing the RESP income before becoming non-residents in Canada and pay the appropriate tax and penalties to rescue funds that they and their relatives may never be able to use before the income is stranded. Non-residents may withdraw principal from RESPs without difficulty or penalty. However, if you did establish the RESP for a Canadian relative such as a grandchild, it will be much easier if you simply give the RESP to the parent of the grandchild or directly to the grandchild before you exit Canada.

CROSS-BORDER Q&A

MARRIAGE TO CANADIAN WITH AN RRSP

I bought a copy of your book, The Border Guide. *I am an American citizen, and my fiancé is coming to the U.S. from Canada to get married. I have a couple of questions: In reading the chapter "The Grass Is Always Greener," I found I completely agreed with your ten reasons why one should liquidate RRSPs before leaving Canada. I have a question, though: if we sell all of my fiancé's RRSPs, should we convert to a RRIF? My fiancé invested at the tail end of the boom and is suffering losses. What is the best way of minimizing taxes on his withdrawals? Do we have to do a staged withdrawal, and what are the matching foreign tax credits you refer to in your book? Of course, we would like to have a 0% tax liability.*

Your book did not mention what to do with life insurance. Should we liquidate before we leave? Will the Canadian government view this as a tie?

Finally, my fiancé owns a house with his parents: joint ownership with right of survival. Should he have his name removed from the title? His parents still live in the house. Will the Canadian government view this as a tie?

Your help would be greatly appreciated.

— Marry Y., San Jose, California

Thank you for your inquiry, and congratulations on your upcoming marriage.

Your questions are quite common for your situation, and there are even many questions that you have not yet asked but will likely also need answered. However, I will need more information before I can provide advice, so I suggest you review the section Withdraw Your RRSP Tax Free! in this chapter, giving special attention to the factors listed there. Without knowing these factors and completing an analysis, my answers could be off considerably.

Notwithstanding these factors, you are right in wanting to get answers to your questions before you are married and your future husband becomes a U.S. resident. One bit of positive tax news is that your fiancé, if the planning is done and executed correctly, should be able to write off the losses in his RRSP portfolio in the U.S.

A U.S. resident may maintain life insurance from Canada without income tax or other major problems; but there may be some estate tax issues, as covered in Chapter 4. The death benefits will be in Canadian dollars, so you will need to continually monitor the exchange rate to make sure your husband has enough insurance.

It is difficult to say what your fiancé should do with the ownership of his parents' home without more information, but it should not be of concern with respect to residential ties to Canada.

As I recommended in my book, anyone in your situation will benefit greatly from having a cross-border financial plan.

DEFERRING TAX ON RRSP UNDER TREATY

Greetings: I just found your book and read it cover to cover. I want to offer thanks for a job well done. I have one or two issues which I didn't see specifically covered (or perhaps I missed them).

I am a dual citizen, my wife is Canadian with a green card, and my children are dual citizens. We have been residing in Washington state for five *years now. I am a physician. We figured most things out on our own when we moved to the U.S., and fortunately it looks like we did pretty well. My wife and I have about $85,000 in RRSPs in Canada. We have nothing else there, except a chequing account to pay insurance premiums (which is only funded by me with after-tax U.S. dollars and used for no other reason). I have been filing elections to defer tax in the U.S. on the RRSPs as per the treaty. We do not know if we will ever return to Canada, but would never close that door. You are the first person I have ever heard to recommend taking the RRSPs out of Canada. What is the most tax-efficient way to approach the process, since I am over 30 years away from being able to take distributions and I have a high income in the U.S.? I never did anything to step up the cost basis before leaving the country, but have since consolidated our RRSPs all in one place. (As you know, Washington state was an early adopter of legislation that allowed us to manage our RRSPs from the U.S.). We use Phillips, Hagar and North, an excellent company with regards to management fees and returns, even when compared with U.S. fund managers. Since it is a small amount of money, would it be better just to leave it, not knowing where we will live in the future? Might that be akin to hedging currency risk for future retirement? This is really my only outstanding issue. Whether to do it, and if so, how? Is there more information on this particular scenario, or do I require professional help to make a judgment?*

My second question relates to being a high income earner in the U.S. and moving back to Canada. I believe there would be onerous tax implications for me, since I would trigger AMT on the U.S. return, and would have to pay 10% of the AMT regardless of the tax treaty and credits (at least this is my understanding). This is in addition to an already high Canadian tax rate. It sounds like I would have issues with my Roth IRAs as well. As an aside, your book has depressed me a bit, because I realize that it may be incredibly prohibitive to ever go back.

— *Andrew J., Snohomish, Washington*

Thank you for your kind comments on *The Border Guide*.

My question to you is why complicate your investment strategy and your income tax filing by leaving a small RRSP in Canada at all? It is costing you more than you think and every year the file you need to keep for the IRS keeps getting thicker and thicker. After 20 or more years this will become quite unwieldy.

Yes, PH&N are a very good company, but if you go to Vanguard or Fidelity in the U.S., you can get excellent funds for about one-tenth the cost. Over the life of your investment, the approximately 1% more per year that you are paying to PH&N can amount to a 10% tax equivalent each year (when you are averaging even a 10% total return, which is a stretch currently). This extra cost of investment and trying to keep up with the U.S. tax complications every year removes any benefits you might get from tax deferral.

Waiting to withdraw the funds until after you are back in Canada guarantees you will pay higher taxes than the 25% you would currently pay in the U.S. — not much of a reward for deferring. Don't forget you can use the 25% non-resident withholding tax not needed to pay all the deferred taxes now on your U.S. return to reduce U.S. taxes for up to ten years through foreign tax credits. This makes a current withdrawal even more beneficial, whereas the longer you defer, the larger your tax bill will be. Eventually the 25% non-resident withholding tax will not even cover the U.S. tax on withdrawal, and you will need to pay out of pocket. In addition, what happens if Canada Revenue Agency decides to increase the non-resident withholding tax to more than 25% as they easily could?

Don't be discouraged about going back to Canada to retire. If you do some advance planning, as I mention in Chapter 10, you can minimize taxes. Some new IRS rules that took effect in October 2004 make AMT using foreign tax credits no longer an issue.

CONVERTING E-2 VISA STATUS AND HOLDING CANADIAN RRSPs

In August of 1990, after obtaining an E-2 visa, I moved to the United States and purchased a business and a home. I am a Canadian citizen, residing in the United States with my wife and children, and would like to establish permanent immigrant status. I own a rental property in Florida through a numbered Ontario corporation. My income is derived from the business in the United States and from dividends received from less-than-arm's-length Canadian corporations. As of 1991, I have elected to be taxed in the United States. I still hold an RRSP in Canada and own a private Canadian corporation.

I realize these are rather complex issues, but I would like to hear from you.

1. *In whose name should any U.S. assets be held?*

2. *What should I do with my Canadian assets?*

3. *What should I do with my Canadian RRSP?*

4. *What should I do with my U.S. rental property?*

5. *What can be done to convert my E-2 non-immigrant status to immigrant status? My sister is a U.S. resident and holds a green card.*

— Jimi H., Wilmington, North Carolina

Your questions cover some very complicated issues. Consequently, the answers will also be complex, depending on your ultimate objectives and other extenuating circumstances.

1. The titling of your U.S. assets generally would follow the same procedures you would use in Canada. Business assets would likely best be owned by the business itself, depending on whether you are operating under a sole proprietorship or are incorporated. Personal assets would be in your and/or your spouse's name. You should also look into using a family living trust with provisions for a qualified domestic trust to own all your assets. This trust would help organize your estate to help avoid probate in Florida, North Carolina and Ontario, and make better use of the U.S. estate tax exemptions.

2. Unless your Canadian assets are of such a nature that there are no comparable assets available in the United States that can produce a similar return on your investment, your life will be greatly simplified if you liquidate all your Canadian assets. Maintaining a Canadian corporation when your intentions are to reside permanently in the United States can create double income and estate tax, possibly subject you to a higher rate of income tax and force you into special Internal Revenue Service reporting on your Canadian personal holding companies.

3. RRSPs and what to do with them when you move to the United States will be explained in the next cross-border question below.

4. Your U.S. rental property in the Ontario company should be moved out of the Ontario company into either your own name or possibly a U.S. corporation similar in purpose to the Ontario one. On the U.S. side of the border, there is no tax advantage to holding small rental properties in holding companies. In fact, you would likely be at a tax disadvantage by using a U.S. holding company, not to mention all the extra costs involved with corporations. There are both Canadian and U.S. tax implications in taking this rental property out of the Ontario corporation, which are too complex to be discussed here. I recommend you seek professional help with this and any other changes you are contemplating, as mistakes can be costly.

5. If your sister has been married to a U.S. citizen and has resided in the United States for more than three years, she can become a U.S. citizen and sponsor your green card immigrant status. The waiting time for this type of sibling sponsorship of the green card is around 15 years from application, so you would need to keep renewing your E-2

visa until that time. You have some other options to obtaining immigrant status through your company, which may require a somewhat difficult labour certification. I would advise a consultation with a good immigration attorney.

MAKING RRSP CONTRIBUTIONS FOR THE YEAR YOU LEAVE CANADA

My husband and I are moving from Toronto to take up new positions in Florida and will be leaving Canada on what appears to be a permanent basis. Do you have any recommendations as to what to do with our RRSPs before we leave Canada? Is it to our advantage to make RRSP contributions in the year we leave? What will happen once we leave Canada if we keep our RRSPs in Canada? Can they be transferred to a retirement plan in the United States, or should we cash them in before we leave?

— *Lucetta S., Safety Harbor, Florida*

You didn't mention how much or what types of investments you had in your and your husband's RRSPs, so I will explore most of the options with you, since this is a very common problem.

First, let's deal with the question of what to do with your RRSPs before you leave Canada. Assuming you both have employment income in the same year you are leaving, cashing in your RRSPs would add greatly to your total income for the year, and likely be taxed at your maximum marginal tax rates of 46% in Ontario. Unless you want to lose half of all your accumulated RRSPs' savings to CRA, you should explore other alternatives to cashing them in before you leave Canada.

There are some alternatives that may allow you to withdraw the full balance of your RRSPs at no or very low Canadian taxes.

If your RRSPs consist of mutual funds, stocks or other appreciated assets, we recommend you realize these gains before you become U.S. residents. You would realize the gains by either liquidating all the investments and transferring the proceeds directly into a new RRSP savings account or short-term deposits. If you have mutual funds, this transaction can be accomplished generally at no cost by merely switching from one fund to another, within the same family of mutual funds. This exercise to realize your gains does not affect your Canadian tax one bit, because your investments remain sheltered within your RRSP. However, for American tax purposes, should you liquidate them while you are United States residents, you will pay more U.S. tax unless you complete this gain realization process. The United States can tax capital gains on your investments, so by realizing these gains before you take up residency you are establishing a higher cost basis, and hence lower U.S. capital gains when the investments are eventually sold.

Before you leave Canada, I recommend you make your maximum contribution to your RRSPs for the current year. With Canada's new RRSP rules, which base this year's contributions on last year's income, you can take advantage of some great tax savings. For example, if you and your husband each earned up to $27,000 from your Canadian employment in the current year before you left the country, and could make the maximum RRSP contributions of $18,000 each, based on last year's earnings, you could eliminate any tax on your income in Canada during your year of exit. Your RRSP contributions and your personal credits should qualify you for a full refund of any tax withheld. At these levels of income, we would estimate a refund of more than $9,000 in the short year of your exit.

After taking up residency in the United States, withdrawals from your RRSPs, if planned correctly, can be a great source of tax savings. Without proper planning, they can create unnecessary U.S. taxes, and could be taxed by both the United States and Canada.

There are no provisions between Canada and the United States for a direct transfer of your RRSP to the U.S. equivalent, an Individual Retirement Account (IRA). However, you can cash out your RRSPs and pay as little as zero taxes on a net basis, once you leave Canada, and use the net proceeds to contribute your maximum to your IRAs or other tax-deductible qualified plans in the United States.

The background of how Canadian RRSPs are looked at by the U.S. Internal Revenue Service will help explain the problem and how to plan around it. The IRS considers your RRSP an ordinary investment, without the deferral of tax that CRA provides. Consequently, as a U.S. resident, if you were to leave your RRSPs in Canada, the IRS would tax you on all interest, dividends and capital gains on your account, even though you may not have actually received them. Income on which you are taxed but that you do not actually receive is called phantom income. The Canada/U.S. Tax Treaty allows you to make an election annually on your U.S. return to defer the payment of U.S. federal tax (individual states generally do not and are not required to follow tax treaties) on the RRSP phantom income, until it is actually withdrawn. Withdrawals of your principal contributions to the RRSP are not taxed by the IRS at any time.

You should know that CRA will tax all lump-sum RRSP withdrawals by non-residents at a flat 25% withholding rate, and periodic withdrawals at a 15% rate.

The question of what to do now should be somewhat easier to explain, now that you have some background. Since CRA has made it next to impossible for younger RRSP holders to have their withdrawals classified as periodic payments, a series of lump-sum withdrawals at the 25% withholding rate is probably the best alternative. If you arrange for a series of annual lump-sum withdrawals, and the total of these withdrawals is less than $9,000, you can file, as a non-resident, under Section 217 of the Canada Income Tax Act, to get a full refund of the withholding tax each year. To qualify for the Section 217 filing, the RRSP withdrawal and other reportable income on this must be very low (less than $25,000 total world income), so if you are working or have significant investment income this option would not be a useful one for you. If the payouts are more than $9,000 but less than $25,000, you could receive a partial refund of the withholding tax under Section 217.

Other than the withholding tax, you have no further Canadian obligations with respect to your RRSPs. However, you are going to have to reconcile the income earned on this RRSP with the IRS, by adding it to your U.S. taxable income. You will receive foreign tax credits for the tax withheld by Canada on your U.S. return. There are a number of alternatives to consider when reporting the income on your U.S. return, but without knowing your U.S. tax information it is difficult to speculate as to which alternative would be best. You will likely need some professional help in this area.

RECOVERING WITHHOLDING TAX ON CANADIAN INCOME

My two brothers and I own a family farm in Saskatchewan, rented out since 1952. One brother lives in Ottawa, the other in San Diego. We all depend on the income from the wheat sales.

My previous year's U.S. taxes gave me no tax relief on my Canadian income and I got no relief from my Canadian taxes. Did the Canada/U.S. Tax Treaty change that much recently? I am a widow living on Social Security plus a small income, so I feel I should have gotten some refund.

— Freda M., Tampa, Florida

While you are in a unique situation, it should not be difficult to resolve. You may file a short-form Canadian tax return to get back some of the withholding tax from CRA. On this return, you should include only the portion of income from the Saskatchewan farm allocated to you, deduct any expenses you have related to this income, and then collect any refund due. The deadline for filing such returns is July 1 following the year end, so you may be out of luck for the previous year, but will likely benefit for the current filing year.

SHOULD YOU COLLAPSE YOUR CANADIAN RRSP?

I read an article entitled "Don't Collapse Your RRSP if You Move to the U.S." It stated that I would lose money if I moved my RRSP and it would be to my advantage to leave my RRSP in Canada as a U.S. resident. I have been a U.S. resident green card holder for two years, and my wife and I have $350,000 in RRSP mutual funds in Canada. We are unlikely to return to Canada in the foreseeable future.

As you can see, due to the size of our RRSP, this is an important issue and the advice in the article appears to conflict with the advice you and others have given us in the past, which is to cash in my RRSPs in 2005. Is this something new or is there some other reason for the advice given in this article? My wife's U.S. income is about $20,000 and mine is about $90,000. Would a Section 217 filing apply to us and could we get a refund of the non-resident withholding from CRA?

— *Kurt K., Seattle, Washington*

There are some good reasons why this strategy mentioned in the article will not work for the majority of Canadians moving to the United States with RRSPs.

Stepping up the basis in your RRSP by buying the assets from your own RRSP would be considered a non-event by the IRS. This kind of transaction would be similar to changing brokerage firms by transferring your RRSP from one firm to another. To qualify for a step-up in basis in your RRSP before you enter the United States, the securities must be sold to a third party (your spouse doesn't count, either). You can switch mutual funds to other funds in the same family to get a step-up in your cost basis before you take up a U.S. residency without transaction cost. Since you are already in the United States this would not apply to you.

In addition, a Section 217 filing won't help obtain refunds of the non-resident withholding tax for those with incomes of more than $20,000. This is generally practical only for those with world incomes around $15,000 including the RRSP withdrawals, not the $30,000 mentioned in the article. For those with incomes of more than $20,000, it becomes more practical to use foreign tax credits in the United States rather than to look for a refund from CRA. The article overlooked several other key issues that I believe would lead most people to conclude that they should take their RRSPs out of Canada soon after departing for the United States:

1. Leaving your RRSP in Canada exposes you to significant government risk. In other words, you are at the mercy of CRA or the IRS's ability to change the rules on these investments and greatly increase your tax. The withholding tax on RRSP lump-sum withdrawals used to be 15%; now it is 25% and we expect it to keep rising even higher. Make hay while the sun is shining! The current 25% withholding on lump-sum RRSP withdrawals may be the lowest you'll ever get.

2. Getting your RRSP out of Canada greatly simplifies your financial life. You will be subject only to U.S. tax rules and you won't need the specialized tax and investment advice that comes with maintaining an RRSP as a U.S. resident. This specialized advice is not only expensive, but hard to find since most U.S. advisors don't have any experience with RRSPs and don't have the time required to get up to speed.

3. The article failed to address the complications of state income tax rules, which vary somewhat from state to state. American states are not bound by any federal tax treaties, so the election to defer U.S. taxes on income in the RRSP at the federal level would have no effect at the state level in many states. This would result in an unnecessary and added level of tax.

4. Once your RRSPs are withdrawn, you can put the net proceeds in the United States into a very broad range of tax-free or tax-deferred investments without all the restrictions of an RRSP.

5. On average, mutual funds in Canada charge about double what they do in the United States. Management expense ratios average 2% to 3% in Canada, while in the United States you have a large selection of no-load mutual funds with expense ratios as low as 0.1%. Based on the size of your RRSPs, the savings in expenses alone could be close to $10,000 a year.

There are at least five other reasons why you should not leave your RRSPs in Canada once you are a U.S. resident, but the ones I've listed should be sufficient to convince you what to do with yours.

CROSS-BORDER RRIFs CAN BE A TRICKY BUSINESS

I am at present considering cashing in $350,000 Canadian RRIFs and investing the proceeds in the United States.

Our bank in Canada advises me that a Canadian withholding tax of 25% applies to all payments above the minimum, which has 15% withheld.

The RRIF withdrawals will also be taxed in the United States, of course, but subject to tax credits. From what I have been able to deduce, it would be advantageous for me to move at least some of the RRIFs from GIC investments to mutual funds to be able to utilize these tax credits fully. Our Canadian bank is prepared to make this switch of assets.

We are inclined to bite the bullet and pay the 25% Canadian tax. Is there a way to avoid the 25% Canadian tax and instead pay 15%?

— G.N., Fort Myers, Florida

You can withdraw twice your annual minimums or up to 10% of the value at the beginning of the year from your RRIFs at the 15% non-resident withholding tax rate. Up to twice the minimum RRIF or the 10% withdrawals are considered periodic under the Canada/U.S. Tax Treaty. Lump-sum withdrawals over the two-times-annual minimum are taxed at the 25% non-resident rate. The only part of your RRIF that is taxable by the United States is your earnings — interest, dividends and capital gains in your plan each year. The rest is considered tax-free withdrawal of principal. You'll need some help from a fee-only financial planner to help you plan these withdrawals. Doing it on your own can mean you miss out on tax credits and could make costly mistakes, as there is more to consider than meets the eye when making these RRIF withdrawals as a U.S. resident.

U.S. RESIDENT WITH CANADIAN INCOME TRUSTS

I am now a U.S. resident and am doing my U.S. taxes for the first time. I have several Canadian energy trusts that I have been buying and selling, and I have received investment income from them. How do I report these investments on my U.S. tax return?

— Dana L., Phoenix, Arizona

Canadian income or energy trusts present some unique concerns for U.S. tax reporting requirements. Some of them are registered as a corporation in the U.S. and therefore taxed as such, and others are trusts that are taxed in the same manner as U.S. Real Estate Investment Trusts (REITs) — with the full flow-through of the tax liability to the individual owners of the trust whether the income is interest, dividends or capital gains. As a consequence, the investors would normally receive a 1099 income slip from the corporate registered income trusts and a K-1 from the others. However, most of the Canadian income trusts don't issue a U.S. K-1 because they are Canadian. You may have to do a bit of detective work to translate the Canadian interest, dividends, capital gains, ordinary income and return of capital amounts from each of your income trusts based on the Canadian tax information provided from the income trusts themselves into an equivalent U.S. K-1 that you can report on your U.S. tax return. This may be difficult; I suggest visiting the websites for each of the trusts you own and looking for the information you need. Canadian income trusts should be withholding 15% non-resident withholding tax on all distributions they send to a U.S. resident, including distributions which are returns of your capital.

Don't Let the Tax Door Hit You in the Behind on the Way Out

9

DEALING WITH DEPARTURE TAX

WHAT IS A DEPARTURE TAX?

It would be nice to be able to say that the Canadian departure tax (also known as the exit tax) is much ado about nothing, but most Canadians give it a great deal of thought when considering moving to or retiring to the U.S. Sunbelt. This chapter will undertake to show the departure tax does get more attention than it deserves. We can start by defining what departure tax is. Departure tax is the tax that the Canada Revenue Agency levies on a taxpayer's capital assets when they become non-residents of Canada. The CRA requires that a taxpayer who is exiting Canada has to go through a deemed disposition or a deemed sale of certain assets on the date of departure. For tax purposes, under the CRA rules, a deemed sell is always taxed as an actual sale of assets. As noted in earlier chapters, Canada taxes residents on their world income only while they are actually living within its borders. Consequently, all one has to do is to depart Canada and no longer be subject to Canadian tax rules. Canada's answer to this simplistic method of avoiding Canadian tax is to collect all the taxes due on any capital gains that have not yet been taxed prior to the taxpayer's departure, hence the departure tax. The best way to understand the departure tax is to understand what is not subject to the tax, since there are many myths and misunderstandings as to what is included in this tax. The following is a list of assets that are NOT subject to any departure tax when moving from Canada:

1. Canadian real estate or resource properties

2. Canadian business capital property(including inventory) if the business is carried on through a permanent establishment in Canada

3. Pensions, all registered plans including RRSPs, registered retirement income funds, locked-in retirement accounts, retirement compensation arrangements and deferred profit-sharing plans

4. Employee stock options subject to tax in Canada

5. Interest in life insurance policies or annuities in Canada

6. Rights to certain benefits under employee profit-sharing plans, employee benefit plans, employee trusts, retirement allowances and salary deferral arrangements

7. Interests in certain trusts in which the trustee and the trust assets will remain in Canada

Now that we've looked at what is not subject to tax, it is a little bit easier to understand what is subject to the departure tax. This is the list of what is subject to departure tax:

1. All stocks (including closely held Canadian-controlled private corporations), bonds, mutual funds, exchange traded funds, limited or general partnership interests and other similar securities that are not inside registered plans noted in (3) above

2. U.S. real estate and other foreign real estate

3. Certain rights or interests in foreign trusts

4. Personal property that has appreciated in value such as artwork or antiques

If you compare the two lists above as to what is and what isn't subject to departure tax, you can easily surmise a large number of Canadians would not be subject to any departure tax at all. Those Canadians who may be subject to departure tax have several options to mitigate, defer or eliminate this tax altogether, as noted in the next section.

TAX ON EXITING CANADA

When Canadian residents move to the United States, CRA requires that they file exit tax returns for the year of their departure. This exit return is a regular T1 form filed by the usual April 30 deadline following the year of departure, with the exit date clearly indicated on the first page of the T1 and all the appropriate schedules, forms and disclosures completed as required. The important forms to be filed with an exit T1 are Form T1161, List of Properties by an Emigrant of Canada and Form T1243, Deemed Disposition Property by an Emigrant of Canada, which lists and calculates the net capital gains on those owned items subject to the exit tax. Each property deemed to be disposed of is deemed to have been re-acquired by the individual at the time of emigration at a cost equal to the proceeds of the disposition of the property. Any capital gains tax due may be paid with the return or deferred using the procedures noted in the next paragraph.

To elect to defer this exit tax you must complete and file Form T1244 with your exit tax return. You are required to post suitable security with the CRA equal to the tax due. The tax due need not be paid until the assets subject to the deemed disposition tax are actually sold. It is important to realize that since CRA charges no interest on the tax due, by electing to defer, you are in exactly the same situation as if you stayed in Canada holding the same securities or properties. Given this, why are so many emigrants overly concerned about leaving Canada and paying an exit tax? Unfortunately, all too often, concern with the exit tax is a result of not knowing the basic rules or of relying on advisors who aren't able to or don't want to explain the rules to the taxpayer. Many times during my cross-border planning career I have heard individuals say to me, "My accountant, who has been my advisor for too many years to mention, told me I can't leave Canada because I would have way too much departure tax to pay." If you hear this phrase or something similar, I believe you need to seek out a new advisor who looks out for your best interests.

Using the election to defer taxes is just a worst-case scenario; there are many cross-border options to legitimately minimize or eliminate any exit tax that may be due. These options include, but are not limited to, the following:

- Most investment portfolios at any given time have some securities in a gain position and some in a loss position. On your exit, you may offset the losses against gains and therefore be subject to tax only if there is any net gain on the portfolio.

- Use the Canada/U.S. Tax Treaty to eliminate the tax entirely on a net basis by turning the so-called exit tax into foreign tax credits that can be used to reduce U.S. income taxes on a dollar-for-dollar basis once you've taken up residency in the United States.

- Use the small-business capital gains exemption (for husband and wife this could mean up to $1 million of tax-free capital gains).

- Utilize capital losses carried forward that may be available from previous investment losses or failed investments.

- If your spouse is not emigrating from Canada with you, transfer assets to him or her on a tax-free basis and you would have no exit tax when you departed Canada.

- If you have any assets that are not deemed to be disposed of when you cross the border and that have a net loss built into them — such as a terrible real estate investment — you may elect to go through a deemed disposition of this property on your exit and use the loss to offset other capital gains that are subject to the exit tax.

There is a reporting requirement for those exiting Canada with total property holdings exceeding $25,000. They are required to report all of their property on CRA Form T1161 with their exit returns for the year of departure.

If you did not sell or do not wish to sell your Canadian principal residence before departing Canada, you need to be aware of some special rules under the Canada/U.S. Tax Treaty that can help you reduce future capital gains tax on the sale of your Canadian home while you are a U.S. resident. In Chapter 3, when we compared the basic differences in taxation between the United States and Canada, we saw that Canada does not tax capital gains on the sale of a principal residence while the United States will tax those gains in excess of $250,000 ($500,000 per married couple). The Canada/U.S. Tax Treaty helps you around this problem by making it appear, for tax purposes, that you purchased the Canadian home at its fair market value the day you entered the United States, provided you file the appropriate treaty election with your U.S. tax return for that tax year. As a result, you are responsible to the IRS for gains on this property only from the date that you became a resident. Note that this step-up in basis for your principal residence applies only to non-U.S. citizens or non-green card holders. Other capital property (thanks to proposed changes to the Canada/U.S.Tax Treaty in September 2000) that is subject to the deemed disposition on exit from Canada may also get a new cost basis for U.S. tax purposes equal to the fair market value of the property on the exit date. To receive the special tax treatment, the individual must file a treaty election Form 8833 with the U.S. tax return for the year of departure from Canada. Even though these proposed changes to the treaty have never yet been officially added to the Canada/U.S. Tax Treaty, both the CRA and the IRS have elected to act as if they were already included in the treaty. It is highly recommended that Canadians who keep their principal residences when moving to the United States get a fair market appraisal just before leaving Canada and keep it for future tax reference when making the treaty election.

Upon your exit from Canada, you must either elect a deemed disposition of your principal residence on your exit tax return, or convert it to rental property. This will step up your Canadian cost basis on the ultimate sale of the property to further reduce possible capital gains taxes in Canada, as you would have received the tax-free principal residence exemption had the residence been sold before your departure from Canada.

CANADIAN DEPARTURE CHECKLIST

If you're exiting Canada for the United States or another treaty country, the treaty will generally provide clear rules as to what income can be taxed, at what rate and by which country. Your exit from Canada should be as clean as possible to avoid CRA attacks on your residency or non-residency status. There are several key actions you should follow when exiting Canada, and if you follow these rules you will likely have little problem with CRA attempting to tax your world income in Canada. In the February 1998 federal budget, CRA introduced a new rule that stated that if a Canadian was deemed a resident of another country under a treaty with Canada, he or she would automatically be a non-resident of Canada for all domestic purposes. This new rule makes it much less likely that CRA will ever challenge the fact that you have not exited Canada and try to tax you at Canadian tax rates. However, some items are not covered by treaty provisions, so to avoid paying full Canadian tax rates we've developed a checklist. These tips can assist you in establishing Canadian non-resident status after your departure, thereby avoiding future controversy with CRA. The items are listed in no particular order, but the first five are considered vitally important. Remember that there is no single thing you do but rather the combination of facts and circumstances determines residency.

1. Sell your Canadian principal residence or rent it out on a long-term lease (six months or longer) on or about your date of departure, preferably before your exit date. Having unrestricted access to year-round accommodation in Canada, regardless of whether you own it, is considered having a principal residence in Canada. A cottage or other seasonal residence generally would not be considered a principal Canadian residence. If you buy or rent in the United States, the Canada/U.S. Tax Treaty will cancel out CRA's claim for Canadian residence even if you still own a place in Canada. This principal residence determination is the first rule of the Canada/U.S. Tax Treaty tiebreaker rules (detailed in Chapter 3).

2. Make sure you spend as much time out of Canada after your exit date as possible, particularly in the first two years after your departure. Under no circumstance spend more than six months a year in Canada after your departure. Keep your visits to Canada relatively short in duration (four to six weeks) and as infrequent as possible.

3. If you have a business in Canada or Canadian employment income, develop proof that you are not required to be in Canada on a continuous basis to operate the business. Other employment or business

income should be earned in the same manner that a U.S. person who has never resided in Canada would earn it. Try to do all your work from the U.S. side of the border. You are allowed to earn up to $10,000 in Canada without being subject to Canadian tax under the Canada/U.S. Tax Treaty. If you exceed this amount, you must file Canadian tax returns and pay Canadian taxes at the full rates on your income earned in Canada, even though you may be a non-resident. Please review the Canada/U.S. Tax Treaty tiebreaker rules outlined in Chapter 3; if there is any doubt or concern with any of these first three items, the treaty is always the final determinant.

4. Close all your Canadian bank and brokerage accounts, including RRSPs (review all the issues concerning RRSPs detailed in Chapter 8), and move them to the United States. Maintaining a chequing and/or savings account at a Canadian bank generally is okay, providing it is clearly set up as a non-resident account.

5. Notify any Canadian payers of Canadian-sourced income such as banks, brokers, pension payers and government agencies in writing that you have left Canada and are to be considered a non-resident for all purposes as of your exit date. Give them your U.S. address to forward all future payments and statements to you there.

6. Cancel your Canadian medicare coverage before your exit date or within the provincially allowed grace period after your departure. Make sure you have U.S. health insurance in place before you leave Canada.

7. You must be a legal resident in the United States before you can exit Canada for tax purposes. Ensure that proper U.S. immigration documentation is in place before you depart from Canada.

8. Cancel all church, club or equivalent memberships in Canada or at minimum convert the regular memberships to non-resident memberships. All churches and most clubs will allow you to visit or use their facilities as a non-resident.

9. Cancel all your Canadian credit cards, your driver's licence and your vehicle registration. Establish all of these in the United States (see the next section of this chapter when attempting to establish credit for the first time in the U.S.).

10. Accept no mail deliveries at any address in Canada. Have all mail forwarded to the United States. Do not have personal mail sent to a Canadian relative or business address.

11. Change wills and other legal documents to reflect U.S. residence.

In general, always think and act as a visitor to Canada in all respects. It is sometimes good to just think of yourself as entering Canada as a visitor for the first time and act accordingly.

TRANSFERRING YOUR CREDIT RATING TO THE UNITED STATES

Many Canadians moving to the United States are shocked to discover their hard-earned good credit rating in Canada cannot get them even a simple VISA card there. This problem can usually be overcome by knowing what to tell a credit card company, or whoever you are borrowing from, what they need to do to verify your credit history. The people doing the credit check will normally feed your Social Security Number into various credit bureaus and see what comes back. Since you are a new resident with a new Social Security Number, usually nothing will come up. No credit will be advanced, since lenders usually consider someone with no credit history a poor risk. The trick is to give them your Canadian Social Insurance Number and explain that credit bureaus in Canada operate on a very similar basis. If they call a Canadian reporting agency with your SIN, they can access your complete credit history.

It is important to obtain a hard copy of your Canadian credit rating from one of the Canadian credit services to provide to the U.S. creditor directly. Equifax is a credit bureau in both Canada and the U.S. so they are the easiest to work with in these circumstances. Without some direction from you, clerks at most lending institutions will simply reject you because their rule books don't tell them what to do in this situation. Be persistent with this process and insist on speaking to higher and higher levels of management in the bank or organization you are wishing to receive credit from and eventually you should find someone experienced enough to actually understand the situation and who will act accordingly. American Express is the only credit card company I am aware of that will transfer your Canadian account to the United States, including all member benefits, without cost or hassle just by calling their customer service.

Royal Bank of Canada recently purchased a Florida bank, RBC Centura Bank, which has about 300 branches, primarily in the U.S. Southeast, including several in Florida. This bank does mortgages in all 50 states, so if any Canadian is looking for a mortgage or other service, RBC will automatically transfer your Canadian credit rating to the U.S. To date, RBC Centura Bank has been doing a very good job on this very valuable service.

U.S. ESTATE PLANNING

Necessity is often the mother of invention. Since there is a greater need for comprehensive estate planning in the United States, a number of very good and proven techniques have been developed to help make management of your estate easier while you are alive and then provide for a smooth transition to your heirs. Many of these techniques will work equally well for Canadians who become residents of the United States and can be used to cover assets still remaining in Canada.

When you are moving or contemplating a move to the United States, cross-border estate planning needs to be a top priority, as there are many complex issues that could lead to unnecessary estate settlement costs and death taxes if not addressed before you take up residence in that country.

Normally the first matter of business in cross-border estate planning is doing a comparison of what your estate costs and taxes are in Canada, and then in the United States, to see if there is any advantage in either country. It is not very often in this book that I can state a general rule that applies in almost every case, but I can say that couples with estates of less than US$4 million (this exception is growing to the equivalent of US$7 million by 2009), or about CDN$4.5 million at current exchange rates, have an unquestionable tax advantage as residents of the United States. Since there are spousal trusts in Canada and qualified domestic-marital deduction trusts in the United States to permit the transfer of assets tax-free between spouses, I will concentrate on estate tax and settlement costs at the death of the second spouse, to measure the full impact of these costs and make a proper Canadian-U.S. comparison. Figure 9.1 gives an example of this situation, using a reasonably well-off couple with an estate of CDN$2,230,000 from the province of Ontario.

The Canadian death taxes in Figure 9.1 are calculated by taking the amount subject to the deemed disposition tax at death of the surviving spouse and adding the Ontario probate fee.

The total deemed disposition tax is CDN$498,800; U.S. non-resident estate tax is zero under the new Canada/U.S. Tax Treaty and the probate fee for an estate of this size in Ontario would be CDN$33,450. Thus, a total death tax of CDN$532,250 would be payable by this couple's estate if they were Canadian residents at the time of their deaths. If this couple, or at the very least the surviving spouse, does not undertake some preventive planning, their heirs will pay what amounts to a total of CDN$532,250 in Canadian inheritance or estate tax after the second spouse's death. These taxes will be due within six months of that person's death or by April 30 of the following year, whichever is sooner.

Assets		Amount Subject to Canadian Death Tax
RRSP/RRIF	$800,000	$800,000
Cdn. Residence	$400,000	$0
Mutual Funds	$300,000	
	(Original cost $150,000)	$75,000
U.S. Residence	$400,000	
	(Original cost $100,000)	$150,000
Land	$150,000	
	(Original cost $50,000)	$50,000
Term Deposit	$100,000	$0
Personal	$80,000	$0
Total	**$2,230,000**	**$1,075,000**
Canadian resident death taxes	$498,800	
U.S. resident death taxes	$0	

Figure 9.1

When comparing U.S. and Canadian taxes, many Canadian accountants, financial planners and attorneys are quick to pontificate that Canada does not have an estate tax. I was raised on the Canadian prairies and we had a simple saying: "If it looks like a duck, walks like a duck, quacks like a duck — it is most likely a duck." Just because the CRA doesn't call the tax at death an "estate tax," as Figure 9.1 illustrates, doesn't mean that most Canadians won't face a much higher estate tax in Canada than U.S. residents who own similar estates. The IRS doesn't try to disguise its estate tax, and because of the high exemptions allowed, less than 2% of all U.S. residents are subject to an estate tax.

If this couple took up residence in the United States and had a similar asset mix at the time of death, they would have absolutely no estate taxes due, since the size of their estate would be only about US$2 million, less than their combined total of US$4 million in U.S. estate tax exemptions. In addition, the beneficiaries of the estate from the U.S. residents would receive a free step-up in basis on any appreciated assets left in the estate so they could be sold without capital gains taxes. In Chapter 4, I listed some of the double-tax consequences of having assets in both

Canada and the United States, and earlier in this chapter I listed things to look out for when leaving Canada. The complexity of these issues underscores the necessity of consulting with a cross-border financial planner to ensure you maximize the opportunities and minimize the pitfalls.

For estates of more than US$4 million per couple, or US$2 million for individuals, other estate-planning techniques can be used to deal economically with almost any estate tax (see Figure 4.2 for the estate tax rates). Substantial U.S. residents with estates exceeding their personal estate tax exemptions, and who are concerned about depletion of their estates as discussed in Chapter 4, will use one or more trusts set aside and funded with income tax savings to pay any potential estate taxes, even when they run into millions of dollars.

The January 1, 1996, protocol to the Canada/U.S. Tax Treaty added a very useful provision that allows the executor of a Canadian citizen descendant to opt out of the U.S. unlimited marital deduction on the first spouse's death and receive an extra exemption equivalent to the US$2 million current amount (growing to $3.5 million by 2009). This means that those couples who have estates of between US$6 million and US$7 million, divided equally between the spouses, can escape U.S. estate taxes altogether using this single treaty provision. In addition, there are many other effective estate tax planning techniques for larger estates, which go beyond the general scope of this cross-border guide.

In the section Living Trusts in Chapter 4, we outlined a number of benefits in using a living trust in an estate plan. These trusts are used in the United States for estates of any size, to assist in minimizing probate costs and delays. Combined with wills that are designed to place assets outside trusts into them at death, powers of attorney and living wills, these trusts round out a cross-border estate plan. (Powers of attorney are also explained in Chapter 4.) A living will is a separate document that deals with the possibility of your becoming incapacitated, to the extent of your being connected to life support systems with no hope of recovery. The living will tells your family and medical professionals your wishes under such circumstances.

CROSS-BORDER Q&A

CANADIAN EXIT PROCEDURES

I am currently getting my tax returns done by Cross Border Tax and Accounting in Phoenix. Is there a beneficial purpose in submitting Canadian Form NR73, Determination of Residency Status (Leaving Canada)? Specifically we (I am dual Canadian and American citizen, age 66, and my husband, age 69, is Canadian) are both retired and own a condo in the U.S. We have been renting a small home in rural Saskatchewan. We would like to establish residency in the U.S., and we would like to keep our small rental home as a seasonal residence.

This would mean showing on form NR73 that we are —

1. *leaving personal possessions in Canada?*
2. *keeping a Canadian bank account?*
3. *keeping a brokerage account? and*
4. *keeping our Canadian passports?*

Apart from the above we have — or will — cancel our Saskatchewan driver's licences and replace them with Washington State licences, cancel Saskatchewan vehicle licences, and closed all memberships, our post office box, government medicare, and telephone. We have paid the instalment on our 2005 taxes due, transferred our Auto Club membership to Washington State, notified all payers of change of residency, and sent in a change of address for periodical subscriptions and all others we can think of, including charitable organizations to which we contribute. Mail is being forward to our U.S. address.

With this situation, and those boxes checked on form NR73 mentioned above — assuming it were to be submitted — what might be the response from CRA, after the 12-week current waiting period?

— Darlene G., Yorkton, Saskatchewan

You are not required to file an NR73, and we generally recommend you do not file one unless you are specifically requested to by CRA. If you follow the exit checklist in this chapter, you can generally assume that you have safely exited Canada for tax purposes. Nothing that you listed in your e-mail regarding what you are leaving in Canada would likely cause CRA to classify you as a resident of Saskatchewan.

However, you should move your brokerage account to the U.S. and keep only minimal amounts in your bank accounts. There are securities regulations that make trading in your Canadian brokerage account illegal from your broker's standpoint, unless the firm and broker are also licensed in Washington state. You'll find investment costs involved in trading and holding mutual funds to be a fraction of the costs in Canada, so there is a cost saving for you also to move this account.

It will be the Canada/U.S. Tax Treaty, not CRA Form NR73, that will determine what country you will be a resident of for tax purposes, the exit checklist can help steer you in right direction under the treaty rules.

TRANSFERRING CANADIAN CREDIT HISTORY TO THE U.S.

My husband holds an L-1A visa, and I have an L-2 visa that is valid until April 2008. I took your advice and called American Express to transfer my credit from Canada to America. They told me that they've made some structural changes in that I would have to be the one to call the Canadian office, cancel my card, then call back to the American office and apply for a card again. The information they would need from me would be my employment information and bank information. Obviously, I told them that I do not work, and they refused me a card. Unfortunately, since my husband is not an American Express cardholder, he was refused as well.

I also tried calling Equifax in the States and explained my situation. They told me to call the Canadian branch and get my credit information from Canada. Shouldn't the States have a copy of my credit information? That's the whole point of my not getting any credit here: America doesn't have any credit file on me! They told me that when and if I apply for any type of credit card or anything else I need, I would have to present a copy of my Canadian credit information. I find that ridiculous! Is this the way it works? I am in the process of mailing my personal information to the Canadian Equifax office to get my credit file.

I was also wondering if I need to cancel my Canadian life insurance policy now that I am an American resident.

— Soula P., Vancouver, British Columbia

Some people have managed to get Equifax to make the call to Canada and get the credit history transferred; others have had to do what you are doing. I don't know why there is such inconsistency in the Equifax procedures, but both ways do work.

Also check with RBC Centura Bank in the U.S., a subsidiary of the Royal Bank of Canada because they have been very helpful in assisting Canadians to transfer their credit ratings to the U.S. There is no need to cancel your Canadian life insurance policy, but if you are still able to get new insurance, it will be more convenient to replace your Canadian policy with an American one. Don't cancel your existing policy until the new policy is in place.

KEEPING A CANADIAN COTTAGE AS A U.S. RESIDENT

I enjoyed your book. I am curious about one point, though. On your Canadian Departure Checklist, you mention selling of your principal residence, and you also mention that a "cottage or seasonal residence generally would not be considered a principal Canadian residence." In the next sentence you mention that "if you buy or rent in the United States, the treaty will cancel out CRA's claim for Canadian residence even if you still own a place in Canada."

When looking at CRA Form NR73, Determination of Canadian Residency, I understand that a cottage is indeed considered a "secondary tie" to Canada and thus would not be a principal residence (which would be considered a primary tie). However, if one had enough ties remaining to be considered a resident of Canada (and owned only a cottage and not a home), and if it came down to the residency tiebreaker, and since the first tiebreaker in the treaty is a permanent home, would CRA at that point consider the cottage to be a permanent home in order to send the decision to the next tiebreaker (which is the center of vital interests)? I began thinking about this while reading your book and thought I would ask about it.

— Krista B., Ottawa, Ontario

Keeping a cottage as a secondary tie to Canada has never, to my knowledge, been a problem for any of the clients or *Border Guide* readers with whom I have worked. There are two reasons for this. First, if CRA were to try to tax you as a resident, you could argue that primary residence trumps secondary residence, and therefore you would pass the first treaty test. However, should that fail, the next treaty test is for vital interests, over which you have nearly full control, and you could make these weigh in favour of U.S. residency, thereby passing that test. You should ensure that you can pass at least one test clearly and should have a good backup plan to be able to pass one other, just in case you are declared a resident when you don't want or plan to be.

There's No Place Like Home 10

RETURNING RESIDENTS

There are estimated to be more than two million Canadians living in the United States. Many of these Canadians took jobs there or were transferred there for employment purposes, leaving their families and their roots behind. Many have completed their U.S. employment or are baby boomers now reaching retirement age who are deciding where they would like to live now that they are no longer going to be tied to jobs. Many will decide to stay where they are and have developed new social and family networks; many others will head south to the U.S. Sunbelt while some will head north back to Canada and their Canadian roots. In the past few years my colleagues and I have helped complete cross-border planning for several of these people returning to Canada and we have had many requests to add to *The Border Guide* information that would be of assistance to them and others in the same situation.

Consequently, this chapter discusses issues and suggests solutions to Canadians returning to Canada to live permanently. U.S. citizens being transferred to Canada for employment or wishing to retire in Canada face similar issues to long-term U.S. resident Canadians returning to Canada; however, there are enough differences between these groups that Chapter 11 specifically deals with the cross-border planning issues for U.S. citizens moving to Canada.

As with most cross-border planning, whether you are heading back to Canada or moving there for the first time, the longer you plan in advance the better the return you will get on your time, effort and expenses. In any event, planning must be completed before you cross the border to take advantage of some of the pre-entry techniques to reduce or eliminate taxes and to take advantage of opportunities that are no longer available to you once you are in Canada. In fact, good cross-border planning dictates that no doors should be closed nor bridges burned, and an optional plan to move back to Canada should have been included in your plan to move to the United States in the first place.

Planning for the move north across the U.S.-Canadian border is not necessarily the reverse of a move south.

IMMIGRATION TO CANADA

Those Canadians who have retained their Canadian citizenship or are dual citizens of the United States and Canada will have absolutely no problem or immigration concerns on entering Canada. If you have been out of Canada for a long time and are concerned that by taking up U.S. citizenship you have lost your Canadian citizenship, you need not worry if you took up U.S. citizenship after 1977. In 1977 Prime Minister Pierre Trudeau introduced his "once a Canadian, always a Canadian" policy, which, after that date, allowed Canadians to retain their citizenship when taking up the citizenship of another country unless they made a formal renunciation of their Canadian citizenship. If you obtained your U.S. citizenship prior to 1977 (which means you no longer have Canadian citizenship) or have never been a Canadian citizen, you will need to obtain permanent resident status under one of several Canadian programs or be granted a visa under the North American Free Trade Agreement (NAFTA) before you will be allowed to move into Canada legally. Canadian immigration options for U.S. citizens moving to Canada will be discussed in detail in Chapter 11.

GIVING UP YOUR U.S. CITIZENSHIP OR GREEN CARD

If you are a U.S. green card holder and are making a move to leave the United States for a period exceeding six months, technically you will be deemed to have abandoned your green card status as a legal permanent resident of the U.S. However, in a practical sense, if you don't voluntarily surrender your green card at the border or to a U.S. Citizenship and Immigration (USCIS), office you should be able to retain the use of the card if you follow some basic guidelines. If you have been a green card holder for more than five years and you wish to keep your options open about moving back to the U.S. at some point in your life, it is recommended that you become a U.S. citizen before you move back to Canada. I wish I had a dollar for each of the countless Canadians who have given up their green cards when they moved back to Canada from the U.S. and then regretted doing so or wished they had taken up U.S. citizenship when they had the chance, so that they could to go back to the U.S. for personal or financial reasons.

There are potentially large tax compliance issues if you retain your green card. The IRS taxes green card holders in the same manner that it taxes U.S. citizens regardless of where they live. Consequently, as part of the cross-border plan it is best to review all the implications of retaining or giving up your green card and take the appropriate action. Generally, because part of cross-border planning is to keep the door open to live and pay taxes in either the United States or Canada, we suggest legally retaining your green card or becoming a U.S. citizen unless it is absolutely certain that you will never return to resident status in the United States. Normally you can retain your green card legally if you maintain a presence in the United States such as a home, investments, driver's licences, etc., and if you return to the United States periodically (at least once every six months) and continue to comply with the IRS by filing annual tax returns. Note that filing U.S. tax returns doesn't necessarily mean you end up paying more taxes since the tax rates in the United States are generally lower on nearly all income items. If you definitely will never return to the United States and are giving up or abandoning your green card, you are treated by the IRS like an expatriating U.S. citizen for tax purposes if you have had the green card for more than eight of the past fifteen years. This is detailed in Chapter 3 in the section U.S. Tax Legislation Concerning Expatriation from the U.S.

It is not easy getting U.S. citizenship or a green card, so giving them up should not be taken lightly. Certainly it should not be done without professional advice and analysis by a qualified U.S. tax expert or cross-border financial planner.

INVESTMENT GAINS AND INCOME

In Chapter 3 we compared the major forms of investment income in Canada and the U.S. on a line-by-line basis. On every major form of investment income, Canadian residents pay substantially higher taxes, so those who rely on investment income need to prepare themselves for a large reduction in after-tax investment income after moving back to Canada. Because of the recent increase in the value of the Canadian dollar relative to the U.S. dollar, Canadian residents of the U.S. who move back to Canada without both kinds of currency protection planning (as discussed in Chapter 2) may see their U.S. dollar retirement nest eggs cut by nearly 50%.

Canada Revenue Agency (CRA), under the same rules that force a deemed disposition of all capital property when you exit Canada, allows you a tax-free step-up in the cost basis on entering the country (see Chapter 9). This means, for Canadian purposes, that you are deemed to have sold all your capital assets on the day prior to your entering the country and to have reacquired them at their fair market value on that day. Consequently, a step-up in cost basis is received so that only the gains that accrue after you become a Canadian resident taxpayer are taxable by CRA. This deemed step-up in cost basis on re-entering Canada, for Canadian purposes has no effect for U.S. tax purposes. If you are still a U.S. citizen or green card holder entering to become a Canadian resident, the sourcing rules for capital gains need to be understood clearly. These rules determine in which country the gains will be taxable, under the Canada/U.S. Tax Treaty capital gains sourcing rules (as previously noted in Chapter 8 in Withdraw Your RRSP Tax Free!). All your gains, with the exception of U.S. real property, will be classed as Canadian gains once residency in Canada is established. Consequently, the sale of appreciated stocks and bonds or other capital property after you become a Canadian resident will, in certain circumstances, trigger a U.S. tax with no offsetting Canadian foreign tax credits. In previous chapters, I defined "double tax" and why you need to plan to avoid it. Double tax is when you pay tax in one country and receive no offsetting tax credits to apply against the same income in the other country, so you are taxed by the other country a second time. The bottom line is that you pay tax on the same income two or more times. If this sounds like double-talk that's because unfortunately that's exactly what it is.

Those to whom the expatriating rules noted above and in Chapter 3 do not apply and who have given up their green cards or U.S. citizenship may escape both Canadian and U.S. tax on any gains accrued on assets before entering Canada. If you fit into this situation, having a tax-free holiday on all your capital gains can be an enormous benefit. Those Canadian residents who remain U.S. citizens or who are green card holders generally will find it best to consider triggering the U.S. capital gains before entering Canada to avoid any future double-tax problems on their appreciated assets. In any event, it is very important to obtain fair market value appraisals on all assets on the date you leave the United States and enter Canada, as you will definitely need those cost basis numbers for future tax filings.

Income (dividends and interest) earned or accrued from investments prior to entering Canada will be taxed only in the United States. After entering Canada the investment income will be taxed by Canada only for those who are no longer U.S. citizens or green card holders. U.S. citizens and green card holders will need to report this income annually in both countries on an ongoing basis, paying the highest rate of tax imposed by either country. Because Canada allows foreign tax credits only on U.S. investment income to the extent of the Canada/U.S. Tax Treaty withholding rates, U.S. citizens or green card holders are advised to move their income-producing investments to Canada or employ other investment strategies to avoid paying a double tax on the investment income. The IRS will allow full foreign tax credits for investment income earned in Canada so no double tax should be levied on IRS returns filed after Canadian residency is established.

It should also be noted that Canada does not have tax-free or tax-deferred investments other than RRSP-type registered plans. This means a U.S. citizen or green card holder holding tax-free U.S. municipal bonds or tax-deferred annuities of any type and who is resident in Canada will pay Canadian tax annually on all the interest and dividends earned in these investments, whether he leaves the income to accrue in the United States or not. This kind of investment situation is a perfect example of the potential double-tax situation I defined above that should not be ignored. People with these types of investments should seriously consider liquidating them before becoming Canadian residents, pay the tax on the deferred income inside the annuities at the lower U.S. rates, and invest the proceeds in Canada, where the income will be taxed on a current basis by CRA and create foreign tax credits for future U.S. tax filings.

Also, since as a Canadian resident you will have to pay full taxes on any municipal bonds you own, you may require some professional investment planning help. For example, by cashing the bonds in and reinvesting them, you may be able to obtain higher yields on the non-tax-free bonds, so in effect you will have more interest income to help pay for the taxes due as a Canadian resident.

U.S. RETIREMENT PLANS

Qualified retirement plans and Individual Retirement Accounts (IRAs) in the United States are the equivalent of the Canadian RRSP-type registered plans in Canada. They can consist of any combination of Individual Retirement Accounts (IRAs), Roth IRAs, 401(k) plans, Roth 401(k) plans, 457 plans, 403(b) plans, Simplified Employee Pensions (SEPs) and Savings Incentive Match Plans for Employees (SIMPLEs). Like Canadian RRSPs, contributions to these U.S. plans are deductible, and all of these plans allow interest, dividends and capital gains to accrue on a tax-deferred basis until they must be withdrawn starting at age 70½ (age 69 for RRSPs). The key exception to this rule is the Roth 401(k)s and Roth IRAs, which are after-tax contributions and in which all investment income is tax free in the United States regardless of when it is withdrawn past age 59½, and there is no forced withdrawal at any age. Once U.S. residents holding any of these U.S. retirement plans become Canadian residents, they may continue to defer the taxation on the buildup of the income until withdrawal in a manner similar to that for RRSPs, with the exception of the Roth IRA and Roth 401(k). CRA will tax the annual buildup of income in a Roth IRA or Roth 401(k) as the income is earned or realized. In other words, what was once tax free in a Roth IRA or Roth 401(k) for U.S. purposes would be taxed at full Canadian rates annually and without any deferral or tax-free benefits at all. Consequently, on these Roth plans you go from zero tax close to 50% tax, depending on your province of residence.

It is very kind of Canada Revenue Agency to allow returning Canadians or U.S. citizens to continue to defer tax in almost all of their U.S. retirement plans except the Roth plans. However, the catch is that CRA will tax 100% of any withdrawals from these plans for Canadian residents at full Canadian rates even if withdrawals are made in the first year of Canadian residency. As a result, those moving to Canada with these qualified plans will pay on average twice as much tax on any withdrawals from these plans as they would have paid as U.S. residents, particularly if the withdrawals bump them up into the maximum Canadian tax brackets and make them subject to OAS clawbacks (review Chapter 3 and in particular Figure 3.6 for a comparison of U.S. and Canadian tax rates).

As described in Chapter 9 and illustrated in Figure 9.1, the full value of U.S. qualified plans and IRAs for Canadian residents is taxed at Canadian maximum rates on the date of your death (unless you have a spouse to roll the plan over to). This is in sharp contrast to the option U.S. residents have on their retirement plans, besides the spousal rollover, to have their estates pay out the qualified plan or IRA to their children or grandchildren over their respective lifetimes. This very useful option allows the family to get another twenty to eighty years of deferral out of their qualified plans and IRA plans. This extra deferral period can provide thousands or even millions more dollars to the family of the original U.S. retirement plan holder that will be lost to Canadian residents regardless of citizenship status.

Anyone entering Canada with any of the U.S. retirement plans noted above may be best advised to forego any future tax-free deferrals on the income buildup inside the plans. It makes very little sense to defer income in retirement accounts when the tax on withdrawal is going to be higher than the tax savings realized when the original contributions to the retirement plans were made. If you are retired or have the necessary flexibility, it may be best if you withdraw all the qualified retirement plans and IRAs at U.S. tax rates before you take up Canadian residence if you are never likely to return to the United States before you begin to withdraw from these plans. For example, if you are retired and your chief source of income is from investments, you could convert most of your investment income to tax-free or low-taxed income such as capital gains and then start withdrawing your qualified plan as rapidly as possible, spread over enough years to keep your average tax rates in the United States as low as possible. In the United States, even if you have a very large qualified retirement plan and are over age 59½ you could withdraw up to US$336,000 a year and not even get into the highest U.S. tax bracket for married jointly filing taxpayers. Once you have taken your entire qualified plans or IRAs out at the lower U.S. rates, you can enter Canada with tax-paid funds, invest them in Canada and pay tax only on the earnings from that point on.

The tax savings on this course of action are enormous, and on larger qualified plans you can easily save enough tax to buy yourself a Canadian house free and clear with money that would have gone to CRA in the future. To complete a withdrawal of this type, you will need the help of a qualified cross-border financial planner as there are far too many factors, combinations and permutations that need to be considered to complete it most efficiently alone, and mistakes can be very costly.

U.S. STOCK OPTIONS, BONUSES AND DEFERRED COMPENSATION

Those who have any U.S.-acquired stock options, yet-to-be-paid employment income or bonuses or are members of deferred compensation plans need to be alerted to some potential adverse tax consequences when taking up Canadian residency. Canada Revenue Agency will tax any of this income at full Canadian rates if paid to a Canadian resident even though it was all earned before he or she entered Canada. Consequently, even if you had taken up Canadian residency last week and got that long-awaited hard-earned bonus from your U.S. employer this week, not only will you pay Canadian tax rates on the bonus and lose close to half of it but you still will be taxable on it in the United States. However, CRA will allow a foreign tax credit for the tax paid to the United States but this will usually cover only a portion of the Canadian tax due. This can come as quite a shock to a first-time or returning Canadian resident being whacked with this "welcome to Canada tax." Clearly the best way to avoid this problem is to not take up Canadian residence until you have exercised all your U.S. stock options, received any residual wages or bonuses and have cleared out your deferred compensation plan. This is one area of pre-entry planning where a simple solution applied in a timely manner can save you a great deal of taxes.

U.S. SOCIAL SECURITY

Providing you have qualified under U.S. rules, you and your spouse will continue to be eligible for Social Security and Medicare benefits if you become Canadian residents. Only 85% of any benefits paid to you as Canadian residents will be taxable at your full Canadian tax rates. For most people this will mean a substantial increase in tax paid on Social Security income over their lifetimes. The maximum tax rate on Social Security in the United States (for those with taxable incomes of more than US$336,000) is 30% at the federal level, whereas in Canada as a Canadian resident your maximum tax rate would be about 40% (for those with incomes of more than CDN$120,000 depending on your province of residence and assuming the Social Security payments would not increase or make you subject to the OAS clawback).

CANADIAN OAS AND CPP/QPP

Qualification for the Canada Pension Plan (CPP) and Quebec Pension Plan (QPP) is based on Canadian employment earnings at any time since the CPP/QPP plan was introduced in the early 1960s. So if you worked in Canada during this period up to age 65, you will be eligible for some CPP/QPP pension. If you are retiring to Canada and are still under 65, it would be worth your while to find or create some Canadian employment income each year so that you will receive a CPP/QPP pension at 65. Qualifying for Canadian Old Age Security is based only on the number of years lived in Canada between ages 18 and 65. To receive a full benefit you need to have 40 years in Canada. The full benefit is about $5,600 per year for life, indexed partially for inflation. Partial benefits are paid based on the fraction of the 40 years you have spent in Canada. If you lived 20 years in Canada between 18 and 65, you would receive half the maximum annual OAS benefit. If your total number of years in Canada is less than 20, in order to get a benefit, you will need to apply under the Canada/U.S.

Social Security agreement to get time credit for your time in the U.S. OAS may be clawed back by CRA through a tax rate of up to 100% of the amount of OAS received for Canadian residents beginning at about the CDN$62,000 income level.

CANADIAN FOREIGN REPORTING

Canada Revenue Agency has recently introduced an entire series of reporting requirements designed to try to catch those thousands of Canadians who have parked money offshore and are not reporting the income on their Canadian returns. These rules essentially dictate that Canadian residents who have investments, bank accounts, foreign trusts or corporations (or are beneficiaries thereof), or investment real estate located outside Canada worth a total value of $100,000 or more must list these accounts on a special CRA form T1135 and report all earnings on the appropriate Canadian T1 return schedules. Failure to complete this reporting will invoke penalties for each year of non-compliance, effectively confiscating the foreign assets after only a few years of trying to hide any of these funds from CRA. Consequently, anyone moving from the United States to Canada will likely face these reporting requirements for every year that they maintain U.S. qualified plans, IRAs, investment accounts, bank accounts or U.S. investment property totalling a worth more than $100,000.

Because the penalties are so severe, care must be taken not to miss any items of foreign reporting that CRA requires. Since CRA and the IRS, under the Canada/U.S. Tax Treaty, regularly share information and help each other enforce penalties, it would be very foolish indeed to think CRA wouldn't find out about any U.S. assets or income that were not reported according to these new rules.

UNITED STATES TO CANADA — YOUR ESTATE PLAN

Anyone moving temporarily or permanently across the Canada-United States border in either direction must replace or, at the very least, modify their estate-planning documents. A well-drafted U.S. estate plan can become very ineffective after a move to Canada. For example, a U.S. living trust for which you and/or your spouse are trustees will become a foreign trust for IRS purposes and be subject to many complex tax rules. From a CRA standpoint, the trust would be considered a Canadian resident trust and required to file its own annual tax return in addition to following many other CRA rules discussed later in this section. Generally speaking, a correctly drafted and valid U.S. will would be valid in most Canadian provinces. However, trying to submit what amounts to a foreign will to a Canadian probate court is not very practical. It would be time-consuming and costly convincing a Canadian judge the U.S. will was valid. It would be much more beneficial to have your U.S. will redrafted by a Canadian lawyer in your province of residence, adding any modifications required by that particular province. If you are going to have assets remaining in the United States, it would be best to use a cross-border lawyer trained and experienced in both Canadian and U.S. estate laws to make sure the will can be easily used and probated in all the jurisdictions in which you have assets. As an alternative, if you cannot find a cross-border lawyer, you can have the Canadian lawyer contact a U.S. counterpart in the state(s) in which you have assets to review the Canadian will. Although this is more time-consuming and costly, it could pay off greatly in the ease with which your estate is settled. U.S. citizens and green card holders must include provisions in their wills to deal with potential U.S. estate taxes and related exemptions or options. Some lawyers may try to convince you to have two or more wills, one for each jurisdiction that you have assets in. Although there are some merits to this advice, I do not generally recommend it. It is difficult enough to keep track of one will for most people — to store it and amend it periodically as necessary due to changing family circumstances — never mind two or more wills. In addition, having more than one will increases the number of opportunities for mistakes or challenges from beneficiaries, particularly as to which will should be the governing one.

Powers of attorney (POAs) for both general matters and medical matters are very important, but often neglected, documents in any Canadian or U.S. estate plan. The POAs need to be enduring (Canadian terminology) or durable (U.S. terminology), which means they will still be valid even in the event of the writers' incapacity. Some POAs can be drafted with "springing powers," stating that they have no effect until incapacity occurs. Our recommendations here are very similar to those regarding wills above: use a competent lawyer or lawyers in your province of residence and state(s) where your assets are located to ensure your POAs are effective when and where needed. Since you are still alive when your POAs are to be used, and they can easily be drafted using even the forms provided by the institutions where you have accounts, such as banks, it is generally okay to have a POA for each jurisdiction or even at each financial institution in which you have assets. U.S. medical POAs, from most states include living wills, which have provisions to determine when and who would "pull the plug" if you were in a vegetative state with no hope of recovery. Many Canadian provinces have not yet recognized living wills or even enduring medical POAs, so these documents may be of no legal use there. We still recommend the use of living wills and enduring POAs even if your province of residence does not formally recognize them yet, as they help family members make better decisions for you, and more and more judges are recognizing their validity.

Living trusts of various forms are very common in the United States and therefore are widely accepted by banks, investment firms and other financial institutions. The same cannot be said for Canada, although their use is beginning to catch on, very slowly. For those over age 65, CRA now allows the use of alter ego trusts, which are very similar in design, use and administration to U.S. living trusts. Upon a move to Canada, the trust also takes up Canadian residence if you are its trustee under CRA rules. In addition, CRA imposes certain rules on trusts that U.S. residents do not have to deal with. For example, in Canada, trusts must file their own tax returns to report income (this is not required for most U.S. trusts since the tax liability flows directly to the trust's grantors or creators), and there is a twenty-one-year rule that requires that all assets in the trust be deemed disposed of and any capital gains taxes paid (the IRS has no similar rule at all in the United States). Although these CRA rules dealing with trusts may increase the cost of administering living trusts in Canada, it doesn't mean that you necessarily scrap your U.S. trusts once you cross the border. Living trusts will still be valid in Canada and can be very useful to avoid Canadian probate fees, to ease the administration of your estate and to look after you and/or your spouse if you are incapacitated. Their trusts can help those who remain U.S. citizens or green card holders take advantage of U.S. estate tax and generation-skipping taxes. Some U.S. trusts may require slight modifications once their grantors or creators effectively become Canadian residents, to deal with some of the CRA rules or provincial idiosyncrasies. Simply put, moving from the U.S. to Canada complicates your estate plan, in my estimation, by a factor of at least three. Again, professional legal help from a cross-border lawyer is recommended.

MEDICAL COVERAGE

One item that is easy to deal with in moving to Canada is the ease in applying for and receiving Canadian medicare regardless of your medical condition. Most provinces require you to be a resident for only 90 days or less before full medical coverage takes effect, providing you apply for it through the applicable provincial agency. Alberta allows returning residents immediate access to medical coverage, with no waiting period. Some provinces charge a nominal quarterly fee for the coverage, depending on your age, while others include the costs in the general taxation system to make it appear free. One thing returning or new Canadian residents will appreciate with the Canadian medicare system is the lack of paperwork for patients. However, they may miss the wide range of choices, full access to specialists and modern medical facilities without waiting lines available in the United States.

Some people moving to Canada may have their cake and eat it too with respect to Canadian and U.S. medical coverage, by having full access to all medical facilities and doctors in Canada or the United States. If you are over 65 and have qualified for U.S. Medicare, you can retain this coverage even as a resident of Canada. Consequently, you can have access to the Canadian medical system through your provincial medicare and to the U.S. medical system through U.S. Medicare. For example, if you lived in Vancouver and needed a hip replacement but there was a long waiting list for the surgery there, you could cross the border to Blaine, Washington, a few miles away, and have the surgery and be fully recovered before your wait for surgery in Vancouver was even over. Also, many returning Canadians still winter or travel in the United States, so having U.S. Medicare gives them very economical travel insurance that is not restricted by age or medical condition and is not limited to emergency care only. This certainly is having the best of both worlds, medically speaking.

For both Canadian and U.S. Medicare, supplements are recommended to fill any gaps of coverage and to give you better access to private hospital beds.

Both U.S. Medicare and, to a lesser extent, Canadian medicare are inadequate when providing long-term nursing care benefits. We recommend that both U.S. and Canadian residents have adequate long-term care insurance to protect their assets from having to be consumed by any lengthy stay in a nursing home or similar facility. Some United States long-term insurance carriers will pay benefits for nursing home stays in either Canada or the United States without any additional premium cost. I highly recommend one of these carriers for your long-term care insurance, as my experience indicates that maximum flexibility in choosing a nursing home in either country is most beneficial. You should have a daily benefit in your policy at least equal to the average daily costs in the long-term facilities in the geographical areas you are likely to be in.

DEDUCTIONS LOST

Chapter 3 compared deductions allowed by the IRS directly to CRA rules, so I will only summarize and review these differences. The key deduction most people would miss moving from the United States to Canada would be the mortgage interest deduction on up to two principal residences and property taxes on all properties. The other major deduction lost would be that for the state income taxes allowed by the IRS; CRA doesn't allow any equivalent deduction for provincial taxes paid. Minor deductions allowed by the IRS but not CRA would be for tax-preparation fees, certain legal fees, financial planning fees and motor vehicle licence fees. Although it's not really a deduction, most U.S. tax-payers would also miss the tax-free treatment of interest from municipal bonds and the ability to defer interest, dividends and capital gains income through variable annuities for as much and as long as they want. Also, as noted earlier in this chapter in the section Investment Gains and Income, one can expect that the income taxes on most forms of investment income will increase from about 50% to over 100% of the taxes paid on the same amount of income in the U.S.

U.S. DEPARTING ALIEN INCOME TAX RETURN

All resident aliens — that is, U.S. green card holders, visa holders or visitors deemed resident of the United States under the Substantial Presence Test as noted in Chapter 3 — leaving the country more or less permanently are required to get a Certificate of Compliance (also known as a sailing permit) from the IRS. The sailing permit is obtained by filing IRS Form 1040-C at your local IRS office at least two weeks before your departure date. Form 1040-C is essentially an interim tax return for the year of your departure to ensure the IRS can collect the tax due on term income earned for the departure year before your departure date. If the IRS is satisfied they have collected enough tax from you through withholding or with the 1040-C return, they will issue you the sailing permit to allow you to leave the country. You are still required to file your regular IRS Form 1040, Dual Status return, by June 15 following the year of departure to make a final reconciliation of the taxes due in the year of departure as the 1040-C is not considered a final return.

The surprising thing about filing Form 1040-C is there are no apparent penalties for not filing it and there is no one to review your sailing permit as you cross the border from the United States. As most people who travel internationally know, when you cross the border from the

United States to Canada, the first people you report to are Canadian Customs and Immigration, who are not the least bit interested in whether you have a sailing permit or not from the IRS and would likely laugh at you if you showed it to them. Note that there definitely are penalties levied by the IRS if the final 1040 is not filed and any tax not paid in the required time.

CANADIAN PRE-ENTRY REVIEW

In order to summarize this chapter and to assist those contemplating a move back to Canada or for the first time from the United States, I have listed the key issues of consideration below:

- Higher overall taxes on most sources of income. Review Chapter 3 and Chapter 8 for a detailed analysis of the tax differences between Canada and the United States.

- Loss of the tax-free status of interest on municipal bonds and Roth IRAs or Roth 401(k) plans.

- No tax-deferred income tax on any form of deferred annuities, long-term deposits or compounding interest bonds.

- Allowance to continue to defer tax on income buildup on U.S.-qualified retirement plans and IRAs but that subjects the entire plan's value to full Canadian tax rates when withdrawn.

- OAS clawback of up to 100% of Old Age Security benefits, to which Canadian residents are subject while U.S. residents are not.

- Access to both Canadian and U.S. Medicare possible from the Canadian side of the border.

- Modifications to wills, living trusts, powers of attorney (POAs) and other estate-planning documents required upon moving to Canada.

- The cost of the actual move, the new estate-planning documents and a cross-border financial plan.

- The consequences of giving up U.S. citizenship or a green card and conversely the cost of keeping U.S. citizenship or a green card as Canadian residents may be significant. You must thoroughly investigate prior to taking these kinds of actions.

After reviewing all these factors and consulting with a cross-border financial planner, you may feel the positive attributes outweigh the negative ones, so a move to Canada is in the cards. However, if the negative factors, such as the increased tax burden, are unacceptable, you should stay put in the United States. If the family and social pressures of moving back to Canada are conflicting with your desire to avoid the higher Canadian taxes, perhaps a "have your cake and eat it too" solution is the answer. You can follow the Canada/U.S. Tax Treaty rules to maintain U.S. residency for tax purposes, yet own a second home in Canada, get on Canadian medicare and live there for up to six months (or more in certain circumstances). Regardless of which goal and objectives you are trying to attain, a complete cross-border plan needs to be initiated and implemented in a timely manner.

Although Chapter 11 is written specifically for U.S. citizens moving to Canada for the first time, it also contains relevant information for Canadians returning to Canada after a period of U.S. residency.

CROSS-BORDER Q&A

MOVING BACK TO CANADA

Relocation between Canada and the United States is not just a one-way street to the South. A lot of Canadians return to Canada after years of living and working in Florida as U.S. residents. These people would love to hear something about their tax-planning opportunities as well, such as deferred U.S. annuities. Florida tax planners are in general not really knowledgeable about Canadian tax law and changes in the past.

— Enocho B., Naples, Florida

Great question. Since we live in such an ever-changing society, good cross-border planning will generally keep all doors open so that people moving out of Canada may move back without adverse tax or other consequences.

Tax-planning opportunities and concerns arising when moving from the United States back to Canada are numerous and are not necessarily the reverse of the planning procedure of the original move to the United States.

Unrealized gains on stocks, bonds and investment real estate are best realized before leaving the United States for Canada. The maximum capital gains rate in most provinces is 25% whereas the U.S. maximum is now 15%. If you don't realize the gains prior to your entrance into Canada, you will have a Canadian cost basis equal to the value of the properties or securities on the date of your return to Canada.

If you have a large capital gain built up in the personal residence you own in the United States, you should take advantage of the $500,000 tax exemption by selling the residence before you leave the country, or you could lose it. Canada will not recognize this U.S. exemption, nor will the United States recognize the Canadian capital gains exemption for the principal residence.

If you have acquired IRAs in the United States, which are equivalent to Canadian RRSPs, you may get some good tax breaks when you head back to Canada, providing you cash them in before exiting the United States. (Watch for the IRS 10% withdrawal penalty if you are younger than 59$\frac{1}{2}$.) Canada will tax you at full rates on the principal, interest and dividends on withdrawals from these accounts once you become a resident. If you still own IRAs or other U.S.-qualified plans when you return to Canada, you will pay higher Canadian tax rates on all your withdrawals.

If you own deferred annuities of any type when you move back to Canada, they will lose their ability to shelter income buildup from current Canadian taxation. Canada requires you to report all interest, dividends and realized capital gains on deferred annuities on a current basis and will not allow you to accrue this income to defer the payment of tax. Annuities are best cashed in and invested in term deposits or similar Canadian investments, or converted to annuity payout options.

If you are collecting U.S. Social Security, under the Canada/U.S. Tax Treaty you will be allowed to exclude 15% of this income from Canadian taxation. If you are a U.S. green card holder when you take up permanent residency back in Canada, you will be required to surrender it. If you don't, not only are you going against U.S. Immigration regulations but the Internal Revenue Service will continue to tax you as a resident. If you have become a U.S. citizen or a dual Canadian/U.S. citizen, much of what I outline here as planning opportunities will apply differently to you, unless you directly and formally surrender your U.S. citizenship. If you are a dual citizen and are a resident of Canada, you will need to file full returns in both Canada and the United States on your world income and take allowable credits back and forth to avoid being double-taxed on that income.

When you re-enter Canada, be prepared for a tax shock. There is no tax-free or tax-deferred income available in Canada. There are fewer deductions and the marginal tax rates are much higher and the amount of income required to reach the highest rates is much lower. If your primary sources of income are interest and pensions, you can expect your income tax bill to nearly double. You will, of course, benefit from Canada's comprehensive, although deteriorating, medical care system and more generous social welfare systems. So what you give up in taxes, you may well recover in social security, particularly if you are in the lower income brackets.

In any case, when you are moving cross-border in either direction, you need a detailed plan with the assistance of a professional who is fully knowledgeable about both sides of the border, to direct you through the maze of opportunities and pitfalls.

GREEN CARD MUST BE GIVEN UP

I am a Canadian citizen and have been a U.S. resident for the last five years. I plan to return to Canada. I am 75 years old. My assets will be two U.S. bank accounts, U.S. Treasury bills worth about $300,000, a mobile home in Alabama, Canada Pension and Old Age Pension. My plan is as follows:

1. *Enter Canada formally on January 1, 2007.*

2. *Apply for OHIP in Ontario.*

3. *Keep my U.S. bank accounts.*

4. *Keep my U.S. Treasury securities.*

5. *Apply for W-8BEN designation of my assets to be U.S. tax exempt.*

6. *Give up my green card to qualify.*

7. *Keep my mobile home in Alabama for now.*

Is my plan satisfactory? Any pitfalls? When do I give up my green card?

— J.B., Elberta, Alabama

There appears to be no reason why you can't go through with your plan to return to Canada on January 1, 2007. OHIP will require a 90-day waiting period before it will cover you. CRA will be happy to see you back as they will collect tax on your OAS, CPP and the interest on your U.S. Treasury bills. There is no requirement for you to file a W-8BEN form for your U.S. Treasuries, as they are not subject to non-resident withholding tax, but you will need to file the W-8BEN for your bank accounts. Remember that exemption from U.S. taxes does not mean exemption for Canadian purposes. You must report all of your U.S. income to CRA. You will have to give up your green card to make all of this work, but make certain you will never need it again before you give it up as they are difficult to obtain these days. Good luck!

RETURNING CANADIAN RESIDENT LOSES HOMESTEAD EXEMPTION

I am a Canadian citizen and live in Florida six months of the year. I have a green card. I have a residence in Ontario where I live for the other six months. I would like to return to Canada as a full-time resident. What is the procedure? Should I sell my house here as I would no longer get the Homestead and widow's allowance exemptions? What should I do with the green card?

— D.S., Boynton Beach, Florida

The procedure to become a Canadian resident, since you are already a Canadian citizen, is simply moving back to Canada and re-establishing your residential ties, such as applying for OHIP, a driver's licence and filing a Canadian tax return. You will need to effectively give up your green card by mailing it to U.S. Citizenship and Immigration Services (USCIS) or surrendering it at the border. Make sure you are prepared for possibly higher Canadian income taxes before you give up U.S. residence.

If keeping your Florida Homestead Exemption is the only reason for your keeping your property, you should sell it as you will lose your exemption if you are no longer a resident of Florida. However, it certainly is not necessary to sell this residence if you still want to visit Florida during the winters and need a place to stay.

MOVING BACK TO CANADA — THE SEQUEL

In 1982 we were transferred to the United States by a subsidiary of a large Canadian company. My husband worked there until retiring in 1992.

We applied for and received our resident alien status in June 1987. In 1992 we returned and resumed Canadian residency in order to take advantage of OHIP. We did not apply for or receive Medicare. Our ages are 68 and 69.

We own a home in the United States where we spend six months every year. My husband has a small company pension, Social Security, stock, investments and IRAs. Our total U.S. assets amount to approximately $400,000 and we file a 1040NR and a Form 8840. Our assets in Canada exceed this amount and include our home, property, company stock, investments, RRSPs, GICs, company pension, OAS and CPP.

We regret our decision to return to Canada and we wish to reinstate our U.S. resident alien status. We still have our green cards and, since purchasing The Border Guide, *are now aware of the implications. Would you advise us or inform us as to where we can obtain information on the following:*

1. *How we do reactivate our NR status?*

2. *Can Medicare be secured prior to reestablishing residency?*

3. *Do we need an estate planner and legal counsel?*

4. *Should we begin using our green cards upon entry to the United States and reinstate residency?*

— Sid and Nancy V., Holiday, Florida

Since you have been living six months every year in the United States and still have your green cards, you are probably permanent legal residents there and have likely not abandoned your green card status. However, you have been filing the wrong returns with the IRS for residents and should go back and re-file all the returns that were completed incorrectly. You need to file Form 1040, not 1040NR returns and not Form 8840. This should get you in compliance with both IRS and USCIS and may also get you some tax benefits to top it off.

1. As noted above, you may have retained your U.S. status.

2. Medicare can be applied for from January 1 through March 31 every year and will become effective July 1 of the year in which you apply, so you may have to cover the gap from January to July with alternative coverage.

3. You definitely do need professional help, but not just for estate planning as you have several other financial, tax, investment and insurance issues to address. A good cross-border financial plan can save you a lot of money and aggravation in these areas.

4. I have to answer this one with a conditional yes after you have covered all the other issues discussed above.

TAX TREATY CAN REDUCE WITHHOLDING ON 401(K) PLANS

I am a 59-year-old retired Canadian citizen who, while living in the United States, participated in a 401(k) plan and who now wishes to commence monthly plan withdrawals.

The plan managers, T. Rowe Price, advise they are required to withhold tax at the rate of 30%. Your guide discusses the Canada/U.S. Tax Treaty and leaves me with the feeling the 30% withholding tax is too high.

If I am correct, can you refer me to the current IRS bulletin so that I can give it to T. Rowe's taxation group?

P.S. Including this withdrawal, my wife and I would have a total gross U.S. income of about $4,000, which includes some common stock dividend payments.

— *P.F.L., Caledonia, Ontario*

T. Rowe Price is technically correct with its withholding rate of 30% according to IRS domestic rules. However, you should qualify for a treaty reduction under the Canada/U.S. Tax Treaty to 15%, providing your withdrawals are periodic by IRS definition. To apply for the treaty-reduced withholding, you will need to file IRS Form W-8BEN with T. Rowe Price.

For residents of Canada, all IRA, 401(k), 403(b) and other qualified U.S. plan withdrawals are 100% taxable by CRA at your marginal Canadian rates. Any U.S. non-resident withholding tax you pay will become a credit for you on filing your annual Canadian T1 return, provided the withholding was done at the correct Canada/U.S. Tax Treaty rates. Consequently, if you are in the 50% Canadian tax bracket and have 15% non-resident withholding by the IRS on 401(k) withdrawals, you will pay an additional tax to CRA equivalent to 35% of your U.S. plan distributions.

Moving to Canada, Eh 11

U.S. CITIZENS OR RESIDENTS
MOVING TO OR INVESTING IN CANADA

It is estimated by the U.S. embassy in Ottawa that there are more than a million Americans living in Canada on a regular basis. Canada welcomes thousands of new immigrants and visitors from the U.S. every year. Just as Canadian visitors fall in love with certain areas of the U.S. and purchase property there, for similar reasons Americans visiting Canada often want to either purchase Canadian property for recreational use or as an investment.

Chapters 1 through 6 have dealt with Canadians visiting and investing in the U.S. and Chapters 7 to 9 have addressed Canadians moving and immigrating to the U.S. Although many of the issues discussed in these chapters are not relevant to Americans immigrating to or investing in Canada, Americans face many similar cross-border issues when they move north. I therefore recommend that American readers review these chapters, paying particular attention to the concerns of U.S. citizens and green card holders living in Canada and the differences in both income and estate taxation between Canada and the United States. Chapter 10 and this chapter discuss the residency status of new or returning immigrants to Canada and certain Canadian tax regulations that apply to Americans who invest in Canada. To get the full picture, both these chapters should be read by Americans moving to Canada for the first time.

We will begin by addressing American visitors wishing to invest in real estate or other securities in Canada. Later in the chapter, we will discuss issues of particular interest to Americans immigrating to Canada.

AMERICANS PURCHASING PROPERTY AND INVESTING IN CANADA

Thousands of Americans currently own or are in the process of buying Canadian real estate. The Vancouver real estate board estimates that one-third to one-half of all new condos in downtown Vancouver are owned by

Americans. Similarly, there are many areas around the Canadian side of the Great Lakes where the majority of the property owners are Americans. Unfortunately, though, just as most Canadian visitors purchasing property in the U.S. are unfamiliar with U.S. income and estate tax implications, so too are American visitors investing in Canada unfamiliar with Canadian income tax, goods and services tax, land transfer taxes, probate fees and the Canadian equivalent to estate taxes. Here are the key concerns Americans buying and holding real estate in Canada need to be aware of:

- When you purchase Canadian real estate for your own personal use, you may pay a goods and services tax (GST), currently equal to 6% of the purchase price. Whether GST applies depends on the type and ultimate use made of the property.

- When you sell your Canadian property you are subject to Canadian capital gains tax, which will normally be withheld by the buyer's attorney until you get a clearance certificate by completing Form T2062, Request by a Non-Resident of Canada for a Certificate of Compliance Related to the Disposition of Taxable Canadian Property, from the Canada Revenue Agency (CRA). Whether you file for a clearance certificate or not — to reduce the withholding tax — you must still file a Canadian non-resident tax return by April 30 following the year of the sale. In most provinces and territories, Canadian capital gains tax is higher than U.S. capital gains tax. However, the Canada/U.S. Tax Treaty will provide you with a tax credit for any taxes paid in Canada, so at least you are not double-taxed.

- Most Canadian provinces and territories have a probate fee (review Chapter 4 for details about these fees), so if you die owning Canadian property, you will be subject to probate fees as well as the cost of probate in Canada. The cost of probate may be substantial, as you will likely need both a Canadian and a U.S. attorney. If you have a U.S. will, it must be submitted to a Canadian court to prove its validity under Canadian rules. If you do not have a will, your Canadian property will be subject to Canadian intestate rules, which may be substantially different from intestate rules in the state where you are resident.

- If you die owning Canadian property, you are subject to the Canadian equivalent of an estate tax. Known as a deemed disposition tax on death, this is a Canadian capital gains tax on the increased value between when a property was bought and its value on the date of your death. You may also be subject to U.S. estate taxes. If so, you will need to know how to use the Canada/U.S. Tax Treaty to prevent double-taxation on death. (Review Chapter 4 for information on estate tax benefits relating to the treaty.)

- Some provinces, such as British Columbia, have a land transfer tax that must be paid every time a property changes ownership.

- The title on your property — such as sole ownership or joint ownership with right of survivorship — is very important, as each form of ownership has specific tax and estate implications. Americans who have U.S. living trusts may be well advised to purchase their Canadian property in the name of the trust. This could avoid Canadian probate fees, estate settlement costs and deemed disposition taxes at death.

- If you already own a Canadian property and wish to transfer it to your U.S. living trust, the Canada Revenue Agency considers the transfer a "taxable event" (it is treated as if the property were sold on the date of transfer). Consequently, capital gains taxes are due in the year of transfer to the trust. In addition, if the property is in a province that has a land transfer tax, this tax will also be due at the same time.

- If you are going to rent out your Canadian property, you are subject to full Canadian income tax on the rental income. You have the option, under the Canada/U.S. Tax Treaty, to pay a flat 25% of the gross rental income directly to the CRA as the rent is received. Alternatively, under Section 216 of the Canadian Income Tax Act, you may elect to file Canadian non-resident tax returns annually and pay regular Canadian tax on the net rental income. Under Section 216, in addition to the annual tax return, you must file CRA Form NR6 each year before you begin receiving rental income to establish the non-resident withholding rate the CRA calculates for you or your agent to collect on the monthly rental checks.

Even though I have attempted to simplify the above property owner-ship issues, you have probably gathered that these issues can be extremely complicated for Americans owning property in Canada. I highly recom-mend that any American wishing to purchase property in Canada get ad-vice from a cross-border planning professional before making the purchase.

Other popular Canadian investments by Americans who are not res-idents of Canada are such securities as Canadian stocks, income trusts, exchange traded funds (ETFs) and private equity investments in closely held Canadian businesses.

Canadian stocks and bonds are available to most Americans through any U.S. brokerage firm. Many Canadian stocks are actually listed on both Canadian and U.S. stock exchanges, which makes trading easier for Americans wishing to buy or sell such stocks. Interlisted Canadian stocks can be tracked in either Canadian or U.S. funds, but the Canadian stocks that are only available through the Canadian stock exchanges are generally available in Canadian dollars only, which means that Americans purchasing the stocks must bear the currency risk in addition to the nor-mal investment risk when buying stocks. However, as non-residents, Americans will normally not be able to open a brokerage account in Canada because of securities regulations. Under the Canada/U.S. Tax Treaty, American residents are exempt from any capital gains tax on trad-ing of Canadian stocks; such gains are only taxable in the U.S. If any of the Canadian stocks pay dividends, the treaty will allow CRA to withhold 15% non-resident withholding tax and to provide a full foreign tax credit for the U.S. resident's tax return.

Income trusts in Canada have recently become very popular for Americans looking for investments that primarily provide income but also have some potential for growth and reasonable liquidity. Canadian income trusts operate very much like U.S. real estate investment trusts (REITs). Like REITs, Canadian income trusts pay no tax at the entity level, so all income flows through to the trust owners. Consequently, all income is only taxed once at the personal level of the trust shareholders. The key differences with the Canadian income trusts — which have more favourable tax rules — are that they are not restricted to investments in commercial real estate as are U.S. REITs and they come in a variety of businesses in all industries, including the energy sector, which is the most popular sector of the Canadian economy. Canadian income trusts trade much like Canadian stocks on the Canadian stock exchanges, and the CRA withholds 15% non-resident withholding tax for American residents on any income distributed from them. The IRS taxes the income from the Canadian income trusts as dividends. However, since income trusts are relatively new and were not included in the Canada/U.S. Tax Treaty, new withholding rules may come into effect with future treaty negotiations.

Canadian exchange traded funds (ETFs) are very similar to American exchange traded funds. They resemble indexed mutual funds but trade like individual stocks. Barclays Bank is the primary supplier of the iShares family of ETFs in Canada. Canadian ETFs can be purchased on major Canadian stock exchanges through most U.S. brokerage firms.

Many successful U.S. business people have significant holdings in Canada. They continue to invest in Canada as opportunities arise through personal and business contacts. Such investments can create significant U.S. tax burdens if the business person does not correctly structure his or her ownership in private Canadian businesses. Many private Canadian companies are considered Controlled Foreign Corporations (CFCs) or Passive Foreign Investment Companies (PFIC) under IRS rules. For U.S. residents, U.S. citizens or green card holders, owning CFCs or PFICs can result in considerably higher taxes, double-taxation and loss of foreign tax credits on the Canadian income in the corporation. To avoid these negative tax consequences of owning closely held Canadian businesses, U.S. business investors must seek to structure their corporate deals in the form of joint ventures, partnerships or limited liability partnerships that flow all income directly to them, without any corporate tax. In addition, U.S. investors can use a relatively new corporate form called Unlimited Liability Companies, which exist in the provinces of Nova Scotia and Alberta. Unlimited Liability Companies are taxed by the CRA as regular Canadian corporations but for U.S. tax purposes there is a flow-through of corporate income directly to the U.S. shareholder, in the same manner as with Limited Liability Corporations and S-Corporations in the U.S.

IMMIGRATING TO CANADA

Canada, like the United States, has many business and family categories by which people can apply for immigration. The key categories used by Citizenship and Immigration Canada (CIC) are outlined below:

1. **Skilled Workers**

    Skilled workers with good education, work experience and knowledge of English or French may immigrate to Canada based on the number of points they receive from a scoring formula based on six factors. Total score from the primary six factors must exceed 75 out of 100 before one may be considered for immigration to Canada in this category. The six factors are Education (maximum of 25 points); English and French Language Ability (maximum 24 points); Work Experience (maximum 21 points); Age (maximum 10 points); Arranged Employment (maximum 10 points); and Adaptability (maximum 10 points). For example, if you had a PhD with work experience of at least four years, spoke English and French, were under the age of 30, had a job offer in Canada and a well-educated spouse who also spoke English or French, your score would be close to 100 and immigration to Canada would likely be straightforward. However, if your education, language ability, and/or work experience were weak, your chances of reaching the minimum score to immigrate in this category would be very poor.

2. **Business Immigrants**

Business immigrants may be selected for immigration to Canada based on their ability to become economically established in Canada. Simply put, this means that if you have enough money and some business experience, you may become a permanent resident of Canada relatively easily. Citizenship and Immigration Canada has three classes of business immigrants each with separate eligibility criteria: investors, entrepreneurs and self-employed persons. Investors must demonstrate business experience and a legally obtained minimum net worth of CDN$800,000, and must make an investment of CDN$400,000. The CIC will return the $400,000 investment, without interest, approximately five years and two months after payment.

Entrepreneurs must demonstrate business experience with a minimum legally obtained net worth of CDN$300,000 and commit to managing and owning at least one-third of a business of a defined size for at least one year within three years of landing in Canada. Self-employed persons are required to have either relevant experience that will enable them to make a significant contribution to the cultural or athletic life of Canada or experience in farm management and the intention and ability to purchase and manage a farm in Canada.

3. **Provincial Nomination**

Most Canadian provinces and territories have programs that encourage immigrants to settle in their jurisdictions. These Provincial Nominee Programs (PNPs) are primarily employment driven, allowing the provinces to select immigrants to assist in the developing specific areas of provincial economies. For example, a province may want to hire a foreign doctor to cover a particular rural area in the province and will nominate that physician to the CIC for immigration. If the selected physician fulfills the provincial requirement to remain and serve in that rural setting for the specified number of years, usually about three years, that physician can become a permanent resident of Canada and may move or live anywhere in the country. This person also becomes eligible for Canadian citizenship after living in Canada for at least 1,065 days.

4. **Family Class Immigration**

   Canadian citizens and permanent residents living in Canada who are 18 years or older may sponsor close relatives or family members who want to become permanent residents of Canada. Sponsors must promise to support the relative or family member and their accompanying family members for a period of three to ten years, depending on their age and relationship to the sponsor, to help them get established in Canada.

5. **Quebec Immigration**

   Quebec is responsible for selecting immigrants who wish to settle in Quebec. In fact, Quebec has a special status with Citizenship and Immigration Canada that allows it to set its own immigration criteria, almost like a separate country. Quebec skilled workers are not assessed on the six selection factors of the Federal Skilled Workers Program. Quebec sets its own criteria for skilled workers, which are normally less restrictive than the federal factors and focus the language skills on French only, with very little emphasis on the ability to speak English.

6. **North American Free Trade Agreement (NAFTA)**

   Under NAFTA, U.S. business people get quicker and easier temporary entry into Canada than other applicants. NAFTA applies to four specific categories of business people: business visitors, professionals, intra-company transferees and traders and investors. Each of these categories has its own requirements to gain temporary access to Canada to conduct business. In general, unless the individuals qualify for permanent resident status under one or the other categories noted above, they will have to return to the U.S. when their temporary visas expire.

Once you become a permanent resident of Canada, you may apply for Canadian citizenship after living in Canada for at least 1,065 days. If you are a U.S. citizen, the United States does not require that you give up your U.S. citizenship to become a Canadian citizen. Therefore, in effect, when you become a Canadian citizen you are considered a dual citizen of Canada and the United States.

WHEN DO YOU PAY TAXES IN CANADA

As noted earlier in this chapter, visitors are taxed in Canada only when they have income that is sourced in Canada. They pay Canadian income tax to the Canada Revenue Agency directly or through a non-resident tax withholding system under the Canada/U.S. Tax Treaty. Visitors who have sojourned in Canada for periods that total 183 days or more in a year are deemed to have been a resident in Canada throughout that taxation year. This deemed residency rule could potentially subject visitors to Canadian income tax on their world income. It is important that visitors who spend 183 days or more in a year in Canada protect themselves from being taxed on their worldwide income by filing Form T1 with CRA for the tax year in question. On this tax return they may claim Canada/U.S. Tax Treaty protection from full taxation on their world income because the treaty considers them residents of the U.S. under the residency tiebreaker rules. (Review Chapter 3 for the treaty tiebreaker rules to ensure that under these rules you would be considered a non-resident of Canada.)

Generally speaking, the Canada Revenue Agency considers any immigrant who becomes a permanent resident of Canada as taxable on their world income on the day they obtain their status and apply for Canadian medical coverage. Permanent residents must then file their first Canadian tax return, a Form T1, by April 30 of the following year, using the date they became permanent residents as the start date on the return. If you are both a permanent resident of Canada and a U.S. citizen, you must file tax returns in both countries and use the many facets of the Canada/U.S. Tax Treaty to ensure that you are not taxed twice on the same income. U.S. citizens must file annual U.S. tax returns regardless of where they live in the world.

In almost all circumstances, once you become taxable by the CRA as a resident of Canada you will pay higher to significantly higher income taxes than you would in the United States, depending on the amounts and sources of your taxable income. (Review Chapters 3 and 8 for more information on specific differences between Canadian and U.S. taxation systems and to learn about ways to take advantage of tax-saving opportunities.)

Some important tax considerations for first-time residents of Canada are outlined in the three sections that follow.

COST BUMP ON PROPERTY UPON IMMIGRATING TO CANADA

Once an individual enters Canada to become a resident for tax purposes, under Canada Revenue Agency rules he or she is deemed to have sold each property owned immediately before entering Canada — for proceeds equal to the property's fair market value — and purchased it back at that same value on the same day. This deemed disposition is called the "cost bump" or "step-up in cost basis" because, for Canadian tax purposes, it's as if the property was sold and then repurchased on the day before the person entered Canada. CRA taxes only those gains that accrue after the individual becomes a resident of Canada.

However, this cost bump does not apply to property that is already taxable Canadian property. For example, if you already own a residence in Canada that you purchased sometime before entering Canada as a resident for tax purposes, that property will retain its original cost for Canadian tax purposes. If you sell the property in the future, you'll pay capital gains tax based on the difference between the purchase price and the price for which you sell it. If you make this property your principal residence, any capital gains that accrue while you are a Canadian resident would be tax free.

U.S. citizens immigrating to Canada have some important issues to consider regarding their capital property when they enter Canada as residents. If they fail to work through these options, they could be double-taxed when they sell properties and investments owned at the time they entered Canada. This potential for double-taxation is best illustrated by a simple example. Assume you, as a U.S. citizen, immigrated and became a Canadian resident owning a stock that you paid $1,000 for and that had a fair market value of $10,000 on the date that you entered Canada. For U.S. tax purposes the purchase price would be $1,000; for Canadian tax purposes the cost basis would be $10,000, the value of the stock when you entered Canada. If, after you had been a resident of Canada for a year, you decided to sell the stock, which had reached a value of $20,000, you would have a Canadian capital gain of $10,000 (the $20,000 fair market value less the Canadian cost basis of $10,000 equals a $10,000 gain), on which you would be taxed in Canada, paying about $2,500 in income tax. You would have a U.S. taxable gain of $19,000 (the $20,000 fair market value less the original cost of $1,000 equals a gain of $19,000), on which you would pay about $2,850 tax in the United States. Under the Canada/U.S. Tax Treaty, once you become a resident of Canada, capital gains are considered "sourced": originated in your country of residence. Because of the sourcing rule, the profit on the sale of this stock is considered a Canadian taxable gain and therefore no foreign tax credits for the taxes paid to the U.S. would be allowed (because from a Canadian tax perspective the gain is not foreign). This means you end up paying capital gains taxes in both countries, totalling $5,350. If you had done some tax planning before entering

Canada, you could have avoided paying tax on the same income in both countries.

This situation is referred to as double-taxation. The tax may not be exactly double; in fact, often it is more than double. Double-taxation really hurts when it hits unexpectedly, especially when it amounts to many thousands of dollars. In the example given above, you could have eliminated double-taxation if you had sold the stock before you entered Canada as a resident and bought it back on the same day. In this circumstance you would pay the U.S. tax on the capital gains, but thereafter your U.S. and Canadian cost bases would be the same, and you would not pay double tax.

Individuals who own considerable investment portfolios and properties located outside Canada are well advised to consult a cross-border planning specialist before entering Canada as residents.

CANADIAN PRE-IMMIGRATION TRUST

An immigration trust is one of the few tax breaks Canada Revenue Agency provides immigrants (other than the bump-up to fair market value of appreciated assets discussed above). To qualify as an immigration trust, a trust must be set up before the immigrant moves to Canada or within the first five years of coming to Canada. When an immigration trust is set up, the new immigrant is exempt from Canadian taxation on the income and capital gains from the assets held in the trust for up to 60 months from the date of arrival in Canada. Consequently, if the country in which the immigration trust is "settled" (the technical term for "set up") does not tax income in the trust, the income will accumulate free of tax for up to 60 months. Upon expiry of the 60 months, the income and capital gains from the trust can be distributed to Canadian beneficiaries without any Canadian income tax being paid. However, U.S. citizens who settle an immigration trust prior to coming to Canada will have to use tax-free investments (such as municipal bonds) or low-taxed investments in the trust because as U.S. citizens they will continue to be taxed on the income of the trust at U.S. tax rates.

For a trust to qualify as an immigration trust, each person or persons contributing directly or indirectly to the trust must have resided in Canada for less than a total of 60 months during their lifetimes. The trust must be non-resident in Canada, which suggests the trustee should be someone who is not a Canadian resident, since CRA generally considers the trust to be resident where the trustee is also resident.

IMPORTANT TAX CONCERNS FOR AMERICANS MOVING TO CANADA

Chapter 10 discusses many important tax considerations for Canadians returning to Canada after a long period of residence in the U.S. Since many people in this situation are also U.S. citizens or long-term green card holders, most of these important tax considerations also apply to Americans moving to Canada for the first time. Rather than repeat tax issues discussed in Chapter 10, I recommend that Americans immigrating to Canada review that chapter. However, I will also summarize these considerations in this chapter and point out any peculiarities that may apply to Americans immigrating to Canada for the first time.

- U.S. citizens heading to Canada with IRAs, 401(k) plans or other qualified plans are, on average, going to double the amount of income taxes they will need to pay when they eventually withdraw income from these plans. In Chapter 10, the section U.S. Retirement Plans provides several solutions to mitigate this doubling of the tax obligations on deferred income plans.

- Income tax on an investment portfolio can increase dramatically when a U.S. taxpayer becomes a Canadian taxpayer. Tax-free and tax-deferred income from investments becomes fully taxable annually in Canada. Capital gains in Canada are taxed at slightly higher rates than in the U.S., but it is important to watch out for potential double-tax situations noted earlier in this chapter.

- Any U.S. resident immigrating to Canada with bonuses, severance payments, vacation pay or deferred compensation earned in the U.S. but not yet collected should delay immigration and collect this income while still a U.S. taxpayer. If a person moves to Canada with any of this or similar kinds of employment income, he or she will pay Canadian tax rates on this income, which in almost all cases will be significantly higher than the taxes paid by U.S. taxpayers.

- U.S. stock options accrued while you are a resident of the U.S. are best exercised before entering Canada and becoming a Canadian taxpayer. The Canada Revenue Agency will tax the stock options even though they were from U.S. employment.

- Americans immigrating to Canada will continue to qualify for U.S. Social Security and Medicare at age 65 (or to continue to receive benefits if they are already receiving them) while they are in Canada, providing that they have qualified under U.S. rules before they left the United States. Under the Canada/U.S. Tax Treaty, when you collect U.S. Social Security benefits in Canada, 15% of the benefit will be tax free and the balance is taxed at Canadian rates. Chapter 13 discusses receiving both Canadian and U.S. Social Security benefits at the same time, whether living in Canada or the U.S. Americans moving to Canada should review that chapter if they wish to maximize these benefits.

- Americans working in Canada will, under normal circumstances, pay into the Canada Pension Plan (CPP) or Quebec Pension Plan (QPP) and be eligible for a pension when they reach age 65. Canadian Old Age Security (OAS) is not based on work history; benefits are accrued to anyone who has lived in Canada between the ages of 18 and 65. Full OAS benefits are paid at age 65 to those with annual incomes less than $62,000 and who have lived in Canada for 40 years between the above-noted ages. If you live in Canada for only 20 years before the age of 65, you could receive up to half the current maximum benefit of $6,000 per year.

- American citizens working in Canada and participating in Canadian deferred income plans such as Registered Retirement Savings Plans (RRSPs) or employer-sponsored pension plans cannot assume they will receive a U.S. deduction or be exempt from paying tax on the income earned in these plans (although their fellow Canadians won't pay until the money is withdrawn from RRSPs). Since American citizens must file U.S. tax returns each year, the IRS will not recognize tax-deferred status of Canadian registered retirement plans. In Chapter 8, in the section Withdraw Your RRSP Tax Free!, there is a discussion of how the IRS views and taxes Canadian RRSPs and similar plans. Review this and the unique tax filing requirements for U.S. citizens in Canada later in this chapter. Special reporting forms need to be completed and attached to your IRS Form 1040 and your Canadian T1 tax form each year.

- If you continue to own U.S. life insurance policies that accumulate cash values after you have moved to Canada, you need to be aware of how CRA will tax these plans. CRA will only allow the tax-free accumulation of income in a Canadian-exempt insurance policy. CRA will require a Canadian resident to annually report the growth of a U.S. insurance policy under the foreign investment entity rules, using the market-to-market approach. This means you will pay income tax annually on any income earned inside the U.S. insurance policy.

- Americans wishing to give up their U.S. citizenship when immigrating to Canada should review Chapter 3, which details the tax implications of completing an expatriation.

CONVERTING YOUR U.S. ESTATE PLAN TO A CANADIAN ESTATE PLAN

Generally speaking, if an American immigrates to Canada, with a valid will from their U.S. state of residence, their will would be recognized as a valid will in Canada. However, ancillary estate documents such as living wills and powers of attorney, which are extremely important documents when you are incapacitated either permanently or temporarily, will likely not be usable in Canada. Consequently, it is highly recommended that you draft a new set of estate-planning documents as soon as possible after entering Canada. These documents should be drawn up by a Canadian attorney intimately familiar with the needs of U.S. citizens living in Canada.

Any American who immigrates to Canada leaving property, investments, retirement plans and/or family members in the U.S. will complicate their estate plan considerably. For example, if you own properties in the U.S. and are living in Canada, your will or testament will need to go through probate in each jurisdiction in which any of the property is located. That means your executor would normally have to hire an attorney to assist with the probate process and filing the required federal and state estate tax returns in each jurisdiction. The executor would then have to try to coordinate all the attorneys to close out the estate. Anyone who has been an executor of a friend's or relative's estate understands the settling of an estate can be a very lengthy, complex process even when only one provincial or state jurisdiction is involved. Adding additional jurisdictions — especially between two countries — makes the executor's job more difficult and increases the cost of estate settlement.

Intelligent use of cross-border trusts and titling of assets can mitigate the complications and the costs of estate settlement, but these options sometimes create additional complications of their own. The use of the standard U.S. "living trust" can avoid probate in multiple jurisdictions; however, once the settler and/or trustee becomes a resident of Canada, an new set of complicated tax rules applies to the trust. Unlike the IRS, which allows a complete flow-through of income to the creator or settler of the trust without any tax at the trust level, CRA treats living trusts as separate taxpayers from the settler. This means that Form T3 must be completed annually in Canada for the trust and care must be taken to distribute the trust income correctly to the beneficiaries so they are not double-taxed. In addition, CRA requires a deemed disposition of all the assets in the trust every 21 years, requiring capital gains tax to be paid on any appreciation on the assets in the trust at that time. Americans moving to Canada with existing U.S. living trusts must at the very least amend their trusts to adjust for these Canadian tax rules. They may want to consider distributing all the assets of a trust to themselves and closing down the trust before entering Canada.

A major consideration in your estate plan is where your executor is located. If you choose one of your children as executor of your estate and they are not located in the same province or even the same country as you are, they could run into obstacles that can delay the settlement of the estate and increase the cost of the settlement. Most provinces or states require outside non-resident executors to post large bonds to ensure all taxes are paid by the estate before the executor distributes any assets. In short, your estate will be settled much more quickly if the executor is located in the same jurisdiction in which you are resident at death.

If your beneficiaries are spread between Canada and the U.S. (or even among other countries abroad) special provisions should be considered in your estate documents to account for the differences in tax rules between the countries to ensure beneficiaries are treated fairly. For example, let's consider the tax rules that affect a U.S. child inheriting a U.S. IRA from a parent. This U.S. child is not taxed on income until it is withdrawn over a lifetime, whereas a Canadian child beneficiary would need to pay the income tax in Canada on the date of death of the parent (receiving only the amount left after the tax is paid). Several other differences need to be accounted for in an estate plan with beneficiaries in multiple countries. Some differences in taxation offer Americans living in Canada great opportunities to reduce or eliminate estate taxes and settlement costs; other differences will have costly consequences.

Americans immigrating to Canada and leaving IRAs, 401(k) plans or other U.S.-qualified plans in the United States should review all their beneficiary designations at the brokerage firm or bank where the plans are held. They must ensure that at death these plans can be rolled over to a spouse or transferred directly to a child or other beneficiary without having to go through probate in either Canada or the U.S. Another complication created by leaving these plans and other portfolio investments in the U.S. is a simple administrative issue that can develop into a major problem for Canadian residents. Most U.S. brokerage firms and other investment companies will refuse to deal with non-residents of the U.S., even if you are a U.S. citizen. Consequently, your U.S. portfolios either inside of IRAs and qualified plans or outside of these plans become frozen and no transactions other than complete liquidation can happen. Because banks and trust companies are regulated differently than the brokerage firms, you will likely have more success leaving your IRA accounts in one of these institutions than with a brokerage firm if you are moving to Canada.

For the purposes of understandability and legibility, I have greatly simplified the complexities of cross-border estate planning in this discussion. If some of the issues mentioned above seem confusing and difficult to understand, this only underlines the importance of consulting a good cross-border planning professional to assist you in dealing with all such issues.

UNIQUE TAX FILING REQUIREMENTS FOR U.S. CITIZENS IN CANADA

As discussed earlier in this chapter and in several previous chapters, U.S. citizens and green card holders living in Canada must continue to file annual U.S. tax returns (Form 1040), whether or not they have any U.S.-sourced income. A married U.S. couple would normally be used to filing just one tax return annually, a "married filing joint" return. After moving to Canada, they will have to file three tax returns: the joint U.S. return plus individual Canadian returns for each of the spouses, since CRA does not allow jointly filed returns. Of the estimated one million U.S. citizens living in Canada, I suspect that considerably less than half meet this requirement of filing U.S. tax returns to keep in compliance with the IRS. The main reason for non-compliance is simply a lack of knowledge.

Many U.S. citizens living in Canada don't know that U.S. tax returns must be filed or if they do know, they don't understand the consequences of failure to file. Many of these people have a misconceived idea that they don't need to file if they have no U.S.-sourced income, and they believe exemptions under the Canada/U.S. Tax Treaty will protect them. They may have filed U.S. tax returns in the past and, as is most often the case, zero taxes were due to the IRS. They concluded there was no need to continue filing in the U.S. This is an entirely false sense of security; many IRS and CRA forms must be filed simply for reporting purposes, with typically no tax due. However, the penalties for not filing these reporting forms in a timely fashion can be so onerous the non-filer may as well give the tax authorities a blank check or an open door invitation to take every asset they own.

Although the Canada/U.S. Tax Treaty provides a great deal of protection to U.S. citizens living in Canada (and vice versa), it can also be used to assist the IRS in collecting penalties if you fail to file the required reporting forms correctly and on time. In addition, if you fail to file a U.S. return and then try to invoke treaty protection, you they may lose treaty protection altogether and face massive double-taxation because a great number of treaty elections cannot be filed retroactively. The Canada Revenue Agency also has some special reporting forms to report foreign income and assets; if these forms are not filed, the penalties can be equally or even more onerous than IRS penalties. The importance of knowing what to file and when with both the CRA and the IRS cannot be overemphasized. The following section outlines the unique forms that the U.S. citizen or green card holder living in Canada needs to consider in addition to the normal forms and schedules when filing annually in both countries.

Canada Revenue Agency forms to be completed with the main tax return, Form T1

- **Form T1135,** Foreign Income Verification Statement

  On this form you must list any foreign property when the total value of such foreign property exceeds CDN$100,000. (If a U.S. citizen left behind any property or investments in the U.S. or other countries, this information must be identified on this form.) Failure to file this form can result in a penalty equal to or even greater than the value of the foreign property, particularly when reporting has been missed for several tax years.

- **Form T1141,** Information Return in Respect of Transfer or Loans to a Non-resident Trust

  This form needs to be completed if you or your controlled foreign affiliate has transferred owned property to a foreign trust or a non-resident corporation controlled by the trust. The penalties for failure to file this form are substantial.

Internal Revenue Service forms to be completed with Form 1040

- **Form TD F 90-22.1,** Report of Foreign Bank and Financial Accounts

This form is actually a Treasury Department form, not an IRS form, and it is completed from information on Form 1040 but is filed separately with the Treasury Department by June 15 every year when required. For each and every Canadian bank account, investment account, retirement savings account or corporate account on which you are a signing authority in Canada or any other foreign country and where the balance of that account exceeded US$10,000 at any point in the calendar year must be fully disclosed on this form.

The penalty for failure to file this form can be up to US$500,000 or five years in jail for each account and for each year the account was not reported. I have yet to see any penalties assessed as high as US$500,000 for not completing this form, but I have heard of penalties levied in excess of US$100,000. This is one form that you should not fail to file under any circumstances. As you can see, the penalties can add up very quickly and can be very severe.

- **Form 5471,** Information Return of U.S. Persons with Respect to Certain Foreign Corporations

  This form is for U.S. citizens owning more than 10% of the shares in a Canadian or other foreign company. This form is filed separately with the IRS international office in Philadelphia and a copy is attached to Form 1040 by the normal 1040 filing date, with extensions. The normal filing date for Form 1040 for U.S. citizens living outside the U.S. is June 15; they get an automatic extension from the regular April 15 deadline. However, U.S. citizens in Canada can extend their returns up to October 15 if required.

  Taxes may have to be paid based on your share of the accrued earnings and profits from inside a Canadian corporation as calculated by completing Form 5471. Completing this form is complicated and time-consuming, as it basically takes the Canadian tax data and translates it into the equivalent of a full U.S. corporate tax return. Double-tax can result from the flow-through of undistributed income from a Canadian company because a corporation is a separate taxpayer from an individual and no foreign tax credits apply to a corporation. Penalties for failure to file a Form 5471 on each and every Canadian corporation you own or control is $10,000 for each annual accounting period for each foreign corporation plus penalties and interest for any taxes that were due.

- **Form 5472,** Information Return of a 25% Foreign-Owned U.S. Corporation or a Foreign Corporation Engaged in a U.S. Trade or Business

  If you are living in Canada and still own 25% or more of a U.S. closely held corporation, the corporation is required to file Form 5472 to disclose ownership by a foreign person or a U.S. citizen living abroad. Penalties for U.S. corporations with foreign ownership who fail to file Form 5472 are $10,000 for each failure to file.

- **Form 8891,** U.S. Information Return for Beneficiaries of Certain Canadian Registered Retirement Savings Plans

  This form is filed with Form 1040 by U.S. citizens in Canada who wish to defer U.S. tax on the income buildup inside any Canadian RRSP or similar registered plan that they have accumulated while in Canada. There is no penalty per se for not filing this form, but if you fail to elect to defer tax buildup on RRSPs and then you fail to report the income earned inside RRSPs on Schedule B or Scheduled D, as applicable, on your Form 1040, you may have to pay penalties and interest on any tax due on this income. One Form 8891 must be filed for each RRSP owned.

- **Form 1116,** Foreign Tax Credit

  Filing this form is important to eliminate double-taxation and is required when a U.S. taxpayer is claiming credit under a treaty for taxes paid to a foreign country such as Canada. This form has several versions for different forms of foreign income and for alternative minimum tax calculations. It is fairly difficult to complete accurately. Form 1116 accounts for unused foreign tax credits and allows you to carry forward unused credits for up to ten years. Since a credit is a dollar-for-dollar reduction in tax, it is very important to continue to file these forms to track accumulated foreign tax credits. There is no penalty for failure to file this form, but if you don't file, you get no credit for taxes paid in Canada, which in itself could be very costly.

- **Form 2555,** Foreign Earned Income

  This form is for U.S. citizens earning employment income while living in Canada or other foreign jurisdictions. It allows the taxpayer to exclude up to $82,400 of income earned from employment in Canada each year. If you are filing as "married filing joint" and your spouse also has employment income, he or she will also qualify to exclude up to $82,400 of employment income each year.

There is no penalty for failure to file this form, but you would lose a very nice exemption.

- **Form 3520,** Annual Return to Report Transactions with Foreign Trusts and Receipt of Certain Foreign Gifts

  These forms are required if, during the current tax year, a U.S. citizen receives a distribution from or makes a contribution to what the IRS considers a foreign trust. Form 3520 is also used to report gifts of $100,000 or more from a non-resident individual or a foreign estate or gifts of more than $12,375 from foreign corporations or foreign partnerships. Penalty for failure to file a required Form 3520 can be as high as the entire value of the distributions, contributions or gifts, even if they are in the hundred thousands or millions of dollars.

- **Form 3520A,** Annual Information Return of Foreign Trusts with a U.S. Owner

  A foreign trust with the U.S. owner must file Form 3520A in order for the U.S. owner to satisfy the annual information reporting requirement. The owner of any portion of a foreign trust is responsible for ensuring that the foreign trust files this form and furnishes the required annual statements to its U.S. owners and U.S. beneficiaries. The U.S. owner is subject to a penalty equal to 5% of the gross value of the portion of the trust assets treated as owned by the U.S. person at the close of the year.

- **Form 8833,** Treaty-Based Return Position Disclosure Under Section 6144 or 7701(b)(also referred to as Treaty Election Form)

  Any U.S. taxpayer who wishes to receive benefits from any tax treaty the IRS is party to must file this form with the IRS to provide full disclosure of all details of the treaty benefit desired. For example, under the Canada/U.S. Tax Treaty, a U.S. citizen living in Canada who is collecting Social Security income is not required to pay tax in the U.S. on this income. The taxpayer would have to disclose this treaty benefit on Form 8833. There are no penalties for failure to file this form, but failure to do so may jeopardize substantial treaty benefits.

The above list of forms should not be considered all-inclusive; however, these are the most common forms that people either fail to file or file incorrectly. U.S. citizens living in Canada — even those with more basic tax filing requirements — should seek professional assistance for their tax preparation as there are far too many opportunities for mistakes when self-filing. There are many tax preparation firms in Canada that claim they can do U.S. tax returns; however, only a few do a reliable job consistently; the majority of these are listed in Appendix E at the back of this book. As you can see from the large penalties or missed exemptions mentioned above, the cost of not filing or making mistakes when filing can be prohibitive. It is not unusual for a high net worth U.S. citizen living in Canada — especially someone with complex business arrangements — to have Canadian and U.S. tax returns several inches thick to keep in compliance with all these tax rules and forms.

OTHER POINTS TO CONSIDER

Here are a few other things you may need to consider or execute when immigrating to Canada:

- **Social Insurance Number (SIN)**

  This number is the equivalent of the U.S. Social Security Number and must be used when filing Canadian tax returns, for payroll records, for opening bank accounts and in general when dealing with the government and other bureaucracies. You need to apply for your SIN as soon as you get your immigration status approved. Citizenship and Immigration Canada will provide the forms to apply for a SIN.

- **Establishing a credit rating in Canada**

  Since you are new to Canada and Canada has a separate credit reporting system, you can expect that banks and credit card companies will be reluctant to loan you money. Chapter 9, in Transferring Your Credit Rating to the United States, outlines what a Canadian needs to do when moving to the U.S. to establish a credit rating there. Since the issues are very similar for an American moving to Canada, please review this section and apply the suggested recommendations on the north side of the Canada/U.S. border.

- **Applying for Canadian medicare**

  Depending on which province or territory you are immigrating to, you will be eligible to apply for Canadian medical benefits as soon as you receive your permanent resident or visa status. Some provinces and territories have a waiting period of 30 to 90 days; others have no waiting period before you are covered. Make sure you are covered with a supplementary plan until your full coverage takes effect. Three out of the ten Canadian provinces charge a small premium for their medical benefit plans. Please review Chapter 5 for information on how to contact your provincial or territorial medicare office and for ideas about how to cover your medical needs when travelling back to the U.S.

CROSS-BORDER Q&A

U.S. PERSONS RENTING OUT THEIR CANADIAN COTTAGE

I am an American citizen and my wife is a Canadian citizen (with green card status) and we reside permanently in the U.S.

Five years ago, we purchased a cottage in Canada that we rent out every summer to various tenants. We have not filed any Canadian tax returns and have not included any income or costs related to the cottage on our U.S. tax returns.

I am looking for some advice in this matter.

— Ray S., New York, NY

It is very important that you get into compliance with both the Canada Revenue Agency and the IRS by filing tax returns for the entire five-year period and continue to do so for all future years. If you do this on a voluntary basis you will find penalties and interest will be much more reasonable than if either tax department comes after you based on information they have collected — for example, from a disgruntled tenant.

Since the property is located in Canada, CRA gets first crack at the tax. You must file a Section 216 T1 tax return in Canada, reporting all your rental income, taking allowed deductions and then paying the applicable Canadian tax on any net profits. You would then take the same information, translate it into U.S. funds and U.S. depreciation schedules, and place it on Schedule E of your U.S. Form 1040. The taxes you paid to the CRA can be taken as a credit on Form 1116, applied against any taxes due on the rental income on your U.S. return so that you are not double-taxed on this income. For future years, in Canada you will need to complete a CRA Form NR 6 each year before you collect any rent for the year.

CANADIAN RESIDENT DAUGHTER GIVING UP U.S. CITIZENSHIP

My daughter, who is 40, became a dual U.S./Canadian citizen in 1987. Each year since she has filed a U.S. tax return declaring her salary and income investments (interest and dividend income, but not the amount and type of her investment portfolio). She has elected not to be taxed on her RRSP income (based on the 1980 Canada/U.S. tax treaty).

She is now considering revoking her U.S. citizenship. What U.S. tax implications should she expect as a result of this action? Do all the gains in her RRSP become taxable in the U.S.? Are there other taxes she has to consider?

— Alan D., Cambridge, Ontario

Your daughter's thoughts of giving up her U.S. citizenship deserve serious consideration before she makes that decision. I wish I had a dollar for every person who came to me who had given up their U.S. citizenship or their U.S. green card and then later in life wished they hadn't. Often my clients spend thousands of dollars and a great deal of time trying to get back into the U.S. or to sponsor their children into the U.S. Depending on your daughter's net worth — i.e., if it is over US$2 million or if her annual income is over US$131,000 — there are considerable tax consequences from giving up U.S. citizenship. In addition, the IRS/U.S. State department are keeping a blacklist since 1996 which they say is to deny entry into the U.S. to anyone who gave up their U.S. citizenship for tax reasons. To date they have never used this blacklist and it would be very difficult for them to enforce it, but nonetheless it exists.

Filing an annual U.S. tax return is time-consuming, but I would recommend your daughter seriously consider not giving up her U.S. citizenship so that she does not regret her decision later.

PRINCIPAL RESIDENCE EXEMPTION FOR U.S. GOVERNMENT EMPLOYEE WORKING IN CANADA

I am one of many U.S. government officials living and working in Canada. Like some of my colleagues, I bought my own house in Canada to live in. I understand my U.S. government salary is exempt from Canadian tax under the Canada/U.S. Tax Treaty, as I am considered a resident of the United States. I am a deemed non-resident of Canada under the Canada Income Tax Act.

My question is: Is it possible for a deemed non-resident of Canada who is a U.S. citizen to elect to file an income tax return in Canada as a resident, similar to a non-resident alien in the United States electing to file a U.S. tax return as a resident alien? If so, would I be able to retain the exemption of my government salary under the tax treaty? Even though my worldwide income would be exposed to Canadian taxation, in my case, I do not think my non-salary income will be significant compared to the advantage of being able to utilize the principal residence exemption when I sell my home.

—Jack W., Ottawa, Ontario

You are exempt from taxation in Canada on your U.S. government income under Article XIX of the Canada/U.S. Tax Treaty.

You can apply for permanent resident status in Canada. If you become a permanent resident, you would file a normal Canadian T1 tax return, exclude your government pension under the treaty, and then be eligible for the full Canadian capital gains exemption on your residence as well as the U.S. capital gains exemption on the principal residence (up to $500,000 for you and your wife on the U.S. return you file).

Give My Regards to Wall Street 12

INVESTING AS A U.S. RESIDENT

A sound investment strategy should be built around the basic concepts of asset allocation, risk allocation, risk control and performance tracking. Risk control and performance tracking are easily understood. Due to the cyclical nature of our economy, attention to asset allocation is necessary. A country's economy changes from periods of prosperity and low interest rates to times of recession and high rates. Proper asset allocation strategies allow portfolios to contain different types of investments that will perform well in various economic environments. Regardless of which way the economy of the United States or Canada is headed, you have a relatively steady return with good safety of principal.

If you were one of the many investors who lost substantial wealth during the three-year market crash of March 2000 to March 2003, when major market indicies fell 30% to 70%, your portfolio was likely not diversified to correspond with your goals. We at our cross-border financial planning firm manage more than $300 million dollars of client total net worth, and virtually none of our clients lost money during this three year period. This is not because we have a crystal ball or inside knowledge, but because we insist on developing diversified strategies focussed on achieving client goals. This chapter is only the first step of many you will need to take to obtain the portfolio that will help you achieve your goals and let you sleep at night.

In Chapter 6, I wrote a great deal about investment types, investment risk and currency fluctuations mainly from the perspective of the non-resident Canadian. Canadians who take up residency in the United States need to consider all these factors, make some necessary adjustments and position their investments in such a way that the proper balance between assets is achieved to realize their financial goals. In addition, most Canadians moving to the U.S. require specialized assistance in their portfolios, because they normally have a considerable amount of foreign tax credits that will expire unless their investments produce the income needed to use those credits efficiently. Proper investment design can turn each dollar of foreign tax credit into a dollar of tax reduction. Most people find this a difficult task, because not only are they treading new ground in the United States, but there are interlocking factors that need to be addressed simultaneously among the financial planning areas of taxation, estate, cash flow and investments. In other words, changes in one segment of your financial plan may require modification to several other areas as well. There are also cross-border considerations, since most Canadians moving to the United States leave several investments in Canada. These investments need to be integrated into their U.S. investment programs for their investors' maximum benefit.

INVESTMENT PRIORITIES

The first step is determining what your actual objectives and needs are from your investment portfolio. Ask yourself what you want the money to do, how it will make your life better, and if there is enough for you to maintain your lifestyle. This may be restating the obvious, but my experience in financial planning has proven that many people neglect doing even a basic analysis of exactly what they want or need from their investment portfolios. Consequently, their current investments do not match their needs. Figure 12.1 is a quick exercise designed to help you determine your priorities.

INVESTMENT PRIORITY CHECKLIST

Inflation	❑
Tax advantages	❑
Safety	❑
Diversification	❑
Professional management	❑
Growth	❑
Liquidity	❑
Income now	❑
Income later	❑

Figure 12.1

The investment characteristics listed in Figure 12.1 are the main attributes you should consider when looking at investments. In the boxes on the right, rank these characteristics by assigning a numerical value from 1 to 9, 1 being the most important to you, and 9 the least. Use the same number only once, so that, when you are finished, you will have a list of the nine main characteristics, in order of their importance. Now you will have a guide against which you can measure how well your investments meet your priorities.

For example, if liquidity and inflation protection are the two most important characteristics, and you have most of your money locked into term deposits or GICs, your investments are mismatched to your own needs, since those investments will provide neither inflation protection nor liquidity.

Professional money managers use some sophisticated computerized asset allocation programs that can compare your current portfolio with twenty or more years of historical data to determine the overall level of risk or variability your investments have and their expected rates of return, assuming you leave the investments as they are. These programs can also recommend changes or "optimize" a portfolio, to achieve greater returns at reduced levels of risk. Of course, historical data cannot guarantee future results, but this sort of analysis is very useful in quantifying levels of risk, determining the relation between one investment and another, and looking at how changes to an individual portfolio can affect the risk and return parameters. More forward-looking advisors will use simulation tools to assist in the design of a portfolio customized to your needs and goals. Simulation tools, such as Monte Carlo analysis, can help your advisor develop a portfolio for you that will have the highest probability of meeting your goals over the balance of your life or some other specified period. Monte Carlo analysis simulates thousands of lifetime scenarios and investor preferences to forecast different forward-looking investment returns. When setting up your U.S. investment program, this type of analysis should be routine and can help provide you with greater security and increased return. You should understand, however, that no system of portfolio design is going to guarantee a predictable outcome. There are far too many variables for even supercomputers and superhuman minds to accurately predict the future.

The next step in developing your portfolio is to determine your overall objectives. There are four key objectives or modes that can realistically be achieved by an investment portfolio.

1. OBJECTIVE — INCOME

The Income and Preservation of Principal objective seeks a high level of current income with liquidity and relatively low annual principal fluctuation. It does not seek to maintain purchasing power against inflation.

Who Should Consider This Objective?

- Investors whose primary concern is current income.
- Investors who will tolerate only minor erosions of principal in any given year.
- Investors who are not concerned with the long-term effects of inflation on their purchasing power.

Typical Investors

- Retired individuals looking to enhance their income in order to live more comfortably.
- Conservative investors willing to accept a relatively small degree of principal fluctuation.
- Families who need to supplement their income.

Management Technique

Use mutual funds that invest in U.S. or foreign government securities, investment-grade corporate debt securities, high quality mortgage securities, investment grade and/or insured municipal bonds. Equity exposure is limited to 30% of the total portfolio.

2. OBJECTIVE — GROWTH AND INCOME

The Income with Growth objective seeks to provide an income stream that on the average increases annually to compensate for the loss of purchasing power, due to rising inflation. This objective also strives to maintain portfolio purchasing power. This objective will entail some year-to-year volatility in portfolio values.

Who Should Consider This Objective?

- Investors with long investment horizons (three years or longer).
- Investors who want some long-term growth along with stability of principal.
- Investors who want current income that could increase each year to offset inflation.

- Investors who can live with the possibility of some losses as well as gains in any given year.

Typical Investors

- Retired individuals concerned about the effects of inflation on their retirement income.
- Conservative working people looking to build a nest egg.

Management Technique

Use mutual funds that invest in large-capitalization stocks and investment-grade debt securities. Investments in cash/short-term debt and fixed income funds will make up at least 20% of the portfolio for each category. Thus, maximum exposure to equity markets will be 60%.

3. OBJECTIVE — GROWTH

The Growth objective is to seek capital appreciation over the long run (three to ten years). Current income is not a consideration.

Who Should Consider This Objective?

- Investors with long-term investment horizons (five years or more).
- Investors who can live with the possibility of large losses as well as gains in any given year.
- Investors who do not have to live on all the income generated from their investments.

Typical Investors

- Working people who are looking to aggressively build an asset base.
- Retired individuals who at present require little or no investment income to live on.
- Bank savers who realize that by keeping their investments solely in bank accounts they may be sacrificing opportunities for superior long-term investment returns.

Management Technique

Use mutual funds that will not be limited by size or type of company. Investments in cash and fixed income funds will usually be minimal, but must make up at least 10% of the portfolio. Thus, maximum exposure to equity markets will be 90%.

4. OBJECTIVE — AGGRESSIVE GROWTH

The Aggressive Growth strategy offers potentially high long-term re-turns (five to ten years) at the cost of year-to-year volatility. This offers the highest potential for growth over the long run, but will probably be the most volatile of all the objectives in any given year.

Who Should Consider This Objective?

- Investors with long-term investment horizons (three to ten years).
- Investors who want a chance to maximize long-term growth.
- Investors who can tolerate potentially large year-to-year volatility in the value of their investments.

Typical Investors

- Aggressive retirees not needing investment income to live on.
- Aggressive middle-aged investors working to build a retirement nest egg.
- Young investors not "now" oriented.

Management Technique

Use mutual funds that will not be limited by size or type of company. In-vestments in cash and fixed income funds will usually be minimal. Equity exposure can range as high as 100%. It is anticipated that this objective will make use of small company funds in both developed countries and emerging markets to a greater degree than the Growth objective.

Once you have determined your own objectives, you are probably 90% of the way toward developing your investment portfolio. The final 10% is important — the actual investment selection. A professional money manager can select and maintain the investments that match your objectives, making future modifications as your objectives change. Refer back to Choosing an International Investment Manager in Chapter 6, which will help you locate the best management firm to meet your needs.

The United States provides a wide variety of investments to achieve any investment objective, many of which are tax-advantaged. These in-vestments allow investors to achieve greater tax savings without sacrific-ing liquidity, diversification or increased risk.

Social Security and Medicare $\boxed{13}$

THE ART OF DOUBLE DIPPING

MAXIMIZING SOCIAL BENEFITS WHEN MOVING TO THE U.S.

For many people, a major objective in cross-border financial planning is to position yourself to qualify for both Canadian and U.S. government social programs: Canada Pension Plan (CPP), Quebec Pension Plan (QPP) and Old Age Security (OAS) in Canada, and Social Security in the United States. Qualifying for these benefits requires careful long-term planning. Canada Pension Plan benefits are earned by being employed in Canada for ten years or longer. Once you have exited Canada, the benefit goes with you. Similarly, if you return to Canada or are immigrating to Canada for the first time from the U.S. after qualifying for U.S. Social Security, these benefits also go with you. You can apply for CPP at age 60 or wait longer to qualify for increased benefits. But the longer you wait, the more zero-income years you will have, reducing your average monthly earnings, offsetting potential increases by delaying the payment of benefits. Widows, whether living in Canada or the U.S., can qualify for a reduced benefit based on their spouses' earnings records.

To qualify for full Old Age Security benefits, you need to be a resident of Canada for 40 years past the age of 18. Anything less will result in a proportionate reduction in benefits. For example, if you had only 30 years in Canada after age 18, you would receive 75% of the maximum $500 monthly benefit.

Those receiving CPP/QPP and OAS may recall from Chapter 8 that there are great tax savings for you while receiving these benefits as a resident of the United States. The same cannot be said for those collecting U.S. Social Security in Canada because the tax rate on this income is higher depending on your Canadian tax bracket.

Before I explain how to qualify for U.S. Social Security, I want to make you aware of another, sometimes very beneficial, treaty between Canada and the United States, the Canada-U.S. Social Security Agreement. This provides for a coordination of benefits between the two countries, so that citizens spending time in both countries are not disadvantaged by any loss of benefits.

As a result of this agreement, a Canadian moving to the United States can qualify for a minimal U.S. Social Security monthly benefit as early as age 62, by working as few as 18 months and earning as little as $450 per month. The normal qualifying time without the benefit of the Canada-U.S. Social Security Agreement is ten years of earnings. With U.S. Social Security, the spouse of the qualifying person also automatically qualifies to receive approximately 50% of the amount of the qualifying person, even though he or she may never have contributed to the system. A Canadian over 62 who marries a U.S. resident who is receiving or who qualifies for Social Security from U.S. employment can, after one year of marriage, receive 50% of the spouse's monthly amount and U.S. Medicare for life, indexed for inflation.

Even retired Canadians up to age 70 who become U.S. residents should attempt to put in the minimum amount of qualifying time for Social Security and Medicare. This can be accomplished by earning about $5,000 a year (even if the entire $5,000 was earned on the first day of the year), working part time, doing some consulting work, or by holding a seat on a board of directors, even if it is your own company's board or that of a friend or family member. It doesn't matter whether or not the company is in Canada or the U.S. You need legitimate employment earnings equivalent to 18 months, or six quarters, of work to qualify for minimum pension benefits, and up to 120 months to qualify for free U.S. Medicare Part A. Even a Canadian past age 70 (but more optimally 55) can continue to easily accumulate quarters of coverage to get a Social Security pension and U.S. Medicare. The pension, unless you have substantial employment earnings well over the minimum, will not be significant; however, qualifying for U.S. Medicare is a major goal, since once one spouse qualifies, both spouses can get coverage at today's value of nearly $12,000 tax free per year for life. Of all the investments you could make, this will provide you the best return you will ever get from any retirement plan. In my opinion as a long-time cross-border financial planner, all Canadians retiring in the U.S. should obtain Medicare at or as soon after age 65 as possible, even if they are covered by a good employer medical plan. Unfortunately, as many retired employees have discovered, employer-sponsored medical plans can change or be eliminated after retirement.

The U.S. health care system is undergoing constant change and there are many government-sponsored proposals to improve the system. These proposed changes may take many years to materialize, but the ultimate goal is to improve access to health coverage for all legal residents and citizens of the United States. Canadians often tend to downplay the fact that they've worked in the United States or for an American company. If you worked in the United States anytime after 1933 when Social Security began, you likely will have accumulated useful quarters toward a monthly Social Security pension benefit and, with enough quarters, Medicare. You can easily find out if you have any quarters of coverage by simply logging on to the Social Security website, www.ssa.gov, and following the instructions.

The maximum U.S. Social Security pension benefit for an individual who has contributed at maximum rates for 30 years or more is approximately $2,000 per month. The benefit for a spouse without a work history is an additional $1,000 per month; a spouse with his or her own work history would qualify for a separate pension, and would receive the higher amount of that pension or the $1,000 spousal benefit. U.S. Social Security benefits are entirely tax free for a married couple with less than $34,000 total income; 50% of the benefits are tax free if their total income is more than $34,000 but less than $46,000; at incomes above that, up to 85% of the benefits must be included in taxable income.

Canadians who have made contributions to a company pension plan will be able to claim a portion of their pensions as tax-free returns of principal while they are residents in the United States. (Refer to the George and Susan example in Chapter 8.) The exact amount of tax-free pension is determined according to the size of the pension annuity purchased, your age and the IRS tables.

U.S. MEDICAL COVERAGE

Canadians routinely hear about Americans being denied medical treatment because they have no money or insurance. Americans hear about the evils of Canada's socialist medical system, patients dying from inadequate care or long waiting lists for surgery. In reality, things are seldom as grim as the media portrays them, and many of these horror stories have been exaggerated or taken out of context by special interest groups and advocates of one particular system. The most important thing to remember about the U.S. medical system is that it is not inherently more or less humane than the Canadian system; it is just different.

American hospitals and health care providers usually operate on a profit-making basis, unlike their Canadian counterparts. They compete for patients and this competition results in improved access to the most sophisticated medical technology. A medium-sized American city often has more specialized diagnostic equipment such as MRI or CAT scanners than is available in all of Canada. The downside of the equation is that patients under age 65 must either pay for the services out of their own pockets or buy health insurance to cover medical expenses. Those without either insurance or the funds to pay generally have access to free medical care through non-profit, government-provided county hospitals, which operate in much the same way that Canadian hospitals do, on a modified first-come first-served basis. County medical facilities provide the full range of medical services required, but they are certainly not as convenient as those in the pay-for-service system. As with many Canadian hospitals, there are often waits for services and a limited choice of doctors. U.S. medical care can vary greatly from state to state, just as it does in Canada from province to province, where there are numerous interprovincial differences in applying federal medicare guidelines.

For a new Canadian resident in the United States, we recommend you purchase private health insurance. Those under age 65 with no pre-existing conditions will find many insurance companies that provide coverage at reasonable cost. The cost will vary from state to state, with California and Florida tending to be more expensive. The best value by far is what is known as catastrophic coverage — insurance that pays only when a claim exceeds a specified dollar amount such as $2,500, $5,000, $10,000 or even $25,000. Coverage can cost from $150 to $750 per month, depending on your age and the deductible level you choose. I cover my entire family of five with $2 million of individual insurance coverage with a highly rated company, a $5,000 deductible and on a preferred provider network, for a $675 premium per month. For most people these insurance premiums are tax deductible, so the cost of the programs can be greatly reduced. In addition, the U.S. has introduced a new savings program called Health Savings Accounts (HSAs). This program works much like a registered retirement savings plan. You can put up to $5,500 per year into the program, take a full tax deduction and then allow the contributions to accumulate in an investment account on a tax-free basis. Withdrawals from the HSA account are tax free as long as they are used for qualified medical expenses.

Some Canadian retirees may find their pension plans will provide full or partial U.S. coverage. Retired federal government employees are eligible through their group plan, the Public Service Health Care Plan (PSHCP), for supplemental coverage that will pay all reasonable doctors' costs up to three times the Canadian rates. Prescription drug costs as well as a small amount toward daily hospital expenses in the United States are also covered. This plan can work well when combined with U.S. Medicare or a very good hospital indemnity policy.

For those over age 65, the choices are more limited, since most Americans at that age go onto U.S. Medicare. Because of this, there is little demand for individual plans other than Medicare supplements. Consequently, the key cross-border financial planning strategy is to ensure Canadian residents living in the United States become eligible for American Medicare. Figure 13.1 outlines the key means to qualify for U.S. Medicare.

U.S. MEDICARE ELIGIBIITY

Age 65 or older, and one or more of the following:

- Five years or longer as a legal U.S. resident or green card holder; or
- U.S. citizen (including derivative citizen); or
- Married to a U.S. citizen or resident on Social Security who qualified through his or her own employment

---

Figure 13.1

There are insurers who will provide supplements to fill in gaps left by Medicare coverage. These "medigap" policies currently cost from $100 to $300 a month, depending on the level and type of medigap chosen. Canadians who have not contributed the minimum 40 quarters (120 months) to U.S. Social Security through employment, or who are not married to a U.S. resident or citizen who has made the necessary contributions, can expect to pay around $500 per month for U.S. Medicare coverage Part A (hospital care: $420 per month) and Part B (doctors and outpatient care: $90 per month). In 2006, the U.S. introduced new rules concerning Medicare Part B: those in higher income brackets will pay anywhere from two to four times the regular Part B premium in 2007 and future years. In 2005, Medicare Part D was introduced as an optional benefit to cover drugs.

For those Canadians over 65 who do not yet meet the five-year-residency requirement for Medicare, there are few options. Chapter 5 referred to several international insurers that provide worldwide coverage at reasonable costs. Premiums are approximately $300 to $500 per month depending on age, for $1 million in coverage, with deductibles ranging from $500 to $25,000. Another solution is to self-insure by setting aside all or a portion of your annual tax savings into a highly liquid investment account. In Chapter 8, Figure 8.7, our couple saved nearly $46,000 a year in taxes. If they set aside these tax savings in a money market account, within a few years they would build a self-insurance fund sufficient to cover most major hospital stays. For higher-income persons or those who have large RRSPs, the tax savings can provide a six-figure self-insurance fund in the first year of U.S. residency. Those who choose to self-insure can always leave the door open to return to Canada and be back on Canadian medicare within 90 days (returning Alberta residents get immediate medical coverage). Refer also to Have Your Cake and Eat It Too! in Chapter 5.

U.S. health insurance and Medicare do not cover extended care in nursing homes or similar facilities, and a separate policy is needed to cover these expenses. Many insurance companies offer this coverage, but great caution is advised. The minimum recommended coverage is $150 per day (this varies from state to state) for up to four years of benefits and with an inflation rider. People over age 75 could eliminate the inflation rider, as it tends to nearly double premiums. Premiums from a good A+ rated insurance company can range between $200 and $500 per month, depending on your age at the time the policy is taken out. This coverage can be applied for at any time, beginning at about age 40, and should be in place well before you reach age 60, whether you are a resident of Canada or the U.S. at that time.

Any medical coverage insurance premiums are deductible as an itemized medical expense on your U.S. tax return. However, total monthly premiums can be substantial, especially for those who do not qualify for free U.S. Medicare. This added cost must be weighed against the potential income tax and other savings of becoming a U.S. resident. In George and Susan's example in Chapter 8, they are able to save over $1,000 a month in taxes just from their CPP tax reduction and OAS clawback — enough to pay for good medical insurance coverage in the United States.

APPLYING FOR SOCIAL SECURITY

Imagine the dismay of a couple who have done ten years of planning so that they qualify for U.S. Social Security and Medicare benefits, only to be told, upon filing the application, that they do not qualify. This scenario has happened to several readers of *The Border Guide*. In fact, in a couple of cases not only did the Social Security clerk tell applicants that they did not qualify, they also wiped out years of quarters of credits, which meant that these people had to start over in the qualifying process — not something one wants to do at age 70+.

So far, we're batting 1.000 in taking on the Social Security Administration with respect to these situations. The clerks were wrong in what they did, but did not (I think) err on purpose, but rather because they didn't understand how the Canada-U.S. Social Security Agreement applied to these people. In this section I want to make you aware of some of these issues so that you can avoid the complications that can arise.

First, the Canada-U.S. Social Security Agreement states that if you have less than 40 quarters of work but more than 6, you can use time spent in Canada to help qualify for benefits. To do so, you must file Form SSA-2400-BK, Application for Benefits Under a U.S. International Social Security Agreement, at the same time as you submit your normal Social Security application. Form SSA-2400-BK, if completed properly, will solve many problems and force clerks who have never seen such a form to send it through the appropriate channels to be processed. Processing can take some time, as U.S. Social Security will contact the Canadian government to confirm your qualifying time for Canadian benefits.

The Canada-U.S. Social Security Agreement also allows U.S. citizens in Canada to use Canadian employment earnings to qualify for benefits, provided that with the annual filing of their U.S. tax returns they paid Social Security taxes on their Canadian income. (Even though the Canada-U.S. Social Security Agreement allows this, internal Social Security rules do not deal with it.) These Canadian earnings helped some of our clients who were U.S. citizens get many quarters of benefits earned while they were still in Canada, and we were even able to re-file up to three past years of returns and pay the Social Security taxes to get 12 additional quarters immediately.

AVOIDING THE WINDFALL ELIMINATION PROVISIONS

The final key benefit of the Canada-U.S. Social Security Agreement is that it can help you avoid the Windfall Elimination Provision (WEP), which can reduce a person's Social Security pension by up to 60%. The WEP applies to people who have earned pensions by working for an employer that did not withhold Social Security taxes (i.e., a government agency or an employer outside the U.S.), but who also worked for other employers that did withhold Social Security taxes long enough for them to qualify for Social Security benefits. The WEP was brought in to prevent such people from gaining an unfair advantage in the Social Security system. So what does the WEP have to do with people who have spent a good deal of their working careers in Canada and are applying for benefits? The Social Security clerks have a sad tendency to apply the WEP because they feel such applicants may gain a similar unfair advantage through not having contributed to Social Security for their entire working careers. However, hidden in the WEP rules — which the clerks seldom read — is a statement that the WEP *doesn't* apply to benefits under a Social Security agreement with the U.S. Even if it did, the Canada-U.S. Social Security Agreement would still exempt persons from WEP who had a total of 30 years working and living in Canada and/or the U.S. while qualifying for either Canadian or U.S. Social Security benefits.

As you can see, most of these concerns arise because Social Security personnel do not apply the rules correctly. In their defence, however, I must state that most Social Security personnel seldom encounter these rules; in fact, yours may be the first and last case ever handled at the particular office with which you are dealing. Thus, you have a strong advantage if you can help the staff interpret the agreement rules. If the staff continue to misapply the rules, you can appeal their rulings once they send them to you in writing. The appeal goes to an administrative judge, who usually does a much better job with international agreements. But you must do your homework and be very prepared or have the assistance of someone who has experience with such hearings.

Because of the increasing number of *Border Guide* readers who seem to be facing this WEP problem, I would like to point out a few of the more technical reasons why WEP does not normally apply to Canadians qualifying for U.S. Social Security. These technical points, which are derived from the U.S. Social Security Act and the Canada-U.S. Social Security Agreement, are also available on the Social Security website, www.ssa.gov. These documents, although written in dense legalese, should be reviewed for supporting information for any petitions or appeals you might want to present before the Social Security Administration. By providing this information, I hope my readers can prevent the Social Security clerks and administrative judges from taking them hopelessly down the wrong path and reducing their Social Security benefit entitlements. Here are the key points to read up on and present to Social Security Administration personnel:

- The Canada-U.S. Social Security Agreement Part 1, Article 1, paragraph 6 defines the period of coverage as: "A period of payment of contributions or a period of earnings from employment or self-employment, as defined or recognized as a period of coverage by the laws under which such period has been completed, or any similar period in so far as it is recognized by such laws is equivalent to period of coverage." Under this definition, an individual's period of coverage in Canada is clearly a period of coverage of earnings under the Canada-U.S. Social Security Agreement. When combined with the U.S. earnings period of coverage, the Canadian period of earnings coverage totals well over 30 years of substantial earnings. Consequently, any Canadian in this position qualifies for the WEP exemption. "The WEP 30 years of coverage exemption" can be found in the Social Security Act section 210(a)(D).

- The Canada-U.S. Social Security Agreement Part 1, Article 1, paragraph 7 defines benefit as "any benefit provided for in the laws of either contracting State." Since the 30 years substantial earnings exemption from the Windfall Elimination Provision is clearly a benefit to Canadians and also Americans who have worked at least part of their careers in Canada, they are certainly entitled to it. Based on the Canada-U.S. Social Security Agreement definition of both benefits and period of coverage, this article clearly confirms that the agreement considers periods of coverage in Canada equivalent to periods of coverage in the U.S. for the purpose of determining whether or not a Canadian is entitled to benefits.

- The Canada-U.S. Social Security Agreement Part 4, Article 29, paragraph 4 states "this agreement shall not result in the reduction of benefit amounts because of its entry into force." By attempting to deny benefits, the Social Security Administration goes against both the spirit and the letter of this article and therefore the agreement in its entirety. The WEP should not result in reduced Social Security benefits, as most Canadians have sufficient earnings to qualify for the 30-year exemption.

- If you have a pension other than OAS that Social Security is attempting to use to reduce your Social Security benefits, you may be able to use some additional support for your petition. This additional defence may be available because the Canadian pension is based on "covered employment," and therefore the WEP does not apply. "Covered employment" is defined in Section 210 (a)(C) of the Social Security Act and clearly states that "employment" includes service rendered abroad for an employer when the service is designated as employment or recognized as equivalent to employment under a totalization agreement such as the Canada-U.S. Social Security Agreement. Although "employment" is not defined in the Canada-U.S. Social Security Agreement, we would respectfully suggest that working in Canada, particularly when Canadian social security taxes are withheld from the wages, should be considered employment almost anywhere. Because the service underlying the foreign pension is "covered employment," the standard benefit formula when calculating the Social Security benefits must be applied without a WEP reduction.

Working with the Social Security Administration on these cross-border issues can be quite time-consuming and frustrating, and I can guarantee you that your patience will be tested to its fullest. You must be prepared to be persistent: appeals can take from a minimum of one year up to two or three years. I would not recommend this as a do-it-yourself project. Because there are few people in the U.S. who ever deal with these issues, it is also hard to get legal or other assistance. In addition, people who fight Social Security and win do not necessarily set precedents for other cases because each appeal judge makes his or her own decision. Generally, appeal cases are not even available for public review. The final level of recourse, once your case goes through all Social Security appeals, is to take the Social Security Administration to court. But if you are sure you are correct, persistence will usually make you victorious.

We have a very good U.S. attorney who lives in Toronto and who has agreed to help me with one of these WEP appeals to get an actual court judgment that can be used as a precedent for not only *Border Guide* readers but all other Canadians and Americans working in Canada who get hit unfairly with WEP.

E-mail us if you run into a brick wall: bobk@keatsconnelly.com.

CROSS-BORDER Q&A

SOCIAL SECURITY SPOUSAL BENEFIT GOOD FOR CROSS-BORDER WORKER

I'm looking for advice on Social Security planning. I am a Canadian citizen with a U.S. green card and have been living in Florida since 1999. I commute to work in Canada from Florida, and my wife works solely in Florida. I pay quarterly taxes to the IRS and have some tax withheld by Canada, which I use as a credit on my U.S. return. To date, I have not paid anything to U.S. Social Security, although my wife pays into the system on her salary, and my Canadian source income has CPP deductions. I have eleven years to retirement and am wondering what the benefit of paying additional monies to the U.S. Social Security would be.

I've put this in a nutshell so that you might decide whether or not you can provide advice. Alternatively, perhaps there is someone with whom you are affiliated in Florida to whom you can refer me.

I enjoyed reading The Border Guide *when I left Canada in 1999. I have used several sections as reference material, yet I feel my situation might require unique advice.*

— Douglas E., Ft. Lauderdale, Florida

It is difficult to give you a specific answer without knowing all the details, but I can give you some general direction.

If you are looking for the best return on your money, you are better off with only one spouse paying into U.S. Social Security. This is because a non-contributing spouse gets a benefit equal to 50% of the contributing spouse's Social Security pension, as well as free Part A Medicare, which would otherwise cost about $420 per month. Consequently, if you started contributing now to Social Security, you would get a very poor return on your contributions, since you have already qualified for major benefits under your wife's plan. Your Social Security pension would be the higher amount of either 50% of your wife's pension or 100% of your benefits through your own contributions, but you would not get both amounts, and you only need to qualify for Medicare once.

However, if your income were high, and if you were to contribute long enough yourself, your 100% could eventually be more than your 50% spousal benefit, and the combined pensions between the two of you could be higher than if you contributed nothing. Therefore, it depends whether you are trying to get the best return on your investments in Social Security or the maximum pension possible.

My experience tells me that you are best off contributing the maximum to CPP and nothing to Social Security while your wife contributes the maximum to Social Security, but I do recommend that you have someone run the numbers for you.

FIGHTING THE WINDFALL ELIMINATION RULES WITH SOCIAL SECURITY

This letter will be of much interest to you for one of these reasons:

(1) There is a major omission in your book, The Border Guide. *My explanation will help you correct the oversight for future editions.*

OR

(2) All the information in your book is correct and complete. Therefore, the Social Security Administration (SSA) is wrong in its handling of my application for a U.S. Social Security pension. In that case, I need your specific advice and request a copy of your fee schedule.

I am a U.S. citizen who lived and worked in the U.S. until I was 30. I was a USAF officer for four years, from 1964 to 1968. When I was 28, I married a Canadian, and two years later, in 1971, we moved to Winnipeg, where we have since resided. I taught in Winnipeg for 25 years, until my retirement at age 55.

We bought the 1992 and 1995 editions of The Border Guide *and, acting on its advice, I took a part-time job in North Dakota after retirement from teaching. When I moved to Canada in 1971, I had already earned thirty-three quarters toward my U.S. Social Security pension. By working in North Dakota from 1995 to 1998, I earned twelve more quarters. This, according to the information in your book, meant I qualified for a U.S. Social Security pension and Medicare benefits for my wife and myself.*

The last statement of benefits I received from the SSA came in 2003, and it indicated my pension would be about $403 a month at age 62, and should I predecease my wife, the widow's benefit would be about $513 monthly.

My wife and I carefully planned our retirement income, buying your books and visiting U.S. SSA offices for information. Imagine our shock when I had my interview for the Social Security pension recently (I became eligible for it in January 2004) and was told I will receive only about 40% of the earned pension because of the Windfall Elimination Provision! I was told to expect a monthly pension of $190 (and my wife will receive $95). In addition, I was told my wife would be eligible for Medicare only after five years of U.S. residency.

Nowhere in your book did we read about the Windfall Elimination Provision! Nor did anyone at an SSA office ever even hint at it.

Of course, we are desperately hoping the SSA clerk who is processing my application is wrong and you are right!

Please advise. Is the SSA clerk correct, which means you will be adding this information to your next book; OR, is the SSA clerk wrong, which means we need your professional advice as to what to do next?

I am sharing this information with TRAF, the teachers' pension group here, and will suggest they recommend your book to Manitoba teachers who are eligible for an SSA pension. (There are a surprising number of U.S.-citizen teachers in Manitoba.)

— Kimber H., Winnipeg, Manitoba

The Windfall Elimination Provision is real, and the Social Security Administration has changed the application of the rules in the past few years to try to bring CPP benefits into its forms. The application forms for Social Security have been modified to ask questions on foreign benefits (question 8. (a) and (b)) that were never asked before; consequently, more people seem to be getting caught up in these rules.

However, I believe that the Windfall Elimination Provision should not apply to you because of the Canada-U.S. Social Security Agreement, Article IV, which states that you must receive treatment equal to that given other U.S. citizens. The Windfall Elimination Provision is not supposed to apply to you if you have 30 or more years of "substantial" earnings in a job where you paid Social Security taxes. Under the agreement, your time in Canada when you were paying into the Canadian Social Security plan is supposed to be added to the time you paid into the U.S. Social Security system, so you would have more than 30 years of combined contributions. Along with your Social Security application, you should complete Form SSA-2490-BK, Application for Benefits Under a U.S. International Social Security Agreement, to apply for the 30-year exemption from this Windfall Elimination Provision. State that Social Security is using this rule to reduce your benefit inappropriately. If this additional form does not work, you can appeal it to a Social Security judge, and I think you would have a decent chance of success. Since this situation is very complicated, it will be pure luck if you can get someone at the lower levels in the Social Security Administration to remove the Windfall Elimination Provision, so you may need to go to appeal within 60 days of receiving the incorrect amount of benefits.

With respect to your wife on Medicare, she should immediately be covered under the spousal benefit of a U.S. citizen. Some offices apply this correctly, and others don't, so it is the luck of the draw working against you here. This too can be appealed if necessary.

I wish you luck in getting this straightened out.

SOCIAL SECURITY WEP 30-YEAR EXEMPTION

I recently bought The Border Guide *from Amazon.com and have read through much of it, some sections more than once. My question is specific to pensions. I have been a Canadian permanent resident of the U.S. since 1976. I receive a small CPP benefit, and last year I started getting Social Security. Due to being one year short of 30 years of "substantial earnings" and the fact that I receive CPP, I am subject to the WEP reduction. After extensive research on the Social Security website, I came to the conclusion that my benefits are probably correct. The research included the totalization agreement with Canada. I also reconfirmed the pension amount using the WEP Online Calculator available on the website and came up with the same dollar amount as my official benefit award. However, in your book, you indicate that the totalization agreement "would still exempt persons from WEP who had a total of 30 years in Canada and/or the U.S" (which I do) based on "a statement that the WEP doesn't apply to benefits under a Social Security agreement with the U.S." I am unable to find any such statement other than that WEP definitely does not apply to Canadian Old-Age Security pension. Incidentally, I recently received an increase in my award after protesting vigorously when my Social Security award was not recalculated after my 2004 earnings had been posted.*

— Dr. Y., San Diego, California

Without sending you into a complicated and lengthy appeal, my recommendation to you, since you are only one year short of your 30 years WEP exemption, is to get one more year of earnings that are subject to Social Security taxes. To do this you only need someone to pay you about $5,000 before the end of this year for legitimate employment of any kind. It could be something as simple as performing as a director of a corporation or some form of consulting/self employment. This is by far easier and less costly than anything else I can recommend for you.

SOCIAL SECURITY APPLICATION DENIED — NO 1099 SLIPS

I was a client of yours some nine years ago, and you were a great help in my moving from Canada to the U.S.

Each year, your office prepared my tax return, and based on your advice, certain self-employment fee income of approximately $4,000 was included as business income each year since 1994, with the objective of attaining 40 quarters for Medicare purposes.

This year, I applied for certain benefits and was told that my last three years' earnings did not qualify because I didn't have Form 1099s, the income slip similar to the Canadian T4s. I never had 1099s from the start. Is there any good reason to appeal this ruling?

Many thanks for any help you can give me on this matter.

— John S., Palm Harbor, Florida

Good to hear from you. I believe someone at the Social Security Administration is just giving you a hard time. Your income is self-employment income, for which no 1099s are normally issued. You have an obligation to report self-employment income and pay Social Security tax, and the IRS rules ensure that you do: you have no choice. I have never heard of this rule, and if one really does exist, it is likely only at an administrative level in Social Security. Ask the person there with whom you are dealing for a copy of the chapter and verse that says this is so. If there is such a procedure, you can ask for reconsideration and/or appeal it once they officially turn you down. The appeals judges normally ignore these internal procedures, as such procedures are not, in fact, the law.

Good luck. Please let me know how you make out.

KNOW SOCIAL SECURITY RULES

I worked for three years as a professor in the United States. The U.S. Social Security office tells me I have 12 quarters of qualifying time toward a U.S. monthly Social Security pension but I must have a minimum of 40 quarters of employment history before I may receive any benefits. I also have nearly $70,000 U.S. accumulated in a TIAA-CREF [this is similar to a Canadian Registered Retirement Savings Plan] that I contributed to while I was in the United States to take a deduction against my teaching salary. The questions I would like to ask are as follows:

1. *As a Canadian resident, can I continue to pay into Social Security so my wife and I can collect Social Security benefits in our retirement years?*

2. *If not, how can I get my money back from them?*

3. *Do you have any other suggestions? What should I do about my TIAA-CREF?*

— Walter J., Saint John, New Brunswick

1. Yes, you can continue to pay into Social Security, but only if you earn $5,000 or more per year of qualifying employment-type income sourced and taxable in the United States. The $5,000 of earnings will give you four quarters of Social Security credit per year. Once you have your total of 40 quarters of benefits or credits, or 28 more than you currently do, both you and your wife can receive U.S. Social Security and Medicare at age 65 even if you don't wish to become U.S. residents in the future under the Canada-U.S. Social Security Agreement. You will need some form of legal immigration status in the United States before you can earn employment-type income in that country.

2. You can get the Social Security money back by applying for a reduced monthly benefit under the Canada-U.S. Social Security Agreement through any U.S. Social Security office once you reach age 62 or older even if you do not contribute any more to the U.S. Social Security system.

3. The tax treatment of the Teachers Insurance and Annuity Association-College Retirement Equities Fund (TIAA-CREF) and other

RRSP-type, U.S.-qualified plans in Canada has recently been changed retroactively. The new Canadian rules, as outlined in Section 243(1), reg S.6803 of the Canada Income Tax Act, state that the income earned on these U.S. accounts is not taxable on a current basis until actual withdrawals are made from the plan. At the time of withdrawal, both income and principal are taxed at the current Canadian rates as income. Therefore, withdrawals should be made at times when income is lower, such as retirement, in a similar manner to your Canadian RRSPs. You are also subject to U.S. rules and taxes on the withdrawals from your TIAA-CREF. You must commence your withdrawals during or before the year in which you become age 70½. Any tax that you may pay to the IRS would be a credit to you on your Canadian return, so you should not be double-taxed on this income.

WORK FOR U.S. SOCIAL SECURITY

I am in the process of obtaining my green card. I shall be sponsored by my son who is an American citizen and will work for him for three or more years. My question concerns Medicare and health insurance at the age of 65. Does the agreement on Social Security between the United States and Canada offer any credits toward Medicare coverage?

— *F.W., Orillia, Ontario*

In order to qualify for U.S. Medicare paid by Social Security at age 65 or later, you need to have forty quarters or ten years of contributions to Social Security through employment income in the United States. You would be eligible for U.S. Medicare after you have had your green card for five years and have reached age 65. However, if you do not have the required 40 quarters of contributions to Social Security, you will have to pay approximately $500 in premiums per month for the coverage instead of $90. If you are married, your wife will qualify for Medicare at age 65 as well as a monthly Social Security payment based on your employment contributions to the plan. Consequently, making the effort to earn $5,000 each year, the minimum amount to get four quarters of qualification during a year, for the total of ten years can give you both a total of more than $12,000 of Medicare benefits plus a small pension for each of you per year for life. This is quite a return on your investment, considering that the Social Security tax on $5,000 of earnings is only about $375 ($750 if you are self-employed).

You can make contributions to Social Security through your earnings at any age, so the sooner you get started the sooner you will qualify. If you work only three years, the agreement on Social Security between the United States and Canada will help you receive a reduced monthly Social Security pension, but since U.S. Medicare is not part of this agreement you will get none of your Medicare premiums paid by the Social Security.

If you are not married and find a U.S. citizen spouse (one who has qualified for Social Security based on her own earnings), after one year of marriage you will get not only a spouse's Social Security pension equal to about 50% of her monthly benefit but you will get U.S. Medicare as well.

MEDICARE COMES FASTER THROUGH MARRIAGE

I have read your answer to a question, in which you write: "If you marry a U.S. citizen sponsor you would get a temporary green card for two years, which would become permanent if you are still married after two years. You may also be eligible for U.S. Social Security and Medicare after one year of marriage, providing your wife had her own employment for ten years or more."

I came to Florida in October 2003, after I got a temporary green card following my marriage to a U.S. citizen. My "permanent" green card was issued in November 2005 and is valid for ten years.

I am 71 years old and my wife retired two years ago, after 40 years of work in the United States. She receives her Social Security pension and is covered by Medicare. I have had a Social Security card since 2005. I have been covered by my wife's health insurance until now, but the end of that coverage comes in October 2006. I applied for Medicare after I read your column in the newspaper, and the Social Security Administration told me I would not be eligible before I have been a "U.S. resident for five consecutive years."

— G.G., Marco Island, Florida

The Social Security Administration (SSA) is not correct in its assessment of your eligibility for Social Security and Medicare. It appears to be applying the rules for immigrants/green card holders who do not have a U.S.-citizen spouse sponsor who has qualified for Social Security and Medicare. You need to stress that you are applying for a spousal benefit and have been married for more than one year. The spousal benefit does not require a five-year presence in the U.S. It may be difficult to convince the lower level of SSA to read their own rules, but if you can get an experienced representative you should be able to clear this up without having to appeal your application. If you don't get satisfaction, you can appeal before an administrative judge to review the law as it applies to you. If your case reaches this point, I recommend you get some legal advice.

AGREEMENT BETWEEN UNITED STATES AND CANADA CAN WORK TO SNOWBIRDS' INCOME ADVANTAGE

Can work in Canada (as landed immigrants) contribute to U.S. credits for Social Security?

We have our U.S. Social Security records and the years 1967–1983 are "non-income" years for my husband and me due to employment in Canada. We have 25 employment years in the United States, which we accumulated before and after our time in Canada.

As I understand it, the complex formula used in determining U.S. benefits takes an average of earnings over one's working lifetime. The "zero income" years presumably would affect that average in a negative way. If the earnings in Canada are factored in, the benefits should be greater.

Please advise if there is a possibility of combining these earning years.

— D.M., Ocala, Florida

The Canada-U.S. Social Security totalization agreement would allow you to use time spent working in Canada (if you need it) to assist you to qualify for Social Security benefits. For example, you need ten years of employment in the United States to qualify for a Social Security pension and Medicare. However, if you had worked only eight years in the United States, but had worked at least two years in Canada, this time in Canada would help you qualify for the Social Security Pension. However, since you already have more than ten years of employment in the United States, you cannot use time in Canada to increase your Social Security benefit. However, technically you would not lose benefits since you contributed to the Canada Pension Plan for the time you were in Canada and will receive a pension from the plan as well as a partial OAS based on the number of years you lived in Canada. Since you had less than 20 years in Canada you will need to use the totalization agreement to get an OAS benefit for each of you. Consequently, you will get some benefits from the totalization agreement, but not from the U.S. Social Security as you expected.

PRIVATE INSURANCE FILLS GAP UNTIL MEDICARE COVERAGE STARTS

I am 67 and my wife is 58 and we are both Canadian citizens. We spent more than four years in Georgia some time ago and I contributed to Social Security for approximately 17 quarters while there. I now receive pensions from both Social Security and the Canada Pension Plan.

Our original intent was to spend six months here in our home in Tucson and six months in Canada so that we could maintain Canadian medical coverage as both my wife and I have pre-existing conditions.

We both received green cards last year and as a CA I am well aware of the tax complications and costs arising from our present plan.

Our family situation in Canada has recently changed and if we can find satisfactory U.S. medical insurance, there is no longer any reason for us to return to Canada other than for family vacations.

My concerns are (1) When will my wife and I be eligible to purchase Medicare insurance? Do my contributions to Social Security reduce the five years' residence requirement? and (2) Are there insurance carriers you can recommend in addition to Ingle Health?

— P.F.D., Tucson, Arizona

Since you did not obtain 40 quarters of credit from Social Security, you are not eligible for U.S. Medicare until you have had your green card for five years. So until then, you will need private insurance. Your wife will not be eligible for Medicare until she turns 65 and also has five continuous years of residence in the United States on a green card.

Since you are nearly halfway to having your full 40 quarters, you should consider working in the United States for the next six years and earn a minimum of approximately $5,000 per year so both you and your wife will get U.S. Medicare Part A for free.

Until you can get Medicare there are several non-U.S. insurance carriers you may be able to get coverage with. It may be very difficult for your wife to get coverage depending on the nature of her pre-existing condition. Insurance carriers that could provide coverage are Lloyd's of London, Danmark and Global. Contact a good international insurance broker for assistance. Cross-border tax issues are quite complex and I know of only a handful of CAs who can deal with them adequately, so I still recommend you get some help in this area rather than try to do it yourself.

EXTRA WORK TRIGGERS SOCIAL SECURITY FOR CANADIAN

I am a U.S. citizen and my residence since 1960 has been Ontario, Canada. To receive Social Security I need 40 credits, and at this time I have 39. I can earn the extra credit by going on my ex-employer's payroll for one month (associate for U.S. company), earning $1,000 U.S., paying tax and Social Security.

Would this trigger a U.S. tax return and future returns? Would the Social Security income received be taxed by either government?

— *R.H.T., Fort Pierce, Florida*

Since you are a U.S. citizen, you are required by the IRS to file U.S. tax returns every year that your income exceeds the personal exemption and standard deduction amount (approximately $10,300 for a single person over age 65). Consequently, earning $1,000 doesn't trigger any new filing requirements since you likely already have an obligation to file. You must file to get the Social Security quarter credited.

Your plan to earn one more credit toward your 40 quarters should enable you to get a Social Security pension and U.S. Medicare at age 65, providing the work is done in the United States. As a U.S. citizen in Canada, you can also complete the work in Canada, but you will need to use the Canada-U.S. Social Security Agreement when you apply for benefits. According to the 1996 amendment to the Canada/U.S. Tax Treaty, Canada would be the only country to tax your Social Security benefit, with 15% of it being totally tax free.

Taking Care of Business 14

HOW SMALL BUSINESS OWNERS
CAN REAP HUGE REWARDS

There is no other area of cross-border financial planning that offers owners of small, closely held businesses more income tax-saving potential than moving to the United States. Consequently, a good cross-border financial plan can save a business owner between several thousand and several million dollars, depending on the size or the nature of the business. Most of these planning opportunities arise solely because a cross-border move is contemplated and possible. They would not be available to business owners if they were not in the process of moving across the border or at least willing and able to relocate to the U.S. for a few years. Unfortunately, the business owner's trusted advisors of many years often become the major deterrent to making these savings happen. Financial advisors may operate under some popular misconceptions because very few of them are aware of cross-border financial planning techniques, and therefore they tend to discourage the business owner from moving. As a result, the business owner is misled or discouraged from taking advantage of great opportunities to realize a much higher net value after taxes on the sale of their business — a business that they worked hard on for many years of their career. Consequently, the business owner must look elsewhere for cross-border advice and use his or her trusted advisors as part of the new team that will work in the owner's best interest to make the move successful. Chapter 15 will be of assistance to you in finding a cross-border planning advisor.

The major considerations that small business owners need to be aware of are outlined in the next four sections.

A CANADIAN CORPORATION CAN ASSIST WITH U.S. IMMIGRATION

Many successful entrepreneurs have worked long and hard to establish businesses. Later, when they want to retire or sell the businesses to try something new, they apply the same amount of diligence to disposing of their businesses. When the money from the sale is sitting in the bank and all the income taxes are paid, they start thinking about retiring to the American Sunbelt where they may have been wintering for many years. Unfortunately, our hypothetical business owners may have just sold off their simplest and best means of U.S. immigration.

As you may recall, the U.S. immigration procedures outlined in Chapter 7 all require some form of business or a family connection for U.S. immigration. So if you have no close family members in the United States or you have sold your principal business, you may need to establish a new business in order to complete your immigration. A better route for business owners would be to complete cross-border plans before the sales of their businesses. A sale could either be delayed for a short period of time or structured in such a way as to incorporate the necessary means to acquire a visa or a green card. This forward planning could save the business owner a great deal of time and money. In addition, the failure to complete a cross-border plan before a business is sold could mean that both vendor and purchaser paid thousands or even millions more in income tax on the sale than was necessary, as outlined in the next section.

HOW TO TAKE A CAPITAL GAINS TAX HOLIDAY

Canadian small business owners are currently limited to a once-in-a-lifetime tax-free capital gains exemption of $500,000. If the proper planning has been done, then this exemption may be effectively doubled by including a spouse as a co-owner of the business(es). What happens if you have no exemption remaining, you need to sell the assets of your company rather than shares, your business doesn't qualify for the exemption or your capital gains exceed the $500,000 exemption limitations? A tax rate, which is currently nearly 25% in most provinces, is applied to the amount of capital gains not eligible for the exemption, and when assets are sold, often there is recapture of previous depreciation write-offs that attract an even higher rate of tax, close to 50%.

So how much tax can you save by making the sale using cross-border planning techniques? A properly drafted cross-border financial plan can legally reduce this tax liability to just 15% or even 5%, using certain provisions included in the Canada/U.S. Tax Treaty. The 5% or 15% tax paid to the CRA may then be recovered in the United States through foreign tax credits on income generated by a properly designed investment portfolio or other foreign tax credit planning methods. Between the Canada/U.S. Tax Treaty and the IRS's generous rules concerning foreign tax credits, this tax paid on the sale of the business can normally be fully recovered over about ten years. The net result is that a successful business owner can sell his or her business and effectively pay no net tax. This no-net-tax scenario can apply if the proceeds from the business are $500,000, $5 million, $50 million or more!

These potentially enormous tax savings can be obtained based on sound legal precedents, but the rules are much too complex to even attempt to explain in a general guide such as this book. The key point is that business owners should be aware that major tax savings are still possible and available. To use a cross-border plan to their maximum advantage, business owners need to seek out the services of a qualified cross-border financial planning specialist early in the process of retiring and/or selling their businesses. In fact, if the cross-border planner is brought in early enough, the planning can actually facilitate the retirement process — or transition to family members or third parties — while simultaneously providing major tax advantages to the purchaser as well as the owner. Often, the business owner's current advisors just don't have the answers to assist the business owner and the family members to do what they want to do in the manner they want to do it.

A good example of such a situation is a case we dealt with in which two brothers equally owned a multi-million-dollar business in Calgary. The younger of the two brothers wanted to retire to his winter home in Arizona, but a study the brothers had commissioned from one of four big accounting firms in Calgary (and for which they had paid thousands of dollars) told them there wasn't enough cash flow from the business for the older brother to buy out the younger one and pay all the taxes due. The accountants and company bankers also told them that if they borrowed the money to complete the sale, the debt load would likely sink the business. For more than two years these brothers sought someone to help them through this dilemma. They were referred to us by another client, and within a year the younger brother was golfing in Arizona, free and easy, the older brother owned the business, and because the tax burden on the sale between the brothers was reduced dramatically, there was more than enough cash flow to pay out the retired brother and allow the business to carry on unimpeded by debt. Now, nearly ten years later, the older brother has transitioned this very successful business to a third party and his son used cross-border planning to save several million dollars in income taxes for himself and his family.

Another client from Vancouver who owned a $15 million business had long-time advisors who were unable to help him successfully retire and transfer the business to a son who was actively involved in the running of the business. With our assistance, he was able to utilize several cross-border planning techniques to transition the business to his son free from income tax on the net basis and save himself and his family nearly $500,000 per year in income taxes.

We have helped many other business owners in a similar manner. The key is that cross-border planning can provide business owners with a new set of options to help them keep their hard-earned business assets and achieve their retirement goals. Most advisors who do not have cross-border experience will not be aware of these possibilities.

TAX RAMIFICATIONS OF MAINTAINING A CANADIAN CORPORATION

If a Canadian business owner wishes to maintain a Canadian corporation after becoming a resident of the United States, he must deal with a number of issues. First of all, the departure tax rules noted in Chapter 9 require a deemed disposition of the corporation shares on exit. Tax would either have to be paid at that time or other arrangements, including collateral, would need to be made with CRA to defer the tax to the time the shares are actually sold. Consequently, the sale of the corporate shares after you become a U.S. resident may be subject to both Canadian and U.S. capital gains tax, as calculated based on the increase in share value since their original acquisition or the creation of the corporation. Business advisors who are not familiar with how to use new exit rules to advantage often cite this fact as the key reason not to move to the U.S. Far too frequently I am approached by frustrated Canadian business owners whose Canadian advisors have told them the only option is to pay a huge tax on the sale of their business or an exit tax if they wish to immigrate to the U.S. If you are a frustrated business owner or know someone who is, it could be extremely beneficial for to pursue a cross-border planning scenario.

The Canada/U.S. Tax Treaty does, however, make some provisions for sufficient tax credits to prevent outright double taxation on gains on exit or sale of a cross-border business. The timing of any foreign tax credits created in the liquidation of the corporate shares and departure from Canada are extremely critical. If the owner were to die in the United States, the estate might still be subject to the double estate tax, a syndrome outlined in Chapter 4. Proper cross-border planning can help eliminate or at least greatly reduce any capital gains tax or estate tax due on the sale or wind-up of a business or the death of the business owner.

Another issue that a Canadian business owner living in the United States needs to address is that if the Canadian company is largely a passive one earning income from rentals and investments, it will likely be considered a foreign personal holding company by the IRS and be subject to a myriad of reporting and other requirements. For example, if the company's fiscal year is not December 31, calendar-year reporting of the corporate income must be provided, and tax must be paid as if the shareholder(s) personally owned the corporate assets. This tax must be paid whether or not income is actually distributed to the shareholders during that year. Considering all of the IRS reporting requirements on foreign holding companies, there is little or no advantage, and there are many disadvantages, including higher taxes, to maintaining a Canadian company of this type. We would normally recommend the company be unwound before or shortly after U.S. residence is taken up, or that it be converted to a Nova Scotia or Alberta Unlimited Liability Company (NSULC or ABULC). A NSULC/ABULC is taxed like a partnership for U.S. purposes, so all income follows the owner, to be taxed only once in the U.S. with full foreign tax credits for taxes paid in Canada by the corporation.

Canadian companies owned by U.S. residents or citizens that are reporting active business income are also subject to special rules on reporting income. The earnings and profits from an active Canadian company that are retained in the company will not flow through to the U.S. shareholder on an accrual basis, and generally the tax to this shareholder may be deferred until the earnings and profits are withdrawn. However, deferring tax on the accrued income in the corporation does not eliminate the double-tax problem on this income unless the corporation is converted to an unlimited liability company as noted above. There is usually a current tax liability on the income from the holding company, and the U.S. reporting and filing requirements are the same for most companies. With an active Canadian company, and to a lesser extent a holding company, one very good method to reduce corporate income from the operation is to collect a reasonable management fee, which could zero out the corporate net income. The Canadian corporation would be able to deduct the management fee in full, and under the Canada/U.S. Tax Treaty management fees are subject only to a maximum 15% withholding tax, as long as the management services were provided from the U.S. side of the border. The 15% withholding tax is fully recoverable in the United States, through the foreign tax credits allowed by the IRS.

If the actual management work is done on the U.S. side of the border, the Canadian company can pay a reasonable management fee to the owner, or to a related U.S. company exempt from Canadian withholding. Care must be taken when paying these kinds of fees on a cross-border basis in order not to violate Canada Revenue Agency transfer pricing rules. The net result is that income can be removed from the Canadian company without Canadian tax and taxed at the lower U.S. rates. The final tax rate paid will be determined by the owner's marginal tax rate and his or her state of residence. If Canadian salaries are taken by U.S. resident shareholders for services provided in Canada, the shareholders would have to file non-resident Canadian returns and pay tax on the Canadian salary. The Canada/U.S. Tax Treaty states that if the salary is under $10,000 annually, no Canadian return need be filed or Canadian tax paid.

U.S. ESTATE TAX CONSIDERATIONS FOR BUSINESS OWNERS

One final misconception perpetuated by many Canadian advisors to business owners is that nothing can be done to protect business owners from U.S. estate taxes when they immigrate to the U.S. Just as there are many ways to deal with or avoid the Canadian exit tax, there are many strategies to mitigate or eliminate U.S. estate taxes for wealthy business owners who wish to enjoy reduced taxes on the sale of their business or on their business income.

What are the estate-planning considerations of a Canadian corporation owned by a U.S. resident? As we have seen in Chapter 4, U.S. residents are taxed at death on their worldwide assets. Canadians who become residents of the United States without proper planning could subject all their Canadian holdings to the U.S. estate tax. In addition, they might face double taxation from the Canadian deemed disposition tax at death.

A proper cross-border plan would use one or more living and/or spousal trusts to eliminate or greatly reduce both levels of tax by either Canada or the United States. Again, this kind of planning needs to be completed before a business owner immigrates to the United States. Once you become a U.S. resident, the number of planning choices for a business owner to avoid unnecessary estate taxes is significantly reduced.

Business advisors who do not have cross-border knowledge often caution business owners against a move to the U.S. because of the burden of U.S. estate taxes. The real fact, as noted in Chapters 4 and 9, is that proper planning and the larger U.S. estate tax exemptions make the tax paid at death by a U.S. resident substantially less than that paid by a Canadian resident.

In God We Trust 15

Choosing a Cross-Border Planning Professional

Individuals in Canada or the United States who have financial interests only in the country they reside in face a single set of rules, making it relatively easy to obtain the services of a competent financial planner, accountant or lawyer who can provide the necessary expertise when required. As soon as a Canadian spends time or purchases real estate or a business in the United States, there are two new sets of tax rules — the Canada/U.S. Tax Treaty and the U.S. Internal Revenue Code — that need to be considered. In addition, other cross-border factors start to come into play such as immigration, estate planning, investment, currency exchange, medical coverage and various forms of insurance for home, auto and personal liability.

There are many other cross-border financial issues that must be dealt with. These rules and considerations are complex, far-reaching and often in conflict with one another. Even a knowledgeable person may have difficulty grasping all the implications, and potentially costly mistakes are easily made. To make things more difficult, cross-border rules are so complex and highly specialized that adequate professional advice is not easy to find. It can be an arduous job for most professionals just to learn and keep current with a single country's rules, let alone making the effort to learn both Canadian and U.S. rules and the implications of the Canada/U.S. Tax Treaty. Consequently, there are few financial planning professionals who have undertaken the task of becoming proficient in both American and Canadian immigration, financial and estate-planning matters as they apply to Canadians living, working or visiting in the United States or Americans doing the same in Canada. In fact, in order to become fully conversant with all these complex cross-border financial considerations, the planning professional needs to actually practise in both countries for extended periods to be immersed in the different environments — somewhat like someone trying to become truly bilingual.

There is no school or college in North America that one can go to to become a cross-border financial planner, making it very difficult to determine how qualified an individual truly is in these matters. Likewise, there are very few publications for cross-border planning professionals or members of the public who wish to do research on the subject.

THE TEAM APPROACH

Any Canadian with assets in the United States or vice versa, and certainly anyone who moves across the 49th parallel in either direction, will require the assistance of one or more professionals from either Canada or the United States. Because there are so many separate areas of expertise required to complete a valid cross-border financial plan, no one professional or planning firm can successfully cover all areas of implementation. Consequently, our recommendation is that you opt for a team approach.

The cross-border financial planning team may consist of two or more professionals from either country, depending on the complexity of your situation. Picking the right members of your team is critical and should be done in a manner similar to choosing a doctor or medical team. You would go first to a general practitioner or family doctor, who would assess your total health, provide the treatment that is within his scope of care and then recommend or refer you to a specialist(s) as required. The general practitioner monitors and coordinates all the other medical services, to ensure that treatments are not being duplicated or in conflict with one another. He will ensure that everyone is focusing on the same objective, your best interests. Once your medical condition has been treated, the general practitioner will probably monitor your condition to watch for any future complications.

Your first step in obtaining prudent cross-border financial planning should be to find a good general financial practitioner, specifically a cross-border financial planner. The cross-border financial planner can draw up a written cross-border plan for you, refer you to the individual experts you may require, and then assist you in implementing the plan by acting as your team leader. He or she can coordinate other team members to complete your plan in a timely and effective manner. Unfortunately, finding such a planner is much more difficult than you might think. To my knowledge, because of time, effort and expense involved, there are only about a dozen individuals in North America that have become Certified Financial Planner® both in Canada and the U.S. This important dual professional certification demands at least a minimum knowledge of both Canadian and U.S. financial planning concerns simultaneously. I personally have been involved in training seven past and four future professionals with this certification, including myself, and I generally know who the qualified planners are and what their expertise is. To confuse the issue, there are also numerous accounting and law firms that are competent and have expertise in one of the many specific tasks involved in cross-border planning. Their expertise lies normally in tax law or tax preparation matters — a small portion of the expertise necessary for cross-border planning. None of them, however, has the expertise to actually do a cross-border plan that covers all the necessary issues such as immigration, taxation, risk management, medical planning, estate planning, and cross-border investment strategies. Figure 15.1 displays one possible organizational chart for a typical cross-border financial planning team.

Figure 15.1

Not everyone is going to need all the advisors listed in Figure 15.1. Some may require more or fewer. For example, a winter visitor may require only a cross-border financial planner to find a U.S. estate attorney or provide investment advice for his assets, while someone moving to the United States might require the assistance of both a Canadian and an American accountant, in addition to all the other advisors. Even though Figure 15.1 indicates separate advisors for eight different services, several of them may be obtained from the same person or firm. For example, an experienced cross-border financial planner would likely have the necessary level of expertise in the areas of investment, tax and insurance, to eliminate the need for separate advisors in these areas.

LOCATING A GOOD CROSS-BORDER PROFESSIONAL

For those moving to the United States, it may be best to choose your financial planning team on the U.S. side of the border, particularly the cross-border financial planner who is your team leader. The converse would be true for Americans moving to Canada or Canadians moving back after a long stay in the United States. Once you have a team leader in place, she should be given the names of all your existing advisors to assess the situation, and determine what other team members, if any, are required.

The best way to proceed is by referral. If you have a friend or relative, or know of someone who has used a cross-border financial planner in a similar situation, ask for a referral. If not, check with professional organizations such as Advocis, the former Canadian Association of Financial Planners (CAFP), in Toronto, the Institute of Advanced Financial Planners (IAFP), also in Toronto, the Financial Planning Association (FPA), in Denver or the National Association of Personal Financial Advisors (NAPFA) in Illinois. These are the key professional associations that educate and license financial planning professionals in Canada and the United States. Advocis has local chapters in most major Canadian cities, and the FPA or NAPFA are located in major American cities. Each has free consumer referral services and can be located through the business listings in the telephone book or on the World Wide Web. The Advocis website is www.advocis.ca, the IAFP is at www.iafp.ca, the FPA website is at www.fpanet.org and NAPFA is at www.napfa.org.

The IAFP in Canada controls the use of the Registered Financial Planner (RFP) professional designation in Canada. They are responsible for establishing standards and conducting courses and examinations for those wishing to make financial planning their career. To become an RFP, one must first pass the three-year, six-course Certified Financial Planner

(CFP) program, or an equivalent professional program, have at least two years' experience in financial planning, write a very comprehensive examination, submit a written financial plan and be an active member of the IAFP. To maintain full membership in IAFP, the Registered Financial Planner must meet continuing education requirements, have errors and omissions insurance, follow the association's code of ethics and pay membership dues.

In 1996, several existing Canadian institutions got together and agreed that the Certified Financial Planner™ (CFP), because of its international recognition, would be adopted as Canada's financial planning designation of choice. A Canadian CFP board, the Financial Planners Standards Council of Canada, was set up as a licensee under the founding and current licenser, the U.S. International Board of Certified Financial Planners (IBCFP). The IBCFP, as noted below, licenses all U.S. CFPs and has licensed the use of the CFP designation in 20 separate countries. Canada's adoption of the Certified Financial Planner™ designation is a great start toward creating higher and more uniform standards, as well as better public confidence in and recognition of the financial planning profession. The Financial Planners Standards Council of Canada has a very good referral system on their website for those looking for planners with the CFP™ designation in Canada at www.cfp-ca.org. The RFP will still be the key designation of the IAFP for planners who can meet the special education and experience requirements. For Advocis, the basic CFP™ was originally deemed as its key designation; however, due to the large insurance sales contingent in its membership, insurance sales designations such as the Certified Life Underwriter (CLU) have in effect "hijacked" the CFP™. I believe this is to the detriment of the Canadian consumer. We recommend that any Canadian planner you engage have a minimum of a CFP™ or RFP designation and be an active member of the IAFP or similar organization with high standards of ethics to provide consumer protection.

The FPA in the United States works closely with the College for Financial Planning in Denver, establishing standards and requirements for those wishing to become Certified Financial Planners® in that country. Once the CFP® education and experience requirements have been met, a separate board, the IBCFP, licenses individuals to use and maintain the CFP® designation in the United States. The IBCFP requires minimum of annual continuing-education and adherence to a comprehensive code of ethics to maintain the CFP® licence. Canadian CFPs™ cannot legally use their Canadian CFP™ designation in the United States, unless they have met the additional education and licensing standards of the IBCFP in that country. The College for Financial Planning has also developed a post-graduate Master's of Science degree in Financial Planning (MSFP) for those who wish to further their studies in the United States. We recommend that any planner you engage in the United States have a CFP® designation, preferably hold a Master's degree in Financial Planning or possess the equivalent experience and be an active member of NAPFA or the FPA.

Although it may be hard to believe, of all the professional financial planning organizations in Canada and the U.S., NAPFA is the only one that puts the consumers' interests first. All NAPFA members must act in a fiduciary relationship with all clients, be fee-only, sell no financial products and disclose any potential conflicts of interest. All the other planning organizations in Canada and the U.S., to various degrees, allow their members to sell products, earn commissions and generally be beholden to their company's products and services rather than acting at all times in the financial consumer's best interest. Consequently, if you can find a NAPFA member to assist you in your cross-border financial planning needs you have the greatest chance of receiving independent quality advice.

The cross-border financial planner selected to be your team leader should have a minimum RFP or CFP™ designation in Canada, or a CFP® in the United States. Although rare, the ideal cross-border financial planner would have both a Canadian CFP™/RFP and an American CFP®, with financial planning experience in both countries. Unfortunately, many Canadian, and to a lesser extent U.S., CFPs™ or RFPs use their licences as a means to sell investment or insurance products and they focus their practices primarily on sales rather than planning. Consequently, it is important to look beyond the designations to what the planners primarily focus on. To be sure it is aligned with your best interest, see the section What Does a Cross-Border Financial Plan Cost? In general, avoid planners who are licensed to sell investments or securities for commissions as you may be sold expensive financial products you do not need.

When interviewing a prospective cross-border financial planner, do not hesitate to ask for references from other Canadians for whom they have successfully completed cross-border financial plans, or developed U.S. non-resident estate plans. Figure 15.2 provides a summary checklist to use when you are interviewing potential candidates.

WHAT ABOUT USING AN ACCOUNTANT?

Many people assume that Chartered Accountants (CAs) in Canada and Certified Public Accountants (CPAs) in the United States are qualified to

```
┌─────────────────────────────────────────────────────────────┐
│                                                               │
│              CHOOSING A CROSS-BORDER                          │
│                 FINANCIAL PLANNER                             │
│                                                               │
│  Designations held:          CFP™ (Canada)        ❏          │
│                               CFP® (U.S.)          ❏          │
│                               RFP (Canada)         ❏          │
│                               Other                ❏          │
│                                                               │
│  Education:                   Degrees              ❏          │
│                               Postgraduate         ❏          │
│                               Other                ❏          │
│  Experience: ___ yrs Canada; ___ yrs U.S.                     │
│  Professional association member:    Advocis       ❏          │
│                                      FPA           ❏          │
│                                      NAPFA         ❏          │
│                                      Other         ❏          │
│  Can provide references:          Yes ❏     No ❏              │
│  Provides written fee agreement:  Yes ❏     No ❏              │
│  Does not sell investments of insurance  Yes ❏  No ❏          │
│                                                               │
└─────────────────────────────────────────────────────────────┘
```

Figure 15.2

do financial planning. While CAs and CPAs are skilled in preparing financial statements and are generally qualified to give tax advice in their own country, problems arise when it comes to investment selection, insurance counselling and estate planning. To make your cross-border financial plan effective, all these issues must be professionally coordinated on a cross-border basis or serious consequences or missed opportunities may result. Professional accountants, by training and temperament, are neither investment counsellors nor estate planners, nor do they generally have a good working knowledge of insurance matters. Even though your Canadian accountant may have been your trusted advisor for many years, it is both unrealistic and unfair for you to ask this person to provide cross-border financial planning services. Some of the most outrageous tax situations I have seen in cross-border financial planning were set up by Canadian accounting firms both big and small. Due to their lack of cross-border planning experience, these accountants structure U.S. businesses like Canadian businesses and end up costing clients hundreds of thousands of dollars of unnecessary taxes.

Professional accountants make excellent cross-border financial planning team members, but because of their narrow focus they are not always suitable as team leaders. For that role, you need someone who can coordinate and implement all the immigration, tax, insurance, risk management, estate and investment issues necessary for a cross-border plan.

WHAT TO EXPECT FROM CROSS-BORDER FINANCIAL PLANNERS

Many people have never heard of cross-border financial planning. As a result, they have no concept of what it entails or what they should expect. By reading this far in this book, you should now have a pretty good grasp of the number and complexity of problems you'll encounter in preparing any good cross-border financial plan. The sheer number of possibilities can be overwhelming.

A professional cross-border financial planner can very quickly sort through this myriad of rules and regulations, and very expeditiously tell you which rules apply to your situation, and how to incorporate them into your planning objectives. Expect a written plan that will address all your concerns, along with a detailed analysis with specific recommendations. No matter which country you're moving to, the cross-border plan should —

- tell you how each of your assets will be taxed by either country before and after leaving your current country of residence.

- show you the best way to keep residences in both Canada and the U.S. and to spend time at each country without tax or immigration consequences.

- provide a Canadian or U.S. net worth and cash flow statement.

- provide detailed tax projections of all the tax options, both personally and for businesses, available to you.

- provide a risk management plan to safeguard you from any financial disasters in medical or liability expenses.

- provide a complete cross-border estate plan that looks after all your assets, whether they are located in Canada or the United States or both countries, and takes into account who your beneficiaries are, where they are located and what your personal desires are.

- provide a complete investment program that takes into consideration your income needs, your tax bracket, your risk tolerance, the location and liquidity of your assets, and the size of your estate. (This should not be confused with purchasing investments from your planner; I believe you will get the best advice from a planner who does not earn commissions or other fees from the investments he or she recommends for you.)

- provide a retirement and benefit plan to maximize CPP/QPP, OAS and Social Security benefits, and ensure your income and assets are not depleted during your and your spouse's lifetimes.

Clear and easy-to-understand oral and written communications are imperative. Nothing is more frustrating than hiring a technically competent professional and then not being able to understand his or her directions. Developing a good rapport with any professional you hire is critical, in order that a fair and open exchange of ideas takes place. If you do not feel comfortable with the person you are considering as your planner, address it up front or seek another person for the job. The second-to-last section of this chapter, The Consumer Bill of Rights for Financial Planning, provides more detailed information about what to look for and how to work with a financial planning professional.

WHAT DOES A CROSS-BORDER FINANCIAL PLAN COST?

Financial planners are compensated by four key methods: by fee only, by commission only, by a combination of fee and commission, or by salary. If you are dealing with a professional financial planner, he or she should provide you with a full written disclosure of the amounts of all fees or commissions you will be charged and the method by which she is compensated for services. If this information was not voluntarily provided, make certain you ask for the full disclosure or avoid using him or her. If you are considering a planner who belongs to one of the professional organizations such as the IAFP, Advocis, FPA or NAPFA, their codes of ethics require that planners provide clients with full disclosure of how they are compensated before any engagement. Planners who take all or part of their compensation through commissions seem to have the hardest time disclosing what they and their firms are taking as direct or indirect commissions: trips to exotic places as sales incentives, price spreads or markups on security trades and trail or residual commission payments. These commissions and incentives are quite complicated and can be easily hidden, so "buyer beware." NAPFA will give you a great deal of free information on fee-only versus commissions-type planning to assist you in making a better, more informed choice of the type of planner you employ.

Which method of compensation is best for the client is the subject of much debate. In cross-border financial planning, I have found that most clients prefer a fee-only basis. They find it reassuring to know that they do not have to buy any financial products to get the necessary advice and that there are no hidden costs or motives. Since other cross-border financial planning team members such as accountants and attorneys are usually compensated by fees, there is often a better rapport between the team members if the financial planner/team leader is paid the same way. There are far too many potential areas of conflict of interest if your planner is compensated either fully or partially on commissions, no matter how hard he or she may try to convince you otherwise.

Regardless of how you pay for your cross-border financial plan, a good general rule is that you get what you pay for. A budget plan could get you budget results and may end up costing you thousands of dollars more in lost benefits, higher-than-necessary taxes and poor investment results. Cross-border financial planning is much too complex an endeavour to take chances by cutting corners. Consider the fee you are paying as an investment and expect a return on that investment. You should find that a good cross-border plan offers you many more opportunities to give you a much greater return on your investment than do basic planners on either side of the border.

You can expect a cross-border financial plan from an experienced fee-only planner to cost a minimum of $10,000 or more, depending on the experience and credentials of the individual. Depending on the size and complexity of your estate, many plans can cost more than $100,000 and be worth every penny. A complete cross-border financial plan takes a considerable number of person-hours to complete and can include from 50 to 100 pages of analysis and recommendations. Implementation of the plan takes an equal or greater amount of professional assistance, so it is often best to get a planner who will include both the planning and the implementation in one all-encompassing fee. Once the cross-border plan has been completed and implemented, there usually are ongoing costs to maintain the plan, manage investment portfolios, update estate documentation and prepare tax returns. Generally, legal and accounting fees for implementation are not included in the cross-border planning fee but your planner can negotiate on your behalf to minimize these costs.

To put the cost of a cross-border plan in perspective, it is useful to compare it to other financial transactions such as the purchase of a house. For example, if you were to purchase a home in the U.S. for $500,000 you would pay real estate agent commissions and other expenses totalling close to $35,000. For that $35,000 in costs you utilize anywhere from a few hours to a few weekends of the realtor's time. That particular realtor may have had very little experience or training and may have just been recently licensed. Once you own the home you have to pay for annual maintenance, taxes and insurance costs. Cross-border financial planning is a bargain compared to those kinds of financial transactions for the following reasons:

- From years of experience in cross-border financial planning I have found that it takes anywhere from 150 to 500 person-hours to complete a proper cross-border financial plan for a client, depending on the complexity of the client's financial situation and goals.

- The person or persons putting together a cross-border plan are required to have a high degree of technical training and many years of experience.

- The cross-border financial plan may save you many times its initial costs in tax savings, lower investment costs, better access to medical professionals or facilities and a more enjoyable retirement. In general, a target that I like to set in a cross-border plan is that, in the first five years, total savings of taxes, fees, commissions and other benefits should be five times or more the actual investment in the cost of the cross-border financial plan. An additional home is more likely to be an added expense and it will not save you money or give you additional benefits other than providing another place to live and hopefully some profit when you eventually sell it.

- You may purchase several houses during your lifetime but you are likely to only need one cross-border financial plan.

- A cross-border plan can not only make your retirement life more enjoyable but it can actually substantially reduce or even eliminate the risk of running out of money in retirement.

The bottom line in a cross-border plan is: Does it create value for you? Value can mean many things to different people. For example, some people might consider that value is just being able to have the cross-border lifestyle that they desire, while others would like to see value that can be measured in dollars and cents. Would you invest a hundred thousand dollars in a plan that would save you a million dollars in income taxes? Most people, including myself, would jump at the chance to get that kind of return on an investment. However, over the years in cross-border planning I have seen many people turn that opportunity down just because they've never paid any professional accountant, attorney or financial planner that amount of money for any reason in their entire lives. Therefore, based on principle alone, they will not make such an investment, regardless of the logic in this kind of value-based decision.

Cross-border financial planners can usually provide assurances that their work will achieve tax or other savings in excess of their fees. Ask for this type of commitment from your chosen planner.

The highest paid member of the cross-border financial planning team should be the one who can save you the most money, and in most cases that will be the team leader/cross-border financial planner.

A CONSUMER BILL OF RIGHTS FOR FINANCIAL PLANNING*

As a consumer, you have a right to know. Whether you are just investigating your options or have already engaged a financial planner, knowing your rights will help ensure that you have a successful working relationship with a competent, trustworthy financial planner who can help you achieve financial independence.

Article I

You have the right to receive competent financial advice from a qualified, knowledgeable professional, with financial training, education and experience. Look for a person who has at least one of the following education credentials:

- A designation in the United States such as Certified Financial Planner® (CFP), Chartered Financial Consultant (ChFC), Certified Public Accountant (CPA), Personal Financial Specialist (PFS) or Chartered Financial Analyst (CFA). In Canada, look for the Certified Financial Planner™ (CFP), Registered Financial Planner (RFP) or Chartered Accountant (CA)

- A law degree (JD) in the United States and/or (LL.B. or LL.M.) in Canada

- A Bachelor's or graduate degree in financial planning, money management or related business from an accredited institution

- A firm commitment to continuing education activities to ensure the planning professional is at the leading edge of their profession

---

*Reprinted with permission from *The Consumer Book of Rights for Financial Planning*, published by the International Association for Financial Planning (IAFP), now the FPA. The FPA website is at www.fpanet.org.

Article II

You have the right to work with a planner who is registered as an investment advisor with the Securities and Exchange Commission (SEC) in the U.S., or an equivalent state, provincial or other federal registration.

It is important to know if the planner is registered in the United States as an investment advisor, because that is the minimum step a planner can take to comply with regulatory requirements unless he or she works directly for a bank or trust company. Unless your planner is fee-only and does not sell any financial products, he or she must be licensed with the National Association of Securities Dealers (NASD) in the U.S. and appropriate state insurance departments to sell investments and insurance. In Canada, provincial registration and licensing are required to sell these products. A fee-only planner does not need to be licensed to sell investment or insurance products since he or she has nothing to sell you but his or her services.

Article III

You have a right to be comfortable with your planner. Most planners will provide references. Ask for names and phone numbers of clients whom the planner has worked with, as well as other financial service professionals. Don't expect the referrals to reveal their confidential financial data and plan but instead focus on asking did the planner meet your expectations and did they treat you with respect and give you good value. A thorough Internet search on the planner and their firm can also yield valuable background information that can help you choose the right planner.

There are very strict rules in the United States on giving investment performance results, so referrals based on past investment results of an investment advisor are not legally available in most circumstances.

Article IV

You have the right to receive financial planning advice that is tailored to your financial needs. Look for a planner who prepares a financial plan based on the accepted industry-wide, six-step process:

1. Information gathering
2. Goal setting
3. Identifying financial problems
4. Preparing written recommendations
5. Implementing recommendations

6. Reviewing and revising the plan

You have the right to expect that this process will provide clear explanations for all recommendations and thorough answers to your questions.

Article V

You have the right to receive a financial plan that is cost-effective. The cost to implement the plan should be within your financial means. You also have the right to obtain an estimate of the total costs involved in financial planning from your planner, and to know exactly what services the planner will provide.

Article VI

You have the right to receive from the planner sufficient information on the risks and benefits of each recommended action to implement the financial plan.

Make sure the planner explains everything thoroughly, including the "worst case" and "middle of the road" investment, tax and other scenarios. You should reject high pressure tactics aimed at getting you to purchase financial products, and be wary of promises of very high rates of return on investments.

Article VII

You have the right to receive full disclosure in writing about how the planner will be compensated. Inquire about the following four methods of compensation: fee-only, fee-and-commission, commission-only and salary. If you are concerned about conflict of interest in the planner's method of compensation, do not hesitate to ask the planner to explain.

Article VIII

You have the right to receive a full explanation about how the final plan is to be implemented and to have an estimate cost of the implementation. Ask whether the recommended investments come from one company or from several different companies. Find out if the planner sells only those products on which he or she makes a commission. And ask whether the plan can be implemented by buying financial products from other sources on a no-load, no-commission basis.

Article IX

You have the right to receive assurances that the planner has the resources to serve your needs for the next year or more. Find out whether the planner has a network of related professionals — such as tax accountants, attorneys and/or brokers — to consult with you on any special needs that you may have. A good financial planner will pinpoint areas of potential financial difficulty (such as an outdated will) and relate the financial consequences to you. If the planner is a sole practitioner, ask what will happen to his or her plan for you if he or she dies prematurely or is disabled and unable to work. A good planner will have a written contingency plan and will be happy to let you see it.

Article X

You have the right to receive regular written and oral updates on the status of your financial plan and the actions you taken to implement it.

Work with your planner to keep track of your investments on a regular basis. Make sure you understand how your investments are performing. If you are in doubt, keep asking questions.

Article XI

You have a right to confidentiality concerning all the information you provided to your planner. Your goals and concerns should rightfully be treated with respect, without your planner making value judgements about them.

KEEPING IN TOUCH

One of the best ways I have found to keep our readers current on changing issues and planning ideas is through our website, www.keatsconnelly.com. Because of the open nature of the website it should not be relied upon as the final source of information before taking action. It can never be overstated that cross-border planning is far too complex to attempt to execute without direct professional help designed for your specific situation, goals and objectives. In addition, we have a quarterly newsletter to keep you updated on the latest financial happenings. We will be glad to mail *Border Guide* readers a sample copy of the newsletter for their examination at no charge.

Numerous *Border Guide* readers have requested additional information regarding specific cross-border services, referrals to health insurance providers, or other professionals and for updates on matters that are pending at the time of publication. In response to these requests, we are making the toll-free number of Keats, Connelly & Associates, Inc. available to you along with our website. You can use it to request information about the materials presented in this book. There will be no charge, provided of course that you do not expect us to offer any planning advice without an official engagement.

We are a fee-only planning firm that does not sell commission-paying products of any kind. We are the largest firm in North America specializing in cross-border financial planning. We have consistently been rated as a top financial planning firm in the U.S. by several financial planning magazines and we have won ethics awards from the Better Business Bureau. We have professional training specifically in the area of Canada and U.S. cross-border financial planning, including immigration, legal, estate, insurance and investment matters.

Providing free cross-border planning information would make it impossible for us to remain in business. So if you need specific advice or services we will be happy to forward our fee schedule. We would also appreciate hearing your comments and suggestions about the book, so we can make future editions of *The Border Guide* even more informative and valuable.

You can call or write to us at —
Keats, Connelly & Associates, Inc.
3336 N. 32nd Street, Suite 100
Phoenix, AZ 85018-6241

Call toll free from Canada or the United States:
1-800-678-5007

Our e-mail address is
bobk@keatsconnelly.com

You can also visit the Keats, Connelly & Associates website at
www.keatsconnelly.com

Appendix A
List of Useful Free Publications

FROM THE U.S. INTERNAL REVENUE SERVICE (IRS)

All of the following IRS publications are available free of charge at any IRS office or U.S. embassy, or by calling toll free 1-800-TAX-FORM anywhere in the United States or from the IRS website, www.irs.gov.

#54 TAX GUIDE FOR U.S. CITIZENS AND RESIDENT ALIENS ABROAD

This publication discusses tax situations for U.S. citizens and resident aliens who live and work abroad. In particular, it explains the rules for excluding income and deduction of certain housing costs. Answers are provided to the questions that taxpayers abroad ask most often.

Forms 2555, 1116 and 1040, Schedule SE (Form 1040)

#513 TAX INFORMATION FOR VISITORS TO THE UNITED STATES

This publication briefly reviews the general requirements of U.S. income tax laws for foreign visitors. You may have to file a U.S. tax return during your visit. Most visitors who come to the United States are not allowed to work there. Check with the U.S. Citizenship and Immigration Service before you take a job.

Forms 1040C, 1040NR, 2063 and 1040-ES (NR)

#514 FOREIGN TAX CREDIT FOR INDIVIDUALS

This publication may help you if you paid foreign income tax. You may be able to take a foreign tax credit or deduction to avoid the burden of double taxation. The publication explains which foreign taxes qualify and how to figure out your credit or deduction.

Form 1116

#515 WITHHOLDING OF TAX ON NON-RESIDENT ALIENS AND FOREIGN CORPORATIONS

This publication provides information for withholding agents, who are required to withhold and report tax on payments to non-resident aliens and foreign corporations. Included are three tables listing U.S. tax treaties and some of the treaty provisions that provide for certain types of income.

Forms 1042 and 1042S, 1001, 4224, 8233, 1078, 8288, 8288-A, 8288-B, 8804, 8805, and W-8BEN, 8813 and 8709

#519 U.S. TAX GUIDE FOR ALIENS

This publication gives guidelines on determining your U.S. tax status and calculating your U.S. tax. Resident aliens, like U.S. citizens, are generally taxed on income from all sources. Non-resident aliens are generally taxed only on income from U.S. sources. The income may be from investments or from business activities, such as performing personal services in the United States. An income tax treaty may reduce the standard 30% tax rate on non-resident aliens' investment income. Their business income is taxed at the same graduated rates that apply to U.S. citizens or residents.

Aliens admitted into the United States with permanent immigrant visas are resident aliens, while temporary visitors generally are non-resident aliens. Aliens with other types of visas may be resident aliens or non-resident aliens, depending on the length and nature of their stays.

Forms 1040, 1040C, 1040NR, 2063 and Schedule A (Form 1040)

#593 TAX HIGHLIGHTS FOR U.S. CITIZENS AND RESIDENTS GOING ABROAD

This publication briefly reviews various U.S. tax provisions that apply to U.S. citizens or resident aliens who live or work abroad and expect to receive income from foreign sources.

#597 INFORMATION ON THE UNITED STATES-CANADA INCOME TAX TREATY

This publication provides information on the income tax treaty between the United States and Canada. It discusses a number of treaty provisions that often apply to U.S. citizens or residents who may be liable for Canadian tax.

Treaty provisions are generally reciprocal (the same rules apply to both treaty countries). Therefore, a Canadian resident who receives income from the United States may refer to this publication to see if a treaty provision may affect the tax to be paid to the United States.

FROM THE CANADA REVENUE AGENCY (CRA)

- Capital Gains Tax Guide
- Pension and RRSP Tax Guide

- Tax Guide for Canadians Living in Other Countries
- Tax Guide for Emigrants

CRA INTERPRETATION BULLETINS

IT-29	United States Social Security tax and benefits
IT-31	Foreign exchange profits and losses
IT-76R2	Exempt portion of pension when employee has been a non-resident
IT-161R3	Non-residents — Exemption from tax deductions at source on employment income
IT-163R2	Election by non-resident individuals on certain Canadian-source income
IT-171R	Non-resident individuals — Taxable income earned in Canada
IT-181	Foreign tax credit — Foreign-tax carryover
IT-194	Foreign tax credit — Part-time residents
IT-221R2	Determination of an individual's residence status
IT-262R	Losses of non-residents and part-year residents
IT-270R2	FOREIGN TAX CREDIT
IT-298	Canada-U.S. Tax Convention — Number of days "present" in Canada
IT-370	Trusts — Capital property owned on December 31, 1971
IT-372R	Trusts — Flow-through of taxable dividends and interest to a beneficiary (1987 and prior taxation years)
IT-395R	Foreign tax credit — Foreign-source capital gains and losses
IT-399	Principal residence — Rental non-resident owner
IT-420R2	Non-residents — Income earned in Canada
IT-465R	Non-resident beneficiaries of trusts
IT-506	Foreign income taxes as a deduction from income
IT-520	Unused foreign tax credits — Carry forward and carry back

Appendix B
Provincial/Territorial and State
Tax Rates

2006 CANADIAN PROVINCIAL TAX RATES

In the wake of recent provincial budgets, new tax rates are now in effect. Here is what you pay if you are in the highest marginal income tax bracket, federal and provincial taxes combined. The table includes the provincial surtaxes that are applied to higher incomes in some provinces.

Newfoundland and Labrador	48.6%
Prince Edward Island	47.4%
Nova Scotia	48.3%
New Brunswick	46.8%
Quebec	48.2%
Ontario	46.4%
Manitoba	46.4%
Saskatchewan	44.0%
Alberta	39.0%
British Columbia	43.7%
Northwest Territories	43.0%
Yukon	42.4%
Nunavut	40.5%
Non-resident	42.9%

SUNBELT STATE INDIVIDUAL INCOME TAXES

The following is a summary of state income taxes to which individuals may be subject in popular Sunbelt states. It is not our intention to provide detailed information with respect to the taxation system of each particular state. The state income tax laws summarized here were those in effect for the 2006 taxation year.

ARIZONA
Individuals Liable to Taxation

Residents of Arizona are taxed on all income, whereas non-residents are taxed on Arizona-source income only. A non-resident's taxable income does not include income from intangibles (interest, dividends, etc.) unless derived from a trade or business carried on in the state.

Allowable Deductions

Taxpayers are allowed the standard deduction. In lieu of the standard deduction, taxpayers can elect to use the revised itemized deductions. Deductions allowable under Arizona law are similar to those allowable for federal tax purposes. You must itemize these deductions on the federal return (Form 1040 only) for Arizona purposes.

Rates for Married Filing Jointly or Head of Household

From	To	Tax Rate
$0	$20,000	2.6%
20,001	50,000	2.9%
50,001	100,000	3.3%
100,001	300,000	4.2%
300,001	More	4.5.%

All taxpayers are allowed credits for net taxes paid to other states or Canada. As of 1999, Arizona allows Canadians credit for taxes withheld on Canadian-sourced income without filing net tax returns.

CALIFORNIA

Individuals Liable to Taxation

Residents of California are taxed on taxable income (adjusted gross income [AGI] minus either the itemized or standard deduction). Non-residents and part-year residents are also taxed on taxable income, but their California tax liability is determined based on the ratio of California AGI to worldwide AGI, multiplied by the California tax on worldwide income. A non-resident's AGI does not include income from intangibles (interest, dividends, gains from sales of securities, etc.) unless the property has a business status in the state.

California is a community property state. If a married couple is domiciled in California, one-half of the community income earned by one spouse is legally owned by and taxable to the other spouse.

Allowable Deductions

Deductions allowable under California law are similar to those allowable for federal purposes, except that state income taxes are not deductible. Federal income tax is also not deductible. In lieu of itemized deductions, single and married taxpayers may claim standard deductions of $2,750 and $5,800 respectively.

Rates for Married Filing Jointly

From	To	Tax Rate
$0	$12,638	1.0%
12,638	29,958	2.0%
29,958	47,282	4.0%
47,282	65,638	6.0%
65,638	82,852	8.0%
82,952	and over	9.3%

Rates for heads of households range from 1% on the first $12,644 to 9.3% on income of more than $56,456. For others, the rate on the first $6,319 is 1%, and on income of more than $41,476 it is 9.3%. California has an 7% alternative minimum tax (AMT). All taxpayers are allowed credit for taxes paid to other states but not for Canada.

FLORIDA

Individuals Liable To Taxation

No individual income tax is imposed by Florida.

HAWAII

Individuals Liable To Taxation

Residents of Hawaii are taxed on their gross income, whereas non-residents are taxed only on their Hawaii-source income. A non-resident's taxable income does not include income from intangibles (interest, dividends, etc.) unless derived from a trade or business carried on in the state.

Allowable Deductions

Deductions allowable under Hawaii law are similar to those allowable for federal income tax purposes.

State income taxes are deductible but federal income taxes are not. Non-residents must allocate their itemized deductions based on the ratio of Hawaii Adjusted Gross Income to total AGI.

Rates for Married Filing Jointly

From	To	Tax Rate
$0	$4,000	1.4%
4,001	8,000	3.2%
8,001	16,000	5.5%
16,001	24,000	6.4%
24,001	32,000	6.8%
32,001	40,000	7.2%
40,001	60,000	7.6%
60,001	80,000	7.9%
80,001	and over	8.3%

Special rate tables are provided for other filing statuses. Credit is given only to residents for taxes paid to other states.

Appendix C
Canadian Embassy and Consulates in the United States

The Embassy of Canada
501 Pennsylvania Avenue, N.W.
Washington, DC 20001-2114

(202) 682-1740

www.canadianembassy.org

Territory: Eastern Pennsylvania, Delaware, Maryland and Virginia, District of Columbia

Anchorage
The Consulate of Canada
310 K Street, Suite 200
Anchorage, AK 99501

(907) 264-6734

Atlanta
The Consulate General of Canada
1175 Peachtree Street
100 Colony Square, Suite 1700
Atlanta, GA 30361-6205

(404) 532-2000

Territory: Georgia, Alabama, Mississippi, North Carolina, South Carolina, Tennessee

Boston
The Consulate General of Canada
Three Copley Place, Suite 400
Boston, MA 02116

(617) 262-3760

Territory: Massachusetts, Maine, New Hampshire, Rhode Island, Vermont (other: Saint-Pierre-et-Miquelon)

Buffalo
The Consulate General of Canada
HSBC Center, Suite 3000
Buffalo, NY 14203-2884

(716) 858-9500

Territory: Western, Central and Upstate New York State, Western and Central Pennsylvania, West Virginia

Chicago
The Consulate General of Canada
Two Prudential Plaza
180 North Stetson Avenue, Suite 2400
Chicago, IL 60601

(312) 616-1860

Territory: Illinois, Missouri, Wisconsin, Quad-Cities portion of Iowa

Dallas
The Consulate General of Canada
750 North St. Paul Street, Suite 1700
Dallas, TX 75201

(214) 922-9806

Territory: Texas, Arkansas, Kansas, Louisiana, Oklahoma

Denver
Consulate General of Canada
1625 Broadway, Suite 2600
Denver, CO 80202

(303) 626-0640

Territory: Colorado, Montana, Wyoming, Utah

Detroit
Consulate General of Canada
600 Renaissance Center, Suite 1100
Detroit, MI 48243-1798

General enquiries: (313) 567-2340

Immigration enquiries:
  (313) 567-2085

Territory: Michigan, Indiana, Kentucky, Ohio

Houston
The Consulate of Canada
5847 San Felipe Street, Suite 1700
Houston, TX 77057
(713) 821-1440

Los Angeles
Consulate General of Canada
550 South Hope Street, 9th Floor
Los Angeles, CA 90071-2627
(213) 346-2700
Territory: California, Arizona,
Hawaii, New Mexico, Nevada

Miami
Consulate General of Canada
Suite 1600, First Union Financial
  Center
200 South Biscayne Blvd.
Miami, FL 33131
(305) 579-1600
Territory: Florida, Puerto Rico, and
the U.S. Virgin Islands

Minneapolis
Consulate General of Canada
701 Fourth Avenue South, Suite 901
Minneapolis, MN 55415-1899
(612) 332-7486
Territory: Minnesota, Iowa (except the
Quad-Cities portion which is covered
by the Chicago Consulate General),
Nebraska, North Dakota, South Dakota

New York
Consulate General of Canada
1251 Avenue of the Americas
New York, NY 10020-1175
(212) 596-1628
Territory: South and Eastern
New York State, Connecticut,
New Jersey (other: Bermuda)

Philadelphia
The Consulate of Canada
1500 John F. Kennedy Blvd.
Suite 200, Two Penn Center

Philadelphia, PA 19102
(215) 854-6380

Phoenix
The Consulate of Canada
2415 East Camelback Road, Suite 740
Phoenix, AZ 85016
(602) 508-3572

Princeton
Canadian Government Trade Office
10 Skyfield Drive
Princeton, NJ 08540-7403
(609) 333-9940

Raleigh
The Consulate of Canada
3737 Glenwood Avenue, Suite 100
Raleigh, NC 27612
(919) 573-1808

San Diego
The Consulate of Canada
402 West Broadway, Suite 400
San Diego, CA 92101
(619) 615-4286

San Francisco/Silicon Valley
Consulate General of Canada
580 California Street, 14th Floor
San Francisco, CA 94104
(415) 834-3180

333 West San Carlos Street, Suite 945
San Jose, CA 95110
(408) 289-1157

Seattle
Consulate General of Canada
412 Plaza 600 Building
(Sixth Avenue and Stewart Street)
Seattle, WA 98101-1286
General inquiries: (206) 443-1777
Immigration and visa inquiries:
  (206) 443-1372
Territory: Washington State, Alaska,
Idaho, Oregon

Appendix D
U.S. Embassy and Consulates in Canada

The Embassy of the United States of America
Street Address:
U.S. Embassy
490 Sussex Drive
Ottawa, ON

Mailing Address:
PO Box 866, Station B
Ottawa, ON K1P 5T1
(613) 238-5335
http://canada.usembassy.gov
American Consular Services:
www.amcits.com

Calgary
615 Macleod Trail S.E., Room 1000
Calgary, AB T2G 4T8
(403) 266-8962

Halifax
Street Address:
Suite 904, Purdy's Wharf Tower II
1969 Upper Water Street
Halifax, NS B3J 3R7

Mailing Address:
PO Box 2130, CRO
Halifax, NS B3J 3B7

for appointments:
(902) 429-2480 ext. 2991

Montreal
Street Address:
1155 St. Alexandre Street
Montreal, QC H3B 1Z1

Mailing Address:
PO Box 65, Postal Station
  Desjardins
Montreal, QC H5B 1G1
(514) 398-9695
http://montreal.usconsulate.gov

Quebec City
Street Address:
2 Place Terrasse Dufferin
(behind Château Frontenac)
Quebec, QC

Mailing Address:
B.P. 939
Quebec, QC G1R 4T9
(418) 692-2095
http://quebec.usconsulate.gov

Toronto
360 University Avenue
Toronto, ON M5G 1S4
(416) 595-0228
http://toronto.usconsulate.gov

Vancouver
1095 West Pender Street
Vancouver BC V6E 2M6
(604) 685-4311
http://vancouver.usconsulate.gov

Winnipeg
860 – 201 Portage Avenue
Winnipeg, MB R3B 3K6
(403) 266-8962
http://winnipeg.usconsulate.gov

Appendix E
Canadian Tax Services and
Newsletters in the United States

CANADIAN TAX SERVICES IN THE U.S.

Cross Border Tax and Accounting, LLC
3336 North 32nd Street, Suite 113
Phoenix, AZ 85018-6241
(602) 956-4661
toll free: 1-800-394-9462
www.cbta.net

Brunton-McCarthy CPA Firm
4710 N.W. Boca Raton Blvd.,
Suite 101
Boca Raton, FL 33431
(407) 241-9991
www.taxintl.com

Serbinski Partners, P.C.
8770 West Bryn Mawr, 13th Floor
Chicago, IL 60631
1-888-US TAXES
(1-888-878-2937)
www.serbinski.com

CANADIAN FINANCIAL NEWSLETTERS IN THE UNITED STATES

Keats, Connelly & Associates Newsletter
3336 North 32nd Street, Suite 100
Phoenix, AZ 85018-6241
(602) 955-5007
toll free: 1-800-678-5007
www.keatsconnelly.com

Brunton's U.S. Taxletter for Canadians
4710 N.W. Boca Raton Blvd.,
Suite 101
Boca Raton, FL 33431
(407) 241-9991
www.taxintl.com

CROSS-BORDER TAX & ACCOUNTING NEWSLETTER

Cross-Border Tax and Accounting, LLC
3336 North 32nd Street, Suite 113
Phoenix, AZ 85018
(602) 956-4661
toll free: 1-800-394-9462
www.cbta.net/newsletter.shtml

Appendix F
Private Travel Insurance Carriers

AARP Canada Travel Medical Insurance
1-888-813-8888
www.aarp.org

Association of Mature Canadians
1-800-667-0429
www.maturecanadians.ca

Blue Cross (Ontario)
1-800-873-2583
www.bluecross.ca

Blue Cross (Quebec)
1-888-588-1212
www.qc.croixbleue.ca

Canada Life
1-800-268-6703
www.canadalife.com

Canadian Association of Retired Persons (CARP)
1-877-450-7587
www.carp.ca

Canadian Automobile Association (CAA)
Check local clubs.
www.caa.ca

CAA Quebec Travel Agency
1-800-CAA-4357
  (1-800-222-4357)
www.caaquebec.com

Canadian Snowbird Association
1-800-563-5104
www.snowbirds.org

TIC Travel Insurance
1-800-663-4494
www.travelinsurance.ca

Appendix G
Immigration Services

U.S. Department of State
Public Communication Division
2201 C Street N.W.
Washington, DC 20520

(202) 647-6575

www.state.gov

American Immigration Lawyers Association
918 F Street N.W.
Washington, DC 20004-1400

(202) 216-2400

www.aila.org

U.S. CITIZENSHIP AND IMMIGRATION SERVICES (USCIS)

The best source of information about U.S. immigration services is the website www.uscis.gov, which provides links to all immigration field offices as well as to immigration forms and instructions. (You can also call 1-800-870-3676 to have forms mailed to you.) There are "district offices" and "sub offices" in most states, but there are only four service centers that handle applications for immigration services and benefits. Please make sure your form will be accepted by the service center of your area.

CALIFORNIA SERVICE CENTER

www.uscis.gov/graphics/fieldoffices/california/

Jurisdiction: Arizona, California, Hawaii, Nevada

Street Address:
U.S. Citizenship and Immigration Service
24000 Avila Road
2nd Floor, Room 2312
Laguna Niguel, CA 92677

Mailing Address:
U.S. Citizenship and Immigration Services
California Service Center
PO Box 30111
Laguna Niguel, CA 92607-0111

NEBRASKA SERVICE CENTER

www.uscis.gov/graphics/fieldoffices/nebraska/

Jurisdiction: Alaska, Colorado, Idaho, Illinois, Indiana, Iowa, Kansas, Michigan, Minnesota, Missouri, Montana, Nebraska, North Dakota, Ohio, Oregon, South Dakota, Utah, Washington, Wisconsin, Wyoming

Please go to their website for the correct PO Box number to which to mail your application/petition.

TEXAS SERVICE CENTER

www.uscis.gov/graphics/fieldoffices/texas/

Jurisdiction: Alabama, Arkansas, Florida, Georgia, Kentucky, Louisiana, Mississippi, New Mexico, North Carolina, Oklahoma, South Carolina, Tennessee, Texas

U.S. Citizenship and Immigration Service
Texas Service Center
PO Box 851488
Mesquite, TX 75185-1488

VERMONT SERVICE CENTER

www.uscis.gov/graphics/fieldoffices/vermont/

Jurisdiction: Connecticut, Delaware, Maine, Maryland, Massachusetts, New Hampshire, New Jersey, New York, Pennsylvania, Puerto Rico, Rhode Island, Vermont, Virginia, West Virginia, District of Columbia

U.S. Citizenship and Immigation Services
Vermont Service Center
75 Lower Welden Street
St. Albans, VT 05479